First Edition

Author: One Exam Prep (1-877-804-3959)
www.1examprep.com

TABLE OF CONTENTS

Scope

"Solar contractor" means a contractor whose services consist of the installation, alteration, repair, maintenance, relocation, or replacement of solar panels for potable solar water heating systems, swimming pool solar heating systems, and photovoltaic systems and any appurtenances, apparatus, or equipment used in connection therewith, whether public, private, or otherwise, regardless of use. A contractor, certified or registered pursuant to this chapter, is not required to become a certified or registered solar contractor or to contract with a solar contractor in order to provide services enumerated in this paragraph that are within the scope of the services such contractors may render under this part.

Examination Outline

Construction Industry Licensing Board Examination At A Glance

Solar Contractors General Trade Knowledge Examination Content Information

Approved References

The answers to the examination questions will be based on the editions listed below. Some of the questions will also be based on field experience and kno wledge of trade practices. Editions earlier or later than those listed below can be brought to the examination but AT YOUR OWN RISK. However, only one copy of each reference will be allowed into the examination.

1. Solar Water and Pool Heating Manual FSEC
2. NRCA Roofing Manual: Membrane Roof Systems, 2019
3. NRCA Roofing Manual: Steep-Slope Roof Systems, 2021
4. NRCA Roofing Manual: Metal Panel and SPF Roof Systems, 2020
5. Photovoltaic System Design, (Course Manual), 3rd Edition
6. Solar Construction Safety
7. Photovoltaic Systems, 3rd Edition
8. Walker's Building Estimator's Reference Book, 32nd Edition **Effective for testing January 1, 2022*
9. NFPA 70: National Electrical Code (NEC) Handbook, 2017
10. 2020 Florida Building Code - Residential
11. 2020 Florida Building Code - Plumbing
12. OSHA 29 CFR 1926 Construction Industry Regulations

Important Notes

- Only original edition reference materials will be allowed for use at the site, except for the references specifically indicated on the reference list as available as PDF.
- All reference materials and PDF copies MUST be bound and remain bound during the exam. Bound refers to materials permanently bound, as by stitching or glue, and materials securely fastened in their covers by fasteners that penetrate all papers. PDF copies of references MUST be bound with ring binders, brads, plastic snap binders, spiralbound notebooks, and screw posts, but not with staples. Writing or electronic tablets are not allowed.
- References containing underlining with pen or highlighter may be used.
- Hand-written and typewritten notes are NOT allowed.
- Existing hand-written notes must be blackened out or whitened out completely, by the candidate, prohibiting legibility.
- Moveable tabs (e.g., Post-it Flags) are NOT allowed. You will not be permitted to make any marks in your references during the examination.

Frequenty Asked Questions

- Frequently Asked Questions - Examination Scheduling and Fees

Special Testing Accommodations

- State of Florida Instruction Booklet Request for Examination Accommodations for Examinees with Disabilities
- Application for Candidate's Requesting Special Testing Accommodations

STRATEGIES FOR TAKING A CONTRACTOR'S EXAM

The amount of time spent studying is not the only factor in being prepared. It is also very important to study efficiently. If you want to retain what you are studying you must set up a system. You are better off if you study for one hour in a quiet, private and relaxed atmosphere than if you study for 15 minutes at a time, 6 or 8 times a day. So start your exam preparation by setting up a schedule and picking an appropriate area.

Rules to help you study more effectively

1. Make sure that you know the meaning of words that are unfamiliar to you. Keep a list of the unknown words, look up their definitions and then keep going back to review the list.

2. Always try to follow your study schedule and plan.

3. Practice the rules for answering multiple choice questions while you are doing practice questions.

4. Find your weakest areas and then concentrate your study in those areas.

5. Write down problem questions and go back over them at a later date. Bring them to the class and ask the instructor to review questions.

6. Be sure to tab the books and become familiar with the tabs, indexes, and table of contents so you can find things quickly.

7. Time yourself, so you know how long you are spending on each question.

The Test Day

- Remind yourself how well you will do on the exam.

- Get a good night's rest. Get up early and remind yourself how well you will do on the exam. Eat a good breakfast. Remind yourself how well you will do on the exam.

- Be sure to wear comfortable clothes. Wear or bring a sweater that you can add or remove depending on the room temperature. Remind yourself how well you will do on the exam.

• Get to the exam site early. If you have to rush to find the site or get to the room you may not do as well on the exam. Remind yourself how well you will do on the exam.

• Don't get nervous or excited. Remember, if all else fails, there is always another day.

General rules to answer multiple choice questions

1. Read the directions carefully and be sure that you understand them.

2. Look over the answer sheet and be sure you understand how to mark your answers.

3. Be carefully when transferring answers from the test to the answer sheet. Be sure to:

• Mark answer completely,

• Only mark one answer per question,

• Make no extra marks on the answer sheet,

• If you make an error, erase,

• Be sure to mark the answer in the correct spot on the answer sheet. Repeat the answer to yourself as you transfer it to the answer sheet. And then check it again on the test sheet, repeating it.

4. Read the question carefully and be sure you understand what it is asking. Cross out any extraneous information. Read the question again.

5. Read all the answers before you make a choice. Quite often a "possible" answer is listed before the correct answer. **Don't be caught by this trap.**

6. Eliminate all choices that are wrong choices. After you read all the answers then cross out the wrong answers and chose from the remaining.

7. Never pick an answer because of a pattern to the answers on previous questions. There is no pattern. Just pick the answer you feel is correct.

8. Be aware of key words that may help select an answer. Absolute words, such as: always, never, only, all or none. These words usually indicate an incorrect answer. Limiting words such as: some, many, most, sometimes, usually, normally, occasionally, will often indicate the correct answer.

9. Skip over a question that gives you trouble or is taking too long to solve. Mark it in the question book so you can find it later. Continue through the exam and come back to the question after you are completed. Be sure to save five minutes at the end of the test period, so that if there are any unanswered questions, you can at least guess at the answer.

10.Never leave a question unanswered. There is no penalty for a wrong answer.

11. Watch for negative question, such as, "Which of the following would make the statement false?"

12.How to make an educated guess. If there are four choices you have a 25% chance to pick the correct answer. But you may be able to improve those odds.

• Eliminate the incorrect answers.

• Look for answers with absolute or limiting words.

• Look for answers with obviously the wrong sign (+ or -).

• Look for two answers with the same meaning, they are probably both wrong.

• Look for two answers with the opposite meaning, one of them may be correct.

• If all else fails and you have to guess, always guess the same choice.

13.Be careful changing answers. Remember that your first guess is normally the best. If you have time at the end of the exam you should go back through the test. But, only change answers if you are sure that your first choice is incorrect, *ie.* you find a calculation error.

GOOD LUCK. Remember to keep reminding yourself that you will do fine and pass the exam!

If you have no confidence in yourself, you are twice defeated in the race of life. With confidence you have won before you've started-----MARCUS GARVEY

STRATEGY FOR TEST TAKING

The preparation for an exam starts at the beginning of the course. It is essential to have the subject's program, become aware of the program, know it, review the books and support materials, and attend classes or tutoring sessions. The greater the time invested in preparing for your exam,the more likely you will pass it the first time around. The exam is just the first goal of a long career.

Prepare Mentally and Physically

Preparing for the exams depends, to a large extent, on the way you study. But other factors directly influence your academic performance, such as diet and exercise. Although the idea is to maintain a healthy and balanced diet throughout the year and exercise regularly, it is even more essential when preparing for your exams.

It is about eating breakfast that gives us the energy to face the day and supply the brain with enough glucose to get the most out of our study hours. Hydrating correctly for the day with water, dividing meals into five or six, and not overdoing it with caffeine will enhance our ability to pay attention and improve memory.

The same thing happens with exercise: Exercising will help us remove stress, rest better, and wake up feeling refreshed and more alert. Regular exercise also improves learning on two levels: it boosts cognitive function and memory retention. The more oxygenated nutrients the brain gets, the better it can perform, especially during exams.

Study planning: The first step to successfully passing the exams is planning well. This involves studying the subjects or content areas that will be on the exam daily. As the day of the exam approaches, we will only have to do an in-depth review of the entire exam scope to reach the exam date with all the suitably prepared subjects.

Reading: It is the general way to get in touch with a topic. When reading the scope of the exam, we must identify different phases for reading comprehension. First, we must understand the text's ideas and then expose our doubts or convey to the instructor what we have not understood. After examining what we read, we will achieve a broad vision of the whole, and it will only be enough for us to look for the general ideas.

Highlighting the text: Highlighting will help us focus on the relevant information in the text, and later, will help us structure and organize for the actual exam. We will avoid overloading the text excessively with highlights, not to hinder the ability to find the right answers during the exam. Note: Most testing companies allow the references for open book exams to be highlighted and tabbed with permanently affixed tabs. Be sure to check with your State or Local Jurisdiction regarding your exam.

Organizational techniques: Organizing the study material is key to understanding the concepts that we have previously highlighted in the text. These techniques will help us clarify the subject's structure, order the ideas hierarchically, and shorten the text's length to facilitate review and active study.

Study sheets: Using study cards or flashcards may sound like a very old-fashioned technique, but it is quite an effective learning method for assimilating specific data. It is about making a 'mini summary' of an entire topic, which allows you to save a lot when creating them, and they are straightforward to consult.

Take Practice Tests: The practice tests are an excellent way to review before an exam; in addition to that, with these, you can check what you are failing and focus efforts where necessary. It is, without a doubt, one of the best study strategies!

How Can You Improve Your Exam Preparation?

Make sure:

- Study daily to make sure you understand the subject.
- Study each subject listed on the exam scope: highlight, make outlines, and summaries.
- When a topic is well learned, it is not easily forgotten. In studying the following topics, you will have to rely on the previous ones, serving as a review and consolidation.
- When the exam approaches, we have to review to anchor them more in memory.

How Can You Improve Taking the Exam?

- Losing the nerve before the exam: "nerves are useless and they are in the way of everything."
- Try to relax. Practice relaxation techniques.
- Do not try to check if you remember all the exam subjects; before the exam, your mind is in tension, you can no longer reinforce your memory, so concentrate on what you will do.
- Being physically and mentally fit: You must sleep well and get enough rest before the exam.
- Do not leave everything for the last moment; if you do, you give the memory time to settle the information it receives. The memory needs rest, and your memory will be more clear if there is order.

How Fully Understand the Exam Questions?

- Leave the nerves at home.
- Take your time to read the questions well. Read them all. Sometimes there may be more than one referring to the same topic, and you will have to decide the focus and content for each one.
- Before answering each particular question, read it several times until you make sure you understand it. Look for the keyword that tells you what to do: explain, demonstrate, define, calculate, find. If your exam is open book, look for keywords that will indicate which book to find the answer in — Practice Comprehensive Reading.
- After answering, reread the question and answers and double-check your selection.

How to Organize the Time You Have During the Exam?

- It is necessary to know each question's value since the same amount of time may not be devoted to each question or subject.
- Quick distribution of time is made. We must allow time for review.
- It would be best to start with the questions that you are familiar with and know the answers quickly. The best way to answer is by making, in the beginning, an outline that guides us during the exam.
- When there is no time to answer a question, don't leave the question not answered. It will be an automatic wrong answer rather than taking a 1 out of 4 chance of getting the answer correct.

How to Review and Correct the Exam?

- Before submitting the exam, you should review:

The content: Make sure that you have answered all the questions.

The form:

It is more than obvious to say that to pass any exam depends a lot on how you study, the time you dedicate, and the information retention capacity you have.

- However, it also requires taking into account many other factors, so the best we can do is use effective study techniques to help you pass that stressful exam.
- It is expected that as the exam approaches, nerves can begin to take over due to the lack of constant study. That is why it is essential to discover an ideal technique that will lead you to achieve success and pass.

Preparation to Examinations

As we previously mentioned, preparation for your exam starts at the beginning of the course. It is essential to have the subject's program, become aware of the program, know it, review the books and support materials, and attend classes or tutoring sessions. The more time invested in preparing for your exam, the more likely you will pass it the first time.

It is also essential to keep motivation high when studying and have a learning strategy for each subject. Above all, you should not fear exploring different study methods.

Conclusively, We Can Develop the Following Strategies

Method One:

You should not "jump" on the exam task immediately after you received it. It would also be best if you didn't go through the questions one at a time in their original order.

Observe the following procedure:

Read the directions very carefully. The exam instructions often contain valuable data. Always examine all guidelines carefully to make sure you understand what's being requested.

Take a deep breath, and then slowly scan your eyes throughout the exam to familiarize yourself with all the questions.

In the process, answer the questions to which you know the correct answer.

Tackle more difficult tasks, but don't spend too much time on them. Leave the most difficult questions for the end.

Your task is to give as many correct answers to questions that you are sure of. Scientists have proven that when you skim through the entire test, unresolved questions are already "looming" in your head even before seriously tackling its solution. This is very useful for a variety of reasons.

First, you subconsciously start thinking about a solution to the most challenging test questions.

Secondly, tests often come across questions containing hints and sometimes even a complete answer to other test questions.

In any case, before proceeding with the solution of exam tasks, first, review the questions and give answers where you can do it. Then start to puzzle over more complicated tasks.

Method Two:

Read each test question at least twice.

This is a handy tip because trick questions are widespread in tests. When we are in the exam, we want to solve the tasks as quickly as possible, as there is not enough time. Therefore, many students make a widespread mistake because they glimpse a question and immediately start sorting out the answers.

The fact is that test developers try to outwit the exam takers and dilute the standard tasks with tricky questions. Let's take a look at some of them:

In tests, you can often come across the following question: Which of the following does not contain "a," "b," or "c"? If you read the task inattentively, it is quite possible to quickly skip the "not" particle and give a wrong answer.

Other questions may contain several correct answers, and your task involves choosing the most correct one.

Summing up, you should not lose your vigilance since inattention often leads to mistakes. So, do not be lazy and reread the questions at least twice.

Method Three:

Double-check the answers right away, rather than postpone checking until the end.

The fact is that once you have answered the question, the information is still very fresh in your head. Therefore, by quickly checking your answers, you will significantly reduce the chances of accidentally missing one silly mistake. On the other hand, you will increase your chances of receiving a passing exam score.

However, this does not mean that you should not recheck your answers after solving all the tests. On the contrary, try to always leave some time for final checking. By adding this technique to your arsenal, you can undoubtedly increase the chance of getting a decent grade.

Method Four (for closed book exams):

If you come across a question, the answer to which you do not remember, or you feel that it literally "spins on the tongue" but does not come to mind, try to mentally transfer yourself to the place where you first heard about it.

There are 24 hours in a day. If 8 of them are spent sleeping, that gives you 16 hours to get some efficient and productive study done, right?

It seems simple enough. There are plenty of hours in a day, so why is it so hard to use this time effectively, especially around exam time?

We've found that managing their time effectively is one of the things that students struggle the most with around exam time. However, time management is also one of the things that schools never teach – how frustrating?!

In the weeks leading up to study leave, every teacher you have for every class you go to seems to pile on the work: Mrs Gibb from English class tells you that you have to prepare 3 practice essays for both your visual and written texts, your Geography teacher Miss Wood expects you to do every past exam paper for the last three years before the exam, Mr West your Maths teacher says that you have to finish all of the questions in that darned AME textbook if you want to do well on the exam.

But they expect you to do all of this without giving you any time management tips. Mrs Gibb, Miss Wood and Mr West all fail to tell you how it's humanly possible to complete all of this work without collapsing when you walk into the exam hall.

That's where we come in!

Read on for the time management tips that your teachers never gave you!

1. Focus on what you have to study – not what you don't.

It seems obvious, but think of all the times you've sat down to study and you've ended up spending 2 hours studying the concepts you already know like the back of your hand.

It's easier to study the subjects you like. Studying the concepts that you're already confident in is a lot less challenging than studying the concepts that you find the most difficult, as your brain will have to work less to learn this information.

Studying what you already know is a bad time management strategy because you'll leave all the important stuff to the last minute meaning you won't have the time to cover these concepts in depth.

The trouble with this tip is that it's often hard to decipher what you know and what you don't.

To figure out what you concepts you already know, and what concepts you still need to learn, complete a subject audit. A subject audit involves breaking down a particular subject into several points or sections and then analysing how well you know each of these points. You should spend most of your time studying those concepts that you have rated the most difficult. Find our study audit outline form here.

The key for effective time management is to review the easier material, but allow enough time to cover the harder concepts in depth so you're not left to study all of the most difficult concepts the night before the exam.

2. Work in sprints.

You may think that to have good time management skills you have to spend all of your time studying. However this is a misconception that many students hold.

Think of studying for exams like training for a marathon.

On your first day of training, you wouldn't go out and run 42kms. You would burn-out quickly due to a lack of prior training, and you would probably be put off running for a long time. This would not be a good way to manage your time. The better route to success would be to slowly work up to running the 42kms by running a bit further every day.

This simple idea of training in short bursts has been proven effective in all areas of human performance. You don't have to be a marathon runner to use this strategy!

When studying, you should start out small by studying in short, focused 'sprints' followed by brief breaks. Start by studying in 15 minute bursts followed by one 10 minute break. Over time, slowly increase the length of time you're studying (and breaking) for.

This strategy is effective because studying for short bursts promotes more intense focus, and will give your brain the time to process and consolidate information as opposed to studying for long periods of time which is not effective and may increase your chances of burnout.

Don't think of effective time management as studying for three hours straight with no breaks, think of effective time management as using your time wisely and in ways that will best promote retention of information.

Follow these steps to practice effective time management and become an expert studier (or marathon runner!) in no time:

1. **Set a timer for 15 minutes.**
2. **Put in some solid study until the timer goes off, making sure you're spending every minute working with no distractions.**
3. **Have a ten-minute break to check your phone, walk around, stretch, get outside etc.**
4. **Rinse and repeat.**
5. **Increase the amount of time you're studying for as you begin to feel more comfortable studying for extended lengths of time.**

3. Make a study system.

I'm sure you've been lectured by every teacher you've ever had to "make a study plan!!!" Study plans are effective for your time management, however they're sometimes hard to stick to.

Here at StudyTime, we find that the 'study system' is an effective strategy for really getting to the root of what you're studying. A study system is easier to stick to, and therefore fosters better time management skills, because it breaks tasks down into small chunks.

A study system is basically a simple list of steps that you can make to outline the steps you're going to take when you study. The list should start simple (4-5 things), but over time it should become more complex as you add steps to it.

Just like a workout plan at the gym or for sport, it will give you a clear direction of what action to take, making study much more efficient.

Over time, you can experiment with new study methods, and add them in to optimise the system.

Below is an example study formula that you could use when studying:

1. **Download the "Achievement Standard" from the NCEA website**
2. **Turn this into a checklist for what you already know and what you need to know**
3. **Break the checklist into main themes using a mind map**
4. **For each theme, make a summary sheet**
5. **After that, break down the key points of each summary and put these onto flash cards**
6. **Read through your notes and ensure you understand them, and then hit the flash cards**
7. **Test yourself on all of them first, then make two piles, one that's wrong and one that's right. Then redo the wrong pile again**
8. **Get someone else to test you**
9. **Practice exam papers – test yourself using exam papers from the past 2-3 years and time yourself**
10. **Work through the answers**
11. **Write a sheet of all tips/tricks i.e. things you got wrong in the practice exam papers**
12. **Redo exam paper and make model answers**
13. **Adjust flashcards if necessary i.e. make new ones based on the exam papers**
14. **Re-test all your flashcards**

Creating a study system will keep you on track and it will allow you to effectively plan out your time while studying.

4. Practice distributed learning.

Imagine your Maths teacher gave you seven equations to do for homework. How would you answer these questions? Would you do one question per day for seven days, or would you do all seven questions in one day?

You may think that it would be a better time management strategy to do all seven questions at once and get them over and done with. However, this is an ineffective way to manage your time.

The brain works better when it has time to process information. Neuroscience has shown that your brain needs time to consolidate information that has been newly learned, in order to form strong links between neurons and thus strong memories.

If the learning is done in one big chunk, you'll just forget it after three days. However, if you review it a day after, then you'll retain it for seven days.

When making a study schedule, you should space out when you study for each subject. For example, don't spend one day studying English, then the next day studying Maths, then the next day studying Biology. Instead, you should alternate studying for these subjects throughout the day. Do one hour of Maths, then one hour of English study, then one hour of Biology, and so on.

This is a much better way to manage your time, because the more often you review a concept, the more solidified it will be in your mind. This is because there will be more time to consolidate this into your memory. Also, taking breaks between reviewing certain concepts will give your brain time to process the information.

Try it out!

Photovoltaic System Design Course Manual
Tabs and Highlights

These 1 Exam Prep Tabs are based on the *Photovoltaic System Design Course Manual.*

Each Tabs sheet has five rows of tabs. Start with the first tab at the first row at the top of the page, and proceed down that row placing the tabs at the locations listed below. Place each tab in your book setting it down one notch until you get to the bottom of the page, and then start back at the top again. After you have completed tabbing your book (the last tab is the glossary, appendix, or index), then you may start highlighting your book.

1 Exam Prep Tab	**Page #**
Table of Contents	
Introduction	1
Solar Radiation	2
Electrical Fundamentals	2a
Photovoltaic Cells	3
Modules, Panels and Arrays	4
Photovoltaic System Components	5
Stand-Alone System Sizing Procedures	6
Electrical Design	7
Mechanical Design and Building Integration	8
Maintenance and Troubleshooting	9
Economic Analysis	10
Photovoltaic Lighting Systems	10a
Utility Interconnection Considerations	11
Glossary	G
Appendices	A-1

******This concludes the tabs for this book. Please continue with the highlights on the following page.******

A.M. 03/25/2021

1 Exam Prep

Solar Water and Pool Heating Manual

Tabs and Highlights

These 1 Exam Prep Highlights are based on the Solar Water and Pool Heating Manual, 2006 Edition.

Each 1 Exam Prep Tabs sheet has five rows of tabs. Start with the first tab at the first row at the top of the page; proceed down that row placing the tabs at the locations listed below. Place each tab in your book setting it down one notch until you get to the bottom of a page. Then start back at the top again.

After each 1 Exam Prep Tab, under "Reason" is a brief explanation of the purpose of the tab, and / or items to highlight in the section.

1 Exam Prep Tab	Page #	Highlight
Table of Contents	iii	Table of Contents
Solar Concepts	1-1	
	1-3	"Isolation is the amount of the sun's electromagnetic energy that "falls" on any given object."
	1-5	"Conduction occurs when a solid material is heated. Molecules exposed to a heat source become energized."
	1-6	Figure 4: Illustration of Conduction, Convection and Radiation
	1-9	Figure 6a and 6b: Collected Energy varies with Time of Year and Tilt
	1-11	Figure 8: Various Collector Tilt Angles
	1-11	Table 1: Solar Radiation for Flat-Plate Collectors Facing South at a Fixed Tilt
Solar Water Heating Systems	2-1	
	2-1	"Solar water heating systems fall into two general categories: 1) Active Systems: which use a pump to control water flow. 2) Passive Systems: which use no pump."
	2-1	Figure 1: Direct and Indirect solar water heating systems

1 Exam Prep Tab	Page #	Highlight
	2-2	"Active systems incorporate the following components: water storage tank, solar collector, controller to regulate pump operation, a pump or circulator to transfer water from the storage tank to the collector."
	2-3	Figure 2: Additional system components
	2-4	Figure 3: Active direct system with differential controller
	2-6	"Indirect systems are typically used in areas of freezing…can accelerate scale build-up in system piping, fittings, and valves."
	2-8	Figure 6: Active indirect system with tank internal heat exchanger
	2-9	Passive and Indirect Systems: "use no pumps or controllers."
	2-12	List/highlight the five basic methods used to prevent freezing
	2-14	Figure 12: Drain-down system configuration
	2-15	"The pump used in these drain-back systems must be capable of overcoming fairly large static heads, since the collector may be mounted several stories above the pump."
	2-16	Collectors
	2-20	Figure 5: Batch collector
	2-22	Figure 6: Vertical solar storage tank
	2-22	"Gas back-up systems may use passive solar pre-heating…with gas back-up heating systems."
	2-24	List/highlight factors in centrifugal pump selection
	2-25	Table 1: Pump Applications
	2-29	Photovoltaic Controller
	2-35	List/highlight the most common heat-transferred fluids
	2-37	Figure 24: Solar water heating system valves and monitoring equipment

1 Exam Prep Tab	**Page #**	**Highlight**
	2-46	Flow meters
Solar Water Heating System Installation	3-1	
	3-1	Collector Positioning
	3-1	Figure 1: Solar window
	3-4	Roof Mounted Collectors
	3-8	Figure 10: A method of locating mounting points
	3-9	Figure 11: Tile roof mount
	3-12	Figure 15: Spanner mounting
	3-13	Figure 16: Lag-bolted mounting assembly
	3-20	Module: Component Installation
	3-25	Pump Installation
	3-25	Differential Controller: List/highlight where high-temperature sensor may be placed
	3-26	List/highlight what installation practices should be observed
	3-27	Photovoltaic Controller
	3-28	Testing the Pump and Controls
	3-31	Table 1: Temperature and Thermistor Resistance
	3-33	Table 2: Temperature and RTD Resistance
Solar Water Heating System Troubleshooting	4-1	
	4-3	Contractor Liability
	4-4	Overall Checkout

1 Exam Prep Tab	Page #	Highlight
	4-6	Light/highlight most common problems
	4-7	Freeze Damage
	4-8	System Checkout
	4-12	"Warning: many pump motors are very hot after operating continuously for some time."
Troubleshooting Checklist	4-21 – 4-28	
Solar Swimming Pool Heating Systems	5-1	
	5-1	Evaporative Losses
	5-2	Convective Losses: "occur when air cooler than the pool water blows across the pool surface."
	5-3	Figure 1: Swimming pool heat loss mechanisms
	5-3	List/highlight three features in new pool construction to minimize expense of supplementary energy for pool heating
	5-5	Pool covers
	5-8	Plumbing Schematics: Flow Control Devices
	5-9	Figure 7: Plumbing schematics
	5-11	Figure 8: Automatic control plumbing schematic
	5-21	Table 1: Pool Heating Options
	5-22	Table 2: Friction Losses
	5-26	Piping
1 – Crome-Dome Collector	A-1	

1 Exam Prep Tab	**Page #**	**Highlight**
2 – Sizing Procedure For Hot Water Sys.	A-3	
3 – Electric Water Heater Circuitry	A-7	
4 – Volt-Ohmmeter or Multimeter Operation	A-8	Table 1: Measuring Resistance with the Volt-Ohmmeter
	A-8	Table 2: Measuring AC Voltage with the Volt-Ohmmeter
	A-8	Table 3: Measuring DC Voltage with the Volt-Ohmmeter
	A-11	Table 4: Temperature and Thermistor Resistance
	A-12	Table 5: Temperature and RTD Resistance
5 – Solar Sys. Flow rates	A-13	
6 – Tools for Svc. and Repairs	A-16	Tools for Service and Repair

Solar Construction Safety
Tabs and Highlights

These 1 Exam Prep Highlights are based on the *Solar Construction Safety Manual*.

Each Tabs sheet has five rows of tabs. Start with the first tab at the first row at the top of the page, and proceed down that row placing the tabs at the locations listed below. Place each tab in your book setting it down one notch until you get to the bottom of the page, and then start back at the top again. After you have completed tabbing your book (the last tab is usually the glossary, appendix, or index), then you may start highlighting your book.

This concludes the tabs for this document. Please continue with the highlights on the following page.

A.M. 02/24/2021

Photovoltaic Systems
Tabs and Highlights

These 1 Exam Prep Tabs are based on the *Photovoltaic Systems, Third Edition*.

Each Tabs sheet has five rows of tabs. Start with the first tab at the first row at the top of the page, and proceed down that row placing the tabs at the locations listed below. Place each tab in your book setting it down one notch until you get to the bottom of the page, and then start back at the top again. After you have completed tabbing your book (the last tab is usually the glossary, appendix, or index), then you may start highlighting your book.

1 Exam Prep Tab	**Page #**
Contents	
Introduction	3
Solar Radiation	29
Site Surveys & Preplanning	61
Systems Components & Configurations	97
Cells, Modules, and Arrays	123
Batteries	159
Charge Controllers	187
Inverters	217
System Sizing	247
Mechanical Integration	275
Electrical Integration	307
Utility Interconnection	351
Permitting & Inspection	375
Commissioning, Maintenance, & Troubleshooting	397
Economic Analysis	425
Appendix	457
Glossary	483
Index	493

******This concludes the tabs for this book. Please continue with the highlights on the following page.******

A.M. 03/25/2021

Page # **Highlight**

4 **Photovoltaics:** *Photovoltaics* is a solar energy technology that uses the unique properties of certain semi-conductors to directly convert solar radiation in electricity.

A *photovoltaic* (PV) *system* is an electrical system consisting of a PV module array and other electrical components needed to convert solar energy into electricity usable by loads.

Advantages: the PV system may save the consumer a great deal of money.

Photovoltaics is an environmentally friendly technology that produces energy with no noise or pollution.

Since there are no moving parts, PV systems are extremely reliable and last a long time with minimal maintenance. PV system reduces the consumer's vulnerability to utility outages, and a stand-alone system eliminates it.

Disadvantages: Currently, the most significant issue is the high initial cost of a PV system.

5 **Figure 1-1. Typical Utility-Connected PV System**

6 **Electricity Distribution:** *Distributed generation* is a system in which many smaller power… A distributed generation system may serve as the only source of power for the consumer (a stand-alone system), or as backup or supplemental power for a utility grid connection.

11 **PV Applications:** Today, PV systems can be used in almost any application where electricity is needed and can support DC loads, AC loads, or both.

Portable Applications: Portable PV systems power mobile loads such as vehicles, temporary sign and lighting, and handheld devices.

12 **Remote Applications:** Remote PV systems power loads that are permanently fixed but too distant to be connected to the utility power grid.

Lighting. The availability of low-power DC lamps makes PV energy ideal for remote lighting applications.

13 **Utility-Interactive Applications:** Systems that are connected to the utility grid and use PV energy as a supplemental source of power offer the greatest flexibility in possible system configurations.

A PV system may or may not save in money in the short-term when competing against relatively inexpensive utility power.

14 PV systems can be used to provide supplemental power to any utility-connected building or structure, including residences, commercial buildings, factories, and institutions.

Utility-Scale Applications: The only moving parts of a PV system are in the tracking system, if one is used.

Unfortunately, PV electricity still costs considerably more in the United States than electricity generated by conventional plants.

15 **Figure 1-14. PV Industry**
Manufacturers: A *balance-of-system (BOS) component* is an electrical or structural component, aside from a major component, that is required to complete a PV system. BOS components include…or interface between the primary devices such as the array, inverter and battery system.

Page # **Highlight**

Integrators: An *integrator* is a business that designs, builds, and installs complete PV systems for particular applications by matching components from various manufactures.

16 **Silicon:** Silicon is the primary raw material for producing PV cells.

Installers: All PV system installers should meet the following criteria: (14 Bullets)

17 **Figure 1-15. Quality PV System Characteristics**

21 **Collectors:** A *solar energy collector* is a device designed to absorb solar radiation and convert it to another form, usually heat or electricity.

Flat-Plate Collectors. A *flat-plate collector* is a solar energy collector that absorbs solar energy on a flat surface without concentrating it, and can utilize solar radiation directly from the sun… Nearly all commercial and residential solar energy installations use flat-plate collectors.

22 **Concentrating Collectors.** A *concentrating collector* is a solar energy collector that enhances solar energy by focusing it on a smaller area through reflective surfaces or lenses.

23 **Solar Thermal Energy:** Solar thermal energy systems convert solar radiation into heat energy.

Solar Thermal Heating. Solar thermal heating systems can be classified as passive or active. In passive systems, the working…In active systems, fans and pumps are used to circulate the fluid.

Solar Thermal Cooling. The heat energy is used to compress a gas…system, cools a set of coils.

Solar Thermal Electricity. *Concentrating solar power (CSP)* is a technology that uses mirrors and/or lenses to reflect and concentrate solar radiation from a large area onto a small area.

30 **THE SUN:** An astronomical unit (AU) is the average distance between Earth and the sun (93 million mi).

SOLAR RADIATION

Solar Irradiance (Solar Power): *Solar irradiance* is the power of solar radiation per unit area… expressed in units of watts per square meter (W/m^2) or kilowatts per square meter (kW/m^2).

31 Solar irradiance is used as a reference input condition to evaluate…equipment such as PV modules.

Figure 2-3. Solar Irradiance

Figure 2-4. Inverse Square Law

32 **Solar Irradiation (Solar Energy):** *Solar irradiation* is the total amount of solar energy accumulated on an area over time.

Solar irradiation is commonly expressed in units of watts-hours per square meter (Wh/m^2) or kilowatts per square meter (kWh/m^2). Solar irradiation quantifies the amount of energy received on a surface over time, and is the principal data needed for sizing and estimating the performance of PV systems.

Solar irradiation can be calculated from average solar irradiance by applying the formula:
$H = E_{avg} \times t$
Figure 2-5. Solar Irradiance and Irradiation

Page #	Highlight
34	**Figure 2-6. Electromagnetic Spectrum**
	Direct Radiation. *Direct radiation* is solar radiation directly from the sun that reaches Earth's surface without scattering.
	Diffuse Radiation. *Diffuse radiation* is solar radiation that is scattered by the atmosphere and clouds.
	Albedo Radiation. *Albedo radiation* is solar radiation that is reflected from the Earth's surface back up through the atmosphere, where it is scattered or escapes back into space.
35	**Figure 2-8. Atmospheric Effect**
	Air Mass. *Zenith* is a point in the sky directly overhead a particular location. The *zenith angle* is the angle between the sun and the zenith.
36	**Figure 2-9. Air Mass**
37	**Terrestrial Solar Radiation:** *Terrestrial solar radiation* is solar radiation reaching the surface of Earth.
	Peak Sun. *Peak sun* is an estimate of terrestrial solar irradiance. *Peak sun hours* is the number of hours required for a day's total solar irradiation to accumulate at peak sun condition.
	the total irradiation for a day may be expressed in units of peak sun hours by dividing by 1000 W/m^2 (peak sun irradiance).
	Figure 2-10. Peak Sun Hours
	knowing the average number of peak sun hours on a given surface at a given location is used to determine PV system performance.
40	**Solar Radiation Measurement**
	Pyranometers. Solar irradiance is typically measured with a pyranometer. A *pyranometer* is a sensor that measures the total global solar irradiance in a hemispherical field of view.
41	**Pyrheliometers.** Direct solar radiation is measured with a pyrheliometer. A *pyrheliometer* is a sensor that measures only direct solar radiation in the field of view of the solar disk (5.7°).
	they must be pointed directly at the sun and installed on sun-tracking devices.
42	**Reference Cells.** A *reference cell* is an encapsulated PV cell that outputs a known amount of electrical current per unit of solar irradiance. Since current output from a PV device varies linearly with the incident solar irradiance, the output current can be used to indirectly measure irradiance.
	Reference cells are highly accurate precision instruments…to measure the output of PV modules.
	Sun-Earth Relationships: Earth's axis is tilted at 23.5°. The amount of solar radiation received at a particular location on Earth's surface is a direct result of Earth's orbit and tilt.
42 & 43	**Earth's Orbit:** *Perihelion* is the point in Earth's orbit that is closest to the sun. *Aphelion* is the… The *equatorial plane* is the plane containing earth's equator and extending outward into space. Because Earth's tilt, the angle between these planes is 23.5° and remains constant as Earth's makes its annual orbit around the sun.

Page # **Highlight**

43 **Solar Declination.** *Solar declination* is the angle between the equatorial plane and the rays of the sun. The angle of solar declination changes continuously as Earth orbits ranging from -23.5° to +23.5°.

Figure 2-18. Ecliptic Plane

Figure 2-19. Solar Declination

44 **Solstices.** A *solstice* is the Earth's orbital position when solar declination is at its minimum or maximum. The summer solstice is at its maximum solar declination (+23.5°) and occurs around June 21.

The winter solstice is a at minimum solar declination (-23.5°) and occurs around December 21.

Figure 2-20. Solstices

Equinoxes. An *equinox* is the Earth's orbital position when solar declination is zero. There are two equinoxes in a year. The spring (vernal) equinox occurs around March 21 and the fall (autumnal) equinox occurs around September 23.

Figure 2-21. Equinoxes

45 **Solar Time.** *Solar Time* is a timescale based on the apparent motion of the sun crossing a local meridian.

Standard Time. *Standard time* is a timescale based on the apparent motion of the sun crossing standard meridians. A *standard meridian* is a meridian located at a multiple of 15° east or west of zero longitude.

Figure 2-22. Standard Time

46 The longitude time correlation is calculated with the following equation: (**equation**)

The *Equation of Time* is the difference between solar time and standard time at a standard meridian. This difference varies over the course of a year and can be as much as +16 min or -14 min.

Using both time correlations, local standard time can be converted to solar time, or vice versa, with the following equations: (**equation**)

Figure 2-23. Equation of Time

47 **Sun Path:** An *analemma* is a diagram of solar declination against the Equation of Time.

Figure 2-24. Analemma

Sun Position. The *solar altitude angle* is the vertical angle between the sun and the horizon.

The *solar azimuth angle* is the horizontal angle between a reference direction (typically due south in the Northern Hemisphere) and the sun.

48 **Figure 2-26. Sun Paths**

49 **The Solar Window.** The *solar window* is the area of sky between sun paths at summer solstice …Knowing the solar window at a given site is critical in properly locating and orienting PV arrays to achieve optimal energy performance and to prevent shading from trees and other obstructions.

Page # **Highlight**

Array Orientation: The *array tilt angle* is the vertical angle between horizontal and the array surface. *The array azimuth angle* is the horizontal angle between the reference direction and the direction an array surface faces.

Figure 2-27. Solar Window

Figure 2-28. Array Orientation

50 **Array Tilt Angle**

51 **Array Azimuth Angle**

Sun Tracking: Sun tracking is continuously changing the array tilt angle, the array azimuth angle, or both, so the array follows the position of the sun.

Single-axis tracking is a sun-tracking system that rotates one axis to approximately follow the position of the sun.

Dual-axis tracking is a sun-tracking system that rotates two axes independently to follow the position of the sun.

53 **Solar Radiation Data Sets:** Solar radiation data indicates how much solar energy trikes a surface at a particular location on Earth during a period of time.

Figure 2-31. NREL Solar Radiation Data Set Excerpt

54 **Solar Radiation for Flat-Plate Collectors Facing South at Fixed Tilt:** The section on flat-plate collectors at fixed tilt is applicable to most installations.

56 **Solar Radiation for Flat-Plate Collectors with Two-Axis Tracking:** The section on two-axis trackers represents solar irradiation on a surface that always faces the sun.

Two-axis tracking enables greater receiving of solar irradiation than either fixed or single-axis tracking surfaces.

62 **Customer Development:** Sales persons, designers, and installers of PV systems must identify customer needs, concerns, and expectations.

Solar Resource: The solar radiation resource should be researched before visiting the site.

63 When reviewing the solar resource data, the installer should note the differences for various array …This information is important when evaluating potential mounting orientations for PV arrays.

64 **Hazard Assessment and Safety Training**

Personal Protective Equipment (PPE). PPE is the equipment and garments worn by workers to protect them from workplace hazards.

Safety glasses, hard hats, safety shoes, gloves, hearing protection, and fall protection gear are common types of PPE required for PV system work.

65 **Electrical Safety.** Preventing injury due to electrical hazards involves wearing appropriate PPE
…equipment should be conducted in a de-energized state, using lockout and tagout procedures.
66 Flexible extension cords must be of the 3-wire type (…conductor) and designed for hard use.

Page # **Highlight**

Fall Protection. OSHA requires fall protection for work taking place more than 6' above a lower level., which includes the vast majority of areas where PV modules are installed on buildings.

A *personal fall arrest system (PFAS)* is a fall prevention system that prevents a worker from falling and consists of anchorage and connectors, a body harness, and a lanyard/deceleration device.

67 **Ladder Safety.** OSHA requires that a stairway or ladder be used at points of access on a construction site with an elevation change of 19" or more.

68 **Hand and Power Tools Safety.** All power tools must be fitted with guards and safety switches.

Site Surveys: Site surveys identify suitable locations for the array and other equipment. The most appropriate array locations have enough surface area for…and are not excessively shaded.

Site Survey Equipment

70 **Solar Shading Calculator.** A *solar shading calculator* is a device that evaluates the extent of shading obstruction interfering in the solar window for a given location.

71 **Array Location:** The primary task of the site survey is to determine whether there is a suitable location for a PV array.

Array Area. The required overall area for any given array is based on the desired peak-rated output, the efficiency of the modules, and how densely the modules are installed in the array. For an initial site survey, the required array area can be estimated with the following: **(formula)**

72 Allowing for space between the modules for access and maintenance, sloped-roof PV systems… about 9 m^2 (100 ft^2) per kilowatt of peak array power. (*Found in blue box in top left corner*)*

Array Orientation. The roof slope orientation must be measured during a site survey for a rooftop installation. The easiest way to measure the slope is with an angle finder, or inclinometer.

The slope is then calculated from the following formula: **(formula)**

73 The azimuth orientation of the roof is the direction, such as southwest or due south, that the sloped surface faces, and is determined with a magnetic or electronic compass.

75 **Shading Analysis:** Preferably, arrays should be installed in location with no shading at any time.

At a minimum, arrays should have an unobstructed solar window from 9 AM to 3 PM (solar time) throughout the…string inverters can help improve system performance under partial shading.

77 **Solar Shading Calculators.** The Solar Pathfinder consists of a latitude specific solar shading diagram…It is leveled and oriented to true south with the built in compass and bubble level.

78 the SunEye directly acquires a digital photo of the sky and includes many analysis features… fish-eye lens that photographs the entire hemisphere of the sky and surroundings in one image.

Using the location information, the SunEye generates and displays a solar window diagram specific to the local latitude. The photo is…It then calculates the total monthly solar access (…).

79 **Altitude Angle Method.** A simple method to evaluate shading at a particular location is by measuring or calculating the altitude angle of each obstruction.

Altitude angles can be calculated with the following formula: **(formula)**

Page #	Highlight
80	**Figure 3-23. Determining Altitude Angle**
	Profile Angle Method. The *profile angle* is the projection of the solar altitude angle onto an imaginary plane perpendicular to the surface of the obstruction.
	The profile angle is calculated with the following formula: (**formula**)
81	**Figure 3-25. Profile Angle**
82	**Figure 3-26. Inter-Row Shading**
83	**Accessibility:** Accessibility to rooftop mounted PV arrays is a critical concern for firefighters in allowing access pathways and ventilation opportunities on the roof in the event of a fire.
	Roofing Evaluation
	Roof Surfaces. Arrays are installed on many types of roof surfaces, although the type of roof… attachment methods that are feasible. The expected life of the roof covering is also very important.
84	A primary concern is the condition of the roof covering, particularly its weather sealing.
	For conventional asphalt shingles, deterioration includes brittleness, cracking, loss of granular… Asphalt shingles generally are the least expensive…and corrosion and pitting on aluminum roofs.
	The thickness of the roof decking dictates the appropriate length of the fasteners needed to install the array. The thickness can usually be determined by looking under the eave drip edge or flashing along the edge of the roof.
85	**Structural Support.** First, a visual inspection determines the flatness of the roof surface. A string line stretches across the roof in various directions reveals dips wherever there is a gap between the string and the roof surface.
	Next, the installer should walk carefully across the roof and check for movement of the surface.
	Arrays must be securely attached to the roof's underlying structural members in order to resist wind and other loads.
86	**Electrical Assessment:** Most inverters can be installed either indoors or outdoors, as long as they have the appropriate enclosure ratings, are kept cool and dry, and have enough…Inverters should be kept out of direct sunlight or other environments that can raise operating temperatures.
	Batteries should be installed within well-ventilated and protective enclosures.
	Site Layout Drawings: Site layout diagrams and sketches should identify the shape and dimensions of the structure, and the locations between major system components.
	Energy Audit: Some PV installations require a detailed electrical load analysis, especially for… estimated or measured peak power demand, average daily time of use, and total energy consumed.
87	**Figure 3-32. Site Layout Drawing**
	Figure 3-33: Load Analysis
90	**Installation Planning:** The installer completes the final design' prepares construction drawings …makes other preparations to complete the installation in the most efficient and timely manner.

Page #	Highlight
98	**Modules and Arrays:** An array consists of individual PV modules that are electrically connected to produce a desired voltage, current, and power output. Modules and arrays produce DC power… used to charge batteries, directly power DC loads, or be converted to AC power by inverters.
	Energy Storage Systems: Energy storage systems balance energy production and demand.
	Batteries, particularly lead-acid types are by far the most common means of energy storage in PV systems.
99	**Batteries.** A *battery bank* is a group of batteries connected together with series and parallel… Batteries in a PV system are charged by the array when sunny and discharged by loads when… starting requirements, which PV modules (as current-limited power sources) cannot provide.
	Flywheels. Flywheels are large, spinning rotors and are commonly used to transfer power from motors and engines to pumps and other rotational loads.
100	**Supercapacitors.** Capacitors store energy in an electrical field developed by two oppositely charged a parallel conductive plates separated by a dielectric (insulating) material.
	Supercapacitors are a suitable replacement for batteries in many low-power applications.
	Power Conditioning Equipment: Power conditioning equipment converts, controls, and otherwise processes DC power produced by a PV array to make the power compatible with other equipment or loads.
101	**Inverters.** An *inverter* is a device that converts DC power to AC power. In PV systems, inverters convert DC power from battery banks or PV arrays to AC power for AC loads to export to the utility grid.
	Battery-based inverters are used in stand-alone PV systems and operate directly from the battery banks to their input source.
	The AC output is typically 120V or 240V single-phase power, with power ratings from a few hundred watts to over 10 kW.
102	Utility-interactive inverters draw power directly from PV arrays and operate in parallel with the utility grid.
	Typical AC output voltages are 120 V or 240 V single-phase units with power outputs up to 10 …is determined by the DC input from the array, unlike the output from battery-based inverters.
	Charge Controllers. A *charge controller* is a device that regulates battery charge by controlling the charging voltage and/or current from a DC power source, such as a PV array.
103	Charge controllers regulate battery charging by terminating or limiting the charging current when the battery bank reaches a full state of charge.
	Rectifiers and Chargers. A *rectifier* is a device that converts AC power to DC power. A *charger* is a device that combines a rectifier with filters, transformers, and other components to condition DC power for the purpose of battery charging.
	DC-DC Converters. A *DC-DC converter* is a device that converts DC power from one voltage to another.

Page #	Highlight
	Maximum Power Point Trackers. A *maximum power tracker (MPPT)* is a device or circuit that introduces electronics to continually adjust the load on a PV device under changing temperature and irradiance conditions to keep it operating at its maximum power point.
104	**Electrical Loads:** An electrical load is any type of device, equipment, or appliance that consumes electricity.
105	**DC Loads.** The most common DC Loads used in PV systems are lighting fixtures and motors for fans and pumps. Many DC loads operate at 12 V, 24 V, or 48 V.
	AC Loads. Most residential and commercial loads are AC loads, including refrigerators, air conditioners, televisions, lighting, and motors.
	Balance-of System Components: Balance-of-system components are all the remaining electrical and mechanical components needed to integrate and assemble the major components in a PV system.
	Mechanical BOS Components. Mechanical BOS components include fasteners, brackets, enclosures, racks, and other structural support…reliable installation of PV system components.
	Electrical BOS Components. Electrical BOS components include conductors, cables, conduits, …between modules, controllers, batteries, inverters, and other electrical systems and equipment.
106	**Electrical Energy Sources:** Besides the PV array, an electric utility grid is the source of electricity that is far by far most commonly connected to PV systems.
110	**PV System Configurations:** The simplest PV system configuration is a PV module or array connected directly to a DC load.
	Stand-Alone Systems: A *stand-alone PV system* is a type of PV system that operates autonomo… Stand-alone PV systems are most popular for meeting small- to intermediate-size electrical loads.
	Direct-Coupled Systems. A *direct-coupled PV system* is a type of stand-alone system where the output of a PV module or array is directly connected to a DC load.
	DC motors are the most common loads for direct-coupled systems, including water…Direct-coupled PV systems are common for pumping potable water and agricultural water supplies.
110 & 111	While direct-coupled systems are the simplest form of any PV system in terms of equipment, they are perhaps the most complex to design properly dues to lack of energy storage or system control.
111	**Self-Regulated Systems.** A *self-regulating PV system* is a type of stand-alone PV system that uses no active control systems to protect the battery, except through careful design and component sizing.
	To protect the battery from over charge, the battery system must be oversized in relation to the size of the array, which keeps charging current low. **Charge-Controlled Systems.** If loads are variable or uncontrolled, charge control is required to prevent damage to the battery from overcharge or discharge. Charge control typically involves interrupting or limiting the charging current to a fully charged battery to prevent overcharge.
	Charge control is required by the NEC® if the maximum array current is equal to 3% or more of the rated battery capacity in ampere-hours.

Page # **Highlight**

113 **Utility-Interactive Systems:** A *utility-interactive system* is a PV system that operates in parallel with and is connected to the electric utility grid.

These systems are the simplest and least-expensive PV systems that produce AC power because they require the fewest components and do not use batteries. The primary component of a utility-interactive system is the inverter.

Net Metering. *Net metering* is a metering arrangement where any excess energy is exported to the utility is subtracted from the amount of energy imported from it. Using this system, energy supplied to the utility from a PV system is effectively credited to the customer at full retail value.

114 **Figure 4-19. Utility-Interactive Systems**

Dual Metering: *Dual metering* is the arrangement that measures energy exported to and imported from the utility grid separately.

115 **Multimode Systems:** A *multimode system* is a PV system that can operate in either utility-interactive or stand-alone mode and uses battery storage.

The key component in a multimode system is the inverter, which draws DC power from the battery system instead of the array.

Multimode systems are typically used to back up critical loads, but can also be used to manage the energy supply for different times of the day in order to reduce electricity bills.

116 **Figure 4-21. Multimode Systems**

118 **Hybrid Systems:** A *hybrid system* is a stand-alone system that includes two or more distributed energy sources.

124 **Photovoltaic Cells:** A *photovoltaic cell* is a semiconductor device that converts solar radiation into direct current electricity.

Semiconductors: A *semiconductor* is a material that can exhibit properties of both an insulator and a conductor.

125 **Photovoltaic Effect:** The basic physical process by which a PV cell converts light into electricity is known as the photovoltaic effect. The *photovoltaic effect* is the movement of the electrons within a material when it absorbs photons with energy above a certain level.

A PV cell is a thin, flat wafer consisting of a p-n junction. A *p-n junction* is the boundary of adjacent layers of p-type and n-type semiconductor materials in contact with one another.

Figure 5-3. Photovoltaic Effect

126 **Cell Materials:** PV cells can be produced from a variety of semiconductor materials, though crystalline silicon is by far the most common.

Crystalline silicon (C-Si) cells currently offer the best ratio of…as the semiconductor industry.

Gallium arsenide (GaAs) cells are more efficient than c-Si cells…their use to space applications.

A *multifunction cell* is a cell that maximizes efficiency…different wavelengths of solar energy.

126 & 127 A *thin-film module* is a module level PV device…and make electrical connections between cells.

Page #	Highlight
127	A *photoelectrochemical cell* is a cell that relies on chemical processes to produce electricity from light, rather than using semiconductors.
	Figure 5-4. PV Cell Material Efficiencies
131	**Current Voltage (I-V) Curves:** The *current-voltage (I-V) characteristic* is the basic electrical output profile of a PV device.
	An *I-V curve* is the graphic representation of all possible voltage and current operating points for a PV device at a specific operating condition.
	A PV device can operate anywhere along its I-V curve, depending on the electrical load.
	Certain points on an I-V curve are used to rate module performance and are the basis for the electrical design of arrays.
	Figure 5-10. I-V Curve
132	**Open-Circuit Voltage:** The *open-circuit voltage* (V_{oc}) is the maximum voltage on an I-V curve and is the operating point for a PV device under infinite load or open-circuit condition, and no current output.
	The open-circuit voltage of a PV-device can be measured by exposing the device to sunlight and measuring across the output terminals with a voltmeter or multimeter set to measure DC voltage.
	The open-circuit voltage of a PV device is determined by the semiconductor material properties and temperature.
	Short-Circuit Current: The *short-circuit current* (I_{sc}) is the maximum current on a n IV-curve and is the operating point for a PV device under no load…circuit condition, and no voltage output.
132 & 133	The short-circuit current of a PV device is used to determine maximum circuit design currents… by exposing the device to sunlight and measuring current with an ammeter or multimeter.
133	**Figure 5-12. Short-Circuit Current Measurement**
134	The current of a PV device is directly proportional to surface area and solar irradiance. In other …current output. Likewise, doubling the solar irradiance on the device surface will double current.
	Maximum Power Point: The *maximum power point (P_{mp})* is the operating point on an I-V curve where the product of current and voltage is at maximum.
	The *maximum power voltage* (V_{mp}) is the operating voltage on an I-V curve where the power… Maximum power is calculated using the following formula: **(formula)**
135	Maximum power voltage and current can be measured only while the PV device is connected to a load that operates the device at maximum power.
	Efficiency. The efficiency of PV devices compares the solar power input to the electrical power output.
136	Efficiency is expressed as a percentage and is calculated with the following formula: **(formula)**
	Operating Point: PV cells operate most efficiently at their maximum power points.

Page #	Highlight
137	The electrical load resistance required to operate a PV device at any point can be calculated using Ohm's law. For the maximum power point, the formula is: (**formula**)
138	**Solar Irradiance Response:** Changes in solar irradiance have a small effect on voltage but a significant effect on the current output of PV devices. The current of a PV device increases proportionally with increasing solar irradiance.
139	**Temperature Response:** For most types of PV devices, high operating temperatures significantly reduce voltage output.
139 & 140	**Cell Temperature.** The cell temperature of a PV device refers to the internal temperature at the p-n junction. Cell temperature is influenced…Cell temperature can be estimated by either directly measuring the cell or module surface temperature or applying the temperature-rise coefficient.
140	**Temperature Coefficients.** A *temperature coefficient* is the rate of change in voltage, current, or power output from a PV device due to changing cell temperature.
143	**Modules and Arrays:** A *module* is a PV device consisting of a number of individual cells connected electrically, laminated, encapsulated, and packaged into a frame.
	An *array* is a complete PV power generating unit consisting of a number of individual electrically and mechanically integrated modules with structural supports, trackers, or other components.
144	**Electrical Connections**
	Series Connections. Individual cells are connected in series by soldering thin metal strips from the top surface (negative terminal) of one cell to the back surface (positive terminal) of the next. Modules are connected in series with other modules by connecting conductors between the negative terminal of one module to the positive terminal of another module.
	Only PV devices having the same current output should be connected in series.
145	PV devices with different voltage outputs can be connected in series without loss of power as long as each device has the same current output.
	Figure 5-25. Series Connections
146	The maximum number of modules that can be connected in a series string is limited by the maximum system voltage rating of the modules and other components.
	Parallel Connections. Parallel connections involve connecting the positive terminals of each string together and all the negative terminals together at common terminals or busbars.
151	**Module Selection:** Electrically, the voltage, current, and power output values are the most important considerations because they define the total number of modules needed to meet the desired energy production requirement.
152	On the physical side, among factors that may be considered for module selection are the overall …of the module, the type of frame and laminate construction, the means for structural attachments.
	Arrays: Groups of modules are combined electrically and mechanically, typically in series…The result is a complete array that integrates all the modules into a single power-generating unit.
	Most complete arrays are monopole arrays. A *monopole array* is an array that has one positive terminal and one negative terminal.

Page # **Highlight**

160 **Battery Principles:** A *cell* is the basic unit in a battery that stores electrical energy in chemical bonds and delivers this energy through chemical reactions.

161 **Steady-State:** A cell or battery that is not connected to a load or charging circuit is at steady-state. *Steady-state* is an open-circuit condition where essentially no electrical or chemical changes are occurring.

The *open-circuit voltage* is the voltage of a battery or cell when it is at steady-state. The open-circuit voltage of a fully charged lead-cell is about 2.1 V.

162 **Capacity:** Capacity is commonly expressed in ampere-hours (Ah), but…in watt-hours (Wh).

Discharging

163 **State of Charge (SOC).** The *state of charge (SOC)* is a percentage of energy remaining in a battery compared to its fully charged capacity.

Depth of Discharge (DOD). *Depth of discharge (DOD)* is the percentage of energy withdrawn from a battery compared to its fully charged capacity.

By definition, the depth of discharge and state of charge of a battery add of to 100%.

164 **Allowable DOD.** The *allowable depth of discharge* is the maximum percentage of total capacity that is permitted to be withdrawn from a battery.

Autonomy. *Autonomy* is the amount of time a fully charged battery system can supply power to system loads without further charging.

Charging: A *cycle* is a battery discharge followed by a charge.

165 *Charge rate* is the ratio of nominal battery capacity to the charge time in hours.

167 **Gassing and Overcharge:** *Overcharge* is the ratio of applied charge to the resulting increase in battery charge.

169 **Battery Life:** Battery life is expressed in terms of cycles or years.

170 **Battery Types:** A *primary battery* is a battery that can store and deliver electrical energy but cannot be recharged.

A *secondary battery* is a battery that can store and deliver electrical energy and can be charged by passing a current through in an opposite direction to the discharge current.

171 **Battery Classifications**

172 **Flooded-Electrolyte Batteries**

Captive-Electrolyte Batteries

173 **Lead-Acid Batteries**

174 **Nickel-Cadmium Batteries**

175 **Battery Systems**

Battery Selection: Considerations includes lifetime, deep cycle performance, tolerance to high temperatures and overcharge, and maintenance requirements.

Page # **Highlight**

Battery Banks: A *battery bank* is a group of batteries connected together with series and/or parallel connections to provide a specific voltage and capacity.

176 **Series Connections.** batteries are first connected in a series string by connecting the negative terminal of one battery, to the positive terminal of the next battery, in order to build voltage.

For batteries of similar capacity and voltage connected on series, the circuit voltage is the sum… battery voltages, and the circuit capacity is the same as the capacity of the individual batteries.

177 **Parallel Connections.** Batteries are connected in parallel by connecting all the positive terminals together and all the negative terminals together.

The current of the parallel circuit is the sum of the current from the individual batteries. The voltage across the circuit is the same as the voltage…is the sum of the capacities of each battery.

179 **Battery Installation**

Battery Bank Voltage: Battery banks installed in dwellings must be less than 50 V nominal… maintenance. This usually limits the voltage of lead-acid batteries to no more than 48 V nominal.

180 **Grounding:** Battery systems over 48 V are permitted to be ungrounded but have several requirements. The PV array…and have overcurrent protection for each ungrounded conductor.

Wiring Methods: Battery systems are permitted to use flexible conductors of 2/0 AWG and larger.

Conductor insulation types RHW and THW also meet the…battery installations in PV systems.

188 **Charge Controller Features:** A *charge controller* is a device that regulates battery charge by controlling the…the battery from overcharge by the array and overdischarge by system loads.

Battery Charging: Charge controllers manage the array current delivered to…*Charge acceptance* is the ratio of the increase in battery charge to the amount of charge supplied to the battery.

190 **Overcharge Protection:** *overcharge* is the condition of a fully charged battery continuing to… A charge controller protects a battery from overcharge through charge regulation.

According to the NEC®, any PV system employing batteries shall have equipment to control… 3% of the rated battery capacity in ampere-hours. This equates to a maximum charge rate of C/33.

191 **Overdischarge Protection:** *Overdischarge* is the condition of a battery state of charge declining …without damaging the battery. A charge controller protects a…(low state of charge) condition.

193 **Charge Controller Types**

Shunt Charge Controllers: A *shunt charge controller* is a charge controller that limits charging current to a battery system by short-circuiting the array.

194 **Series Charge Controllers:** A *series charge controller* is a charge controller that limits charging current to a battery system by open-circuiting the array.

196 **Maximum Power Point Tracking (MPPT) Charge Controllers:** A *maximum power point tracking (MPPT) charge controller* is a charge controller…as well as regulates battery charging.

Diversionary Charge Controllers: A *diversionary charge controller* is a charge controller that regulates charging current to a battery system by diverting excess power to an auxiliary load.

Page #	**Highlight**
197	**Hybrid System Controllers:** A *hybrid system controller* is a controller with advanced features for managing multiple energy sources.
	A principle feature of some hybrid controllers is the additional ability to start and control an engine generator.
198	**Ampere-Hour Integrating Charge Controllers:** An *ampere-hour integrating charge controller* ...into and out of a battery and regulates charging current based on a preset amount of overcharge.
199	**Charge Controller Setpoints:** A *charge controller setpoint* is a battery...or switching functions.
	Charge Regulation Setpoints
200	**Load Control Setpoints**
205	**Charge Controller Installation**
	Figure 7-19. Charge Controller Selection Criteria
206	**Location:** To minimize their operating temperature, charge controllers should be installed out of direct sunlight and with unobstructed airflow around the heat sinks.
209	**Self-Regulating PV Systems:** A *self-regulating PV system* is a type of stand-alone PV system... active control systems to protect the battery, except through careful design and component sizing.
	Self-regulating PV systems must be designed so that the battery is never overcharged or discharged under any operating conditions.
211	**Battery and Array Sizing.** According to the NEC®, any PV system with batteries must employ a charge control whenever the charge rate exceeds C/33.
218	**Waveforms:** A *waveform* is the shape of an electrical signal that varies over time. Waveforms are used to represent changing electrical current and voltage.
220	**Three-Phase AC Power:** Three-phase AC power includes three separate voltage and current waveforms occurring simultaneously 120° apart.
223	**Power Factor.** *True power* is the product of in-phase voltage and current waveforms and produces ...True power is also called real power or active power and is represented in units of watts (W).
224	*Reactive power* is the product of out-of-phase voltage and current waveforms...no net power flow.
	Power factor is the ratio of true power to apparent power and describes the displacement of...
	Apparent power is a combination of true and reactive power and is given in units of volt-...(VA).
	Inverters: When a PV system must supply power for AC loads, an inverter is required. An inverter is a device that converts DC power to AC power.
	inverters provide convenience by being able to integrate a PV system with existing electrical systems.
	Static (solid-state) inverters change DC power to AC power using electronics and have no moving parts.
	Inverters used in PV systems are exclusively static inverters.

Page #	Highlight
226	**Stand-Alone Inverters:** Stand-alone inverters are connected to batteries as the DC power source and operate independently of the PV array and the utility grid.
	Utility-Interactive Inverters: Utility-interactive PV inverters are connected to, and operate in parallel with, the electric utility grid.
229	**Multimode Inverters:** Multimode inverters can operate in either interactive or stand-alone (though not simultaneously).
231	**Square Wave Inverters**
233	**Power Conditioning Units:** The physical enclosure that is referred to as an inverter is actually… Power conditioning units perform one…DC-DC conversion, and maximum power point tracking.
234	**Rectifiers:** A *rectifier* is a device that converts AC power to DC power. Rectifiers are used in battery chargers and DC power supplies operating from AC power.
	Transformers: A *transformer* is a device that transfers energy from one circuit to another through magnetic coupling.
	Transformers cannot convert between DC and AC, change the voltage or current of a DC source, or change the frequency of an AC source.
235	**DC-DC Converter:** A *DC-DC converter* is a device that changes DC power from one voltage to another.
	Many PV inverters use DC-DC converters to change the DC input from low voltage to high voltage prior to the power-inverting process.
	Maximum Power Point Trackers: A *maximum power point tracker (MPPT)* is a device or… to keep it operating at its maximum…to the array, all interactive inverters include MPPT circuits.
236	**Power Ratings.** For an interactive inverter, the output power rating limits the power it can handle at its DC input, which limits the size of the PV array.
236 & 237	**Temperature Limitations.** Solid-state switching devices are capable of handling only so much current before they overheat and fail. Parallel switching devices in the design increases the power rating of an inverter.
237	temperature is the primary limiting factor for inverter power ratings.
	Interactive inverters control high temperatures by limiting the array power delivered to the inverter
	Voltage Ratings
	AC Output. For interactive inverters, AC voltage output must be maintained at -10% to +5% of the nominal system voltage. In the case of nominal output, this range is from 108 V to 126 V.
238	**DC Input.** DC input voltage ratings are based on the operating characteristics of either a battery bank (for stand-alone inverters) or a PV array (for interactive inverters).
	The required array voltage increases with increasing grid voltage, and the array must have maximum power voltage in this range to permit MPPT operation.
	The DC voltage from the array is also affected by ambient temperature, which complicates sizing.

Page # **Highlight**

239 **Frequency Ratings:** For nominal 60 Hz operation the, the AC output frequency must be maintained between 59.3 Hz and 60.5 Hz.

Current Ratings: For the DC side, current ratings limit the PV array or battery current that can be applied to the inverter. On the AC side, current ratings...current output for interactive inverters.

240 **Efficiency:** *Inverter efficiency* is the ratio of an inverter's AC power output to its DC power input.

Inverter efficiency is calculated with the following formula: (**formula**)

Inverter efficiency is primarily affected by the inverter load. In stand-alone, the AC load defines the inverter load, and for interactive inverters the PV array defines the load.

248 **Sizing Methodologies**

Sizing Utility-Interactive Systems: The sizing for interactive systems without energy storage generally...80% to 90% of the array maximum-power rating at standard test conditions (STC).

249 Sizing interactive systems begins with the specifications of PV module chosen for the system.

Figure 9-2. Interactive System Sizing

The size of an interactive system is primarily limited by the space available for an array and the owner's budget.

250 **Sizing Stand-Alone Systems:** Stand-alone systems are designed to power specific on-site loads, so the size of these systems is directly proportional to the load requirements.

Sizing stand-alone systems is based on meeting specific load requirements and involves the following key steps: 1 - 4.

251 **Sizing Multimode Systems:** multi-mode systems are typically sized according to the stand-alone methodology.

The stand-alone sizing methodology determines the minimum size of a multimode system.

Sizing Hybrid Systems: The array and battery bank for a PV array and engine generator hybrid ...Finally, battery banks can be sized...also because the generator power is available on demand.

Sizing Calculations: Sizing PV systems for stand-alone operation involves four sets of... Finally, the PV array is sized to fully charge the battery bank under the critical conditions.

252 **Load Analysis:** Analyzing electrical loads is the first and most important step in PV-system sizing. The energy consumption dictates the amount of electricity that must be produced.

A detailed load analysis completed during the site survey lists each load, its power demand and daily energy consumption.

253 **Power Demand.** Peak-power information is usually found on appliance nameplates or in...peak power demand can be estimated by multiplying the maximum current by the operating voltage.

Energy Consumption. Electrical energy consumption is based on the power demand over time.

254 The daily energy consumption for each load is determined by the load's power demand multiplied by the daily operating time.

Page #	Highlight
	Inverter Selection. If the system includes AC loads, an inverter must be selected. Several factors must be considered when selecting an inverter. First…as the largest single AC load.
	Inverter voltage output is another consideration.
255	The inverter DC-input voltage must also correspond with either the array voltage (for interactive systems) or the battery-bank voltage (for stand-alone systems).
	Inverter Efficiency. Both the AC and DC energy requirements from the load analysis are used to determine how much total DC energy will be required. The total amount of DC energy required by the loads is calculated using the following formula: (**formula**)
256	**Critical Design Analysis:** systems are sized for the worst-case scenario of high load and low insolation.
	The *critical design ratio* is the ratio of electrical energy demand to average…during a period.
257	**Array Orientation.** if multiple orientations are possible, separate analyses are performed for each orientation.
	The orientations most commonly used in a critical design analysis are tilt angles equal to the latitude…The greater array tilt angle maximizes the received solar energy…in summer months.
260	**DC-System Voltage:** This voltage dictates the operating voltage and ratings for all…the array.
	The selection of the battery-bank voltage affects system currents.
	Lower current reduces the required sizes of conductors, overcurrent protection…other equipment.
	As a rule of thumb, stand-alone systems up to 1 kW use a minimum 12 V battery-bank voltage, which limits DC currents to less than 84 A.
	System Availability: *System availability* is the percentage of time over an average year that a stand-alone PV system meets the system load requirements.
	System availability is determined by insulation and autonomy.
	Autonomy is the amount of time a fully charged battery can supply system can supply power to the system loads without further charging.
261	**Battery-Bank Required Output.** Batteries for stand-alone PV systems are sized to store enough …length of autonomy without any further charge or energy contributions from the PV array.
	Figure 9-13. Battery-Bank Sizing
262	The required battery-bank capacity is determined from electrical-energy requirements to operate …The required battery-bank rated capacity is calculated using the following formula: (**formula**)
	Battery-Bank Rated Capacity. Most PV systems use deep-cycle lead-acid batteries, which can be discharged to about 80%. This is the maximum fraction of the total rated…battery at any time.
	Most battery rating are specified for operation at 25°C (77°F) at a certain discharge rate.
263	Using the daily operating time calculated in the load analysis, the average discharge rate is calculated using the following formula: (**formula**)

Page #	Highlight
	To calculate the total rated capacity of the battery bank, the required battery-bank output is increased…The required capacity is calculated using the following formula: (**formula**)
264	**Battery Selection.** the number of parallel battery connections should be limited to no more than 3 to 4 strings.
	The nominal DC-system voltage divided by the nominal battery voltage determines the number of batteries in a string.
265	**Battery-Bank Operation:** First, the daily load fraction supplied by the battery bank is estimated.
	The *load fraction* is the portion of load operating power that comes from the battery bank over the course of a day.
	Instead, of load-fraction estimate of 0.75 is a common rule of thumb used for most PV systems.
	With the load fraction estimate, the average battery-bank daily depth of discharge is then estimated with the following formula: (**formula**)
266	**Array Sizing:** For stand-alone systems, the array must be sized to produce enough electrical energy to meet…during the critical design month while accounting for normal system losses.
	Figure 9-18. Array Sizing
	Required Array Output. The required array current is calculated using the following formula: (**formula**)
268	**Array Rated Output.** *Soiling* is the acumination of dust and dirt on an array surface that shades the array and reduces electrical output.
	The rated array maximum-power current is calculated using the following formula: (**formula**)
	High temperature reduces array voltage output.
	The rated array maximum-power voltage is calculated using the following formula: (**formula**)
269	**Module Selection.** For each module, three parameters are needed for sizing: the maximum power …power, the maximum power (operating) current, and the maximum-power (operating) voltage.
	The number of parallel strings of modules required is…The rated array maximum power is calculated by multiplying the rated module maximum power by the total number of modules.
278	**Array Performance.** The *installed nominal operating cell temperature (INOCT)* is the estimated temperature of a PV array operating in a specific mounting system design.
281	**Array Mounting Systems:** The simplest and most common type of array mount for modules is the fixed-tilt type. A *fixed-tilt mounting system* is an…azimuth angles to increase the array output.
	Building Mounting Systems
	Direct Mounts. A *direct mount* is a type of fixed-tilt…finished rooftop or other building surface.
	Temperature-rise coefficients for direct mounts can be as high as 40 to 50º C/kW/m^2 (…).
282	**Roof-Rack Mounts:** A *rack-mount* is a type of fixed- or adjustable-tilt array mounting system with a triangular-shaped structure to increase the tilt angle of the array.

Page #	Highlight
	INOCT for rack-mounted arrays is the lowest among building mounting…15 to 20º C/kW/m^2.
	Standoff Mounts. A *standoff mount* is a type of fixed-tilt array mounting system where modules are supported by a structure parallel to and slightly above the roof surface.
283	In general, standoff mounts should be installed between 3" to 6"…are around 20 to 30º C/kW/m^2.
284	**Ground Mounting Systems**
286	**Sun-Tracking Systems:** A *sun-tracking mount* is an array mounting system that automatically orients the array to the position of the sun.
287	An *active tracking mount* is an array mounting system that uses electric motors and gear drives to automatically direct the array toward the sun.
288	A *passive track mount* is an array mounting system that uses nonelectrical means to automatically direct an array toward the sun.
	Mechanical Integration
	Materials: Any material used should match the expected 20- to 30-year service lifetime of the overall system under the given conditions.
	Stainless steel alloys 316 and 403 are recommended for most fasteners.
	Aluminum structural alloys 6061 and 6063 are…lightweight, and relatively inexpensive.
289	**Structural Loads:** Arrays and their attachment points must be designed and installed to withstand the forces from a combination of structural loads. A *design load* is a calculated structural load used to evaluate the strength of a structure to failure.
290	**Dead Loads.** A *dead load* is a static structural load due to the weight of permanent building members, supported structure, and attachments.
	Live Loads. A *live load* is a dynamic structural load due to…using or occupying the structure.
291	**Wind Loads:** The *basic wind speed* is the maximum value of a 3 sec gust at 33' elevation, which is used in wind load calculations.
295	**Attachment Methods:** Mounting system attachments should be made through the roof cladding and into building structural members, such as rafters.
	Lag Screws. Lag screws are the most common fastenings for attaching array mounts to rooftops.
	Figure 10-22. Allowable Withdrawal Loads
309	**Voltage and Current Requirements**
310	**Maximum PV Circuit Voltage:** the maximum DC voltage of a PV source circuit or output… voltages of the series-connected modules corrected for the lowest expected ambient temperature.
311	The maximum PV source-circuit or output-circuit voltage is calculated using the formula: **(formula)**
312	**Maximum PV Circuit Currents:** For PV source circuits, the maximum current is 125% of the sum of the short-circuit current ratings of parallel-connected modules.

Page #	Highlight
	For PV output circuits, the maximum current is the sum of the maximum currents of the parallel-connected source circuits.
	Maximum Inverter Input Current: Maximum inverter input current is calculated with the following formula: (**formula**)
313	**Maximum Inverter Output Current:** The maximum current for the inverter output is equal to the inverter's maximum continuous output current rating.
	Conductors and Wiring Methods
314	**Figure 11-4. Conductor Sizes**
315	**Figure 11-5. National Ampacities of Insulated Cooper Conductors**
317	**Voltage Drop.** Voltage drop and the associated percentage of the voltage drop of conductors are calculated using Ohm's law: (**formula**)
318	**Conductor Insulation**
319	**Figure 11-10. Recommended Insulation Types for PV Systems**
322	**Wiring Connections:** The following are basic requirements for terminating electrical conductors: (6 Bullets)
	Module Connectors: These connectors must meet the following five requirements from Section 690.33: (5 Bullets)
324	**Junction Boxes**
328	**Overcurrent Protection**
329	**Overcurrent Protection Devices:** devices include fuses and circuit breakers.
331	**PV System Overcurrent Protection:** Circuits must be protected from every source of power.
	every undergrounded conductor must be protected.
	Array Overcurrent Protection. Generally, all undergrounded array conductors must include overcurrent protection. The grounded conductors must not normally include overcurrent protection (or a disconnect).
332	**Inverter-Output Overcurrent Protection**
	Figure 11-25. Inverter-Output Overcurrent Protection and Disconnects
333	**Disconnects:** A *disconnec*t is a device used to isolate equipment and conductors from sources of electricity from the purpose of installation, maintenance, or service.
334	**Array Disconnects:** A disconnect must be provided to isolate all…in a building or structure.
	AC Disconnects: A disconnect must also be installed on the AC side of the PV system to isolate the system from the rest of a building's electrical system.
335	**Equipment Disconnects:** If equipment is connected to one or more power source, each power source must have disconnecting means.

Page #	Highlight
	Grounding
336	**AC Grounding**
	DC Grounding. The DC grounding connection must be made at a single point on the PV output circuit, usually within the inverter.
337	**AC and DC Ground**
	Figure 11-30. AC and DC Grounding Methods
338	**Ground-Fault Protection:** *Ground-fault protection* is the automatic opening of conductors involved in a ground fault.
340	**Equipment Grounding**
341	**Figure 11-35. Grounding Conductor Sizing**
343	**Surge Arrestors:** A *surge arrestor* is a device that protects electrical devices from transients (voltage spikes).
345	**Battery Systems**
	Battery Banks Less Than 50 V
	Battery Banks Greater Than 50 V: Battery systems of greater than 48 V must include a disconnect to divide the system into segments of 48 V or less for maintenance.
346	**Charge Control:** In the case of self-regulated systems, charge control is accomplished through careful sizing and the matching of the array to the…must include active means of charge control.
	Diversion loads are commonly used for charge control…The loads voltage rating must be greater than the maximum battery…the power rating must be at least 150% of the array's power rating.
354	**Utility-Interactive Systems.** The most common type of utility interactive PV system is one that does not use energy storage. The array is connected to the DC input of the utility-interactive inverter.
	When on-site power demand exceeds the supply from the PV system, the power is drawn from the utility.
	Multimode Systems. Multimode systems are interactive systems that include battery storage… back-up power supply for critical loads such as computers, refrigeration, water pumps, or lighting.
	The inverters serve the on-site loads or send excess power back to the grid while the array keeps the battery bank fully charged.
355	Multimode inverters are programmed to supply…minimizing the use of high-priced utility energy.
358	**Interconnection Concerns**
	Islanding. *Islanding* is the undesirable condition where a distributed-generation power source… continues to supply power to the utility grid during a utility outage.
360	**Point of Connection:** The *point of connection* is the location at which the interactive distributed-generation system makes its interconnection with the electric utility system.

Page #	**Highlight**
360 & 361	**Load-Side Interconnections.** The NEC® permits load-side connection for utility interactive… providing the following seven conditions are satisfied: 1 – 7.
363	**Supply-Side Interconnections.** When PV systems are too large to interconnect on the load side …due to the capacity of the distribution equipment, a supply side interconnection must be used.
366	**Utility Interconnection Policies**
383	**Permitting**
	Permit Applications: Permit applications for PV systems should contain site drawings, electrical…specifications for major components and equipment, and array mounting information.
	Site Drawings. A simple drawing of the site should indicate the locations of major PV system… disconnects, and their relationships to electrical services, property lines, streets, and other features.
	Electrical Diagram
385	**Figure 13-5. Electrical Diagrams**
	Array Mounting Design: Most permit applications for PV systems require descriptions and/or …can support the additional weight of the PV array and that the array will be well secured.
387	**Inspection**
388	**Working Space:** PV system inspections also ensure that there is adequate access and safe working space around all electrical equipment.
389	**Live Parts:** Live parts are energized conductors and terminals. Live parts must…50 V or more.
390	**Labels and Marking**
400	**System Functional Testing**
	Verification Testing
402	**System Performance Testing**
404	**Maintenance**
405	**Array Maintenance**
408	**Battery Maintenance**
413	**Monitoring**
417	**Troubleshooting**
426	**Incentives**
431	**Cost Analysis**
433	**Life-Cycle Costs**
438	**Life-Cycle Cost Analysis:** The life-cycle cost for any energy system is the sum of the present values…This is represented in the following formula: (**formula**)

Florida Building Code - Plumbing, 7th Edition, 2020

Tabs and Highlights

These1 Exam Prep Tabs are based on the *Florida Building Code - Plumbing 2020.*

Each 1 Exam Prep tabs sheet has five rows of tabs. Start with the first tab at the first row at the top of the page; proceed down that row placing the tabs at the locations listed below. Place each tab in your book setting it down one notch until you get to the last tab (usually the index or glossary). Then start with the highlights.

1 Exam Prep Tab	Section	Page #
Table of Contents		v
Piping Support	308	13
Minimum Plumbing Facilities	403	19
Materials, Joints & Connections	605	39
Protection of Potable Water Supply	608	47
Healthcare Plumbing	609	53
Joints	705	59
Cleanouts	708	61
Drainage System Sizing	710	65
Vacuum Drainage System	715	67
Permit Schedule Fee	Appendix A	121
Rates of Rainfall	Appendix B	123
Structural Safety	Appendix C	125
Degree Day & Design Temp.	Appendix D	127
Sizing of Water Piping System	Appendix E	133
Turf & Landscape Irrigation	Appendix F	155

******This concludes the tabs for this book. Please continue with the highlights on the following page.******

Section #	Highlight
202	**General Definitions:**

- Backflow
  - Back pressure, low head
  - Backsiphonage
- Backflow Connection
- Bedpan Steamer or Boiler
- Developed Length
- Offset
- Potable Water

305 **Protection of Pipes and Plumbing System Components**

306 **Trenching, Excavation and Backfill**

307 **Structural Safety**

307.5 **Protection of footings:** Trenching installed parallel to footings and walls shall not extend into the bearing plane…at an angle of 45 degrees (0.79 rad) from horizontal, from the outside bottom edge of the footing or wall.

308 **Piping Support**

308.5 **Interval of support:** Pipe shall be supported in accordance with Table 308.5.

Table 308.5 **Hanger Spacing**

308.8 **Expansion joint fittings**

310 **Washroom and Toilet Room Requirements**

310.1 **Light and ventilation:** Washrooms and toilet rooms shall be illuminated and ventilated in accordance with the *Florida Building Code, Building and the Florida Building Code, Mechanical.*

312 **Tests and Inspections**

312.2 **Drainage and vent water test:** If the system is tested in sections, each opening shall be tightly plugged except the highest openings…This pressure shall be held for not less than 15 minutes.

312.6 **Gravity sewer test:** Gravity *sewer* tests shall consist of plugging the end of the *building sewer* at the point of connection…with not less than a 5-foot head of water and maintaining such pressure for 15 minutes.

312.7 **Forced sewer test:** Forced *sewer* tests shall consist of plugging the end of the *building sewer* at the point of connection with the public sewer and applying a pressure of 5 psi greater than the pump rating, and maintaining such pressure for 15 minutes.

318 **Irrigation**

318.1 **General:** Irrigation/sprinkler systems and risers for spray heads shall not be installed within 1 foot of the building sidewall.

402 **Fixture Materials**

Section #	Highlight
402.3	**Sheet copper:** Sheet copper for general applications shall conform to ASTM B152 and shall not weigh less than 12 ounces per square foot.
403	**Minimum Plumbing Facilities**
403.1	**Minimum number of fixtures:** Plumbing fixtures shall be provided for the type of occupancy and in the minimum number shown in Table 403.1.
Table 403.1	**Minimum Number of Required Plumbing Fixtures**
403.1.3	**Potty parity**
403.3.3	**Location of toilet facilities in occupancies other than covered malls:** shall be located not more than one story above or below the space required to be provided with toilet facilities, and the path of travel to such facilities shall not exceed a distance of 500 feet.
403.6	**Sanitary facilities for public swimming pools:** Swimming pools with a bathing load of 20 persons or less may utilize a unisex restroom. Pools with bathing loads of 40 persons or less may utilize two unisex restrooms or meet the requirements of Table 403.6.
403.6.1	**Required fixtures:** Fixtures shall be provided as indicated on Table 403.6. An additional set of fixtures shall be provided in the men's restroom for every 7,500 square feet or major fraction thereof for pools greater than 10,000 square feet.
Table 403.6	**Public Swimming Pool–Required Fixtures Count**
405	**Installation of Fixtures**
405.3.1	**Water closets, urinals, lavatories and bidets:** A water closet, urinal, lavatory or bidet shall not be set closer than 15 inches from its center to any side wall…Water closet compartments shall be less than 30 inches in width and not less than 60 inches in depth for floor-mounted water closets and not less than 30 inches in width and 56 inches in depth for wall- hung water closets.
405.9	**Slip joint connections:** Fixtures with concealed slip-joint connections shall be provided with an *access* panel or utility space not less than 12-inches in its smallest dimension or other *approved* arrangement so as to provide *access* to the slip joint connections for inspection and repair.
409	**Dishwashing Machines**
409.1	**Approval:** Commercial dishwashing machines shall conform to ASSE 1004 and NSF 3.
411	**Emergency Showers and Eyewash Stations**
411.2	**Waste connection:** Waste connections shall not be required for emergency showers and eyewash stations.
415	**Flushing Devices for Water Closets and Urinals**
415.1.1	**Separate for each fixture:** A flushing device shall not serve more than one fixture.
416	**Food Waste Grinder Units**

Section #	Highlight
416.3	**Commercial food waste grinder waste outlets:** Commercial food waste grinders shall be connected to a drain not less than 1½ inches in diameter.
416.4	**Water supply required:** All food waste grinders shall be provided with a supply of cold water. The water supply shall be protected against backflow by an *air gap* or backflow preventer in accordance with Section 608.
421	**Showers**
421.4.1	**Floor and wall area:** Wall materials shall extend to a height not less than 6 feet above the room floor level, and not less than 70 inches above the drain of the tub or shower.
421.5.2.1	**PVC sheets:** Plasticized polyvinyl chloride (PVC) sheets shall meet the requirements of ASTM D4551. Sheets shall be joined by solvent welding in accordance with the manufacturer's installation instructions.
421.5.2.2	**Chlorinated polyethylene (CPE) sheets:** Nonplasticized chlorinated polyethylene sheet shall meet the requirements of ASTM D4068. The liner shall be joined in accordance with the manufacturer's installation instructions.
424	**Urinals**
424.2	**Substitution for water closets:** In each bathroom or toilet room, urinals shall not be substituted for more than 67 percent of the required water closets in assembly and educational *occupancies.*
426	**Whirlpool Bathtubs**
426.3	**Drain:** The pump drain and circulation piping shall be sloped to drain the water in the volute and the circulation piping when the whirlpool bathtub is empty.
501	**General**
501.2	**Water heater as space heater:** Where a combination potable water heating and space heating system requires water for space heating at temperatures higher than 140°F…the potable *hot water* distribution system to a temperature of 140°F or less.
502	**Installation**
502.1.1	**Elevation and protection:** Elevation of water heater ignition sources and mechanical damage protection requirements for water heaters, shall be in accordance with the *Florida Building Code, Mechanical and the Florida Building Code, Fuel Gas.*
502.5	**Clearances for maintenance and replacement:** A level working space not less than 30 inches in length and 30 inches in width shall be provided in front of the control side to service and appliance.
503	**Connections**
503.1	**Cold water line valve:** The cold water *branch* line from the main water supply line to each hot water storage tank or water heater shall be provided with a valve, located near the equipment and serving only the hot water storage tank or water heater.
504	**Safety Devices**

Section #	Highlight
504.4	**Relief valve:** Storage water heaters operating above atmospheric pressure shall be provided with an *approved*, self-closing (levered) pressure relief valve and temperature relief valve or combination thereof.
504.7	**Required pan:** Where a storage tank-type water heater or a hot water storage tank is installed in a location where water leakage from the tank will cause damage, the tank shall be installed in a pan constructed of one of the following: 1 - 3.
504.7.1	**Pan size and drain:** The pan shall be not less than 1½ inches in depth and shall be of sufficient size...having a diameter of not less than ¾ inch. Piping for safety pan drains shall be of those materials listed in Table 605.4.
504.7.2	**Pan drain termination:** The pan drain shall extend full-size and terminate over a suitably located...and terminate not less than 6 inches and not more than 24 inches above the adjacent ground surface.
505	**Insulation**
[E]505.1	**Unfired vessel insulation:** Unfired hot water storage tanks shall be insulated to R-12.5 (h x ft^2 x °F)/Btu (R-2.2m^2 x K/W).
603	**Water Service**
603.1	**Size of water service pipe:** The water service pipe shall be not less than ¾ inch in diameter.
603.2	**Separation of water service and building sewer:** Where the *building sewer* piping is not constructed of materials listed in Table 702.2, the water service pipe and the *building sewer* shall be horizontally separated by not less than 5 feet of undisturbed or compacted earth.
604	**Design of Building Water Distribution System**
604.3	**Water distribution system design criteria:** The water distribution system shall be designed, and pipe sizes shall be selected such that under conditions of peak demand, the capacities at the fixture supply pipe outlets shall not be less than shown in Table 604.3.
Table 604.3	**Water Distribution System Design Criteria Required Capacity at Fixture Supply Pipe Outlets**
604.5	**Size of fixture supply:** The minimum size of a fixture supply pipe shall be shown in Table 604.5.
Table 604.5	**Minimum Sizes of Fixture Water Supply Pipes**
604.7	**Inadequate water pressure:** Wherever water pressure from the street main or other source of supply is insufficient to provide flow pressures at fixture outlets as required under table 604.3, a water pressure booster system conforming to Section 606.5 shall be installed on the building water supply system.
605	**Materials, Joints and Connections**
605.3	**Water service pipe:** Water service pipe or tubing, installed underground and outside the structure, shall have a working pressure rating of not less than 160 psi at 73.4°F.

Section #	Highlight
605.4	**Water distribution pipe:** Water distribution pipe shall conform to NSF 61 and shall conform to one of the standards listed in Table 605.4. Hot water distribution pipe and tubing shall have a pressure rating of not less than 100 psi at 180°F.
Table 605.4	**Water Distribution Pipe**
605.9	**Prohibited joints and connections:** The following types of joints and connections shall be prohibited: 1 - 4.
606	**Installation of the Building Water Distribution System**
606.5.1	**Water pressure booster system required:** Where the water pressure in the public water main or individual water supply system is insufficient...pressure booster pump installed in accordance with Section 606.5.5.
606.5.6	**Potable water inlet control and location:** Potable water inlets to gravity tanks shall be controlled by a fill valve...The inlet shall be terminated so as to provide an *air gap* not less than 4 inches above the overflow.
608	**Protection of Potable Water Supply**
608.9	**Identification of non-potable water:** Where non-potable water systems are installed... in accordance with Sections 608.9.1 through 608.9.2.3.
608.9.2.1	**Color:** The color of pipe identification shall be discernible and consistent throughout the building. The color purple shall be used to identify reclaimed, rain and gray water distribution systems.
608.16.4	**Protection by a vacuum breaker:** The critical level of the vacuum breaker shall be set not less than 6 inches above the *flood level rim* of the fixture or device. Pipe applied vacuum breakers shall be installed not less than 6 inches above the *flood level rim* of the fixture, receptor or device served.
608.17.5	**Connections to lawn irrigation systems:** Where chemicals are introduced into the system, the potable water supply shall be protected against backflow by a reduced pressure principle backflow prevention assembly.
609	**Health Care Plumbing**
610	**Disinfection of Potable Water System**
702	**Materials**
702.2	**Underground building sanitary drainage and vent pipe:** Underground building sanitary damage and vent pipe shall conform to one of the standards listed in Table 702.2.
Table 702.2	**Underground Building Drainage and Vent Pipe**
702.6	**Chemical waste system:** A chemical waste system shall be completely separated from the sanitary drainage system.
704	**Drainage Piping Installation**

Section #	Highlight
704.1	**Slope of horizontal drainage piping:** Horizontal drainage piping shall be installed in uniform alignment at uniform slopes. The minimum slope of a horizontal drainage pipe shall be in accordance with Table 704.1.
Table 704.1	**Slope of Horizontal Drainage Piping**
705	**Joints**
705.1	**General:** The section contains provisions applicable to joints specific to sanitary drainage piping.
705.2	**ABS plastic:** Joints between ABS plastic pipe or fittings shall comply with Sections 705.2.1 through 705.2.3.
705.3	**Cast iron:** Joints between cast iron pipe or fittings shall comply with sections 705.3.1 through 705.3.3.
705.3.2	**Compression gasket joints:** Compression gaskets for hub and spigot pipe and fittings shall conform to ASTM C564 and shall be tested to ASTM C1563. Gaskets shall be compressed when the pipe is fully inserted.
705.3.3	**Mechanical joint coupling:** Mechanical joint couplings for hubless pipe and fittings shall consist of an elastomeric sealing sleeve and a metallic shield that comply with CISPI 310, ASTM C1277 or ASTM C1540. The elastomeric sealing sleeve shall conform to ASTM C564 or CSA B602 and shall be provided with a center stop.
705.9.2	**Wiped:** Joints shall be fully wiped with an exposed surface on each side of the joint not less than ¾ inch. The joint shall not be less than 3/8 inch thick at the thickest point.
705.10.2	**Solvent cementing:** Joint surfaces shall be clean and free from moisture. A purple primer that conforms to ASTM F656 shall be applied.
705.12	**Polyethylene plastic pipe:** Joints between polyethylene plastic pipe and fittings shall be underground and shall comply with section 705.12.1 or 705.12.2.
705.12.1	**Heat-fusion joints:** Joints shall be undisturbed until cool. Joints shall be made in accordance with ASTM D2657 and the manufacturer's instructions.
705.12.2	**Mechanical joints:** Mechanical joints in drainage piping shall be made with an elastomeric seal conforming to ASTM C1173, ASTM D3212 or CSA B602.
705.13	**Polyolefin plastic:** Joints between polyolefin plastic pipe and fittings shall comply with Sections 705.13.1 and 705.13.2.
705.13.1	**Heat-fusion joints:** Joint surfaces shall be clean and free from moisture. The joint shall …until cool. Joints shall be made in accordance with ASTM F1412 or CSA B181.3.
705.13.2	**Mechanical and compression sleeve joints:** Mechanical and compression sleeve joints shall be installed in accordance with the manufacturer's instructions.
705.16	**Joints between different materials:** Joints between different piping materials shall be made with a mechanical joint of the compression or mechanical-sealing type conforming to ASTM C1173, ASTM C1460 or ASTM C1461.

Section #	Highlight
705.16.4	**Plastic pipe or tubing to other piping material:** Joints between different types of… cast-iron hub pipe shall be made by a caulked joint or a mechanical compression joint.
705.19	**Soldering bushings:** Soldering bushings shall be of copper or copper-alloy and shall be in accordance with Table 705.19.
Table 705.19	**Soldering Bushing Specifications**
706	**Connections between Drainage Piping and Fittings**
706.2	**Obstructions:** The fittings shall not have ledges, shoulders, or reductions capable of retarding or obstructing flow in the piping. Threaded drainage pipe fittings shall be of the recessed drainage type.
706.3	**Installation of fittings:** Fittings shall be installed to guide sewage and waste in the direction of flow. Change in direction shall be made by fittings installed in accordance with Table 706.3.
Table 706.3	**Fittings for Change in Direction**
706.4	**Heel- or side-inlet quarter bends:** Heel-inlet quarter bends shall be an acceptable means of connection, except where the quarter bend serves a water closet.
707	**Prohibited Joints and Connections**
708	**Cleanouts**
708.1.1	**Horizontal drains and building drains:** Horizontal drainage pipes in buildings shall have cleanouts located at intervals not more than 100 feet.
708.1.2	**Building sewers:** *Building sewers* smaller than 8 inches shall have cleanouts located at intervals of not more than 100 feet…and at intervals of not more than 400 feet.
708.1.5	**Cleanout size:** Cleanouts shall be the same size as the piping served by the cleanout, except that cleanouts for piping larger than 4 inches need not be larger than 4 inches.
708.1.9	**Required clearance:** Cleanouts for 6-inch and smaller piping shall be provided with a clearance of not less than 18-inches…Cleanouts for 8-inch and larger pipes shall be provided with a clearance of not less than 36 inches.
709	**Fixture Units**
709.1	**Values for fixtures:** *Drainage fixture unit* values as given in Table 709.1 designate the relative load weight…in connection with Tables 710.1(1) and 710.1(2) of sizes for soil, waste and vent pipes for which the permissible load is given in terms of fixture units.
Table 709.2	**Drainage Fixtures Units for Fixture Drains or Traps**
710	**Drainage System Sizing**
710.1	**Maximum fixture unit load:** The maximum number of *drainage fixture units* connected to a given size of *building sewer*…The maximum number of drainage fixture units connected to a given size horizontal *branch* or vertical soil or waste *stack* shall be determined using Table 710.1(2).

Section #	Highlight
Table 710.1(1)	**Building Drains and Sewers**
Table 710.1(2)	**Horizontal Fixture Branches and Stacks**
711	**Offsets in Drainage Piping in Buildings of Five Stories or More**
711.2	**Horizontal stack offsets:** A *stack* with a horizontal offset located more than four *branch intervals* below the stack shall be vented in accordance with Section 907 and sized as follows: 1 - 3.
712	**Sumps and Ejectors**
712.2	**Valves required:** A check valve and a full open valve located on the discharge side of the check valve shall be installed in the pump or ejector discharge piping between the pump or ejector and the gravity drainage system. *Access* shall be provided to such valves.
712.3.2	**Sump pit**
712.3.4	**Maximum effluent level:** The effluent level control shall be adjusted and maintained… sump from rising to within 2 inches of the invert of the gravity drain inlet into the sump.
802	**Indirect Wastes**
802.1	**Where required**
802.1.1	**Food handling:** Equipment and fixtures utilized for the storage, preparation and handling of food shall discharge through an indirect water pipe by means of an air gap.
802.1.2	**Floor drains in food storage areas**
802.1.4	**Swimming pools:** Where wastewater from swimming pools, backwash from filters and water…the discharge shall be through an indirect waste pipe by means of an *air gap*.
802.1.5	**Nonpotable clear-water waste:** Where devices and equipment such as process tanks, filters, drips and boilers discharge nonpotable water to the building drainage system, the discharge shall be through an indirect waste pipe by means of an *air break* or an *air gap*.
802.1.6	**Commercial dishwashing machines:** The discharge form a commercial dishwashing machine shall be through an *air gap* or *air brake* into the standpipe or waste receptor in accordance with Section 802.3.
802.4	**Waste receptors**
802.4.2	**Hub drains.** A hub drain shall be in the form of a hub or pipe extending not less than 1 inch above a water-impervious floor.
802.4.3	**Standpipes:** Standpipes shall be individually trapped. Standpipes shall extend not less… above the trap weir. *Access* shall be provided for all standpipes and drains for rodding.
902	**Materials**
902.2	**Sheet copper:** Sheet copper for vent pipe flashings shall conform to ASTM B152 and shall weigh not less than 8 ounces per square foot.

Section #	Highlight
902.3	**Sheet lead:** Sheet lead for vent pipe flashings shall weigh not less than 3 pounds per square foot…and not less than 2½ pounds per square foot for prefabricated flashings.
903	**Vent Terminals**
903.1	**Roof extension:** Open vent pipes that extend through a roof shall be terminated not less than 6 inches above the roof…shall terminate not less than 7 feet above the roof.
903.5	**Location of vent terminal:** An open vent terminal from a drainage system shall not be located directly beneath any door…shall not be within 10 feet horizontally of such an opening unless it is 3 feet or more above the top of such opening.
904	**Outdoor Vent Extension**
904.1	**Required vent extension:** The vent system serving each *building drain* shall have at least one vent pipe that extends to the outdoors.
905	**Vent Connections and Grades**
905.5	**Height above fixtures:** A connection between a vent pipe and vent *stack* or *stack vent* shall be made at not less than 6 inches above the *flood level rim* of the highest fixture served by the vent.
909	**Fixture Vents**
Table 909.1	**Maximum Distance of Fixture Trap from Vent**
909.3	**Crown vent:** A vent shall not be installed within two pipe diameters of the trap weir.
912	**Wet Venting**
912.1	**Horizontal wet vent permitted:** The wet vent shall be considered the vent for the fixtures and shall extend from the connection of the dry vent along the direction of the flow in the drain pipe to the most downstream *fixture drain* connection to the *horizontal branch drain*.
913	**Waste Stack Vent**
913.2	**Stack installation:** The waste *stack* shall be vertical, and both horizontal and vertical offsets shall be prohibited between the lowest *fixture drain* connection and the highest *fixture drain* connection.
913.4	**Waste stack size:** The waste *stack* shall be sized based on the total discharge to the *stack* and the discharge within a *branch* interval in accordance with Table 913.4.
Table 913.4	**Waste Stack Vent Size**
914	**Circuit Venting**
914.1	**Circuit vent permitted:** A maximum of eight fixtures connected to a horizontal *branch* drain shall be permitted to be circuit vented.
915	**Combination Drain and Vent System**

Section #	Highlight
915.1	**Type of fixtures:** A *combination waste and vent system* shall not serve fixtures other… *Combination waste and vent systems* shall not receive the discharge from a food waste grinder or clinical sink.
1002	**Trap Requirements**
1002.1	**Fixture traps:** The vertical distance from the fixture outlet to the trap weir shall not exceed 24 inches, and the horizontal distance shall not exceed 30 inches measured from the centerline of the fixture outlet to the centerline of the inlet of the trap. A fixture shall not be double trapped. **Exceptions:** 1 - 4.
1002.2	**Design of traps:** Slip joints shall be made with an *approved* elastomeric gasket and shall be installed only on the trap inlet, trap outlet and within the trap seal
1002.4	**Trap seals:** Each fixture trap shall have a liquid seal of not less than 2 inches and not more than 4 inches, or deeper for special designs relating to accessible fixtures.
1003	**Interceptors and Separators**
1003.1	**Where required:** Interceptors and separators shall be provided to prevent the discharge of oil, grease, sand and other substances harmful or hazardous to the public sewer, the private sewage system or the sewage treatment plant or processes.
1003.3.9	**Grease interceptors for on-site sewage treatment and disposal systems:** Grease interceptors are not required for a residence.
1003.5	**Sand interceptors in commercial establishments.** Sand and similar interceptors for heavy solids…access for cleaning, and shall have a water seal of not less than 6 inches.
1003.6	**Clothes washer discharge interceptor:** Clothes washers shall discharge through an interceptor…into the drainage system of solids ½ inch or larger in size, string, rags, buttons or other materials detrimental to the public sewage system.
1004	**Materials, Joints and Connections**
1102	**Materials**
1104	**Conductors and Connections**
1106	**Size of Conductors, Leaders and Storm Drains**
1110	**Controlled Flow Roof Drain Systems**
1110.2	**Control devices.** The control devices shall be installed so that a rate of discharge of water per minute shall not exceed the values for continuous flow as indicated in Section 1110.1.
1113	**Sumps and Pumping Systems**
1301	**General**

Section #	Highlight
1301.2.2	**Filtration required.** Nonpotable water utilized for water closet and urinal flushing applications shall be filtered by a 100-micron or finer filter.
1301.3	**Signage required**
1301.11	**Trenching requirements for nonpotable water piping.** Nonpotable water collection and distribution…pipping underground by 5 feet of undisturbed or compacted earth.
Appendix B	Highlight: **Florida:** Miami and Pensacola
Appendix E	**Sizing of Water Piping System**
E103	**Selection of Pipe Size**
Table E103.3(2)	**Load Values Assigned to Fixtures**
Table E103.3(4)	**Loss of Pressure Through Taps and Tees in Pounds per Square Inch**
Figure E103.3(2)	**Friction Loss in Smooth Pipe (Type K, ASTM B88 Copper Tubing)**
Figure E103.3(3)	**Friction Loss in Smooth Pipe (Type L, ASTM B88 Copper Tubing)**
Figure E103.3(6)	**Friction Loss in Fairly Rough Pipe**
E201	**Selection of Pipe Size**
E202	**Determination of Pipe Volumes**
Appendix F	**Part I: General**
	B. Permits
	D. Definitions
	Part II: Design Criteria
	K. Chemical injection
	Part IV: Materials
	Part V: Installation
	C. Sprinkler installation
	F. Hydraulic control tubing
	Part VI: Testing & Inspections
	C. Final inspection

<u>**Section #**</u>	<u>**Highlight**</u>

<u>Florida Building Code 2020, Building Chapter 1</u>

102	**Applicability**
102.2	**Building.** The provisions of the *Florida Building Code* shall apply to the construction, erection, alteration, modification, repair, equipment, use and occupancy, location, maintenance, removal and demolition of every public and private building, structure or facility or floating residential structure, or any appurtenances connected or attached to such buildings, structures or facilities.
105	**Permits**
[A] 105.1	**Required.** Any *owner* or owner's authorized agent who intends to construct, enlarge, alter, repair, move, demolish, or change the occupancy of a building or structure, or to erect, install, enlarge, alter, repair, remove, convert or replace any impact resistant coverings, electrical, gas, mechanical or plumbing system, the installation of which is regulated by this code, or to cause any such work to be done, shall first make application to the *building official* and obtain the required *permit.*
107	**Submittal Documents**
107.3.5	**Minimum plan review criteria for buildings**
	Commercial Buildings
	Residential (one- and two-family)
108	**Temporary Structures and Uses**

Florida Building Code - Plumbing, 6th Ed, 2017

Tabs and Highlights

These1 Exam Prep Tabs are based on the *Florida Building Code - Plumbing 2017.*

Each 1 Exam Prep tabs sheet has five rows of tabs. Start with the first tab at the first row at the top of the page; proceed down that row placing the tabs at the locations listed below. Place each tab in your book setting it down one notch until you get to the last tab (usually the index or glossary). Then start with the highlights.

1 Exam Prep Tab	Section	Page #
Table of Contents		vii
Piping Support	308	pg. 13
Minimum Plumbing Facilities	403	pg. 19
Materials, Joints & Connections	605	pg. 3
Protection of Potable Water Supply	608	pg. 47
Joints	705	pg. 57
Cleanouts	708	pg. 61
Drainage System Sizing	710	pg. 63
Healthcare Plumbing	713	pg. 65
Vacuum Drainage System	716	pg. 67
Permit Schedule Fee	Appendix A	pg. 121
Rates of Rainfall	Appendix B	pg. 123
Structural Safety	Appendix C	pg. 125
Degree Day & Design Temp.	Appendix D	pg. 127
Sizing of Water Piping System	Appendix E	pg. 133
Turf & Landscape Irrigation	Appendix F	pg. 155

******This concludes the tabs for this book. Please continue with the highlights on the following page.******

A.M. 07/14/2020

Section #	Highlight
202	**General Definitions:** ▪ Backflow ▪ Back pressure, low head ▪ Backflow connection ▪ Backsiphonage ▪ Bedpan steamer or boiler ▪ Developed length ▪ Offset ▪ Potable water
305	**Protection of Pipes and Plumbing System Components**
306	**Trenching, Excavation and Backfill**
307	**Structural Safety**
307.5	**Protection of footings:** Trenching installed parallel to footings and walls shall not extend into the bearing plane…at an angle of 45-degrees from horizontal, from the outside bottom edge of the footing or wall.
308	**Piping Support**
308.5	**Interval of support:** Pipe shall be supported in accordance with Table 308.5.
Table 308.5	**Hanger Spacing**
308.8	**Expansion joint fittings**
Table 308.5	**Hanger Spacing**
310	**Washroom and Toilet Room Requirements**
310.1	**Light and Ventilation:** Washrooms and toilet rooms shall be illuminated and ventilated in accordance with the Florida Building Code, Building and the Florida Building Code, Mechanical.
312	**Tests and Inspections**
312.2	**Drainage and vent water test:** If the system is tested in sections, each opening shall be tightly plugged except the highest openings…This pressure shall be held for not less than 15 minutes.
312.6	**Gravity sewer test:** Gravity sewer tests shall consist of plugging the end of the building sewer at the point of connection…with not less than a 5-foot head of water and maintaining such pressure for 15 minutes.
312.7	**Forced sewer test:** Forced sewer tests shall consist of plugging the end of the building sewer at the point of connection with the public sewer and applying a pressure of 5 psi greater than the pump rating, and maintaining such pressure for 15 minutes.
318	**Irrigation**

Section #	Highlight
318.1	**General:** Irrigation/sprinkler systems and risers for spray heads shall not be installed within 1 foot of the building sidewall.
402	**Fixture Materials**
402.3	**Sheet copper:** Sheet copper for general applications shall conform to ASTM B 152 and shall not weigh less than 12 ounces per square foot.
403	**Minimum Plumbing Facilities**
403.1	**Minimum number of fixtures:** Plumbing fixtures shall be provided for the type of occupancy and in the minimum number shown in Table 403.1.
Table 403.1	**Minimum Number of Required Plumbing Fixtures**
403.1.3	**Potty parity**
403.3.3	**Location of toilet facilities in occupancies other than covered malls:** shall be located not more than one story above…shall not exceed a distance of 500 feet.
403.6	**Sanitary facilities for public swimming pools:** Swimming pools with a bathing load of 20 persons or less may utilize a unisex restroom. Pools with bathing loads of 40 persons or less may utilize two unisex restrooms or meet the requirements of Table 403.6.
403.6.1	**Required fixtures:** Fixtures shall be provided as indicated on Table 403.6. An additional set of fixtures shall be provided in the men's restroom for every 7,500 square feet or major fraction thereof for pools greater than 10,000 square feet.
Table 403.6	**Public Swimming Pool – Required Fixtures Count**
405	**Installation of Fixtures**
405.3.1	**Water closets, urinals, lavatories and bidets:** A water closet, urinal, lavatory or bidet shall not be set closer than 15 inches from its center to any side wall…Water closet compartments shall be less than 30 inches in width and not less than 60 inches in depth for floor-mounted water closets and not less than 30 inches in width and 56 inches in depth for wall hung water closets.
405.8	**Slip joint connections:** Fixtures with concealed slip-joint connections shall be provided with an access panel or utility space not less than 12-inches in its smallest dimension or other approved arrangement so as to provide access to the slip joint connections for inspection and repair.
409	**Dishwashing Machines**
409.1	**Approval:** Commercial dishwashing machines shall conform to ASSE 1004 and NSF 3.
411	**Emergency Showers and Eyewash Stations**
411.2	**Waste connection:** Waste connections shall not be required for emergency showers and eyewash stations.
413	**Food Waste Grinder Units**

Section #	Highlight
413.3	**Commercial food waste grinder waste outlets:** Commercial food waste grinders shall be connected to a drain not less than 1 ½ inches in diameter.
413.4	**Water supply required:** All food waste grinders shall be provided with a supply of cold water. The water supply shall be protected against backflow by an air gap or backflow preventer in accordance with Section 608.
417	**Showers**
417.4.1	**Floor and wall area:** Wall materials shall extend to a height not less than 6 feet above the room floor level, and not less than 70 inches above the drain of the tub and shower.
417.5.2.1	**PVC sheets:** Plasticized polyvinyl chloride (PVC) sheets shall meet the requirements of ASTM D 4551. Sheets can be joined in accordance with the Manufacturer's instructions.
417.5.2.2	**Chlorinated polyethylene (CPE) sheets:** Nonplasticized chlorinated polyethylene sheet shall meet the requirements of ASTM D 4068. The liner shall be joined in accordance with the manufacturer's installation instructions.
419	**Urinals**
419.2	**Substitution for water closets:** In each bathroom or toilet room, urinals shall not be substituted for more than 67 percent of the required water closets in assembly and educational occupancies.
421	**Whirlpool Bathtubs**
421.3	**Drain:** The pump drain and circulation piping shall be sloped to drain the water in the volute and the circulation piping when the whirlpool bathtub is empty.
425	**Flushing Devices for Water Closets and Urinals**
425.1.1	**Separate for each fixture:** A flushing device shall not serve more than one fixture.
501.2	**Water heater as space heater:** Where a combination potable water heating and space heating system requires water for space heating at temperatures higher than 140 F…the potable hot water distribution system of 140 F or less.
502	**Installation**
502.1.1	**Elevation and protection:** Elevation of water heater ignition sources and mechanical damage protection requirements for water heaters, shall be in accordance with the Florida Building Code, Mechanical and the Florida Building Code, Fuel Gas.
502.5	**Clearances for maintenance and replacement:** A level working space not less than 30 inches in length and 30 inches in width shall be provided in front of the control side to service and appliance.
503	**Connections**
503.1	**Cold water line valve:** The cold water branch line from the main water supply line to each hot water storage tank or water heater shall be provided with a valve, located near the equipment and serving only the hot water storage tank or water heater.
504	**Safety Devices**

Section #	Highlight
504.4	**Relief valve:** Storage water heaters operating above atmospheric pressure shall be provided with an approved, self-closing pressure relief valve and temperature relief valve or combination thereof.
504.7	**Required pan:** Where a storage tank-type water heater or a hot water storage tank is installed in a location…galvanized steel pan having a material thickness of not less than 0.0236 inch (No. 24 gage), or other pans approved for such use.
504.7.1	**Pan size and drain:** The pan shall be not less than 1 ½ inches in depth and shall be of sufficient size…having a diameter of not less than ¾ inch. Piping for safety pan drains shall be of those materials listed in Table 605.4.
504.7.2	**Pan drain termination:** The pan drain shall extend full-size and terminate over a suitably located…and terminate not less than 6 inches and not more than 24 inches above the adjacent ground surface.
505	**Insulation**
505.1	**Unfired vessel insulation:** Unfired hot water storage tanks shall be insulated to R-12.5.
603	**Water Service**
603.1	**Size of water service pipe:** The water service pipe shall be not less than ¾ inch in diameter.
603.2	**Separation of water service and building sewer:** Water service pipe and the building sewer shall be horizontally separated by not less than 5 feet of undisturbed or compacted earth.
604	**Design of Building Water Distribution System**
604.3	**Water distribution system design criteria:** The water distribution system shall be designed, and pipe sizes shall be selected such that under conditions of peak demand, the capacities at the fixture supply pipe outlets shall not be less than shown in Table 604.3.
Table 604.3	**Water Distribution System Design Criteria Required Capacity at Fixture Supply Pipe Outlets**
604.5	**Size and fixture supply:** The minimum size of a fixture supply pipe shall be shown in Table 604.5.
604.7	**Inadequate water pressure:** Wherever water pressure from the street main or other source of supply is insufficient to provide flow pressures at fixture outlets as required under table 604.3, a water pressure booster system conforming to Section 606.5 shall be installed on the building water supply system.
Table 604.5	**Minimum Sizes of Fixture Water Supply Pipes**
605	**Materials, Joints and Connections**
605.3	**Water service pipe:** water service pipe or tubing, installed underground and outside the structure, shall have a working pressure rating of not less than 160 psi at 73.4 F.

Section #	Highlight
605.4	**Water distribution pipe:** water distribution pipe shall conform to NSF 61 and shall conform to one of the standards listed in Table 605.4. Hot water distribution pipe and tubing shall have a pressure rating of not less than 100 psi at 180 F.
Table 605.4	**Water Distribution Pipe**
605.9	**Prohibited joints and connections:** The following types of joints and connections shall be prohibited: 1 - 4.
606	**Installation of the Building Water Distribution System**
606.5.1	**Water pressure booster system required:** Where the water pressure in the public water main or individual water supply system is insufficient…pressure booster pump installed in accordance with Section 606.5.5.
606.5.6	**Potable water inlet control and location:** Potable water inlets to gravity tanks shall be controlled by a fill valve…The inlet shall be terminated so as to provide an air gap not less than 4 inches above the overflow.
608	**Protection of Potable Water Supply**
608.8	**Identification of non-potable water:** Where non-potable water systems are installed… in accordance with Sections 608.8.1 through 608.8.2.3.
608.8.2.1	**Color**: The color of pipe identification shall be discernible and consistent throughout the building. The color purple shall be used to identify reclaimed, rain and gray water distribution systems.
608.15.4	**Protection by a vacuum breaker:** The critical level of the vacuum breaker shall be set not less than 6 inches above the flood level rim of the fixture or device. Pipe applied vacuum breakers shall be installed not less than 6 inches above the flood level rim of the fixture, receptor or device served.
608.16.5	**Connections to lawn irrigation systems:** Where systems are under continuous pressure contain chemical additives…backflow prevention assembly or a reduced pressure principle fire protection backflow prevention assembly.
610	**Disinfection of Potable Water System**
702	**Materials**
702.2	**Underground building sanitary drainage and vent pipe:** Underground building sanitary damage and vent pipe shall conform to one of the standards listed in Table 702.2.
702.6	**Chemical waste system:** A chemical waste system shall be completely separated from the sanitary drainage system.
Table 702.2	**Underground Building Drainage and Vent Pipe**
704	**Drainage Piping Installation**
704.1	**Slope of horizontal drainage piping:** Horizontal drainage piping shall be installed in uniform alignment at uniform slopes. The minimum slope of a horizontal drainage pipe shall be in accordance with Table 704.1.

Section #	Highlight
Table 704.1	**Slope of Horizontal Drainage Piping**
705	**Joints**
705.1	**General:** The section contains provisions applicable to joints specific to sanitary drainage piping.
705.2	**ABS plastic:** Joints between ABS plastic pipe or fittings shall comply with Sections 705.2.1 through 705.2.3.
705.4	**Cast iron:** Joints between cast iron pipe or fittings shall comply with sections 705.4.1 through 705.4.3.
705.4.2	**Compression gasket joints:** Compression gaskets for hub and spigot pipe and fittings shall conform to ASTM C 564 and shall be tested to ASTM C 1563. Gaskets shall be compressed when the pipe is fully inserted.
705.4.3	**Mechanical joint coupling:** Mechanical joint couplings for hubless pipe and fittings shall comply with…or ASTM C 1540.
705.10.2	**Wiped:** Joints shall be fully wiped with an exposed surface on each side of the joint not less than ¾ inch. The joint shall not be less than 3/8 inch thick at the thickest point.
705.11.2	**Solvent cementing:** Joint surfaces shall be clean and free from moisture. A purple primer that conforms to ASTM F 656 shall be applied.
705.13	**Polyethylene plastic pipe:** Joints between polyethylene plastic pipe and fittings shall be underground and shall comply with section 705.13.1 or 705.13.2.
705.13.1	**Heat-fusion joints:** Joints shall be undisturbed until cool. Joints shall be made in accordance with ASTM D 2657 and the manufacturer's instructions.
705.13.2	**Mechanical joints:** Mechanical joints in drainage piping shall be made with an elastomeric seal conforming to ASTM C 1173…or CSA B602.
705.14	**Polyolefin plastic:** Joints between polyolefin plastic pipe and fittings shall comply with Sections 705.14.1 and 705.14.2.
705.15.1	**Heat-fusion joints:** Joint surfaces shall be clean and free from moisture…in accordance with ASTM F1673.
705.15.2	**Mechanical and compression sleeve joints:** Mechanical and compression sleeve joints shall be installed in accordance with the manufacturer's instructions.
705.16	**Joints between different materials:** Joints between different piping materials shall be made with a mechanical joint of the compression or mechanical-sealing type conforming to ASTM C 1173, ASTM C 1460 or ASTM C 1461.
705.16.4	**Plastic pipe or tubing to other piping material:** Joints between different types of plastic pipe or between plastic pipe…shall be made by a caulked joint or a mechanical compression joint.
705.19	**Soldering bushings:** Soldering bushings shall be of red brass and shall be in accordance with Table 705.19.

Section #	**Highlight**
Table 705.19	**Soldering Bushing Specifications**
706	**Connections between Drainage Piping and Fittings**
706.2	**Obstructions:** The fittings shall not have ledges, shoulders, or reductions capable of retarding or obstructing flow in the piping. Threaded drainage pipe fittings shall be of the recessed drainage type.
706.3	**Installation of fittings:** Fittings shall be installed to guide sewage and waste in the direction of flow. Change in direction shall be made by fittings installed in accordance with Table 706.3.
Table 706.3	**Fittings for Change in Direction**
706.4	**Heel- or side- inlet quarter bends:** Heel-inlet quarter bends shall be an acceptable means of connection, except where the quarter bend serves a water closet.
707	**Prohibited Joints and Connections**
708	**Cleanouts**
708.1.1	**Horizontal drains within buildings:** Horizontal drainage pipes in buildings shall have cleanouts located at intervals not more than 100 feet.
708.1.2	**Building sewers:** Building sewers smaller than 8 inches shall have cleanouts located at intervals of not more than 100 feet…at intervals of not more than 400 feet apart.
708.1.5	**Cleanout size:** Cleanouts shall be the same size as the piping served by the cleanout … need not be larger than 4 inches.
708.1.9	**Required clearance:** Cleanouts for 6-inch and smaller piping shall be provided with a clearance of not less than 18-inches…Cleanouts for 8-inch and larger pipes shall be provided with a clearance of not less than 36 inches.
709	**Fixture Units**
709.1	**Values for fixtures:** Drainage fixture unit values as given in Table 709.1 designate the relative load weight…in connection with Tables 710.1(1) and 710.1(2) of sizes for soil, waste and vent pipes for which the permissible load is given in terms of fixture units.
709.3	**Values for continuous and semicontinuous flow:** Drainage fixture unit values for continuous and semicontinuous flow into s drainage system shall be computed on the basis that 1 gpm of flow is equivalent to two fixture units.
Table 709.2	**Drainage Fixtures Units for Fixture Drains or Traps**
710	**Drainage System Sizing**
710.1	**Maximum fixture unit load:** The maximum number of drainage fixture units connected to a given size of building sewer…The maximum number of drainage fixture units connected to a given size horizontal branch or vertical soil or waste stack shall be determined using Table 710.(2).
Table 710.1(1)	**Building Drains and Sewers**

Section #	Highlight
Table 710.1(2)	**Horizontal Fixture Branches and Stacks**
711	**Offsets in Drainage Piping in Buildings of Five Stories or More**
711.2	**Horizontal stack offsets:** A stack with a horizontal offset located more than four branch intervals below the stack shall be vented in accordance with Section 907 and sized as follows: 1 - 3.
712	**Sumps and Ejectors**
712.2	**Valves required:** A check valve and a full open valve located on the discharge side of the check valve shall be installed in the pump or ejector discharge piping between the pump or ejector and the gravity drainage system. Access shall be provided to such valves.
712.3.2	**Sump pit**
712.3.4	**Maximum effluent level:** The effluent level control shall be adjusted and maintained …from rising within 2 inches of the invert of the gravity drain inlet into the sump.
713	**Health Care Plumbing**
713.7	**Central vacuums or disposals systems:** Where the waste from a central vacuum (fluid suction) system of the barometric-lag, collection-tank or bottle-disposal type is connected to the drainage system, the waste shall be directly connected to the sanitary drainage system through a trapped waste.
713.9	**Local vents and stacks for bedpan washers:** The local vent for a bedpan washer shall not be less than a 2-inch diameter pipe.
713.9.1	**Multiple installations:** Not more than three bedpan washers shall be connected to a 2-inch local vent stack, not more than six to a 3-inch local vent stack and not more than 12 to a 4-inch local vent stack.
713.11.2	**Boiling-type sterilizers:** The size of a sterilizer vent stack shall not be less than 2 inches in diameter where serving a utensil sterilizer not less than 1 ½ inches in diameter where serving an instrument sterilizer.
802	**Indirect Wastes**
802.1	**Where required:** Health-care related fixtures, devices and equipment shall discharge to the drainage system through an indirect waste pipe by means of an air gap in accordance with this chapter and Section 713.3.
802.1.1	**Food handling:** Equipment and fixtures utilized for the storage, preparation and handling of food shall discharge through an indirect water pipe by means of an air gap.
802.1.2	**Floor drains in food storage areas**
802.1.4	**Swimming pools:** Where wastewater from swimming pools, backwash from filters and water from pool deck drains…the discharge shall be through an indirect waste pipe by means of an air gap.
802.1.5	**Non-potable clear-water waste:** Where devices and equipment such as process tanks, filters, drips and boilers discharge nonpotable water to the building drainage system, the discharge shall be through an indirect waste pipe by means of an air break or an air gap.

Section #	Highlight
802.1.7	**Commercial dishwashing machines:** The discharge form a commercial dishwashing machine shall be through an air gap or air brake into the standpipe or waste receptor in accordance with Section 802.2.
802.3	**Waste receptors**
802.3.2	**Hub drains.** A hub drain shall be in the form of a hub or pipe extending not less than 1 inch above a water-impervious floor.
802.3.3	**Standpipes:** Standpipes shall be individually trapped. Standpipes shall extend…Access shall be provided for all standpipes and drains for rodding.
804	**Materials, Joints and Connections**
902	**Materials**
902.2	**Sheet copper:** Sheet copper for vent pipe flashings shall conform to ASTM B 152 and shall weigh not less than 8 ounces per square foot.
902.3	**Sheet lead:** Sheet lead for vent pipe flashings shall weigh not less than 3 pounds per square foot…and not less than 2 ½ pounds per square foot for prefabricated flashings.
903	**Vent Terminals**
903.1	**Roof extension:** Open vent pipes that extend through a roof shall be terminated not less than 6 inches above the roof…shall terminate not less than 7 feet above the roof.
903.5	**Location of vent terminal:** An open vent terminal from a drainage system shall not be located directly beneath any door…shall not be within 10 feet horizontally of such an opening unless it is 3 feet or more above the top of such opening.
904	**Outdoor Vent Extension**
904.1	**Required vent extension:** The vent system serving each building drain shall have at least one vent pipe that extends to the outdoors.
905	**Vent Connections and Grades**
905.5	**Height above fixtures:** A connection between a vent pipe and vent stack or stack vent shall be made at not less than 6 inches above the floor level rim of the highest fixture served by the vent.
909	**Fixture Vents**
909.3	**Crown vent:** A vent shall not be installed within two pipe diameters of the trap weir.
Table 909.1	**Maximum Distance of Fixture Trap from Vent**
912	**Wet Venting**
912.1	**Horizontal wet vent permitted:** The wet vent shall be considered the vent for the fixtures and shall extend from the connection of the dry vent along the direction of the flow in the drain pipe to the most downstream fixture drain connection to the horizontal branch drain.

Section #	Highlight
913	**Waste Stack Vent**
913.2	**Stack installation:** The waste stack shall be vertical, and both horizontal and vertical offsets shall be prohibited between the lowest fixture drain connection and the highest fixture drain connection.
913.4	**Waste stack size:** The waste stack shall be sized based on the total discharge to the stack and the discharge within branch interval in accordance with Table 913.4.
Table 913.4	**Waste Stack Vent Size**
914	**Circuit Venting**
914.1	**Circuit vent permitted:** A maximum of eight fixtures connected to a horizontal branch drain shall be permitted to be circuit vented.
915	**Combination Drain and Vent System**
915.1	**Type of fixtures:** A combination drain and vent system shall not serve fixtures … combination drain and vent systems shall not receive the discharge from a food waste grinder or clinical sink.
1002	**Trap Requirements**
1002.1	**Fixture traps:** The vertical distance from the fixture outlet to the trap weir shall not exceed 24 inches, and the horizontal distance shall not exceed 30 inches measured from the centerline of the fixture outlet to the centerline of the inlet of the trap.
	A fixture shall not be double trapped.
	Exceptions: 1 - 4.
1002.2	**Design of traps:** Slip joints shall be made with an approved elastomeric gasket and shall be installed only on the trap inlet, trap outlet and within the trap seal
1002.4	**Trap seals:** Each fixture trap shall have a liquid seal of not less than 2 inches and not more than 4 inches, or deeper for special designs relating to accessible fixtures.
1003	**Interceptors and Separators**
1003.1	**Where required:** Interceptors and separators shall be provided to prevent the discharge of oil, grease, sand and other substances harmful or hazardous to the public sewer, the private sewage system or the sewage treatment plant or processes.
1003.5	**Grease interceptors for onsite sewage treatment and disposal systems:** Grease interceptors are not required for a residence.
1003.6	**Clothes washer discharge interceptor:** Clothes washers shall discharge through an interceptor…into the drainage system of solids ½ inch or larger in size, string, rags, buttons or other materials detrimental to the public sewage system.
1003.11	**Sand interceptors in commercial establishments.** Sand and similar interceptors for heavy solids…shall have a water seal of not less than 6 inches.
1004	**Materials, Joints and Connections**

Section #	Highlight
1102	**Materials**
1104	**Conductors and Connections**
1106	**Size of Conductors, Leaders and Storm Drains**
1110	**Controlled Flow Roof Drain Systems**
1110.2	**Control devices.** The control devices shall be installed so that a rate of discharge of water per minute shall not exceed the values for continuous flow as indicated in Section 1110.1.
1113	**Sumps and Pumping Systems**
1301.2.2	**Filtration required.** Nonpotable water utilized for water closet and urinal flushing applications shall be filtered by a 100-micron or finer filter.
1301.3	**Signage required**
1301.11	**Trenching requirements for nonpotable water piping.** Nonpotable water collection and distribution piping…underground by 5 feet of undisturbed or compacted earth.
Appendix B	**Rates of Rainfall for Various Cities**
	Highlight: Florida, Miami and Pensacola
Appendix C	**Structural Safety**
Appendix D	**Degree Day and Design Temperatures**
Appendix E	**Sizing of Water Piping System**
E103	**Selection of Pipe Size**
Table E103.3(2)	**Load Values Assigned to Fixtures**
Table E103.3(4)	**Loss of Pressure Through Taps and Tees in Pounds per Square Inch**
Figure E103.3(2)	**Friction Loss in Smooth Pipe (Type K)**
Figure E103.3(3)	**Friction Loss in Smooth Pipe (Type L)**
Figure E103.3(6)	**Friction Loss in Fairly Rough Pipe**
E201	**Selection of Pipe Size**
E202	**Determination of Pipe Volumes**
Appendix F	**Proposed Construction Building Codes for Turf & Landscape Irrigation Systems**
	Part I- General
	B. Permits
	D. Definitions
	Part II- Design Criteria

Section #	**Highlight**
	K. Chemical Injection
	Part IV- Materials
	Part V- Installation
	C. Sprinkler Installation
	F. Hydraulic Control Tubing
	Part VI: Testing and Inspections
	C. Final Inspection

Florida Building Code 2017, Building Chapter 1

102	**Applicability**
102.2	**Building.** "The provisions of the *Florida Building Code* shall apply to the construction, erection, alteration, modification, repair, equipment, use and occupancy, location, maintenance, removal and demolition of every public and private building, structure or facility or floating residential structure, or any appurtenances connected or attached to such buildings, structures or facilities."
105	**Permits**
105.1	**Required.** Any owner or authorized agent who intends to construct, enlarge, alter, repair, move, demolish, or change the occupancy of a building or structure, or to erect, install, enlarge, alter, repair, remove, convert or replace any impact resistant coverings, electrical, gas, mechanical or plumbing system, the installation of which is regulated by this code, or to cause any such work to be done, shall first make application to the *building official* and obtain the required *permit."*
107	**Submittal Documents**
107.3.5	**Minimum plan review criteria for buildings**
	Commercial Buildings
	Residential Buildings
108	**Temporary Structures and Uses**

Florida Building Code - Residential, 7th Edition, 2020
Tabs and Highlights

These 1 Exam Prep Tabs are based on the *Florida Building Code – Residential, 7th Edition, 2020.*

This book is divided into two main sections: the *Florida Building Code – Residential* and the *Florida Building Code - Building, Chapter 1.*

Each 1 Exam Prep tabs sheet has five rows of tabs. Start with the first tab at the first row at the top of the page; proceed down that row placing the tabs at the locations listed below. Place each tab in your book setting it down one notch until you get to the last tab (usually the index or glossary). Then start with the highlights.

1 Exam Prep Tab	Section	Page #
Table of Contents		v
Protection of Openings	R301.2.1.2	27
Termite Protection	R318	69
Drainage	R401.3	79
Footings	R403	83
Under Floor Ventilation	R408.1	129
Drilling and Notching	R502.8	129
Floor Sheathing	R503	131
Concrete Floors	R506	131
Masonry	R606	143
Bed and Head Joints	R606.3.1	143
Wood Roof Framing	R802	269
Requirements for Masonry Chimneys	Table R1001.1	295
Fireplace Clearances	R1001.11	297
Chimney Clearances	R1003.18	301
Clothes Dryer Exhaust	M1502	321
Chimney Connector Clearances	Table M1803.3.4	333
Water Heater Prohibited Locations	M2005.2	339
Backflow Protection	P2902.3	445

****This concludes the tabs for this book. Please continue with the highlights on the following page.****

Section #	Highlight
R101.2	**Scope:** The provisions of the *Florida Building Code, Residential* shall apply to the construction, *alteration*, movement, enlargement, replacement, repair, *equipment*, use and occupancy, location, removal and demolition of detached one - and two-family dwellings and *townhouses* not more than three stories above *grade plane* in height with a separate means of egress and their *accessory structures* not more than three stories above *grade plan* in height.
R202	**Definitions**
R301.1	**Application:** Building and structures, and all parts thereof, shall be constructed to safely support all loads, including dead loads, live loads, roof loads, flood loads, snow loads, wind loads and seismic loads as prescribed by this code…Buildings and structures constructed as prescribed by this code are deemed to comply with the requirements of this section.
R301.1.3	**Engineered design:** Where a building of otherwise conventional construction contains structural elements exceeding the limit of Section R301 or otherwise not conforming to this code, these elements shall be designed in accordance with accepted engineering practice.
R301.2.1.2	**Protection of openings:** Glazed opening protection for windborne debris shall meet the requirements of the Large Missile Test of ASTM E 1996…shall meet the requirements of an *approved* impact-resisting standard or ANSI/DASMA 115. **Exception:** Wood structural panels with a thickness of not less than 7/16 inch (11 mm) and a span between lines of fasteners of 44 inches (1118 mm) shall be permitted for opening protection in buildings with a mean roof height of 33 feet or less in locations where Vult is 180 mph or less. a. Attachments shall be designed to resist the component and cladding loads determined in accordance with Table R301.2(2) or ASCE 7, with the permanent corrosion-resistant hardware provided and anchors permanently installed on the building.
Figure R301.2(3)	**Weathering Probability Map for Concrete**
Figure R301.2(4)	**Ultimate Design Wind Speeds Vult**
Figure R301.2(6)	**Termite Infestation Probability Map**
Table R301.2.1.3	**Wind Speed Conversions**
R301.2.1.3	**Wind speed conversion**; Where referenced documents are based on nominal design wind speeds…the ultimate design wind speeds, Vult, of Figure R301.2(4) shall be converted to nominal design wind speeds, Vasd, using Table R301.2.1.3.
Table R301.6	**Minimum Roof Live Loads in Pounds-Force per Square Foot of Horizontal Projection**
R310	**Emergency Escape and Rescue Openings**
R310.1	**Emergency escape and rescue opening required:** *Basements, habitable attics* and every sleeping room shall not have less than one operable emergency escape and rescue opening.
R310.2.1	**Minimum opening area:** Emergency and escape rescue openings shall have a net clear opening of not less than 5.7 square feet (0.530 m^2).

Section #	Highlight
	The net clear height opening shall not be less than 24 inches and the net clear width shall not be less than 20 inches (508 mm).
R310.2.3	**Window wells:** The horizontal area of the window well shall not be less than 9 square feet (0.9 m^2), with a horizontal projection and width of not less than 36 inches (914 mm).
R318	**Protection Against Termites**
R318.1.4	If soil treatment is used for subterranean termite prevention, chemically treated soil shall be protected with a minimum 6 mil vapor retarder to protect against rainfall dilution.
R401.3	**Drainage:** Surface drainage shall be diverted to a storm sewer conveyance or other *approved* point of collection that does not create a hazard. *Lots* shall be graded to drain surface water away from foundation walls. The *grade* shall fall a minimum of 6 inches (152 mm) within the first 10 feet (3048 mm).
R401.4	**Soil tests:** Where quantifiable data created by accepted soil science methodologies indicate expansive...This test shall be done by an *approved agency* using an *approved* method.
Table R401.4.1	**Presumptive Load-Bearing Values of Foundation Materials**
R402	**Materials**
R402.1	**Wood Foundations:** Wood foundation systems shall be designed and installed in accordance with the provisions of this code.
R402.1.1	**Fasteners:** Fasteners used below *grade* to attach plywood to the exterior side of exterior *basement* or crawl space wall studs, or fasteners used in knee wall construction shall be of Type 304 or 316 stainless steel.
	Electro-galvanized steel nails and galvanized (zinc coated) steel staples shall not be permitted.
R402.1.2	**Wood treatment:** Where lumber and/or plywood is cut or drilled after treatment ... which shall contain a minimum of 2-percent copper metal, by repeated brushing, dipping or soaking until the wood absorbs no more preservative.
R402.2	**Concrete:** Concrete shall have a minimum specified compressive strength of f'_c, as shown in Table R402.2.
	Materials used to produce concrete and testing thereof shall comply with the applicable standards listed in Chapters 19 and 20 of ACI 318 or ACI 332.
Table R402.2	**Minimum Specified Compressive Strength of Concrete**
R403	**Footings**
R403.1.1	**Minimum size.** The minimum width, W, and thickness, T, for concrete footings shall be in accordance with Tables R403.1(1) through R403.1(3) and Figure R403.1(1) as applicable.
	Footings projections, P, shall not be less than 2 inches (51 mm) and shall not exceed the thickness of the footing.

Section #	Highlight
	Footings for wood foundations shall be in accordance with the details set forth in Section R403.2, and Figures R403.1(2) and R403.1.(3).
R403.1.4	**Minimum depth:** Exterior footings shall be placed not less than 12 inches (305 mm) below the finished grade of ground surface.
R403.1.7.3	**Foundation Elevation:** On graded sites, the top of any exterior foundation shall extend above the elevation of the street gutter at point of discharge or the inlet of an *approved* drainage device a minimum of 12 inches (305 mm) plus 2 percent.
Figure 403.1(1)	**Concrete and Masonry Foundation Details**
Figure R403.1(2)	**Permanent Wood Foundation Basement Wall Section**
Figure R403.1(3)	**Permanent Wood Foundation Crawl Space Section**
R404	**Foundation and Retaining Walls**
R404.1.5	**Foundation wall thickness based on walls supported:** The thickness of masonry or concrete foundation walls shall not be less than that required by Section R404.1.5.1 or R404.1.5.2, respectively.
R404.1.5.1	**Masonry wall thickness.** Masonry foundation walls shall not be less than the thickness of the wall supported, except that masonry foundation walls of at least 8-inch (203 mm) nominal thickness shall be permitted under brick veneered frame walls and under 10 inch wide (254 mm) cavity walls where the total height of the wall supported, including gables, is not more than 20 feet (6096 mm), provided the requirements of Section R404.1.1 are met.
R404.1.6	**Height above finished grade:** Concrete and masonry foundation walls shall extend above the finished *grade* adjacent to the foundation at all points a minimum of 4 inches (102 mm) where masonry veneer is used and a minimum of 6 inches (152 mm) elsewhere.
R404.1.8	**Rubble stone masonry:** Rubble stone masonry foundation walls shall have a minimum thickness of 16 inches (406 mm), shall not support an unbalanced backfill exceeding 8 feet (2438 mm) in height, shall not support soil pressure greater than 30 pounds per square foot per foot (4.71 kPa/m).
R404.3	**Wood sill plates:** Wood sill plates shall be a minimum of 2-inch by 4-inch (51 mm by 102 mm) nominal lumber. Sill plate anchorage shall be in accordance of sections R403.1.6 and Item 1 of Section R403.1.6.1.
R405	**Foundation Drainage**
R405.1	**Concrete or masonry foundations:** Drains shall be provided around concrete or masonry foundations that retain earth and enclose habitable or usable spaces located below *grade.*
	Gravel or crushed store drains shall extend not less than 1 foot (305 mm) beyond the outside edge of the footing and 6 inches (152 mm) above the top of the footing and be covered with an *approved* filter membrane material…and covered with not less than 6 inches (152 mm) of the same material.
R406	**Foundation Waterproofing and Dampproofing**

Section #	Highlight
R406.2	**Concrete and Masonry Foundation Waterproofing:** In areas where a high water table or other severe soil-water conditions are known to exist…Walls shall be waterproofed in accordance with one of the following: (Highlight 1 – 8) **Exception:** Use of plastic roofing cements, acrylic coatings, latex coatings, mortars and pargings to seal ICF walls is permitted.
R407	**Columns**
R407.3	**Structural requirements:** Wood columns shall not be less in nominal size than 4 inches by 4 inches (102 mm by 102 mm). Steel columns shall not be less than 3-inch-diameter (76 mm) Schedule 40 pipe manufactured in accordance with ASTM A53 Grade B or *approved* equivalent.
R408	**Under-Floor Space**
R408.1	**Ventilation:** The minimum net area of ventilation openings shall not be less than 1 square foot for each 150 square feet of under-floor space area…When a Class I vapor retarder material is used, the minimum net area of ventilation openings shall not be less than 1 square foot (0.0929 m^2) for each 150 square feet (14 m^2) of under-floor space area….One such ventilating opening shall be within 3 feet (914 mm) of each corner of the building.
R408.2	**Openings for under floor ventilation:** Ventilation openings shall be covered for their height and width with any of the following materials provided that the least dimension of the covering shall not exceed 1/4 inch (6.4 mm): (Highlight 1 – 6)
R408.4	**Access.** Access shall be provided to all under-floor spaces. Access openings through the floor shall be a minimum of 18 inches by 24 inches (457 mm by 610 mm)…Through wall access openings shall not be located under a door to the residence.
R502	**Wood Floor Framing**
R502.11	**Wood Trusses**
R502.11.1	**Design:** The truss design drawings shall be prepared by a registered professional where required by *Florida Statutes*.
R502.11.2	**Bracing:** Trusses shall be braced to prevent rotation and provide lateral stability in accordance with the requirements specified in the *construction documents* for the building and on the individual truss design drawings.
R502.11.3	**Alterations to trusses:** *Alterations* resulting in the addition of load that exceed the design load for the truss, shall not be permitted without verification that the truss is capable of supporting the additional loading.
R502.11.4	**Truss design drawings:** Truss design drawings shall include, at a minimum, the information specified as follows: (Highlight 1 – 12)
R502.12	**Draftstopping required:** Draftstopping shall be provided in accordance with Section R302.12.
503	**Floor Sheathing**

Section #	Highlight
R504	**Pressure Preservative-Treated Wood Floors (On Ground)**
R504.1.3	**Uplift and buckling:** Where required, resistance to uplift or restraint against buckling shall be provided by interior bearing walls or properly designed stub walls anchored in the supporting soil below.
R504.2	**Site Preparation:** The area within the foundation walls shall have all vegetation, topsoil and foreign material removed, and any fill material that is added shall be free of vegetation and foreign material. The fill shall be compacted to ensure uniform support of the pressure preservative treated-wood floor sleepers.
R504.2.1	**Base:** A minimum 4-inch thick (102 mm) granular base of gravel having a maximum size of ¾ inch (19.1 mm) or crushed stone having a maximum size of ½ inch (12.7 mm) shall be placed over the compacted earth.
R504.2.2	**Moisture barrier**: Polyethylene sheeting of minimum 6-mil (0.15 mm) thickness shall be placed over the granular base. Joints shall be lapped 6 inches (152 mm) and left unsealed.
R506	**Concrete Floors (On Ground)**
R506.1	**General:** Floors shall be a minimum 3 ½ (89 mm) inches thick (for expansive soils, see Section R403.1.8).
R506.2	**Site preparation:** The area within the foundation walls shall have all vegetation, top soil and foreign material removed.
R506.2.1	**Fill:** Fill material shall be free of vegetation and foreign material. The fill shall be compacted…fill depths shall not exceed 24 inches (610 mm) for clean sand or gravel and 8 inches (203 mm) for earth.
R506.2.2	**Base:** A 4-inch thick (102 mm) base course consisting of clean graded sand, gravel, crushed stone, crushed concrete or crushed blast-furnace slag passing a 2-inch (51 mm) sieve shall be placed on the prepared sub-grade where the slab is below *grade.* **Exception:** A base course is not required where the concrete slab is installed on well-drained or sand-gravel mixture soils classified as Group I according to the United Soil Classification System in accordance with Table R405.1.
R506.2.3	**Vapor retarder:** A 6-mil (0.006 inch; 152 µm) polyethylene or *approved* vapor retarder with joints lapped not less than 6 inches (152 mm) shall be placed between the concrete slab floor and the base course or the prepared subgrade where no base course exists.
R602	**Wood Wall Framing**
R606	**General Masonry Construction**
R606.3.1	**Bed and head joints:** Unless otherwise required or indicated on the project drawings, head and bed joints shall be 3/8 inch (9.5 mm) thick, except that the thickness of the bed joint of the starting course placed over foundations shall not be less than ¼ inch (6.4 mm) and not more than ¾ inch (19.1 mm).
R606.3.2	**Masonry unit placement**

Section #	Highlight
R606.5	**Corbeled Masonry:** Corbeled masonry shall be in accordance with Sections R606.5.1 through R606.5.3.
R606.5.1	**Units:** *Solid masonry* units or masonry units filled with mortar or grout shall be used for corbeling.
R606.5.2	**Corbel projection:** The maximum projection of one unit shall not exceed one-half the height of the unit or one-third the thickness at right angles to the wall. The maximum corbeled projection beyond the face of the wall shall not exceed: (Highlight 1-2)
R607	**Glass Unit Masonry**
R609	**Exterior Windows and Doors**
R610	**Structural Insulated Panel Wall Construction**
R610.3	**Materials:** SIP's shall comply with the requirements of ANSI/APA PRS 610.1:
R610.3.1	**Lumber:** The minimum lumber framing material used for SIPs prescribed in this document is NLGA graded No. 2 Spruce-pine-fir. Substitution of other wood species/grades that meet or exceed the mechanical properties and specific gravity of No. 2 Spruce-pine-fir shall be permitted.
R610.3.2	**SIP screws:** The screws shall be corrosion resistant and have a minimum shank diameter of 0.188 inch (4.7 mm) and minimum head diameter of 0.620 inch (15.5 mm).
R610.3.3	**Nails:** Nails specified in Section R610 shall be common or galvanized box unless otherwise stated.
Table R610.5(1)	**Minimum Thickness for SIP Wall Supporting SIP or Light-Frame Roof Only**
R701.1	**Application:** The provisions of this chapter shall control the design and construction of the interior and exterior wall covering for buildings.
R702	**Interior Covering**
R702.1	**General:** Interior coverings or wall finishes shall be installed in accordance with this chapter and Table R702.1(1), Table R702.1.(2), Table R702.1(3)and Table R702.3.5. Interior masonry veneer shall comply with the requirements of Section R703.7.1 for support and Section R703.7.4 for anchorage, except an airspace is not required. Interior finishes and materials shall conform to the flame spread and smoke development of Section R302.9.
R702.2	**Interior Plaster**
Table R702.1(1)	**Thickness of Plaster**
R702.2.3	**Support:** Support spacing for gypsum or metal lath on walls or ceilings shall not exceed 16 inches (406 mm) for 3/8-inch-thick (9.5 mm) or 24 inches (610 mm) for ½-inch-thick (12.7 mm) plain gypsum lath.
R702.3	**Gypsum board and gypsum panel products**

Section #	**Highlight**
Table R702.1(2)	**Gypsum Plaster Proportions**
Table R702.1(3)	**Cement Plaster Proportions, Parts by Volume**
R702.3.7	**Water-resistant gypsum backing board:** Use of water-resistant gypsum backing board shall be permitted on ceilings. Water-resistant gypsum board shall not be installed over a Class I or II vapor retarder in a shower or tub compartment.
Table R702.3.5	**Minimum Thickness and Application of Gypsum Board and Gypsum Panel Products**
R702.5	**Other finishes:** Wood veer paneling and hard board paneling shall be placed on wood or cold-formed steel framing spaced not more than 16 inches (406 mm) on center. Wood veneer and hard board paneling less than ¼-inch (6 mm) nominal thickness…Hardboard paneling shall conform to CPA/ANSI A135.5.
R703	**Exterior Covering**
R703.2	**Water-resistive barrier:** One layer of No. 15 asphalt felt, free from holes and breaks, complying with ASTM D226…Where joints occur, felt shall be lapped not less than 6 inches (152 mm).
R703.5	**Wood, hardboard and wood structural panel siding**
R703.5.2	**Panel Siding:** Vertical joints in panel siding shall occur over framing members…Horizontal joints in panel siding shall be lapped not less than 1 inch (25 mm) or shall be shiplapped or flashed with Z-flashing and occur over solid blocking, wood or wood structural panel sheathing.
R703.6	**Wood shakes and shingles**
Table R703.6.1	**Maximum Weather Exposure for Wood Shakes and Shingles on Exterior Walls**
R703.6.3	**Attachment:** Wood shakes or shingles shall be installed according to this chapoter and the manufacturer's instructions. Where wind pressures determine…The fasteners shall penetrate the sheathing or furring strips by not less than ½ inch (13 mm) and shall not be overdriven.
R703.8	**Anchored stone and masonry veneer, general**
R703.8.5	**Flashing:** Flashing shall be located beneath the first course of masonry above finished ground level above the foundation wall or slab…in accordance with Section R703.8.
R703.8.6	**Weepholes:** Weepholes shall be provided in the outside wythe of masonry walls at a maximum spacing of 33 inches (838 mm) on center. Weepholes shall not be less than 3/16 inch (5 mm) in diameter. Weepholes shall be located immediately above the flashing.
R703.10	**Fiber cement siding**
R703.10.1	**Panel siding:** Panels shall be installed with the long dimension either parallel or perpendicular to framing. Vertical and horizontal joints shall occur over framing members and shall be protected with caulking… or otherwise designed to comply with Section R703.1.

Section #	Highlight
R703.10.2	**Lap Siding:** Fiber-cement lap siding having a maximum width of 12 inches (305 mm) shall comply with the requirements of ASTM C1186, Type A, minimum Grade II or ISO 8336, Category A, minimum Class 2. Lap siding shall be lapped a minimum of 1 ¼ inches and lap siding not having tongue-and-groove end joints shall have the ends protected with caulking, covered with an H-section joint cover, located over a strip of flashing, or shall be designed to comply with Section R703.1.
R802	**Wood Roof Framing**
R802.1.5.4	**Labeling:** Fire-retardant-treated lumber and wood structural panels shall be *labeled.* The label shall contain: (Highlight 1 – 8)
R802.1.10.1	**Truss design drawings:** Truss design drawings shall be provided with the shipment of trusses delivered to the job site. Truss design drawings shall include, at a minimum, the following information: (Highlight 1 – 12)
R803	**Roof Sheathing**
Table R803.1	**Minimum Thickness of Lumber Roof Sheathing**
R806	**Roof Ventilation**
R806.1	**Ventilation required.** Ventilation openings shall have a least dimension of 1/16 inch (1.6 mm) minimum and 1/4 inch (6.4 mm) maximum. Ventilation openings having a least dimension larger than 1/4 inch (6.4 mm) shall be provided with corrosion-resistant wire cloth screening, hardware cloth, perforated vinyl or similar material with openings having a least dimension of 1/16 inch (1.6 mm) minimum and 1/4 inch (6.4 mm) maximum.
R806.2	**Minimum vent area:** The minimum net free ventilating area shall be 1/150 of the area of the vented space.
	Exception: The minimum net free ventilation area shall be 1/300 of the vented space, provided that not less than 40 percent and not more than 50 percent of the required ventilating area is provided by ventilators located in the upper portion or the attic or rafter space. Upper ventilators shall be located not more than 3 feet (914 mm) below the ridge or highest point of space, measured vertically.
R807	**Attic Access**
R807.1	**Attic Access:** Buildings with combustible ceiling or roof construction shall have an *attic* access opening to *attic* areas that have a vertical height of 30 inches (762 mm) or greater over an area of not less than 30 square feet (2.8 m^2).
	The rough-framed opening shall not be less than 22 inches by 30 inches (559 mm by 762 mm) and shall be located in a hallway or other location with *ready access.*
R902	**Fire Classification**
R902.1	**Roofing Covering Materials**
	Exceptions (Highlight 1 – 3)

Section #	Highlight
R903	**Weather Protection**
R903.2	**Flashing:** Flashings shall be used to seal roofing systems, where the system is interrupted or terminated and shall be installed in a manner that prevents moisture from entering the wall and roof through joints in copings, through moisture permeable materials and at intersections with parapet walls and other penetrations through the roof plane.
R903.2.1	**Locations**: Flashings shall be installed at wall and roof intersections, wherever there is a change in roof slope or direction and around roof openings. **Exception:** Flashing is not required at hip and ridge junctions.
Table R903.2.1	**Metal Flashing Material**
R903.3	**Coping:** Parapet walls shall be properly coped with noncombustible, weatherproof materials of a width not less than the thickness of parapet wall.
R903.4	**Roof drainage:** Unless roofs are sloped to drain over roof edges, roof drains shall be installed at each low point of the roof.
R903.4.1	**Overflow drains and scuppers**: When other means of drainage of overflow water is not provided, overflow scuppers shall be placed in walls or parapets not less than 2 inches (51 mm) nor more than 4 inches (102 mm) above the finished roof covering and shall be located as close as practical to required vertical leaders or downspouts or wall and parapet scuppers.
R905	**Requirements for Roof Coverings**
R905.2	**Asphalt Shingles:** The installation of asphalt shingles shall comply with the provisions of this section or RAS 115.
R905.2.2	**Slope:** Asphalt shingles shall be used only on roof slopes of two units vertical in 12 units horizontal (2:12) or greater. For roof slopes from two units vertical in 12 units horizontal (2:12) and less than four units vertical in 12 units horizontal (4:12), double underlayment application is required in accordance with section R905.1.1.
R905.2.5	**Fasteners:** Fasteners for asphalt shingles shall be galvanized steel, stainless steel, aluminum or copper roofing nails, minimum 12-gage [0.105 inch (3 mm)] shank with a minimum 3/8-inch diameter (9.5 mm) head ...and not less than ¾ -inch (19.1 mm) into the roof sheathing.
R905.2.6	**Attachment:** Asphalt shingles shall have the minimum number of fasteners required by the manufacturer, but not less than four fasteners per strip shingle, or two fasteners per individual shingle.
R905.2.8.2	**Valleys:** Valley linings of the following types shall be permitted: (Highlight 1-3)
R905.2.8.5	**Drip edge:** Overlap to be a minimum of 3 inches (76 mm). Eave drip edges shall extend ½ inch (13 mm) below sheathing and extend back on the roof a minimum of 2 inches (51 mm)...Drip edge shall be mechanically fastened a maximum of 12 inches (305 mm) on center.
R905.3	**Clay and Concrete tile**

Section #	Highlight
R905.3.5	**Concrete Tile**
R905.3.6	**Fasteners:** Nails shall be corrosion resistant and not less than 11 gage, 5/16-inch (11 mm) head, and of sufficient length to penetrate the deck not less than ¾ inch (19 mm) or through the thickness of the deck, whichever is less
R905.4	**Metal roof shingles:** The installation of metal roof shingles shall comply with the provisions of this section.
R905.4.2	**Deck slope:** Metal roof shingles shall not be installed on roof slopes below three units vertical in 12 units horizontal (25-percent slope).
Table 905.4.4	**Metal Roof Coverings**
R905.4.6	**Flashing:** Valley flashing shall extend not less than 8 inches (203 mm) from the centerline each way and shall have a splash diverter rib not less than 3/4 inch (19 mm) in height at the flow line formed as part of the flashing. Sections of flashing shall have an end lap of not less than 4 inches (102 mm). The metal valley flashing shall have a 36-inch-wide (914 mm) underlayment running the full length of the valley, in addition to underlayment required for metal roof shingles.
R905.6	**Slate and slate-type shingles**
R905.6.3	**Underlayment:** Underlayment shall be installed in accordance with the manufacturer's installation instructions.
Table R905.6.5	**Slate Shingle Headlap**
R905.6.6	**Flashing:** Valley flashing shall be a minimum of 16 inches (406 mm) wide.
R905.7	**Wood Shingles:** The installation of wood shingles shall be limited to roofs where the allowable uplift resistance is equal to or greater than the design uplift pressure for the roof listed in Table R301.2(2).
R905.7.6.1	**Fasteners**
R905.7.6.1.1	**Nails:** Fasteners to attach wood shingles shall be Type 304 (Type 316 for costal areas) stainless steel ring-shank nails with a minimum penetration of 0.75 inch into the sheathing. Each shingle shall be attached with a minimum of two fasteners.
R905.8	**Wood shakes:** All wood shakes shall be installed in accordance with this chapter…or RAS 130.
R905.9	**Built Up Roofs**
R905.9.1	**Slope:** Built-up roofs shall have a design slope of not less than one-fourth unit vertical in 12 units horizontal (2-percent slope) for drainage
R905.9.2	**Material Standards**: Built-up roof covering materials shall comply with the standards in Table R905.9.2 or UL 55A.
Table R905.9.2	**Built-Up Roofing Material Standards**

Section #	Highlight
R905.10	**Metal Roof Panels**
R905.10.1	**Deck Requirements:** Metal roof panel roof coverings shall be applied to solid or spaced sheathing, except where the roof covering is specifically designed to be applied to spaced supports.
R905.10.2	**Slope:** Minimum slopes for metal roof panels shall comply with the following: (Highlight 1-3)
R905.11	**Modified bitumen roofing:** The installation of modified bitumen roofing shall comply with the provisions of this section
R905.11.2	**Material Standards:** Modified bitumen roof coverings shall comply with the standards in Table R905.11.2.

Table R905.11.2 **Modified Bitumen Roofing Material Standards**

R905.12	**Thermoset single-ply roofing:** The installation of thermoset single-ply roofing shall comply with the provisions of this section.
R905.12.1	**Slope:** Thermoset single-ply membrane roofs shall have a design slope of not less than one-fourth unit vertical in 12 units horizontal (2-percent slope) for drainage.
R905.13	**Thermoplastic single-ply roofing:** The installation of the thermoplastic single-ply roofing shall comply with the provisions of this section.
R905.13.1	**Slope:** Thermoplastic single-ply membrane roofs shall have a design slope of not less than one-fourth unit vertical in 12 units horizontal (2-percent slope).
R905.14	**Sprayed polyurethane foam roofing:** The installation of the sprayed polyurethane foam roofing shall comply with the provisions of this section or incompliance with RAS 109 and 109A.
R905.14.1	**Slope:** Sprayed polyurethane foam roofs shall have a design slope of not less than one-fourth unit vertical in 12 units horizontal (2-percent slope) for drainage.
R905.15	**Liquid-applied roofing:** The installation of the liquid-applied roofing shall comply with this section.
R905.15.1	**Slope:** Liquid-applied roofing shall have a design slope of not less than one-fourth unit vertical in 12 units horizontal (2-percent slope).
R906	**Roof Insulation**
R906.1	**General:** The use of above-deck thermal insulation shall be permitted provided such insulation is covered with an *approved* roof covering and complies with FM 4450 or UL 1256.

Table R906.2 **Material Standards for Roof Insulation**

Section #	Highlight
R1001.2	**Footings and Foundations:** Footings for masonry fireplaces and their chimneys shall be constructed of concrete or *solid masonry* at least 12 inches (305 mm) thick and shall extend not less than 6 inches (152 mm) beyond the face of the fireplace or foundation wall on all sides…In areas not subject to freezing, footings shall be not less than 12 inches (305 mm) below finished *grade.*
R1001.5	**Firebox walls:** Masonry fireboxes shall be constructed of *solid masonry* units, hollow masonry units grouted solid, stone or concrete. Where a lining of firebrick not less than 2 inches (51 mm) thick or other *approved* lining is provided, the minimum thickness of back and side walls shall be 8 inches (203 mm) of *solid masonry*, including the lining. Where a lining is not provided, the total minimum thickness of back and side walls shall be 10 inches (254 mm) of *solid masonry.*
Table R1001.1	**Summary of Requirements for Masonry Fireplaces and Chimneys**
R1001.7	**Lintel and throat:** Masonry over a fireplace opening shall be supported by a lintel of noncombustible material. The minimum required bearing length on each end of the fireplace opening shall be 4 inches (102 mm).
R1001.7.1	**Damper:** Masonry fireplaces shall be equipped with a ferrous metal damper located not less than 8 inches (203 mm) above the top of the fireplace opening.
R1001.10	**Hearth extension dimensions:** Hearth extensions shall extend not less than 16 inches (406 mm) in front of and not less than 8 inches (203 mm) beyond each side of the fireplace opening.
R1001.11	**Fireplace clearance:** Wood beams, joists, studs, and other combustible material shall have a clearance of not less than 2 inches (51 mm) from the front faces and sides of masonry fireplaces and not less than 4 inches (102 mm) from the back faces of masonry fireplaces.
R1003	**Masonry Chimneys**
R1003.2	**Footings and foundations:** Footings for masonry chimneys shall be constructed of concrete or *solid masonry* not less than 12 inches (305 mm) thick and shall extend not less than 6 inches (152 mm) beyond the face of the foundation or support the wall on all sides. In areas not subjected to freezing, footings shall be not less than 12 inches (305 mm) below finished *grade.*
R1003.5	**Corbeling:** Masonry chimneys shall not be corbelled more than one-half of the chimney's wall thickness from a wall or foundation,
R1003.10	**Wall thickness:** Masonry chimney walls shall be constructed of *solid masonry* units or hollow masonry units grouted solid with not less than a 4-inch (102 mm) nominal thickness.
Table R1003.14(1)	**Net Cross-Sectional Area of Round Flue Sizes**
Table R1003.14(2)	**Net Cross-Sectional Area of Square and Rectangular Flue Sizes**

Section #	Highlight
R1003.17	**Masonry chimney cleanout openings:** Cleanout openings shall be provided within 6 inches (152 mm) of the base of each flue within every masonry chimney. The upper edge of the cleanout shall be located not less than 6 inches (152 mm) below the lowest chimney opening. The height of the opening shall be not less than 6 inches (152 mm).
R1003.18	**Chimney Clearances:** Any potion of a masonry chimney located in the interior of the building… shall have a minimum air space clearance of 1 inch (25 mm).
R1004	**Factory-Built Fireplaces**
N1101	**Chapter 11 — Energy Efficiency**
shall	**Energy efficiency.** The provisions of the *Florida Building Code, Energy Conservation,* govern the energy efficiency of residential construction.
M1403	**Heat Pump Equipment**
M1406	**Radiant Heating Systems**
M1406.2	**Clearances:** Clearances for radiant heating panels or elements to any wiring, outlet boxes and junction boxes used for installing electrical devices or mounting luminaires shall comply with Chapter 34 of this code.
M1408	**Vented Floor Furnaces**
M1408.3	**Location:** Location of floor furnaces shall conform to the following requirements: 1. Floor registers of floor furnaces shall be installed not less than 6 inches (152 mm) from a wall.
M1502	**Clothes Dryer Exhaust**
M1502.3	**Duct termination:** Exhaust ducts shall terminate on the outside of the building. Exhaust duct terminations shall be in accordance with the dryer manufacturer's installation instructions. In the manufacturer's instructions do not specify a termination location, the exhaust duct shall terminate not less than 3 feet (914 mm) in any direction from openings into buildings. Exhaust duct terminations shall be equipped with a backdraft damper.
M1502.4.3	**Transition duct:** Transition ducts used to connect the dryer to the exhaust *duct system* shall be a single length that is *listed* and *labeled* in accordance with UL 2158A. Transition ducts shall be not greater than 8 feet (2438 mm) in length.
M1502.4.5	**Duct Length**
M1502.4.5.1	**Specified length:** The maximum length of the exhaust duct shall be 35 feet (10 688 mm) from the connection to the transition duct from the dryer to the outlet terminal.
M1505	**Overhead Exhaust Hoods**
M1505.1	**General:** Domestic open-top broiler units shall have a metal exhaust hood, having a minimum thickness of 0.0157-inch (0.3950 mm) (No. 28 gage) with ¼ inch (6.4 mm) clearance between the hood and the underside of combustible material or cabinets.

Section #	Highlight
Table M1507.4	**Minimum Required Local Exhaust Rates for One- and Two-Family Dwellings**
M1803	**Chimney and Vent Connectors**
M1803.3.1	**Floor, ceiling and wall penetrations:** A chimney connector or vent connector shall not pass through any floor or ceiling. A chimney connector or vent connector shall not pass through a wall or partition unless the connector is *listed* or *labeled* for wall pass-through, or is routed through a device *listed* and *labeled* for wall pass-through and is installed in accordance with the conditions of its *listing* and *label*.
Table M1803.3.4	**Chimney and Vent Connector Clearances to Combustible Materials**
M2005	**Water Heaters**
M2005.2	**Prohibited Locations:** Fuel-fired water heaters not be installed in a room used as a storage closet. Water heaters located in a bedroom or bathroom shall be installed in a sealed enclosure so that *combustion air* will not be taken from the living space.
P2801.6	**Required Pan**
P2801.6.1	**Pan size and drain:** The pan shall be not less than 1 ½ inches (38 mm) deep and shall be of sufficient size and shape to receive dripping or condensate from the tank or water heater.
P2801.6.2	**Pan drain termination:** The pan drain shall extend full-size and terminate over a suitably located indirect waste receptor or shall extend to the exterior of the building and terminate not less than 6 inches (152 mm) and not more than 24 inches (610 mm) above the adjacent ground surface.
P2804	**Relief Valves**
P2804.3	**Pressure-relief valves:** They shall be set to open at not less than 25 psi (172 kPa) above the system pressure and not greater than 150 psi (1034 kPa).
P2804.4	**Temperature-relief valves:** The valves shall be installed such that the temperature-sensing element monitors the water within the top 6 inches (152 mm) of the tank.
P2804.6.1	**Requirements for discharge pipe:** The discharge piping serving a pressure-relief valve, temperature-relief valve or combination valve shall: (Highlight 1 – 14)
P2902.3	**Backflow protection:** A means of protection against backflow shall be provided in accordance with Sections P2902.3.1 through P2902.3.6.
Table P2902.3	**Application for Backflow Preventers**
Table P2903.2	**Maximum Flow Rates and Consumption for Plumbing Fixtures and Fixture Fittings**
R4400	**Chapter 44 - High Velocity Hurricane Zones**
R4600	**Chapter 46 – Referenced Standards**
	ANSI American National Standards Institute

Florida Building Code 2017, Building Chapter 1

Section #	**Highlight**
102	**Applicability**
102.2	**Building.** The provisions of the *Florida Building Code* shall apply to the construction, erection, alteration, modification, repair, equipment, use and occupancy, location, maintenance, removal and demolition of every public and private building, structure or facility or floating residential structure, or any appurtenances connected or attached to such buildings, structures or facilities.
105	**Permits**
105.1	**Required.** Any *owner* or owner's authorized agent who intends to construct, enlarge, alter, *repair*, move, demolish, or change the occupancy of a building or structure, or to erect, install, enlarge, alter, *repair*, remove, convert or replace any impact-resistant coverings, electrical, gas, mechanical or plumbing system, the installation of which is regulated by this code, or to cause any such work to be performed, shall first make application to the *building official* and obtain the required *permit.*
107	**Submittal Documents**
107.3.5	**Minimum plan review criteria for buildings**
	Commercial Buildings:
	Residential (one- and two-family):
108	**Temporary Structures and Uses**

Florida Building Code - Residential, 6th Ed, 2017
Tabs and Highlights

These 1 Exam Prep Tabs are based on the *Florida Building Code-Residential-2017 Edition.*

Each 1 Exam Prep tabs sheet has five rows of tabs. Start with the first tab at the first row at the top of the page; proceed down that row placing the tabs at the locations listed below. Place each tab in your book setting it down one notch until you get to the last tab (usually the index or glossary). Then start with the highlights.

1 Exam Prep Tab	Section	Page #
Table of Contents		vii
Protection of Openings	R301.2.1.2	37
Termite Protection	R318	67
Drainage	R401.3	75
Footings	R403	79
Under Floor Ventilation	R408.1	125
Drilling and Notching	R502.8	135
Floor Sheathing	R503	**137**
Spans and Loads	Table R503.2.1.1(1)	**137**
Concrete Floors	R506	153
Masonry	R606	249
Bed and Head Joints	R606.3.1	251
Wood Roof Framing	R802	373
Requirements for Masonry Chimneys	Table R1001.1	439
Fireplace Clearances	R1001.11	441
Chimney Clearances	R1003.18	445
Clothes Dryer Exhaust	M1502	463
Chimney Connector Clearances	Table M1803.3.4	475
Water Heater Prohibited Locations	M2005.2	481
Backflow Protection	P2902.3	585

******This concludes the tabs for this book. Please continue with the highlights on the following page.******

A.M. 07/16/2020

Section #	Highlight
R101.2	**Scope:** The provisions of the Florida Building Code, Residential shall apply to the construction, alteration, movement enlargement, replacement, repair, equipment, use and occupancy, location, removal and demolition of detached one - and two-family dwellings and townhouses not more than three stories above grade plane in height with a separate means of egress and their accessory structures not more than three stories above grade plan in height.
R202	**Definitions**
R301.1	**Application:** Building and structures, and all parts thereof, shall be constructed to safely support all loads including dead loads, live loads, roof loads, flood loads, snow loads, wind loads and seismic loads as prescribed by this code…Buildings and structures constructed as prescribed by this code are deemed to comply with the requirements of this section.
R301.1.3	**Engineered design:** When a building of otherwise conventional construction contains structural elements exceeding the limit of Section R301…these elements shall be designed in accordance with accepted engineering practice.
Figure R301.2(3)	**Weathering Probability Map for Concrete**
Figure R301.2(4)	**Ultimate Design Wind Speed**
Figure R301.2(6)	**Termite Infestation Probability Map**
R301.2.1.2	**Protection of openings:** Glazed opening protection for windborne debris shall meet the requirements of the Large Missle Test of ASTM E 1996…or ANSI?DASMA 115… **Exception:** Wood structural panels with a minimum thickness of 7/16 inch and a span between lines of fasteners of 44 inches shall be permitted…is 180 mph or less. a. Attachments shall be designed to resist the component and cladding loads determined either in accordance with Table R301.2(2) or ASCE 7, with the permanent corrosion-resistant hardware provided and anchors permanently installed on the building.
Table R301.2.1.3	**Wind Speed Conversions**
R301.2.1.3	**Wind speed conversion**; Where referenced documents are based on nominal design wind speeds…the ultimate design wind speeds, Vult, of Figure R301.2(4) shall be converted to nominal design wind speeds, Vasd, using Table R301.2.1.3.
Table R301.6	**Minimum Roof Live Loads in Pounds-Force per Square Foot of Horizontal Projection**
R310	**Emergency Escape and Rescue Openings**
R310.1	**Emergency escape and rescue opening required:** Basements, habitable attics and every sleeping room shall not have less than one operable emergency escape and rescue opening.
R310.2.1	**Minimum opening area:** Emergency escape and rescue openings shall have net clear opening of not less than 5.7 square feet. The net clear height opening shall not be less than 24 inches and the minimum net clear width shall not be less than 20 inches.
R310.2.3	**Window wells:** The horizontal area of the window well shall not be less than 9 square feet with a horizontal projection and width not less than 36 inches.

Section #	Highlight
R318	**Protection Against Termites**
R318.1.4	If soil treatment is used for subterranean termite prevention ...minimum 6 mil vapor retarder.
R401.3	**Drainage:** Surface drainage shall be diverted to a storm sewer conveyance or other approved point of collection that does not create a hazard. Lots shall be graded to drain surface water away from foundation walls. The grade shall fall a minimum of 6 inches within the first 10 feet.
R401.4	**Soil tests:** Where quantifiable data created by accepted soil science methodologies indicate expansive…This test shall be done by an approved agency using an approved method.
Table R401.4.1	**Presumptive Load-Bearing Values of Foundation Materials**
R402	**Materials**
R402.1	**Wood Foundations:** Wood foundation systems shall be designed and installed in accordance with the provisions of this code.
R402.1.1	**Fasteners:** Fasteners used below grade to attach plywood to the exterior side of exterior basement or crawl space wall studs, or fasteners used in knee wall construction shall be of Type 304 or 316 stainless steel. Electro-galvanized steel nails and galvanized (zinc coated) steel staples shall not be permitted.
R402.1.2	**Wood treatment:** Where lumber and/or plywood is cut or drilled after treatment … minimum of 2-percent copper metal, by repeated brushing, dipping or soaking until the wood absorbs no more preservative.
R402.2	**Concrete:** Concrete shall have a minimum specified compressive strength of f'_c, as shown in Table R402.2. Materials used to produce concrete and testing thereof shall comply with the applicable standards listed in Chapter 19 and 20 of ACI 318 or ACI332.
Table R402.2	**Minimum Specified Compressive Strength of Concrete**
R403	**Footings**
R403.1.1	**Minimum size.** The minimum width, W, and thickness, T, for sizes for concrete footings shall be in accordance with Tables R403.1(1) through R403.1(3) and Figure R403.1(1). Footings projections, P, shall not be less than 2 inches and shall not exceed the thickness of the footing. Footings for wood foundations shall be in accordance with the details set forth in Section R403.2, and Figures R403.1(2) and R403.1.(3)
R403.1.4	**Minimum depth:** Exterior footings shall be placed at least 12 inches below the undisturbed ground surface.
R403.1.7.3	**Foundation Elevation:** On graded sites, the top of any exterior foundation shall extend above the elevation of the street gutter at point of discharge or the inlet of an approved drainage device a minimum of 12 inches plus 2 percent.

Section #	**Highlight**
Figure 403.1(1)	**Concrete and Masonry Foundation Details**
Figure R403.1(2)	**Permanent Wood Foundation Basement Wall Section**
Figure R403.1(3)	**Permanent Wood Foundation Crawl Space Section**
R404	**Foundation and Retaining Walls**
R404.1.5	**Foundation wall thickness on walls supported:** The thickness of masonry or concrete foundation walls shall not be less than that required by Section R404.1.5.1 or R404.1.5.2, respectively.
R404.1.5.1	**Masonry wall thickness.** Masonry foundation walls shall not be less than the thickness of the wall supported, except that masonry foundation walls of at least 8-inch nominal thickness shall be permitted under brick veneered frame walls and under 10 inch wide cavity walls there the total height of the wall supported including gables is not more than 20 feet, provided Section R404.1.1 is met.
R404.1.6	**Height above finished grade:** Concrete and masonry foundation walls shall extend above the finished grade…minimum of 4 inches where masonry veneer is used and a minimum of 6 inches elsewhere.
R404.1.8	**Rubble stone masonry:** Rubble stone masonry foundation walls shall have a minimum thickness of 16 inches, shall not support an unbalanced backfill exceeding 8 feet in height, shall not support soil pressure greater than 30 pounds per square foot.
R404.3	**Wood sill plates:** Wood sill plates shall be a minimum of 2-inch by 4-inch nominal lumber. Sill plate anchorage shall be in accordance of sections R403.1.6 and R602.11.
R405	**Foundation Drainage**
R405.1	**Concrete or masonry foundations:** Drains shall be provided around all concrete or masonry foundations that retain earth and enclose habitable or usable spaces located below grade. Gravel or crushed store drains shall extend at least 1 foot beyond the outside edge of the footing and 6 inches above the top of the footing and be covered with an approved filter membrane material…and covered with not less than 6 inches of the same material.
R406	**Foundation Waterproofing and Dampproofing**
R406.2	**Concrete and Masonry Foundation Waterproofing:** In areas where high water table or other severe soil-water conditions are known to exist…Walls shall be waterproofed in accordance with one of the following: Highlight 1 – 8. **Exception:** Use of plastic roofing cements, acrylic coatings, mortars and parings to seal ICF walls is permitted.
R407	**Columns**
R407.3	**Structural requirements:** Wood columns shall not be less in nominal size than 4 inches by 4 inches. Steel columns shall not be less than 3-inch-diameterSchedule 40 pipe manufactured in accordance with ASTM A 53 Grade B or approved equivalent.
R408	**Under-Floor Space**

Section #	Highlight
R408.1	**Ventilation:** The minimum net area of ventilation openings shall not be less than 1 square-foot for each 150 square feet of under-floor space area…When a Class I vapor retarder material is used, the minimum net area of ventilation openings shall not be less than 1 square foot for each 1,500 square feet. One such ventilating opening shall be within 3 feet of each corner of the building.
R408.2	**Openings for under floor ventilation:** Ventilation openings shall be covered for their height and width with any of the following materials provided that the least dimension of the covering shall not exceed 1/4 inch: Highlight 1 - 6.
R408.4	**Access.** Access shall be provided for all under-floor spaces. Access openings through the floor shall be a minimum of 18 inches by 24 inches…Through wall access openings shall not be located under a door to the residence.
R502	**Wood Floor Framing**
R502.8	**Cutting, drilling and notching:** Structural floor members shall not be cut, bored or notched in excess of the limitations specified in this section. See figure R502.8.
R502.8.1	**Sawn Lumber:** Notches in joists, rafters and beams shall not exceed one-sixth of the depth of the member, shall not be longer than one-third of the depth of the member and shall not be located in the middle one-third of the span. Notches at the ends of members shall not exceed one-fourth the depth of the member…The diameter of holes bored or cut into members shall not exceed one-third of the depth of the member, Holes shall not be closer than 2 inches to the top or bottom of the member or to any other hole located in the member. Where the member is also notched, the hole shall not be closer than 2 inches to the notch.
R502.11	**Wood Trusses**
R502.11.1	**Design:** The truss design drawings shall be prepared by a registered professional where required by Florida Statutes.
R502.11.2	**Bracing:** Trusses shall be braced to prevent rotation and provide lateral stability in accordance with the requirements specified in the construction documents for the building and on the individual truss design drawings.
R502.11.3	**Alterations to trusses:** Alterations resulting in the addition of load that exceed the design load for the truss, shall not be permitted without verification that the truss is capable of supporting the additional loading.
R502.11.4	**Truss design drawings:** Truss design drawings shall include, at a minimum, the information specified below: Highlight 1 – 12.
Figure R502.8	**Cutting, Notching and Drilling**
R502.12	**Draftstopping required:** Draftstopping shall be provided in accordance with Section R302.12.
503	**Floor Sheathing**
R503.1	**Lumber sheathing:** Maximum allowable spans for lumber used as floor sheathing shall conform to Tables R503.1, R503.2.1.1(1) & R503.2.1.1 (2)
Table R503.1	**Minimum thickness of lumber floor sheathing**

Section #	Highlight
R503.2	**Wood structural panel sheathing**
Table R503.2.1.1(2)	**Allowable Spans for Sanded Plywood combination subfloor underlayment**
R503.2.2	**Allowable spans:** The maximum allowable span for wood structural panels used as subfloor or combination floor underlayment shall be set forth in Table R 503.2.1.1(1) or APA E30.
R503.2.3	**Installation:** Wood structural panels used as subfloor underlayment shall be attached to wood framing in accordance with R602.3(1) and shall be attached to cold-formed steel framing in accordance with Section R505.3.1(2).
Table R503.2.1.1(1)	**Allowable Spans and Loads For Wood Structural Panels For Roof and Subfloor Sheathing and Combination Subfloor Underlayment**
R504	**Pressure Preservatively Treated Wood Floors (On Ground)**
R504.1.3	**Uplift and buckling:** Where required, resistance to uplift or restraint against buckling shall be provided by interior bearing walls or properly designed stub walls anchored in the supporting soil below.
R504.2	**Site Preparation:** The area within the foundation walls shall have all vegetation, topsoil and foreign material removed…The fill shall be compacted to assure uniform support of the pressure preservative treated-wood floor sleepers.
R504.2.1	**Base:** A minimum 4-inch thick granular base of gravel having a maximum size of ¾ inch or crushed stone having a maximum size of ½ inch shall be placed over the compacted earth.
R504.2.2	**Moisture barrier**: Polyethylene sheeting of minimum 6-mil thickness shall be placed over granular base. Joints shall be lapped 6 inches and left unsealed.
R506	**Concrete floors (on ground)**
R506.1	**General:** Floors shall be a minimum 3.5 inches thick.
R506.2	**Site preparation:** The area within the foundation walls shall have all vegetation, top soil and foreign material removed.
R506.2.1	**Fill:** Fill material shall be free of vegetation and foreign material. The fill shall be compacted…depths shall not exceed 24inches for clean sand or gravel and 8 inches for earth.
R506.2.2	**Base:** A 4-inch thick base course consisting of clean graded sand, gravel, crushed stone, or crushed blast-furnace slag passing a 2-inch sieve shall be placed on the prepared sub grade when the slab is below grade. **Exception:** A base course is not required when the slab is installed on well-drained or sand-gravel mixture soil classified as Group I.
R506.2.3	**Vapor retarder:** A 6-mil polyethylene or approve vapor retarder with joints lapped not less than 6 inches shall be placed between the concrete floor and the base course or the prepared subgrade where no base course exists.
R602	**Wood Wall Framing**

Section #	Highlight
R602.6	**Drilling and notching of studs:**
	1. Notching: Any stud in exterior wall or bearing partition may be cut or notched to a depth not exceeding 25 percent of its width. Studs in nonbearing partitions may be notched to a depth not to exceed 40 percent of a single stud width.
	2. Drilling**:** Any stud may be bored and drilled, provided that the diameter of the resulting hole is no more than 60 percent of the stud width, the edge of the hole is no more than 5/8 inch to the edge of the stud, and the hole is not located in the same section as a cut or notch.
R602.6.1	**Drilling and notching of top plate:** When piping or ductwork is placed in or partly in an exterior wall or interior load-bearing wall, necessitating cutting, drilling, or notching of the top plate by more than 50 percent of its width, a galvanized metal tie not less than 0.054 inch thick and 1 1/2 inches wide shall be fastened across and to the at each side of the opening with not less than eight 10d having a minimum length of 1 1/2 inches at each side or equivalent. The metal tie must extend a minimum of 6 inches past the opening.
Figure R602.6(1)	**Notching and Bored Hole Limitations for Exterior Walls and Bearing Walls**
Figure R602.6(2)	**Notching and Bored Hole Limitations for Interior Nonbearing Walls**
Figure R602.6.1	**Top Plate Framing to Accommodate Piping**
R602.8	**Fireblocking required:** Fireblocking shall be provided in accordance with Section R302.11.
R606	**General Masonry Construction**
R606.3.1	**Head and bed joints:** Unless otherwise required or indicated on the project drawings, head and bed joints shall be 3/8 inch thick, except…shall not be less than ¼ inch and not more than ¾ inch.
R606.3.2	**Masonry unit placement**
R606.5	**Corbeled Masonry:** Corbeled masonry shall be in accordance with Sections R606.5.1 throughR606.5.3
R606.5.1	**Units:** Solid masonry units or masonry units filled with mortar or grout shall be used for corbeling.
R606.5.2	**Corbel projection:** The maximum projection of one unit shall not exceed one-half the height of the unit or one-third the thickness at right angles to the wall. The maximum corbeled projection beyond the face of the wall shall not exceed:
	1.One-half of the wall thickness for multiwythe walls
	2. One-half the wythe thickness for single wythewalls
R607	**Glass Unit Masonry**
R609	**Exterior Windows and Doors**
R610	**Structural Insulated Panel Wall Construction**
R610.3	**Materials:** SIP's shall comply with the following criteria:

Section #	Highlight
R610.3.1	**Core:** The core material shall be composed of foam plastic insulation meeting one of the following requirements: 1 - 3.
R610.3.2	**Facing:** Facing materials for SIPs shall be wood structural panels…having a minimum nominal thickness of 7/16 inch and shall meet the additional minimum properties specified in Table R610.3.2.
R610.3.3	**Adhesive:** Adhesives used to structurally laminate foam plastic insulation ore material to the structural wood facers shall conform to ASTM D 2559.
R610.3.4	**Lumber:** The minimum lumber framing material used for SIPs prescribed in this document is NLGA graded…No. 2 Spruce-pine-fir shall be permitted.
R610.3.5	**SIP Screws:** The screws shall be corrosion resistant and have a minimum shank diameter of 0.188 inch and minimum head diameter of 0.620 inch.
R610.3.6	**Nails:** Nails specified in Section R613 shall be common or galvanized box unless otherwise stated.
Table R610.5(1)	**Minimum Thickness for SIP Wall Supporting SIP or Light-Frame Roof Only**
R701.1	**Application:** The provisions of this chapter shall control the design and construction of the interior and exterior wall coverings for all buildings.
R702	**Interior Covering**
R702.1	**General:** Interior coverings or wall finishes shall be installed in accordance with this chapter and Tables R702.1(1), R702.1.(2), R702.1(3)and 702.3.5. Interior masonry veneer shall comply with Section R703.7.1 for support and R703.7.4 for anchorage, except an air space is not required. Interior finishes and materials shall conform to the flame spread and smoke development of Section R302.9.
R702.2	**Interior Plaster**
Table R702.1(1)	**Thickness of Plaster**
R702.2.3	**Support:** Support spacing for gypsum or metal lath on walls or ceilings shall not exceed 16 inches for 3/8-inch-thick or 24 inches for ½-inch-thick plain gypsum lath.
R702.3	**Gypsum board and gypsum panel products**
Table R702.1(2)	**Gypsum Plaster Proportions**
Table R702.1(3)	**Cement Plaster Proportions Parts by Volume**
Table R702.3.5	**Minimum Thickness and Applications of Gypsum Board and Gypsum Panel Products**
R702.3.7	**Water-resistant gypsum backing board:** Use of water-resistant gypsum backing board shall be permitted on ceilings. Water-resistant gypsum board shall not be installed over a Class I or II vapor retarder in a shower or tub compartment.
R702.5	**Other finishes:** Wood veer paneling and hard board paneling shall be placed on wood or cold-formed steel framing spaced not more than 16 inches on center, Wood veneer paneling and hard board paneling less than ¼-inch nominal thickness…hardboard paneling shall conform to CPA/ANSI A135.5.

Section #	Highlight
R703	**Exterior Covering**
R703.2	**Water-resistive barrier:** One layer of No. 15 asphalt felt, free from holes and breaks, complying with ASTM D 226…Where joints occur, felt shall be lapped not less than 6 inches.
R703.5	**Wood, hardboard and wood structural panel siding**
R703.5.2	**Panel Siding:** Vertical joints in panel siding shall occur over framing members…Horizontal joints in panel siding shall be lapped a minimum of 1 inch or shall be shiplapped or shall be flashed with Z-flashing and occur over solid blocking, wood or wood structural panel sheathing.
R703.6	**Wood shakes and shingles**
Table R703.6.1	**Maximum Weather Exposure for Wood Shakes and Shingles on Exterior Walls**
R703.6.3	**Attachment:** Wood shakes and shingles, and attachment and supports shall be capable of…each shake or shingle shall be held in place by two hot-dipped, zinc coated, stainless steel, or aluminum nails or staples. The fasteners shall penetrate the sheathing or furring strips by not less than ½ inch and shall not be overdriven.
R703.8	**Anchored tone and masonry veneer, general**
R703.8.5	**Flashing:** Flashing shall be located beneath the first course of masonry above finished ground level above the foundation wall or slab…in accordance with Section R703.8.
R703.8.6	**Weepholes:** Weepholes shall be provided in the outside wythe of masonry walls at a maximum spacing of 33inches on center. Weepholes shall not be less than 3/16 inch in diameter. Weepholes shall be located immediately above the flashing.
R703.10	**Fiber cement siding**
R703.10.1	**Panel siding:** Panels shall be installed with the long dimension either parallel or perpendicular to framing. Vertical and horizontal joints shall occur over framing members and shall be sealed with caulking…to comply with Section R703.1.
R703.10.2	**Lap Siding:** Fiber-cement lap siding having a maximum width of 12 inches shall comply with the requirements of ASTM C 1186. Type A, minimum Grade II. Lap siding shall be lapped a minimum of 1 1/4 inches and lap siding not having tongue-and-groove end joints should have the ends sealed with caulking, installed with an H-section joint cover, located over a strip of flashing or shall be designed to comply with Section R703.1.
R802	**Wood Roof Framing**
R802.1.5.4	**Labeling:** Fire-retardant-treated lumber and wood structural panels shall be labeled. The label shall contain: 1 - 8.
R802.1.10.1	**Truss design drawings:** Truss design drawings shall be provided with the shipment of trusses delivered to the jobsite. Truss design drawings shall include, at a minimum, the following information: Items 1 - 12.
R803	**Roof Sheathing**
Table R803.1	**Minimum Thickness of Lumber Roof Sheathing**

Section #	Highlight
R806	**Roof Ventilation**
R806.1	**Ventilation required.** Ventilation openings shall have a least dimension of 1/16 inch minimum and1/4 inch maximum. Ventilation openings having a least dimension larger than 1/4 inch shall be provided with corrosion-resistant wire cloth screening, hardware cloth, or similar material with openings having a least dimension of 1/16 inch minimum and 1/4 inch maximum.
R806.2	**Minimum vent area:** The minimum net free ventilating area shall be 1/150 of the area of the vented space.
	Exception: The minimum net free ventilation area shall be 1/300of the area of the vented space provided one or more of the following conditions are met:
	2. Not less 40 percent and not more than 50 percent of the required ventilating…Upper ventilators shall be located no more than 3 feet below the ridge or highest point of space.
R807	**Attic Access**
R807.1	**Attic Access:** Buildings with combustible ceiling or roof construction shall have an attic access opening to attic areas that exceed 30 square feet and have a vertical height of 30 inches or greater.
	The rough-framed opening shall not be less than 22 inches by 30 inches and shall be located in a hallway or other readily accessible location.
R902	**Fire Classification**
R902.1	**Roofing Covering Materials**: **Exceptions**: Highlight 1, 2, and 3.
R903	**Weather Protection**
R903.2	**Flashing:** Flashings shall be used to seal roofing systems…installed in a manner that prevents moisture from entering the wall and roof through joints in copings, through moisture permeable materials and at intersections with parapet walls and other penetrations through the roof plane.
R903.2.1	**Locations**: Flashings shall be installed at wall and roof intersections, wherever there is a change in roof slope or direction and around roof openings.
	Exception: Flashing is not required at hip and ridge junctions.
Table R903.2.1	**Metal Flashing Material**
R903.3	**Coping:** Parapet walls shall be properly coped with non combustible, weatherproof materials of a width no less than the thickness of parapet wall.
R903.4	**Roof drainage:** Unless roofs are sloped to drain over roof edges, roof drains shall be installed at each low point of the roof.
R903.4.1	**Overflow drains and scuppers**: When other means of drainage of overflow water is not provided, overflow scuppers shall be placed in walls or parapets not less than2 inches nor more than 4 inches above the finished roof covering and shall be located as close as practical to required vertical leaders or downspouts or wall and parapet scuppers.
R905	**Requirements for Roof Coverings**

Section #	Highlight
R905.2	**Asphalt Shingles:** The installation of asphalt shingles shall comply with the provisions of this section or RAS 115.
R905.2.2	**Slope:** Asphalt shingles shall be used only on roof slopes of two units vertical in 12 units horizontal or greater. For roof slopes from two vertical units in 12 units horizontal, double underlayment application is required in accordance with section R905.1.1.
R905.2.5	**Fasteners:** Fasteners for asphalt shingles shall be galvanized steel, stainless steel, aluminum or copper roofing nails, minimum 12 gage shank with a minimum 3/8-inch diameter head …and a minimum of ¾ -inch into the roof sheathing.
R905.2.6	**Attachment:** Asphalt shingles shall have the minimum number of fasteners required by the manufacturer, but not less than four fasteners per strip shingle, or two fasteners per individual shingle
R905.2.8.2	**Valleys:** Valley linings of the following types shall be permitted: 1. For open valleys lined with metal: at least 16 inches wide 2. For open valleys, valley lining of two plies of mineral surfaced roll roofing…the bottom layer shall be 18 inches and the top layer 36 inches wide. 3. For closed valleys :at least 36 inches wide
R905.2.8.5	**Drip edge:** Overlap is to be a minimum of 3 inches. Eave drip edges shall extend ½ inch below the sheathing and extend back on the roof a minimum of 2 inches…Drip edge shall be mechanically fastened a maximum of 12 inches on center.
R905.3	**Clay and Concrete tile**
R905.3.5	**Concrete Tile**
R905.3.6	**Fasteners:** Nails shall be corrosion resistant and not less than 11 gage, 5/16-inch head and of sufficient length to penetrate the deck a minimum of ¾ inch.
R905.4	**Metal roof shingles:** The installation of metal roof shingles shall comply with the provisions of this section.
R905.4.2	**Deck slope:** Metal roof shingles shall not be installed on roof slopes below three units vertical in 12 units horizontal.
R905.4.6	**Flashing:** Valley flashing shall extend at least 8 inches from the center line each way and shall have a splash diverter rib not less than 3/4 inch high at the flow line formed as part of the flashing. Sections of flashing shall have an end lap of not less than 4 inches. The metal valley flashing shall have a36-inch wide underlayment in addition to the underlayment required for metal roof shingles.
Table 905.4.4	**Metal Roof Coverings**
R905.6	**Slate and slate-type shingles**
R905.6.3	**Underlayment:** Underlayment shall be installed in accordance with the manufacturer's installation instructions.
Table R905.6.5	**Slate Shingle Headlap**
R905.6.6	**Flashing:** Valley flashing shall be a minimum of 16 inches wide.

Section #	Highlight
R905.7	**Wood Shingles:** The installation of wood shingles shall be limited to roofs where the allowable uplift resistance is equal to or greater than the design uplift pressure for the roof listed in Table R301.2(2).
R905.7.6.1	**Fasteners**
R905.7.6.1.1	**Nails:** Fasteners to attach to wood shakes shall be Type 304 stainless steel ring-shank nails with a minimum penetration of 0.75 inch into the sheathing. Each shingle shall be attached with a minimum of two fasteners.
R905.8	**Wood shakes:** All wood shakes shall be installed in accordance with this chapter…or RAS 130.
R905.9	**Built Up Roofs**
R905.9.1	**Slope:** Built-up roofs shall have a design slope of not less than one-fourth unit vertical in 12 units horizontal for drainage.
R905.9.2	**Material Standards**: Built-up roof covering materials shall comply with the standards in Table R905.9.2 or UL 55A.
Table R905.9.2	**Built-Up Roofing Material Standards**
R905.10	**Metal Roof Panels**
R905.10.1	**Deck Requirements:** Metal roof panel roof coverings shall be applied to solid or spaced sheathing, except where the roof covering is specifically designed to be applied to spaced supports.
R905.10.2	**Slope:** Minimum slopes for metal roof panels shall comply with the following: 1. The minimum slope for lapped, non soldered-seam metal roofs…shall be three units vertical in 12 units horizontal. 2. The minimum slope for lapped, non-soldered-seam metal roofs…shall be one-half vertical units in 12 units horizontal 3. The minimum slope for standing-seam roof systems shall be one-quarter unit vertical in 12 units horizontal.
R905.11	**Modified bitumen roofing:** The installation of modified bitumen roofing shall comply with the provisions of this section
R905.11.2	**Material Standards:** Modified Bitumen roof coverings shall comply with the standards in Table R905.11.2.
Table R905.11.2	**Modified Bitumen Roofing Material Standards**
R905.12	**Thermoset single-ply roofing:** The installation of thermoset single-ply roofing shall comply with the provisions of this section.
R905.12.1	**Slope:** Thermoset single-ply membrane roofs shall have a design slope of not less than one-fourth unit vertical in 12 units horizontal.
R905.13	**Thermoplastic single-ply roofing:** The installation of the thermoplastic single-ply roofing shall comply with the provisions of this section.

Section #	Highlight
R905.13.1	**Slope:** Thermoplastic single-ply membrane roofs shall have a design slope of not less than one-fourth unit vertical in 12 units horizontal
R905.14	**Sprayed polyurethane foam roofing:** The installation of the sprayed polyurethane foam roofing shall comply with the provisions of this section or in compliance with RAS 109 and 109A.
R905.14.1	**Slope:** Sprayed polyurethane foam roofs shall have a design slope of not less than one-fourth unit vertical in 12 units horizontal for drainage.
R905.15	**Liquid-applied roofing:** The installation of the liquid-applied roofing shall comply with Section R316.
R905.15.1	**Slope:** Liquid-applied roofing roofs shall have a design slope of not less than one-fourth unit vertical in 12 units horizontal.
R906	**Roof Insulation**
R906.1	**General:** The use of above-deck thermal insulation shall be permitted provided such insulation is covered with an approved roof covering and complies with FM 4450or UL 1256.
Table R906.2	**Material Standards for Roof Insulation**
R1001.2	**Footings and Foundations:** Footings for masonry fireplaces and their chimneys shall be constructed of concrete or solid masonry at least 12 inches thick and shall extend at least 6 inches beyond the face of the fireplace or foundation wall on all sides…In areas not subject to freezing, footings shall be at least 12 inches below finish grade.
R1001.5	**Firebox walls:** Masonry fireboxes shall be constructed of solid masonry units, hollow masonry units grouted solid, stone or concrete. Where a lining of firebrick not less than 2 inches thick or other approved lining is provided, the minimum thickness of back and side walls shall be 8 inches of solid masonry, including the lining. Where a lining is not provided, the total minimum thickness of back and side walls shall be 10 inches of solid masonry.
Table R1001.1	**Summary of Requirements for Masonry Fireplaces and Chimneys**
R1001.7	**Lintel and throat:** Masonry over a fireplace opening shall be supported by a lintel of noncombustible material. The minimum required bearing length on each end of the fireplace opening shall be 4 inches.
R1001.7.1	**Damper:** Masonry fireplaces shall be equipped with ferrous metal damper located at least 8 inches above the top of the fireplace opening.
R1001.10	**Hearth extension dimensions:** Hearth extensions shall extend not less than 16 inches in front of and at least 8 inches beyond each side of the fireplace opening.
R1001.11	**Fireplace clearance:** Wood beams, joists, studs, and other combustible material shall have a clearance of not less than 2 inches from the front faces and sides of masonry fireplaces and not less than 4 inches from the back faces of masonry fireplaces.
R1003	**Masonry Chimneys**

Section #	Highlight
R1003.2	**Footings and foundations:** Footings for masonry chimneys shall be constructed of concrete or solid masonry not less than 12 inches thick and shall extend not less than 6 inches beyond the face of the foundation or support the wall on all sides.
	In areas not subjected to freezing, footings shall be at least 12 inches below finished grade.
R1003.5	**Corbeling:** Masonry chimneys shall not be corbelled more than one-half of the chimney's wall thickness form a wall or foundation.
R1003.10	**Wall thickness:** Masonry chimney walls shall be constructed of solid masonry units or hollow masonry units grouted solid with not less than 4 inch nominal thickness.
Table R1003.14(1)	**Net Cross-Sectional Area of Round Flue Sizes**
Table R1003.14(2)	**Net Cross-Sectional Area of Square and Rectangular Flue Sizes**
R1003.17	**Masonry chimney cleanout openings:** Cleanout openings shall be provided within 6 inches of the base of each flue…The height of the opening shall be not less than 6 inches.
R1003.18	**Chimney Clearances:** Any potion of a masonry chimney located in the interior of the building…air space clearance to combustibles of 2 inches.
R1004	**Factory-Built Fireplaces**
N1101	**Chapter 11 — Energy Efficiency**
	Note: Residential construction energy efficiency is governed by the Florida Building Code, Energy Conservation.
M1403	**Heat Pump Equipment**
M1406	**Radiant Heating Systems**
M1406.2	**Clearances:** Clearances for radiant heating panels or elements…shall comply with Chapter 34 through 43 of this code.
M1408	**Vented Floor Furnaces**
M1408.3	**Location:** Location of floor furnaces shall conform to the following requirements:
	1. Floor registers or floor furnaces shall be installed not less than 6 inch from a wall.
M1502	**Clothes Dryer Exhaust**
M1502.3	**Duct termination:** Exhaust ducts terminate on the outside of the building…the exhaust duct shall terminate not less than 3 feet in any direction from openings into buildings. Exhaust duct terminations shall be equipped with a back draft damper.
M1502.4.3	**Transition duct:** Transition ducts used to connect the dryer to the exhaust duct system shall be a single length…shall not be greater than 8 feet in length.
M1502.4.4	**Duct Length**
M1502.4.5.1	**Specified length:** The maximum length of the exhaust duct shall be 35 feet from the connection to the transition duct from the dryer to the outlet terminal.
M1505	**Overhead Exhaust Hoods**

Section #	**Highlight**
M1505.1	**General:** Domestic open-top broiler units shall have a metal exhaust hood, having a minimum thickness of 0.0157-inch (No. 28 gage) with ¼ inch clearance between the hood and the underside of the combustible material or cabinets.
Table M1507.4	**Minimum Required Exhaust Rates for One- and Two- Family Dwellings**
M1803	**Chimney and Vent Connectors**
M1803.3.1	**Floor, ceiling and wall penetrations:** A chimney connector or vent connector shall not pass through any floor or ceiling…or is routed through a device listed and labeled for wall pass through and is installed in accordance with the conditions of its listing and label.
Table M1803.3.4	**Chimney and Vent Connector Clearances to Combustible Materials**
M2005	**Water Heaters**
M2005.2	**Prohibited Locations:** Fuel-fired water heaters not installed in a room used as a storage closet. Water heaters located in a bedroom or bathrooms shall be installed in a sealed enclosure so combustion air will not be taken from the living space.
P2801.6	**Required Pan**
P2801.6.1	**Pan size and drain:** The pan shall not be less than 1 ½ inches deep and shall be of sufficient size and shape to receive all dripping or condensate from the tank or water heater.
P2801.6.2	**Pan drain termination:** The pan drain shall extend full-size and terminate…not less than 6 inches and not more than 24 inches above adjacent ground surface.
P2804	**Relief Valves**
P2804.3	**Pressure-relief valves:** They shall be set to open not less than 25 psi above the system pressure and not greater than150 psi.
P2804.4	**Temperature-relief valves:** The valves shall be installed such that the temperature-sensing element monitors the water within the top 6 inches of the tank.
P2804.6.1	**Requirements for discharge pipe:** The discharge piping serving a pressure-relief valve, temperature relief valve or combination valve shall: 1 - 14.
P2902.3	**Backflow protection:** A means of protection against backflow shall be provided in accordance with Sections P2902.3.1 through P2902.3.6.
Table P2902.3	**Application for Backflow Preventers**
Table P2903.2	**Maximum Flow Rates and Consumption for Plumbing Fixtures and Fixture Fittings**
R4400	**Chapter 44 - High Velocity Hurricane Zones** — Because HVHZ does "not apply across the entire state" this may not be asked on some **state** exams but must be noted.
R4600	**Chapter 46 – Referenced Standards**: Know what ANSI stands for.

Section #	Highlight
Florida Building Code 2017, Building Chapter 1	
102	**Applicability**
102.2	**Building.** The provisions of the *Florida Building Code* shall apply to the construction, erection, alteration, modification, repair, equipment, use and occupancy, location, maintenance, removal and demolition of every public and private building, structure or facility or floating residential structure, or any appurtenances connected or attached to such buildings, structures or facilities.
105	**Permits**
105.1	**Required.** Any owner or authorized agent who intends to construct, enlarge, alter, repair, move, demolish, or change the occupancy of a building or structure, or to erect, install, enlarge, alter, repair, remove, convert or replace any impact resistant coverings, electrical, gas, mechanical or plumbing system, the installation of which is regulated by this code, or to cause any such work to be done, shall first make application to the *building official* and obtain the required *permit.*
107	**Submittal Documents**
107.3.5	**Minimum plan review criteria for buildings**
	Commercial Buildings
	Residential Buildings
108	**Temporary Structures and Uses**

Walker's Guide to Estimating, 32nd Edition (Roofing Contractors) Tabs and Highlights

These 1 Exam Prep Tabs are based on the *Walker's Building Estimator's Reference Book, Edition No. 32, Frank R. Walker Company, 2020.*

Each Tabs sheet has five rows of tabs. Start with the first tab at the first row at the top of the page and proceed down that row placing the tabs at the locations listed below. Place each tab in your book setting it down one notch until you get to the bottom of the page, and then start back at the top again. After you have completed tabbing your book (the last tab is the glossary, appendix, or index), then you may start highlighting your book.

1 Exam Prep Tab	**Page #**
Waterproofing	451
Weight of Tar & Asphalt Felt	459
Thermal Protection/Insulation	461
Roof Area	471
Asphalt Shingles	473
Wood Shingles and Shakes	477
Clay Roofing Tile	481
Membrane Roofing	489
EPDM Roof Systems	493
Flashing and Sheet Metal	495
Painting Roofs	661
Mensuration	869
Glossary	883
Safety	897
Index	907

******This concludes the tabs for this document. Please continue with the highlights on the following page.******

ABC 09/08/2021

Page # **Highlight**

1 **Introduction**

The Role of the Estimator: The following requisites are essential for the making of a good estimator: (Highlight 1 – 7)

The Role of the Contractor

2 Erecting a building is a complex undertaking and seldom is one firm capable of doing all phases of the work. Yet the owner or developer usually prefers to let one contract and make one firm responsible for the completion of the project.

The average percent of work performed by subcontractors for a general contractor cannot be precisely determined, but surveys conducted by the Associated General Contractors of America indicate from 40% to 70%.

The American Subcontractor Association claims that 90% of the work force in the building construction industry is employed by subcontractors.

Usually there is a retainage of at least 5 to 10% by the general contractor to the subs and in turn by the owner to the general contractor. Retainage is not completely released until the project is substantially complete. It has become common practice to reduce the retainage by 50% when the project is 50% satisfactorily completed.

3 **The Cost of Money**

3 – 4 **Sources of Money:** The main sources of money are: (Highlight 1 – 8)

4 **Mortgage Loans**

Once a loan is approved and accepted, there are certain charges called closing costs, and a part of these costs, known as points, origination fees, or the discount, cover the cost of setting up the loan.

The usual range of points is from 1% to 3%, but in states where there are legal limits set on the interest that may be charged, points have been quoted as high as 7% as a way to get around the usury laws.

Mortgage Banker

For consummating the transaction, they charge a flat fee of around 1% to 2% of the loan placed. This fee is in addition to the usual closing costs that are charged by the lender.

Selling the Lender

5 **Short Term Loans**

The construction loan is a short term loan to cover the building costs during the erection of the project.

One such source is those who loan the difference between the floor and ceiling of the mortgage. This is known as *gap financing*.

6 To obtain such a commitment one must pay in advance a flat fee, usually around 5% of the amount to be loaned. If the project reaches the income level to qualify for the full mortgage, and the gap loan is not needed, the fee is not refundable.

Page # **Highlight**

How much front money, or equity, an owner will need to launch the project will vary with the type of project, the money market, and the owner's reputation. It is often said that an owner with a proven need, a piece of property free of debt, and an architect's set of plans can obtain all the financing they will need.

Interim Financing

Progress, at this point, should place the contractor in a position to obtain from the bank a general commitment as to the limit and terms under which they would participate in granting short term loans (usually 30 to 90 days).

7 **Setting Up the Estimate**

There are various reasons for these failures, but probably the most common one is the inability of the person estimating costs to come up with realistic and profitable estimates.

Some of the most important considerations that such companies make before bonding an applicant are: (Highlight 1 – 3)

8 **Estimate Types**

Budget/Feasibility Estimate: The budget or feasibility estimate, once it has been developed, is effectively cast in stone.

9 **Schematic Design milestone Estimate - 3% to 5% Overall Design Completeness**
Design Development Milestone Estimate - 35% to 50% Overall Design Completeness
70% to 98% Construction Documents Milestone Estimate(s)
Construction Documents Milestone and Bid Cost Estimate - 100% Overall Design Completeness

10 **Project Office Expense**
Small Tools & Consumables
Weather Protection
Home Office Support
Escalation (Cost Growth)
Finance Expense
Profit

On small jobs, alterations, remodeling and similar work, a contractor is justified in adding 20% to 30% profit to the actual cost, but must ask themselves whether they can actually obtain this amount. On new work, where it is possible to estimate cost with a fair degree of accuracy, a contractor is entitled to 10% to 15% on the actual cost of the work (job overhead included in the actual cost of the job), but it is safe to say that competitive figures submitted for many jobs show a 5% instead of a 10% to 15%. A contractor is entitled to a fair profit of 10% profit, but getting it is another matter.

15 **Bidding for a Contract:** Construction contracts are awarded in one of two ways - competitive bidding or negotiation.

Page # **Highlight**

There are various ways this is done, by organizations, governmental bodies, and banks, but in general, the information that must be submitted will follow that contained in AIA Document A-305 Contractor's Qualifications Statement (AIA form A305 Contractor's Qualification Statement).

Invitation to Bid. Once on a bidding list, a contractor will receive an **Invitation to Bid or Bid Notice** for each prospective job.

16 **Instructions to Bidders:** Often the invitation to bid is accompanied by an **Instruction to Bidders** further defining the job restrictions such as completion dates, milestone dates, visiting job site, special conditions, etc.

The bid bond guarantees that the bidding contractor, if awarded a contract, will enter into the contract and furnish a performance and payment bond, if required. If they do not honor their bid, they forfeit the amount of the bond.

Bid bonds–and the later performance, material, labor, maintenance, completion, supply, and subcontractor bonds–are often encountered in public work, but may not be required in private work, where the contractor's reputation is deemed sufficient and the cost of bonds unwarranted. Bid bond costs are customarily minimal, if any, and borne by the contractor.

Construction Management: In Construction Management (CM), a general contractor or engineering company enters into a contract with the owner prior to the bidding period and acts in a managerial and advisory role. Bid packages for the project are usually taken under the construction manager's supervision.

They will provide reports on the project cost status, payment status, and an analysis of each contract and the project cash flow. The construction management approach has gained a wider acceptance in recent times, especially in federally sponsored construction.

17 **Estimate Check Lists and Practices**

A master checklist for every estimator should include the Bid Document Inventory, Estimating Assignment, Direct Estimate, Wage Rate Development, Bid Document Reviews, Takeoff General Practices, Labor Hour General practices, Material Pricing General Practice, Subcontractor Dealings General practices, Formatting the Estimate/Bid, Estimate Reviews along with Bid Statistics/Evaluation.

18 **Federal Unemployment Tax Act (FUTA):** This tax applies to the first $7,000 of wages paid each employee during the calendar year 2013. The rate is 6.0% but a credit of up to a maximum 5.4% of total wages for contributions paid into State Unemployment Funds for a total federal tax rate of 0.6%. Federal Unemployment Tax is imposed on employers and must not be deducted from wages of employees.

State Unemployment Tax.

Worker's Compensation.

Rates vary widely among the states, craft labor and staff labor categories. In states where medical benefits are limited, it may be advisable to carry full or extra-legal medical coverage.

Property Damage Insurance.

Page #	Highlight
19	**Office Overhead Expense**
	This is sometimes referred to as General and Administrative (G&A) costs.
20	Overhead may run 6.00% to 15% for smaller firms. Larger firms may have overheads that are as little as 1% to 2% of the annual volume.
	Office Furniture and Equipment **Insurance**
	Project Indirect Costs
21	**Contract Documents:** Once it is determined which contracting firm is to do the job, a formal contract will be drawn up. The Contract Documents usually should include the Owner-Contractor Agreement; the General Conditions of the Contract; Supplementary Conditions of the Contract (if any); the Working Drawings, giving all sheet numbers with revisions; Specifications, giving page numbers; and Addenda or Bulletins issued prior to contract.
21 – 22	Highlight bold titles for the **AIA documents.** (11 items)
22	**A – Series: Owner – Contractor Document:** **B – Series: Owner – Architect Documents:**
23	**C – Series: Architect – Consultants Documents:** **D – Series: Architect – Industry Documents:** **G – Series: Architect – Industry Document:**
24	**Performance and Payment Bonds.** These are required on a vast majority of contracts. Some owners and most public work require that each contractor to whom a contract is awarded shall furnish bonds which contain two obligations: a performance bond to indemnify the owner against loss resulting from the failure of the contractor to complete the work in accordance with the plans and specifications; and a payment bond to guarantee payment for all bills incurred by the contractor for labor or materials for the work. The federal government, under the Miller act, requires that a contractor furnish two separate bonds, one for the performance and one for the payment of labor and materials.
	Maintenance Bonds.
	Bid Bonds. Bids are invited by advertisements, and the bidder may have to submit with the bid a certified check, usually for a 5% of the bid, or a bid bond, usually for 10% of the bid.
	License or Permit Bonds. Bonds provided by a contractor to a public body, guaranteeing compliance with local codes and ordinances. If the contractor regularly operates within an area requiring such bonds, this cost should be carried under office overhead, because is a normal cost of doing business.
	Supply and Subcontractor Bonds
	Construction Equipment
25	The advantages in renting or leasing include: (Highlight 1 – 5)
	Negotiating a Contract

Page # **Highlight**

A variation of the negotiated contract is fast track, design build construction. In this arrangement the project may be started before all the plans are fully developed. Each phase of the job, such as foundation, masonry, carpentry, etc., is bid separately, just before the phase is required to be installed. Some advantages and disadvantages are: (Highlight 1 – 3)

As the phases are bid, the successful subcontractors may be assigned to a general contractor in the same manner as a lump-sum contract; or the general may act in the role of a project manager, in which case each subcontractor for each phase will have a direct contract with the owner. This variation is referred to as multiple bidding.

26 – 27 **Contracting Definitions:** Addenda, Alternates, Approved Equal, Arbitration, Bid, Bid Bond, Cash Allowance, Certificate of Occupancy, Change Order, Contract Time, Cost Breakdown (or Schedule of Values), Extras, Final Acceptance, Payment and Performance Bond, Letter of Intent, Liens, Liquidated Damages, Maintenance Bond, Punch List, Retainage, Separate Contract, Shop Drawings, Subcontractor Bonds, Substantial Completion, Superintendent, Supplier, Supply Affidavit (Bond), Unit Prices, Upset Price, Warranty

27 **The Working Drawings**

Each sheet should have a title block in the lower right-hand corner with the sheet number (usually “G-” for general information, “C-“ for civil, “A-“ for architectural, “S-“ for structural, “M-“ for heating and ventilating, “P-“ for plumbing, “FP-“ for fire protection, E-“ for electrical, “I-“ for instrumentation and “T-“ for technology); the number of sheet in each set (i.e., A-1 of 7); the date made plus each date it has been revised, and the initials of the person or persons who drew and approved the sheet.

Type of Drawings. Most working drawings for building construction are based on *orthographic projection*, which is a parallel projection to a plane by lines perpendicular to the plane. In this way, all dimensions will be true. If the plane is horizontal, the projection is a plan; if vertical, it is an elevation for outside the building, or a sectional elevation if through the building. The only descriptive drawing that presents a building as the eye sees it is the perspective. But perspectives are used mainly to study the building and present it to the client in an easily understood form. A perspective is seldom useful for presenting information on working drawings.

28 Highlight **Isometric**, **Orthographic**, **Cabinet** and **Elevation** drawings

29 Highlight drawing at the top of the page.

Scale. The architect's scale, with the inch divided into 1/4, 1/8, 1/16, 1/32, is standard for building construction in the United States. The engineer's scale, with the inch divided into tenths, is sometimes used in structural work or on site plans. However, it is advantageous to have architectural, structural, and mechanical drawings all at the same scale for a job. The metric scale is divided into centimeters and millimeters, 2.54 centimeters equaling one inch.

Reproduction.

There were also processes that transfer blueprints to cloth drawings or to *sepia prints,* which could be altered, added to, and printed just like an original tracing.

30 **Symbols**

General Outlets:
Convenience Outlets:

Page #	Highlight
31	Switch Outlets:
	Panels & Circuits:
	Signaling Systems:
	Pipe Fitting Symbols:
	Heating Symbols:
32	Ductwork Symbols:
	Piping Symbols:

Specifications

Arrangement. The Uniform System developed by the Construction Specifications Institute (CSI) has become the accepted industry standard for setting up specifications.

CSI MasterFormat™ 2014 edition by division numbers and titles

55 **Subdivision.**

Materials will list the materials to be used in one of several ways, often found in combination. The closed specification will list a single trade name, and the specified product that must be furnished. The contractor's option specification (or bidder's choice) lists more than one trade name, and the contractor may choose from those listed.

A variation is the product approval specification which asks the contractor to submit any substitutions prior to submitting a bid. If the architect approves the substitute, it will be put in an addenda sent to all contractors. This "or approved equal" type specification is the most common.

The performance specification describes not the material but what work is required to produce strength, mechanical ability, or similar measurable results.

Insurance Taxes & Bonds:
Contractor's Equipment Floater:
56 **Installation Floater:**

Alternates. On the typical lump sum proposal form, the Alternate follows the Statement of the Lump Sum price in a form such as the following: If the following Alternates are accepted, (Highlight Example)

Cash Allowance. Sometimes, the architect does not have a final decision from the owner on certain items. Rather than leave them out of the lump sum proposal, the architect will state a definite budget amount in the specification that is to be included in the bid.
57 **Unit Prices.** Where quantity of materials is in doubt, but quality is known, the specification may ask for unit prices.

For example, unit prices are often asked for concrete per square yard, piling per lineal foot, partition block per square foot, etc. These prices should be complete with all costs, profit, and overhead included.

Addenda. These, plus changes the architect and owner may wish to make after the plans and specifications have been issued but before bids are turned in, are incorporated in the Addenda.

Change Orders: Change orders are modifications issued after the contract is signed.

Page # Highlight

62 **Project Staff:**
Mobilization:

Construction Scheduling: There are three methods of construction scheduling: (Highlight 1 – 3)

Planning
Project Scope and Work Breakdown Structure

63 **Construction Means and Methods**
Drawings and Specifications.
Technology.
Labor Availability and Skills Pool
Procurement Strategy

64 **Institutional Constraints.**
Project Phasing and Staging.
Weather Considerations
Scheduling

Scheduling Methods/Tools. The use of bar charts started the industrial revolution of the late 1800s. An early industrial engineer named Gantt developed these charts to improve factory efficiency. Bar charts are often called "Gantt Charts."

Critical Path Method (CPM) for project scheduling began in the 1950s in two parallel applications. The U.S. Navy developed the Project Evaluation and Review Technique (PERT) to develop the schedule for the construction of its Polaris Program.

There are two methods for CPM calculations, arrow diagramming and precedence diagramming. In the arrow diagramming method, project activities are shown as arrows. Circles at the beginning and end of activities are called nodes. Pairs of nodes or letters are used to identify each activity.

65 In the precedence diagram. activities and their durations are shown "on the node." Sequence between tasks is shown with arrows between related activities.

Precedence diagramming is capable of representing activities that start or end in parallel with other activities.

Identification of Activities. An activity is any significant unit of work within the WBS' work package. There is no one "right" way to define activities for a given project.

CPM calculations: As stated earlier precedence diagramming (also called network diagram) graphically represents the relationships between the project activities.

Early Start (ES)
Early Finish (EF)

66 **Late Finish (LF)**
Late Start (LS)
Forward Pass — Formula (ES + Duration = EF)
Backward Pass
Finish to Start or FS
Start to Start or SS
Finish to Finish or FF

Page #	**Highlight**
	Network Logic Diagram
	Total Float is the amount of time an activity can be delayed without delaying the end date of the project, and is defined as the difference between the LS and ES of an activity. Activities with 0 Total Float are critical activities and are said to fall on the Critical Path.
67	**Critical Activity** **Contingency Time** **Resource Constraints** **Monitoring/Updating**
68	**Measuring Progress** **Activities Started and Finished** **Activities Percent Complete** **Productivity** **Remaining Durations**
80	**Temporary Utilities** **Temporary Buildings & Construction** **Demobilization** **Outside Services**
85	**Concrete**
142	**Steelforms for Joist Constructed Floors and Roofs**
	Estimating Quantities of Steelform. In estimating the area of floor and roof construction requiring removable or permanent forms, the gross floor or roof area is used. No deductions are to be made for beams or for tees of beams or for wide joists.
143	**Ceco Steelform Construction:** Ceco steelform construction is a combination of concrete joist construction and thin top slabs.
	Forms Other Than Wood
	Lightweight Steel Forming Material for Concrete. High-strength corrugated steel forming material is often used for forming reinforced concrete floor and roof slabs.
144	Highlight all tables: **Concrete Quantities** and **Voids Created by Various Size FLANGEforms**
145	**Estimating:** Corrugated steel forming material is sold by the square, with the area determination based on sheet width times actual sheet length.
	Highlight table: Standard Sizes and Weights of Concrete Reinforcing Bars
183	**Finishing Lightweight Concrete Floor and Roof Fill**
	Finishing Concrete Roof Fill: Concrete fill for flat roofs are usually struck off, darbied, and floated. If fill is not over 2" to 3" thick, 2 cement masons with a helper should place screeds, strike off, darby, and float 1,500 to 1,700 s.f. of roof fill per 8-hr. day at the following labor cost per 100 sq.ft.: (Highlight Table)
	Where concrete fill is placed on pitch or gable roofs, finishing is more difficult/ Screeds must be set closer together to help keep the fill rom sliding, and an additional helper is usually required.

Page #	Highlight
219	**Precast Concrete Roof Slabs:** Precast concrete roof slabs are of three general types: rib, flat, and channel. The rib tile is self-weathering. Its attractive red color provides a desirable architectural feature that is often lacking in industrial buildings. Auxiliary pieces are furnished to suit the particular design required, such as ridges, saw-tooth ridges, gables end finishing tile, monitor flashing tile and other specials required in connection with hip or valley.
220	The other two types of precast concrete roof slabs, flat and channel, are used over all roof decks, whether flat or sloping, and present a smooth surface for the application of any type of built-up roofing. **Labor Placing Precast Concrete Roof and Floor Slabs.** Because of their size and weight, it requires 2 workers to handle precast concrete roof or floor slabs. Each piece weighs from 125 to 200 lbs. Ordinarily it requires 2 workers on the ground handling the slabs and getting them to the hoist, 2 more on the floor or roof placing them for the mason, and a mason and helper to lay and caulk the joints.
235	**Cast Decks and Underlayment**
236	**Monolithic or Poured-in-Place Gypsum Roof Construction.** The effective cross sectional area of reinforcing shall be not less than 0.026 sq. in. per ft. of slab width. The weights, excluding sub purlins and insulating values of poured gypsum roof decks are as follows: (Highlight Table) The following are approximate prices only on the various types of poured-in-place gypsum roof decks. (Highlight Table)
340	**Structural Metal Framing** **Estimating Quantities of Structural Steel:** When estimating the quantity of structural steel required for any job, each class of work (column bases, columns, girders, beams, lintels, trusses) should be estimated separately, because each involves different labor operations in fabrication and erection. **Items to Be Included in a Structural Steel Estimate.** (Highlight 1 – 8)
341	**Basis for Estimating All Classes of Structural Steel Work** (Highlight Table: Approximate Constant or Fixed Costs)
346	**Bolting Field Connections:** Most structural steel projects have sections bolted together. The most common bolts are ASTM A-325, high strength bolts for structural steel joints, 3/4" diameter x 2" long, at an approximate cost per bolt unit of $0.95 each. Each bolt unit consists of bolt, washers, and nut. Other grades sometimes required for connections are A490M-04a Standard Specification for High Strength Steel Bolts, Classes 10.9 and 10.9.3, for Structural Steel Joints [Metric] heat treated steel structural bolts (add up to 50% to the cost [er bolt unit), and for secondary bolted connections, Grade *A307-04 Standard Specification for Carbon Steel Bolts and Studs. 60,000 PSI Tensile Strength* carbon steel externally-threaded standard connection (decrease the cost about 15% per bolt unit).

Page #	Highlight
357	**Junior Steel Beams:** Junior beams (M shapes) are lightweight, hot-rolled structural beams that are used as secondary floor and roof beams in schools, stores, apartments, hospitals, and other types of light occupancy building.
	Sizes and properties are given below: (Highlight Table)
	The cost of cutting, punching holes, and coping junior beams will run approximately as given below, but when much fabricating is required, it is advisable to refer plans to a local fabricator or warehouse for a sub bid. (Highlight Chart)
	Metal Joists
358	**Metal Decking**
360	**Lightgage Framing**
362	Lightgage framing systems can supply complete wall, floor, and roof construction for buildings up to four stories in height, or can be used in combination with other framing systems for interior, load bearing partitions, exterior curtain walls, fire separation walls, parapets, penthouses, trusses, suspended ceilings, and mansard roofs.
	Joists come in 6", 8", 10", and 12" depths and in 12, 14, 16, and 18 gauge material.
	Joist bridging, which may be stock "V" units or solid channels, must be supplied in the center of all spans up to 14'; at third points on spans from 14' to 20'; at quarter points on spans from 26' to 32'; and at 8' centers on all spans over 32'.
367	**Wood, Plastics, and Composites**
	Nails Required for Carpentry Work
368	Highlight Table: *Recommended Sizes and Quantities Commonly Used*
	Highlight Table: *Bright Common Nail Specifications*
	Bright box nails are generally of the same length but slightly smaller diameter, see table below.
369	Highlight Table: *Bright Box Nail Specifications*
	Highlight Table: *Recommended Sizes and Quantities Commonly Used*
	Hand-driven nails for roofing-Asphalt and Fiberglass Shingle Nails.
	Roofing nails should be long enough to penetrate ¾" into the wood deck lumber, or completely thru the plywood decking.
370 – 371	Highlight all tables: *Different types of roofing nail specifications*
372	Highlight Table: *Masonry Nail Specifications*
	Metal Roof nails with Rubber Washers **Metal Roof Nails with Silicone Washers**
	Highlight Table: *Metal Roofing Nail Specifications*

Page #	Highlight
373	Highlight Table: *Pole Barn - Post and Framing Nail Specifications*
	Highlight Table: *Nail Reference Data Specifications*
376	**Estimating Lumber Quantities**
	One board foot is always 144 cubic inches. The formula for figuring the number of board feet in a given length of board or lumber is:
	Highlight formula: Width (inches) x Thickness (inches) x Length (feet) ÷ 12 = # of BF
	Estimating Wood Joists.
377	Highlight Table: *Number of Wood Floor Joists Required for any Spacing*
	Highlight Table: *Board Feet Required per 100 Sq. Ft of Surface When Used for Studs, Joists Rafters, Wall and Floor, Furring Strips, etc.*
378	Highlight Table: *Number of Wood Joists Required for any Floor and Spacing*
	Estimating Number of Wood Studs: When estimating the number of wood partition studs, take the length of each partition and then the total length of all partitions.
379	3. Example:
	13 pcs of 2" x 4" @ 8'-0" long = 104'-0" 2 pcs of 2" x 4" @ 16'-0" long = 32'-0" Convert the total lineal feet of lumber to board feet. (2 x 4 x 136) ÷ 12 = 90.67 bd. ft.
380	Highlight Table: *Bd. Ft. of Lumber Required for Wood Stud Partitions 2" x 4" Studs 16" O.C., Single Top and Bottom Plates**
381	**Estimating the number of headers and plywood spacers.**
	Sample Gable End Roof Outrigger or Lookout Estimate
382	**Sample Gable/End Vaulted End Wall Framing Estimate**
383	Highlight Table: *Gable End Framing at 16" o.c. Spacing – Total Length (feet) of Vertical Studs*
386	**To Obtain Area of Roofs for Any Pitch** (Highlight example calculation)
387	**Wood Framing — Hardware Accessories Used for Wood Framing**
388	**Metal Connector Plates (Truss Plates)**
389	**Wood Floor and Roof Trusses:** Wood roof trusses are used for spans as short as 25' - 0" and can be used up to 200' - 0".
390	Prices of wood trusses are governed by the following conditions: (Highlight 1 – 4)
	The spacing of wood roof trusses that directly support roof sheathing roof sheathing is usually 2'0". Where roof loads are light and the installation of a ceiling is not required, spacings of 4' - 0" to 4' - 10" are advantageous.

Page # **Highlight**

Bowstring Bolted Roof Truss

Approximate Prices of Wood Bowstring Truss. (Highlight Table)

Crescent Type Roof Truss: Recommended span is from 20' - 0" to 85' - 0"

391 **Approximate Prices of Crescent Type Wood Roof Trusses:** (Highlight Table)

Belgian Roof Truss: It is used on some higher class store buildings and low cost churches and is recommended for spans from 20' - 0" to 85' - 0". Belgian roof trusses are less efficient than the bowstring type, because the connections generally govern the member sizes. They cost about 50% more than bowstring type trusses. The Double fink truss is also referred to as a Belgian truss and is used for spans from 36' - 0" to 60' - 0".

Flattop Roof Truss: Spans should not exceed 65' where cost is an important factor

Howe Truss: The Howe truss can be used for spans from 16' to 18'.

Parallel Chord 4x2 Truss: This type of truss can be manufactured with duct chase openings so that wiring, piping, and ducts can run within the chords.

392 **Types of Trusses**

Parallel Chord 2”x4” Truss: Roof slopes should be at least 1/4" per foot of span.

Modified Queen Post Truss

Fink Truss: The fink truss is generally suitable for spans from 16' to as long as 46' and for all classes of construction. It is an efficient and cost effective truss configuration, 50% to 60% the cost of a comparable steel truss.

393 **Three-Hinged Arch**

Cantilever Truss: Trusses with single or double cantilever sections are possible. Cantilevers can approach one-fourth of the distance of the main interior truss span.

Clerestory Truss: This type of truss is used extensively in industrial and agricultural buildings, in spans up to 60'.

Inverted Truss; Vaulted Ceiling Truss; Mono-Pitch Truss; Dual-Pitch Truss

Pitched Warren Truss: This truss form is most economical in spans from 30' to 70', on center spacings from 2' to 8'.

The *W-Type* is the most popular type and is adaptable for spans from 18' up to 40'; roof slope from 2 in 12 to 6 in 12 and higher.

The *Triple-W* is used for spans up to 80’ with slopes of 3 in 12 and higher. Centerline spacings can be from 2' to 20', depending on requirements.

The *Kingpost* truss is usually recommended for shorter spans. The economical range is up to 26' under most loading conditions.

Page # **Highlight**

394 **Other Types of Commonly Used Wood Trusses:** The Double Fink truss is generally used for spans from 36' to 60'.

An extremely long truss with cantilevered ends can be manufactured in three sections. Trusses of this type, 128' in overall length, have been fabricated in this manner.

Truss Openings

Installation of Wood Trusses

Table: Center Duct Depth/Opening

397 **Installation Sequence for Temporary and Permanent Bracing of Wood Truss:** Install the first truss with a ground bracing system, which is constructed as follows: (Highlight 1 – 6)

For the first group of three to six trusses, the sequence is as follows: (Highlight 1 – 6)

Note that all bracing lumber should be no less than 2' x 4' x 10'. A minimum of two 16d double head nails should be used at each connection.

Mechanical Erection of Trusses: Highlight Table: **Erecting Roof Trusses Using a Machine**

398 **Hand Erection of Trusses:** Highlight Table: **Erecting Roof Trusses by Hand**

403 **Framing and Erecting Rafters for Gable Roofs**

Framing and Erecting Rafters for Hip Roofs

Framing Light Timbers for Exposed Roof Beam Construction

Framing for Roof Saddles on Flat Roofs

404 **Laying Wood Sheathing on Flat Roofs**

412 **Sheathing — Plywood Roof and Wall Sheathing, Subflooring and Underlayment — Roof and Wall Sheathing:** Nailing of plywood sheathing should be at 6" o.c. along panel edges and 12" o.c. at intermediate supports. Use 6d common nails for panels of ½" or less in thickness, and 8d for greater thickness.

Laying Wood Sheathing on Pitch or Gable Roofs

413 **Insulating Sheathing:** Insulating sheathing is furnished in sheets 4' wide and 6', 7', 8', 9', 10' and 12' long, and 1/2" and 25/32" thick, the same thickness as wood sheathing.

Insulating Roof Decking: Decking should be laid so that cross joints are staggered and occur only over supports. Decking should be face nailed to all framing members. spacing nails 4" to 6" apart and keeping back 3/4" to 1" from edges of plank. Nails should be galvanized common of sufficient length to pass through decking and penetrate supports at least 1½" and should be driven flush but not countersunk.

414 **Labor Placing Insulating Roof Decking**

417 **Wood Board Sheathing - Labor Placing Plywood on a Hip Roof**

418 **Shop-Fabricated Structural Wood - Glued Laminated Beam Construction:** Beams of glued laminated construction are popular where price is not the controlling factor.

Page #	Highlight

They are used in schools, auditoriums, churches, stores, and ranch-style homes and are made of kiln-dried structural woods bonded together by glue, applied under controlled conditions of temperature and pressure.

Roof insulation is accomplished through the use of standard insulating boards placed upon the roof deck and covered with roofing material. Because of the purlin construction generally used, 2" or 4" decking is recommended.

Glue Laminated Three Hinged Arch: Another type of glued laminated construction is the three-hinged arch, which gains its support from floor level, incorporating column and beam in one compact design.

Purlins are generally used to span the resulting bays and are covered with two inch decking and suitable insulating material.

Labor Framing Woof Roof Trusses

419 **Finish Carpentry**

Exterior Finish Carpentry - Placing Corner Boards, Fascia Boards, Etc.

Placing Exterior Wood Cornices, Verge Boards, Etc.

450 **Selective Demolition for Thermal Moisture Protection – Dampproofing and Waterproofing**

457 **Built-Up Bituminous Waterproofing — Estimating the Quantity of Felt or Fabric Required for Membrane Waterproofing**

458 **Weight of Tar or Asphalt Felt for Membrane Waterproofing:** Tar or asphalt felt for waterproofing is currently furnished in 4 sq. rolls of 432 sq. ft. weighing 60 lbs. per roll. Double thickness asphalt felt is also furnished in 60 lbs. per roll containing 216 sq. ft and this felt is known and No.30. When specifying the grade or weight of felt to be used, it is customary to state that "felt shall weigh not less than 15 lbs. per 108 sq. ft". This is known as No. 15 felt. Felt is furnished in 4 sq. rolls of 32 sq. ft, so there are 32 sq. ft per roll or 8 sq. ft per 100 sq. ft allowed for laps. Tar or asphalt saturated fabric is usually sold by the roll containing 50 sq. yds or by the sq. yd.

Applying Membrane Waterproofing

461 **Thermal Protection – Thermal Insulation**

462 Highlight Table: *Different Material R Values*

Heat transfer thru the building enclosure is by three means: convection, conduction, and radiation.

Convection is the thermally produced upward and downward movement of air.

Conduction is the transmission of heat thru a material.

Radiation is the emission of energy from a surface.

463 **Rigid Insulation**

468 **Reflective Insulation:** Where the heat flows down from a hot roof to a ceiling below, 93% of the heat transfer is by radiation and only 7% by conduction.

Page #	Highlight
	Roof & Deck Insulation
469	**Weather Barriers**

Steep Slope Roofing – Shingle and Shakes: Roofing is estimated by the square, containing 100 sq. ft.

Rules for Measuring Plain Double Pitch or Gable Roofs: To obtain the area of a plain double pitch or gable roof as shown in Figure 1, multiply the length of the ridge (A to B), by the length of the rafter (A to C). This will give the area of one-half the roof. Multiply this by 2 to obtain the total sq. ft. of roof surface.

470 **Rule for Measuring Hip Roofs**

Fig. 1 Plain Double Pitch or Gable Roof

Fig. 2 Conical Building and Roof

To obtain the total number of sq. ft. of roof surface, add the area of the two ends to the area of the two sides. This total divided by 100 equals the number of squares in the roof.

Fig. 3 Hip Roofs

To obtain the area of the sides of the roof, the length of the ridge (A to B), is 10'-0" and the length of the eaves (D to H) is 30"- 0":

Fig. 4 Hip Roofs

Rules for Measuring Conical Tower Roofs and Circular Buildings: *Highlight examples given.*

471 **A Short Method of Figuring Roof Areas:** To obtain the number of sq. ft. of roof area, where the pitch (rise and run) of the roof is known, take the entire flat or horizontal area of the roof and multiply by the factor given below for the roof slope applicable and the result will be the area of the roof.

Highlight Table: **Sample Roof Factor Estimate -** Showing different factors to convert flat areas into various slopes.

472 **Asphalt Shingles — Estimating Quantities of Asphalt Shingles:** When measuring roofs of any shape, always allow one extra course of shingles for the "starters" at the eaves. The first or starting course of shingles must always be doubled.

Asphalt shingles must be properly nailed 6 nails to a strip and nailed low enough on the shingle (right at the cut-out); otherwise, they will blow off the roof.

Nails Required for Asphalt Shingles: When laying square butt strip shingles, use 11 ga. aluminum nails, 1" long, with a 7/16" head.

473 **Metal Shingles**

Porcelain Enamel Shingles: Porcelain enamel shingles are manufactured to have an exposed surface of 10"x10" with 144 shingles per square. Weight is 225 lbs. per 100 sq. ft. Finish is fused on at 1500°F and provides a long lasting, self-cleaning finish that will not peel or blister.

Page #	Highlight
474	**Slate Roofing**
	Items to be Included in an Estimate for Slate Roofing: The following items should be included to make a complete and accurate estimate on slate roofing: (Highlight 1 – 4)
475	Highlight Table: *Slate Roofing*
477	**Wood Shingles and Shakes**
	Estimating the Quantity of Wood Shingles
	Highlight Table: *Number of Shingles and Quantity of Nails Required*
	Estimating the Quantity of Wood Shingles
478	Wood shingles are usually sold by the square based on sufficient shingles to lay 100 sq. ft of surface, when laid 5" to the weather, 4 bundles to the square.
480	**Clay Roofing Tile**
483	**Roofing and Siding Panels – Aluminum and Siding:** To provide adequate drainage, the roof surface should never have a slope less than 2½" per ft. and preferably not less than 3" per foot. For roofing, sheets should have a side lap of 1½ corrugations. For sidings, sheets should be lapped 1 corrugation.
485	**Steel Siding:** It is made with various corrugations, varying in width and depth, but the 2-1/2" corrugation width is the most commonly used.
486	When used for siding one corrugation lap is usually sufficient, but for roofing two corrugations should be used and if the roof has only a slight pitch, the lap should be three corrugations.
	When used for siding, a 1" to 2" end lap is sufficient, but when laid on roofs it should have an end lap of 3" to 6" depending on the pitch of the roof. For a 1/3 pitch, a 3" lap is sufficient; for a 1/4 pitch, a 4" lap should be used; and for a 1/8 pitch, a 5" end lap is recommended.
489	**Membrane Roofing**
490	**Figure:** *Fig. 1. Flat Roof with Parapet Walls*
	Rules for Measuring Flat Roof: When measuring flat roof surfaces that are to be covered with composition, tar and gravel, tin, metal, or prepared roofing, the measurements should be taken from the outside of the walls on all four sides to allow for flashing up the side of each wall. The flashing is usually 8" to 1' - 0" high.
	Figure: *Fig. 2. Flat Roof Overhanging Walls*
491	**Quantity of Roofing Gravel Required for Built-Up Roofs:** Roofing gravel should be uniformly embedded into a heavy top pouring of asphalt or pitch so that approximately 400 lbs. of gravel or 300 lbs. of slag is used per 100 sq. ft. of roof area.
493	**EPDM Roof Systems:** Ethylene Propylene Diene Methylene Rubber is popular known in the trade as EPDM.
	EPDM membranes can be produced in various colors, including black, reinforced, reinforced, or non-reinforced, and in thicknesses ranging from 30 to 90 mils.

Page #	Highlight
494	**Roll Roofing**
495	**Flashing and Sheet Metal — Sheet Metal Roofing**
	Copper Roofing —
496	**Standing Seam Sheet Metal Roofing**
497	The following table gives the covering capacity of painted or galvanized steel sheets of the different sizes. (Highlight Table)
	V-Crimped Roofing. When estimating quantities of V-crimped roofing, allow for the end lap but there is no waste in the width as only the actual covering capacity is charged for by the manufacturer.
	The following table gives the quantity of V-crimp roofing required to cover 100 sq. ft of roof with end laps 1" to 6" — (Highlight Table)
499	**Flat Seam Sheet Metal Roofing**
501	**Sheet Metal Flashing and Trim**
551	**Metal-Framed Skylights**
	Erecting and Glazing Metal Skylights: An average skylight (single, double pitch or hip) up to 8'-0" x 12'-0" in size containing 100 sq. ft of area, should be erected and glazed complete by a sheet metal worker and glizer in 8 to 10 hrs. time, at the following labor cost: — Highlight Table
	Erecting Skylights With Side Sash: If the skylights have side sash, the erection cost will vary with the number of sash in the skylight and whether stationary or pivoted. On an average it will require 1 to 1½ hrs. labor time for each sash in the skylight, at the following labor cost per sash. – Highlight Table
660	**Painting and Coating**
	Eaves
	Cornices, Exterior
661	**Roofs:** For flat roofs or nearly flat, measure actual area. For roofs having a quarter pitch, measure actual area and add 25%; roofs having a one-third pitch, measure actual area and add 33 1/3%; roofs having a half pitch, measure actual area and add 50 percent.
869	**Mensuration**
	Highlight formulas
870	**Computing Areas and Volumes**
873 – 874	**Volumes and Pictorials**
875	**Table of Feet and Inches Reduced to Decimals**
880 – 882	**Conversion Factors S.I. Metric — English Systems**
883	**Glossary of Construction Terms:** The test will ask at least one question from here.

Walker's Guide to Estimating, 31st Edition Tabs and Highlights (Roofing Contractors)

These1 Exam Prep Tabs are based on the 31st edition of the *Walker's Building Estimator's Reference Book*, Frank R Walker Company.

Each Tabs sheet has five rows of tabs. Start with the first tab at the first row at the top of the page, and proceed down that row placing the tabs at the locations listed below. Place each tab in your book setting it down one notch until you get to the bottom of the page, and then start back at the top again. After you have completed tabbing your book then you may start highlighting your book.

1 Exam Prep Tab **Page #**

******This concludes the tabs for this document. Please continue with the highlights on the following page.******

Page #	Highlight
1	**Introduction**
1-2	**The Role of the Estimator:** The following requisites are essential for the making of a good estimator: Highlight the first sentence for items 1 thru 7.
2-3	**The Role of the Contractor:** Erecting a building is a complex undertaking and seldom is one firm capable of doing all phases of the work. Yet the owner or developer usually prefers to let one contract and make one firm responsible for the completion of the project.
4	The average percent of work performed by subcontractors for a general contractor cannot be precisely determined, but surveys conducted by the Associated General Contractors of America indicate from 40% to 70%. The American Subcontractor Association claims that 90% of the work force in the building construction industry is employed by subcontractors.
5	Usually there is a retainage of at least 5 to 10% by the general contractor to the subs and in turn by the owner to the general contractor. Retainage is not completely released until the project is substantially complete. It has become common practice to reduce the retainage by 50% when the project is 50% satisfactorily completed.
6-7	**The Cost of Money**
7	**Sources of Money:** The main sources of money are: Highlight items 1 - 8.
8	**Mortgage Loans:** Once a loan is approved and accepted, there are certain charges called closing costs. and a part of these costs, known as points, origination fees, or the discount, cover the cost of setting up the loan. The usual range of points is from 1% to 3%, but in states where there are legal limits set on the interest that may be charged, points have been quoted as high as 7% as a way to get around the usury laws. **Mortgage Banker:** For consummating the transaction, they charge a flat fee of around 1%to 2% of the loan placed. This fee is in addition to the usual closing costs that are charged by the lender.
9-10	**Selling the Lender**
11	**Short Term Loans:** The construction loan is a short term loan to cover the building costs during the erection of the project.
12	One such source is those who loan the difference between the floor and ceiling of the mortgage, this is known as gap financing. To obtain such a commitment one must pay in advance a flat fee, usually around 5% of the amount to be loaned. If the project reaches the income level to qualify for the full mortgage, and the gap loan is not needed, the fee is not refundable.
12-13	How much front money, or equity, an owner will need to launch the project will vary with the type of project, the money market, and the owner's reputation. It is often said that an owner with a proven need, a piece of property free of debt, and an architect's set of plans can obtain all the financing they will need.
14	**Interim Financing:** Progress, at this point, should place the contractor in a position to obtain from the bank a general commitment as to the limit and terms under which they would participate in granting short term loans (usually 30 to 90 days).

Page #	Highlight
15	**Setting Up the Estimate:** There are various reasons for these failures, but probably the most common one is the inability of the person estimating costs to come up with realistic and profitable estimates. Some of the most important considerations that such companies make before bonding an applicant are: Highlight items 1 thru 3
17-21	**Estimate Types**
18	**Budget/Feasibility Estimate:** The budget or feasibility estimate, once it has been developed, is effectively cast in stone.
19-20	**Schematic Design milestone Estimate — 3% to 5% Overall Completeness; Design Development Milestone Estimate — 35% to 60% Overall Design Completeness; 70% to 98% Construction Documents Milestone Estimates; Construction Documents Milestone and Bid Cost Estimate — 100% Overall Design Completeness" The student should highlight the titles only.**
21-22	**Project Office Expense; Small Tools & Consumables; Weather Protection; Home Office Support; Escalation (Cost Growth); Finance Expense.** Highlight the titles only.
23	**Profit -** On small jobs, alterations, remodeling and similar work, a contractor is justified in adding 20% to 30% profit to the actual cost, but must ask themselves whether they can actually obtain this amount. On new work, where it is possible to estimate cost with a fair degree of accuracy, a contractor is entitled to 10% to 15% on the actual cost of the work (job overhead included in the actual cost of the job), but it is safe to say that competitive figures submitted for many jobs show a 5% instead of a 10% to 15%. A contractor is entitled to a fair profit of 10% profit, but getting it is another matter.
29	**Bidding for a Contract:** Construction contracts are awarded in one of two ways — competitive bidding or negotiation.
30	There are various ways this is done, by organizations, governmental bodies, and banks, but in general, the information that must be submitted will follow that contained in AIA document A-305 Contractor's Qualifications Statement). **Invitation to Bid**: Once on a bidding list, a contractor will receive an Invitation to Bid or Bid Notice for each prospective job.
31	**Instructions to Bidders:** Often the invitation to bid is accompanied by an Instruction to Bidders further defining the job restrictions such as completion dates, milestone dates, visiting job site, special conditions, etc. The bid bond guarantees that the bidding contractor, if awarded a contract, will enter into the contract and furnish a performance and payment bond if required. If they do not honor their bid, they forfeit the amount of the bond. Bid bonds and the later performance, material, labor, maintenance, completion, supply, and subcontractor bonds are often encountered in public work, but may not be required in private work, where the contractor's reputation is deemed sufficient and the cost of bonds unwarranted. Bid bond costs are customarily minimal, if any, and the cost of bonds is borne by the contractor.

Page #	Highlight
	Construction Management: In Construction Management (CM), a general contractor or engineering company enters into a contract with the owner prior to the bidding period and acts in a managerial and advisory role. Bid packages for the project are usually taken under the construction manager's supervision.
32	They will provide reports on the project cost status, payment status, and an analysis of each contract and the project cash flow. The construction management approach has gained a wider acceptance in recent times, especially in federally sponsored construction.
33	**Estimate Check Lists and Practices**: A master checklist for every estimator should include the Bid Document Inventory, Estimating Assignment, Direct Estimate, Wage Rate Development, Bid Document Reviews, Takeoff General Practices, etc
35	**Federal Unemployment Tax Act (FUTA):** This tax applies to the first $7,000 of wages paid each employee during the calendar year 2013. The rate is 6.0% but a credit of up to a maximum 5.4% of total wages for contributions paid into State Unemployment Funds for a total federal tax rate of 0.6%. Federal Unemployment Tax is imposed on employers and must not be deducted from wages of employees.
35	**State Unemployment Tax**
36	**Worker's Compensation:** Rates vary widely among the states, craft labor and staff labor categories. In states where medical benefits are limited, it may be advisable to carry full or extra-legal medical coverage.
	Property Damage Insurance
39	**Office Overhead Expense:** This is sometimes referred to as General and Administrative (G&A) costs.
39	Overhead may run 6% to 15% for smaller firms. Larger firms may have overhead that are as little as 1% to 2% of the annual volume.
40-41	**Office Furniture and Equipment; Insurance.** The student should highlight the titles only.
41	**Project Indirect Costs.** The student should highlight the titles only.
42	**Contract Documents:** Once it is determined which contracting firm is to do the job, a formal contract will be drawn up. The Contract Documents usually should include the Owner-Contractor Agreement; the General Conditions of the Contract; Supplementary Conditions of the Contract (if any); the Working Drawings, giving all sheet numbers with revisions; Specifications, giving page numbers; and Addenda or Bulletins issued prior to contract
42-47	Highlight all bold letters titles for the AIA documents.
48	**Performance and Payment Bonds -** a performance bond to indemnify the owner against loss resulting from the failure of the contractor to complete the work in accordance with the plans and specifications; and a payment bond to guarantee payment for all bills incurred by the contractor for labor or materials for the work. The federal government, under the Miller Act, requires that a contractor furnish two separate bonds, one for the performance and one for the payment of labor and materials.
	Maintenance Bonds

Page #	Highlight
49	**Bid Bonds:** Bids are invited by advertisements, and the bidder may have to submit with the bid a certified check, usually for a 5% of the bid, or a bid bond, usually for 10% of the bid.
	License or Permit Bonds: If the contractor regularly operates within an area requiring such bonds, this cost should be carried under office overhead, because is a normal cost of doing business.
	Supply and Subcontractor Bonds.
49-50	**Construction Equipment:** The advantages in renting or leasing include: highlight items 1 thru 5
51	**Negotiating a Contract:** A variation of the negotiated contract is fast track, design build construction. In this arrangement the project may be started before all the plans are fully developed. Each phase of the job, such as foundation, masonry, carpentry, etc., is bid separately, just before the phase is required to be installed. Some advantages and disadvantages are: Highlight items 1 thru 3.
	As the phases are bid, the successful subcontractors may be assigned to a general contractor in the same manner as a lump-sum contract; or the general may act in the role of a project manager, in which case each subcontractor for each phase will have a direct contract with the owner. This variation is referred to as multiple bidding.
52-54	**Contracting Definitions -** Addenda, Alternates, Approved Equal, Arbitration, Bid. Bid Bond, Cash Allowance, Certificate of Occupancy, Change Order, Contract Time, Cost Breakdown, Extras, Final Acceptance. Payment and Performance Bond, Letter of Intent, Liens, Liquidated damages, Maintenance Bond, Punch List, Retainage, Separate Contract, Shop Drawings, Subcontractor Bonds, Substantial Completion, Superintendent, Supplier, Supply Affidavit, Unit Prices, Upset Price, Warranty". The student should highlight the titles only.
55	**The Working Drawings:** Each sheet should have a title block in the lower right-hand corner with the sheet number; the number of sheets in each set; the date made plus each date it has been revised, and the initials of the person or persons who drew and approved the sheet. The student should be familiar with the different letters usually assigned to the drawings.
55	**Type of drawings:** Most working drawings for building construction are based on orthographic projection, which is a parallel projection to a plane by lines perpendicular to the plane. In this way all dimensions will be true. If the plane is horizontal, the projection is a plan; if vertical, it is an elevation for outside the building, or a sectional elevation if through the building.
	The only descriptive drawing that presents a building as the eye sees it is the perspective. A perspective is seldom useful for presenting information on working drawings.
56-58	Highlight drawings in these pages. Isometric, Orthographic, Cabinet and Elevation
59	**Scale:** The architect's scale, with the inch divided into 1/4, 1/8, 1/16, 1/32, is standard for building construction in the United States. The engineer's scale, with the inch divided into tenths, is sometimes used in structural work or on site plans.
	The metric scale is divided into centimeters and millimeters, 2.54 centimeters equaling one inch.
60	**Reproduction** – There were also processes that transfer blueprints to cloth drawings or to *sepia prints,* which could be altered, added to, and printed just like an original tracing.
61-68	Highlights symbols and specifications

Page #	Highlight
69-102	**CSI MasterFormat 2014 edition by Division Numbers and Titles -** This format is ideal for developing estimates and estimating check lists.
102	**Subdivision:** Materials will list the materials to be used in one of several ways, often found in combination. The closed specification will list a single trade name, and the specified product that must be furnished. The contractor's option specification (or bidder's choice) lists more than one trade name, and the contractor may choose from those listed.
	A variation is the product approval specification which asks the contractor to submit any substitutions prior to submitting a bid. If the architect approves the substitute, it will be put in an addenda sent to all contractors. This "or approved equal" type specification is the most common.
	The performance specification describes not the material but what work is required to produce strength, mechanical ability, or similar measurable results.
103-104	**Insurance Taxes & Bonds; Contractor's Equipment Floater; Installation Floater.** The student should highlight the titles only.
105	**Alternates:** On the typical lump sum proposal form, the Alternate follows the Statement of the Lump Sum price in a form such as the following: Highlight the sample given in the book.
106	**Cash Allowance:** Sometimes the architect does not have a final decision from the owner on certain items. Rather than leave them out of the lump sum proposal, the architect will state a definite budget amount in the specification that is to be included in the bid.
	Unit Prices: Where quantity of materials is in doubt, but quality is known, the specification may ask for unit prices. For example, unit prices are often asked for concrete per square yard, piling per lineal foot, partition block per square foot, etc. These prices should be complete with all costs, profit, and overhead included.
	Addenda: These, plus changes the architect and owner may wish to make after the plans and specifications have been issued but before bids are turned in, are incorporated in the Addenda.
107	**Change Orders** are modifications issued after the contract is signed.
115	**Project Staff; Mobilization.**
	Construction Scheduling: There are three methods of construction scheduling: Highlight 1 - 3.
116-119	**Planning; Project Scope and Work Breakdown Structure; Construction Means and Methods; Drawings and Specifications; Technology; Labor Availability and Skills Pool; Procurement Strategy; Institutional Constraints; Project Phasing and Staging; Weather Considerations.** The student should highlight the titles only.
120	**Scheduling Methods/Tools:** The use of bar charts started the industrial revolution of the late 1800s. An early industrial engineer named Gantt developed these charts to improve factory efficiency. Bar charts are often called 'Gantt Charts'.
	Critical Path Method (CPM) for project scheduling began in the 1950s in twoparallel applications. The US Navy developed the Project Evaluation and Review Technique (PERT) to develop the schedule for the construction of its Polaris Program.

Page #	Highlight
	There are two methods for CPM calculations. arrow diagramming and precedence diagramming. In the arrow diagramming method, project activities are shown as arrows. Circles at the beginning and end of activities are called nodes. Pairs of nodes or letters are used to identify each activity.
121	In the precedence diagram. activities and their durations are shown "on the nod." Sequence between tasks is shown with arrows between related activities.
	Precedence diagramming is capable of representing activities that start or end in parallel with other activities.
	Identification of Activities — An activity is any significant unit of work within the WBS' work package. There is no one "right" way to define activities for a given project.
122	**CPM calculations:** As stated earlier precedence diagramming (also called network diagram) graphically represents the relationships between the project activities.
122-123	**Early Start (ES); Early Finish (EF); Late Finish (LF); Late Start (LS); Forward Pass** — Formula (ES + Duration = EF); **Backward Pass; Finish to Start or FS; Start to Start or SS; Finish to Finish or FF; Network Logic Diagram.** The student should highlight the titles only.
124	**Total Float:** is the amount of time an activity can be delayed without delaying the end date of the project, and is defined as the difference between the LS and ES of an activity. Activities with 0 Total Float are critical activities.
125-126	**Critical Activity; Contingency Time; Resource Constraints; Monitoring/Updating; Measuring Progress.** The student should highlight the titles only.
151	**Temporary Utilities.**
152	**Temporary Buildings & Construction; Demobilization; Outside Services.**
	The student should highlight the titles only
159	**Concrete**
252	**Steelforms for Joist Constructed Floors and Roofs**
	Estimating Quantities of Steelform: In estimating the area of floor and roof construction requiring removable or permanent...No deductions are to be made for beams or for tees of beams or for wide joists.
254	**Ceco Steelform Construction:** Ceco steelform construction is a combination of concrete joist construction and thin top slabs.
	Forms Other Than Wood
	Lightweight Steel Forming Material for Concrete: High-strength corrugated steel forming material is often used for forming reinforced concrete floor and roof slabs.
255-256	**Tables** showing Concrete Quantities for LONGform.
256	**Estimating:** Corrugated steel forming material is sold by the square, with the area determination based on sheet width times actual sheet length.

Page #	Highlight
325	**Finishing Lightweight Concrete Floor and Roof Fill**
326	**Finishing Concrete Roof Fill:** Concrete fill for flat roofs are usually struck off, darbied, and floated. If fill is not over 2" to 3" thick, 2 cement masons with a helper should place screeds, strike off, darby, and float 1,500 to 1,700 sq ft of roof fill per 8-hr. day. Where concrete fill is placed on pitch or gable roofs, finishing is more difficult…and additional helper is usually required.
382	**Precast Concrete Roof Slabs:** Precast concrete roof slabs are of three general types: rib, flat, and channel. The rib tile is self-weathering. Auxiliary pieces are furnished to suit the particular design required, such as ridges, saw-tooth ridges, gables end finishing tile, monitor flashing tile and other specials required in connection with hip or valley.
383	The other two types of precast concrete roof slabs, flat and channel, are used over all roof decks, whether flat or sloping, and present a smooth surface for the application of any type of built-up roofing. **Labor Placing Precast Concrete Roof and Floor Slabs:** Because of their size and weight, it requires 2 workers to handle precast concrete roof or floor slabs…2 more on the floor or roof placing them for the mason, and a mason and helper to lay and caulk the joints.
406	**Cast Decks and Underlayment** **Monolithic or Poured-in-Place Gypsum Roof Construction:** The effective cross sectional area of reinforcing shall be not less than 0.026 sq. in. per foot of slab width.
407	The weights, excluding sub purlins and insulating values of poured gypsum roof decks are as follows: Highlight Table. The following are approximate prices only on the various types of poured-in-place gypsum roof decks. Highlight Table.
581	**Metals- Structural Metal Framing** **Estimating Quantities of Structural Steel:** When estimating the quantity of structural steel required for any job, each class of work (column bases, columns, girders, beams, lintels, trusses) should be estimated separately, because each involves different labor operations in fabrication and erection.
581-582	**Items to Be Included in a Structural Steel Estimate:** Highlight 1 - 8.
583	**Basis for Estimating All Classes of Structural Steel Work:** Highlight table.
590	**Bolting Field Connections.** Most Structural steel projects have sections bolted together.
591	The most common bolts are ASTM A-325, high strength bolts for structural steel joints, 3/4" diameter x 2" long, at an approximate cost per bolt unit of $0.95 each. Each bolt unit consists of bolt, washers, and nut. Other grades sometimes required for connections are A490M-04a Standard specification for High Strength Steel Bolts, Classes 10.9 and 10.9.3…Grade *A307-04 Standard Specification for Carbon Steel Bolts and Studs. 60,000 PSI Tensile Strength* carbon steel externally threaded standard connection (decrease the cost about 15% per bolt unit.

Page #	Highlight
605	**Junior Steel Beams:** Junior beams (M shapes) are lightweight, hot-rolled structural beams that are used as secondary floor and roof beams in schools, stores, apartments…Sizes and properties are given below: Highlight chart.
	The cost of cutting, punching holes, and coping junior beams will run approximately as given below, but when much fabricating is required, it is advisable to refer plans to a local fabricator or warehouse for a sub bid. Highlight chart.
606	**Metal Joists**
608	**Metal Decking**
610	**Lightgage Framing**
613	Lightgage framing systems can supply complete wall, floor, and roof construction for buildings up to four stories in height, or can be used in combination with other framing systems for interior, load bearing partitions, exterior curtain walls, fire separation walls, parapets, penthouses, trusses, suspended ceilings, and mansard roofs.
614	Joists come in 6", 8" 10" and 12" depths and in 12, 14, 16, and 18 gauge material.
	Joist bridging, which may be stock 'V' units or solid channels, must be supplied in the center of all spans up to 14'; at third points on spans from 14' to 20; at quarter points on spans from 26' to 32'; and at 8' centers on all spans over 32'.
619	**Wood, Plastics, and Composites**
620	**Nails Required for Carpentry Work**
621	**Table: Recommended Sizes and Quantities Commonly Used**
622	**Table: Bright Common Nail Specifications**
	Bright box nails are generally of the same length but slightly smaller diameter. **See Table below on same page Bright Box Nail Specifications**
623	**Table: Recommended Sizes and Quantities Commonly Used**
	Hand driven nails for roofing-Asphalt and Fiberglass Shingle Nails: Roofing nails should be long enough to penetrate ¾" into the wood deck lumber, or completely thru the plywood decking.
624-627	**Tables: Different types of roofing nail specifications**
627	**Metal Roof Nails with Rubber Washers**
628	**Metal Roof Nails with Silicone Washers**
	Table: Metal Roofing Nail Specifications
629	**Tables: Pole Barn — Post and Framing Nail Specifications & Nail**
	Reference Data Specifications
632-633	**Rough Carpentry - Estimating Lumber Quantities:** One board foot is always 144 cubic inches.

Page #	Highlight
633	Example of calculating board foot - Width (inches) x Thickness (inches) x Length (feet) and divide by 12 – practice calculation
	Estimating Wood Joists
634	**Table - Number of Wood Floor Joists Required for any Spacing**
	Table - Board Feet Required per 100 SqFt of Surface when used for Studs,
	Joists Rafters, Wall and Floor, Furring Strips, etc.
635	**Table — Number of Wood Joists Required for any Floor and Spacing**
636	**Estimating number of Wood Studs** — When estimating the number of wood partition studs, take the length of each partition and then the total length of all partitions.
636-637	Highlight example on how to calculate total quantity of lumber required. Ask your instructor for help if needed.
638	**Table - Board Ft of Lumber Required for Wood Stud Partitions 2"x 4" Studs; 16" o.c. Single Top and Bottom Plates** – see small print bottom of table - (numbers are calculated and then rounded to nearest board ft.)
639	**Estimating the number of headers and plywood spacers**
640	**Sample Gable End Roof Outrigger or Lookout Estimate**
641	**Sample Gable/End Vaulted End Wall Framing Estimate**
642	**Table - Gable End Framing at 16" o.c. Spacing – Total Length (ft) of Vertical Studs**
645	**To Obtain Area of Roofs for Any Pitch - calculation**
648	**Wood Framing – Hardware Accessories Used in Wood Framing; Metal Connector Plates (Truss Plates)**
650	**Wood Floor and Roof Trusses:** Wood roof trusses are used for spans as short as 25'-0" and can be used up to 200'-0".
651	Prices of wood trusses are governed by the following conditions: Highlight 1 - 4.
	The spacing of wood roof trusses that directly support roof sheathing roof sheathing is usually 2'0". Where roof loads are light and the installation of a ceiling is not required, spacings of 4'-0" to 4'-10" are advantageous.
	Bowstring Bolted Roof Truss
651-652	**Approximate Prices of Wood Bowstring Truss – Highlight Table on following page 652.**
652	**Crescent Type Roof Truss** — Recommended span is from 20'-0" to 85'-0"
652-653	**Approximate Prices of Crescent Type Wood Roof Trusses – Highlight Table on following page 653**
653	**Belgian Roof Truss:** It is used on some higher class store buildings and low cost churches and is recommended for spans from 20'-0" to 85'-0".

Page #	Highlight
	Belgian roof trusses are less efficient than the bowstring type, because the connections generally govern the member sizes. They cost about 50% more than bowstring type trusses.
	The Double fink truss is also referred to as a Belgian truss and is used for spans from 36'-0" to 60'-0".
653	**Flattop Roof Truss:** Spans should not exceed 65' where cost is an important factor
	Howe Truss: The Howe truss can be used for spans from 16' to 18'.
	Parallel Chord 4x2 Truss: This type of truss can be manufactured with duct chase openings so that wiring, piping, and ducts can run within the chords.
654	Pictorial — Types of Trusses
	Parallel Chord 2x4 Truss: Roof slopes should be at least 1/4" per foot of span.
	Modified Queen Post Truss
	Fink Truss — The fink truss is generally suitable for spans from 16' to as long as 46' and for all classes of construction. It is an efficient and cost effective truss configuration, 50% to 60% the cost of a comparable steel truss.
655	**Three-Hinged Arch**
	Cantilever Truss — Trusses with single or double cantilever sections are possible. Cantilevers can approach one-fourth of the distance of the main interior truss span.
	Clerestory Truss — is used extensively in industrial and agricultural buildings, in spans up to 60'.
655-656	**Inverted Truss; Vaulted Ceiling Truss; Mono-Pitch Truss; Dual-Pitch Truss**
656	**Pitched Warren Truss** — This truss form is most economical in spans from 30' to 70', on center spacings from 2' to 8'.
	The *W-Type* is the most popular type and is adaptable for spans from 18' up to 40'; roof slope from 2 in 12 to 6 in 12 and higher.
	The *Triple-W* is used for spans up to 80' with slopes of 3 in 12 and higher. Centerline spacings can be from 2' to 20'.
	The *Kingpost* truss is usually recommended for shorter spans. The economical range is up to 26' under most loading conditions.
657	**Other Types of Commonly Used Wood Trusses -** The Double Fink truss is generally used for spans from 36' to 60'
	An extremely long truss with cantilevered ends can be manufactured in three sections. Trusses of this type, 128' in overall length, have been fabricated in this manner.
658	**Truss Openings**
	Installation of Wood Trusses
	Table: Center Duct Depth/Opening

Page #	Highlight
663	**Installation Sequence for Temporary and Permanent Bracing of Wood Truss:** Install the first truss with a ground bracing system, which is constructed as follows: Highlight 1 - 6. For the first group of three to six trusses, the sequence is as follows: Highlight 1 - 6. Note that all bracing lumber should be no less than 2' x 4' x 10'. A Minimum of two 16d double head nails should be used at each connection.
664	**Mechanical Erection of Trusses:** Highlight Table For Erecting Roof Trusses.
664-665	**Hand Erection of Trusses:** Highlight Table for Erecting Roof Trusses By Hand on page 665
672	**Framing and Erecting Rafters for Gable Roofs**
673	**Framing and Erecting Rafters for Hip Roofs** **Framing Light Timbers for Exposed Roof Beam Construction**
673-674	**Framing for Roof Saddles on Flat Roofs**
674	**Laying Wood Sheathing on Flat Roofs**
688	**Plywood Roof and Wall Sheathing, Subflooring and Underlayment- Roof and Wall Sheathing** Nailing of plywood sheathing should be at 6" o.c. along panel edges and 12" o.c. at intermediate supports. Use 6d common nails for panels of ½" or less in thickness, and 8d for greater thickness. **Laying Wood Sheathing on Pitch or Gable Roofs**
689	**Insulating Sheathing:** Insulating sheathing is furnished in sheets 4' wide and 6', 7', 8', 9', 10' and 12' long, and 1/2" and 25/32" thick, the same thickness as wood sheathing.
690	**Insulating Roof Decking:** Decking should he laid so that cross joints are staggered and occur only over supports. Decking should be face nailed to all framing members. spacing nails 4" to 6" apart and keeping back 3/4" to 1" from edges of plank. Nails should be galvanized common of sufficient length to pass through decking and penetrate supports at least 1½" and should be driven flush but not countersunk.
691	**Labor Placing Insulating Roof Decking**
695	**Wood Board Sheathing - Labor Placing Plywood on a Hip Roof**
692	**Insulating Shingle Backer Strips** **Labor Placing Insulating Shingle Backer Strips**
697	**Shop-Fabricated Structural Wood - Glued Laminated Beam Construction:** Beams of glued laminated construction are popular where price is not the controlling factor. They are used in schools, auditoriums, churches, stores, and ranch-style homes and are made of kiln-dried structural woods bonded together by glue, applied under controlled conditions of temperature and pressure.

Page #	Highlight
697-698	Roof insulation is accomplished through the use of standard insulating boards placed upon the roof deck and covered with roofing material. Because of the purlin construction generally used, 2" or 4" decking is recommended.
698	**Glue Laminated Three Hinged Arch:** Another type of glued laminated construction is the three-hinged arch, which gains its support from floor level, incorporating column and beam in one compact design.
	Purlins are generally used to span the resulting bays and are covered with two inch decking and suitable insulating material.
	Labor Framing Woof Roof Trusses
699	**Finish Carpentry**
	Exterior Finish Carpentry - Placing Corner Boards, Fascia Boards, Etc.
700	**Placing Exterior Wood Cornices, Verge Boards, Etc.**
749	**Thermal Moisture Protection – Dampproofing and Waterproofing**
762	**Built-Up Bituminous Waterproofing – Estimating the Quantity of Felt Or Fabric Required for Membrane Required Waterproofing**
763	**Weight of Tar or Asphalt Felt for Membrane Waterproofing:** Tar or asphalt felt for waterproofing is currently furnished in 4 square rolls of 432 sq ft weighing 60 lbs per roll.
	Double thickness asphalt felt is also furnished in 60 lbs per roll containing 216 sq ft and this felt is known and No.30.
	When specifying the grade or weight of felt to be used, it is customary to state that "felt shall weigh not less than 15 lbs per 108 sq ft". This is known as No. 15 felt. Felt is furnished in 4 square rolls of 432 sq ft, so there are 32 sq ft per roll or 8 sq ft. per 100 sq ft allowed for laps.
	Tar or asphalt saturated fabric is usually sold by the roll containing 50 sqyds or by the sqyd.
763	**Applying Membrane Waterproofing**
769	**Thermal Protection – Thermal Insulation**
770	**Table — Different Material R Values**
	Heat transfer thru the building enclosure is by three means: convection, conduction, and radiation.
	Convection is the thermally produced upward and downward movement of air.
771	Conduction is the transmission of heat thru a material.
	Radiation is the emission of energy from a surface.
772	**Rigid Insulation**
782	**Reflective Insulation:** Where the heat flows down from a hot roof to a ceiling below, 93% of the heat transfer is by radiation and only 7% by conduction.

Page #	Highlight
	Roof and Deck Insulation
783	**Weather Barriers**
784	**Steep Slope Roofing – Shingle and Shakes** – Roofing is estimated by the square, containing 100 sq. ft.
784-785	**Rules for Measuring Plain Double Pitch or Gable Roofs:** Multiply the length of the ridge (A to B)… Multiply this by 2 to obtain the total sq. ft. of roof surface.
785	**Fig. 1 - Plain Double Pitch or Gable Roof and Fig. 2 -Conical Building and Roof**
	Rule for Measuring Hip Roofs: To obtain the total number of sq. ft. of roof surface, add… equals the number of squares in the roof.
786	**Fig. 3 Hip Roofs**
	To obtain the area of the sides of the roof…and the length of the eaves (D to H) is 30"- 0":
	Fig. 4 – Hip Roofs
786-787	**Rules for Measuring Conical Tower Roofs and Circular Buildings:** Highlight examples given.
787	**A Short Method of Figuring Roof Areas** — To obtain the number of sq. ft. of roof area, where the pitch (rise and run) of the roof is known, take the entire flat or horizontal area of the roof and multiply by the factor given below for the roof slope applicable and the result will be the area of the roof. See table on following page 788.
788	**Table — Showing different factors to obtain number of sq footage of roofing required based on slope and flat area of roof**
789	**Asphalt Shingles — Estimating Quantities of Asphalt Shingles:** When measuring roofs of any shape, always allow one extra course of shingles for the "starters" at the eaves. The first or starting course of shingles must always be doubled.
	Asphalt shingles must be properly nailed 6 nails to a strip and nailed low enough on the shingle (right at the cut-out); otherwise, they will blow off the roof.
	Nails Required for Asphalt Shingles: When laying square butt strip shingles, use 11 ga. aluminum nails, 1" long, with a 7/16" head.
791	**Metal Shingles**
	Porcelain Enamel Shingles - Are manufactured to have an exposed surface of 10"x10" with 144 shingles per square. Weight is 225 lbs. per 100 sq. ft. Finish is fused on at 1500 deg. F and provides a long lasting, self-cleaning finish that will not peel or blister
792	**Slate Roofing**
793	**Items to be Included in an Estimate for Slate Roofing – Items 1 - 4**
794	**Table: Showing Units per Square and Number of Nails per Square**
798	**Wood Shingles and Shakes**

Page #	Highlight
	Estimating the Quantity of Wood Shingles
799	**Table: Number of Shingles and Quantity of Nails Required**
	Wood shingles are usually sold by the square based on sufficient shingles to lay 100 sq. ft. of surface, when laid 5" to the weather, 4 bundles to the square.
802	**Clay Roofing Tile**
806	**Roofing and Siding Panels – Aluminum Siding** - To provide adequate drainage the roof surface should never have a slope less than 2-1/2" per foot, and preferably not less than 3" per foot.
	For roofing, sheets should have a side lap of 1-1/2 corrugations. For sidings, should be lapped 1 corrugation.
810	**Steel Siding:** It is made with various corrugations, varying in width and depth, but the 2-1/2" corrugation width is the most commonly used.
	When used for siding one corrugation lap is usually sufficient, but for roofing two corrugations should be used and if the roof has only a slight pitch, the lap should be three corrugations.
811	When used for siding, a 1" to 2" end lap is sufficient, but when laid on roofs it should have an end lap of 3" to 6" depending on the pitch of the roof. For a 1/3 pitch, a 3" lap is sufficient; for a 1/4 pitch, a 4" lap should be used; and for a 1/8 pitch, a 5" end lap is recommended.
817	**Membrane Roofing- Built-Up Bituminous Roofing: Fig. 1 - Flat Roof with Parapet Walls**
817-818	**Rules for Measuring Flat Roof :** When measuring flat roof surfaces that are to be covered with composition, tar and gravel. tin, metal, or prepared roofing, the measurements should be taken from the outside of the walls on all four sides to allow for flashing up the side of each wall. The flashing is usually 8" to 1'-0" high.
818	**Fig. 2 - Flat Roof Overhanging Walls**
819	**Quantity of Roofing Gravel Required for Built-Up Roofs** — Roofing gravel should be uniformly embedded into a heavy top pouring of asphalt or pitch so that approximately 400 lbs of gravel or 300 lbs of slag is used per 100 sft of roof area.
823	**EPDM Roof Systems:** Ethylene Propylene Diene Methylene Rubber is popular known in the trade as EPDM. EPDM membranes can be produced in various colors, including black, reinforced, reinforced, or non-reinforced, and in thicknesses ranging from 30 to 90 mils.
826	**Roll Roofing**
	Flashing and Sheet Metal — Sheet Metal Roofing
827-833	**Copper Roofing —Standing Seam Sheet Metal Roofing – Flat Seam Sheet Metal Roofing**
830	The following table gives the covering capacity of painted or galvanized steel sheets of the different sizes. Highlight the table following the paragraph.
	V Crimped Roofing: When estimating quantities of V crimped roofing, allow for the end lap but there is no waste in the width as only the actual covering capacity is charged for by the manufacturer.

Page #	Highlight
830-831	The following table gives the quantity of V-crimp roofing required to cover 100 sq ft of roof with end laps 1" to 6". — Highlight the table following the paragraph.
837	**Sheet Metal Flashing and Trim**
915	**Metal-Framed Skylights - Erecting and Glazing Metal Skylights:** An average skylight (single, double pitch or hip) up to 8'-0"x12'- 0" in size containing 100 sqft should be erected and glazed complete by a sheet metal worker and glazier in 8 to 10 hrs time at the following labor cost — Highlight the table following the paragraph.
916	**Erecting Skylights with Side Sash:** If the skylights have side sash, the erection cost will vary with the number of sash in the skylight and whether stationary or pivoted. On an average it will require 1 to 1-1/2 hrs labor time for each sash in the skylight, at the following labor cost per sash - Highlight the table following the paragraph.
1095	**Painting and Coating**
1096	**Eaves**
	Cornices, Exterior
1097	**Roofs:** For flat roofs or nearly flat, measure actual area. For roofs having a quarter pitch, measure actual area and add 25%; roofs having a one-third pitch, measure actual area and add 33 1/3%; roofs having a half pitch, measure actual area and add 50 percent.
1395	**Mensuration**
1395-1396	**Highlight Conversions, and Examples**
1397-1398	**Computing Areas and Volumes**
1399-1402	**Area and Volume:** Formulas and Pictorials
1404-1405	**Table of Feet and Inches Reduced to Decimals**
1412-1414	**Conversion Factors S.I. Metric — English Systems**
1415	**Glossary of Construction Terms:** The test will ask at least one question from here
1443-1451	**Construction Safety:** OSHA / pit issues
1453	**Index**

NFPA 70: National Electric Code 2017 Handbook Tabs and Highlights

These 1 Exam Prep Tabs are based on *NFPA 70: National Electrical Code 2017 Handbook.*

Each Tabs sheet has five rows of tabs. Start with the first tab at the first row at the top of the page and proceed down that row placing the tabs at the locations listed below. Place each tab in your book setting it down one notch until you get to the bottom of the page, and then start back at the top again. After you have completed tabbing your book (the last tab is usually the glossary, appendix, or index), then you may start highlighting your book.

1 Exam Prep Tab	Page #	Section #
Contents	v	
Definitions	9	100
Electrical Installation Requirements	31	110
Grounded Conductors	57	200
Branch Circuits	61	210
Branch Circuit Feeder & Svc. Calculations	95	220
Outside Branch Circuits & Feeders	113	225
Services	123	230
Overcurrent Protection	147	240
Grounding & Bonding	167	250
Grounding Electrode Conductor	191	250 III
Bonding	201	250 V
Equipment Grounding Conductors	209	250 VI
Surge Arresters	225	280
Wiring Methods & Materials	231	300
Conductors for General Wiring	253	310
Box Fill	291	314
NM Cable	321	334
Service-Entrance Cable	327	338
Rigid Metal Conduit	333	344

1 Exam Prep Tab	Page #	Section #
Flexible Metal Conduit	337	348
Rigid PVC Conduit	341	352
Electric Metallic Tubing	353	358
Metal Wireways	375	376
Cable Trays	387	392
Flexible Cords /Cables	407	400
Switches	421	404
Receptacles & Cord Connectors	427	406
Switch/Panelboards	435	408
Luminaires	445	410
Appliances	463	422
Electric Space-Heating	469	424
Motors	493	430
Motor Tables	533	430 XIV
Air-Conditioning & Refrigeration Equipment	537	440
Transformers	549	450
Equipment Over 1000 Volts	573	490
Hazardous Locations	581	500
Class I Locations	593	501
Motor Fuel Dispensing Facilities	665	514
Health Care Facilities	693	517
Mobile Homes	755	550
Temporary Installations	799	590
Electric Signs & Outline Lighting	803	600
Elevators	823	620
Information Technology Equipment	861	645
Pools & Spas	889	680
Emergency Systems	955	700
Signal Circuits	999	725

******This concludes the tabs for this book. Please continue with the highlights on the following page.******

A.M. 12/09/2021

Section	Highlight
90.1	**Purpose:** (A) **Practical Safeguarding.** The purpose of this *Code* is the practical safeguarding of persons and property from hazards arising from the use of electricity.
90.2	**Scope:** (A) **Covered.** This *Code* covers the installation…for the following. Highlight (1) – (4).
	(B) **Not Covered.** This *Code* does not cover the following: Highlight (1) – (5).
90.4	**Enforcement.** This *Code* is intended to be suitable for…and for use by insurance inspectors.
90.5	**Mandatory Rules, Permissive Rules, and Explanatory Material:**
	(A) **Mandatory Rules.** …characterized by the use of the terms *shall* or *shall not*.
90.7	**Examination of Equipment for Safety.** …examinations for safety made under standard conditions…determination through field inspections.
100	**Definitions: Scope.** Become familiar with all definitions essential to the application of this *Code.*
110.3	**Part I. General – Examination, Identification, Installation, Use, and Listing (Product Certification) of Equipment.**
	(A) **Examination:** Highlight (1) – (8).
110.5	**Conductors.** Conductors normally used to carry current shall be of copper or aluminum unless otherwise provided in the *Code*.
110.12	**Mechanical Execution of Work.**
	(A) **Unused Openings.** …shall be closed to afford protection substantially equivalent to the wall of the equipment.
110.13	**Mounting and Cooling of Equipment:** (A) **Mounting.** Wooden plugs driven into holes in masonry, concrete, plaster, or similar materials shall not be used.
110.14	**Electrical Connections.** Conductors of dissimilar metals shall not be intermixed in terminal… unless the device is identified for the purpose and conditions of use.
	(A) **Terminals.** …shall be made by means of pressure connectors…or splices to flexible leads.
	(B) **Splices.** Conductors shall be spliced or joined…or soldering with a fusible metal or alloy.
110.15	**High-Leg Marking.** …marked by an outer finish that is orange in color.
110.22	**Identification of Disconnecting Means**
110.26	**Part II. 1000 Volts, Nominal, or Less – Spaces About Electrical Equipment.**
	(1) **Depth of Working Space.** The depth of the working space in the direction of live parts shall not be less than that specified in Table 110.26 (A)(1).
	Table 110.26(A)(1) *Working Spaces*
110.31	**Part III. Over 1000 Volts, Nominal - Enclosure for Electrical Installations.** A fence shall not be less than…or more extension utilizing three or more strands of barbed wire or equivalent.

Section	Highlight
110.34	**Work Space and Guarding.**
	(A) **Working Space.** *Exception: Where rear access is required to work on nonelectrical parts… a minimum working space of 30 in. horizontally shall be provided.*
110.36	**Circuit Conductors.** Circuit conductors shall be permitted to be installed in raceways: in cable …conductors provided in 300.7, 300.39, 300.40, and 300.50.
110.54	**Part IV. Tunnel Installations over 1000 Volts, Nominal - Bonding and Equipment Grounding Conductors:** (A) **Grounded and Bonding.** …at intervals not exceeding 1000 ft throughout the tunnel.
	(B) **Equipment Grounding Conductors.** The grounding conductor shall be permitted to be insulated or bare.
110.75	**Part V. Manholes and Other Electrical Enclosures - Access to Manholes:** (A) **Dimensions.** Rectangular access openings…shall not be less than 26 in. in diameter.
200.6	**Means of Identifying Grounded Conductors.**
	(A) **Sizes 6 AWG or Smaller.** Highlight (1) – (8).
	(B) **Sizes 4 AWG or Larger.** Highlight (1) – (4).
	(D) **Grounded Conductors of Different Systems.** The means of identification shall be documented…where the conductor of different systems originate.
200.7	**Use of Installation of a White or Gray Color or with Three Continuous White or Gray Stripes.**
	(B) **Circuits Less Than 50 Volts.**
	(C) **Circuits of 50 Volts or More.** (2) A flexible cord having one conductor identified by a white …by a circuit that has a grounded conductor.
200.10	**Identification of Terminals:** (A) **Device Terminals.**
	(B) **Receptacles, Plugs and Connectors.**
	(1) Identification shall be by a metal or…the letter *W* located adjacent to the identified terminal.
200.11	**Polarity of Connections.** No grounded conductor shall be attached to any terminal or lead so as to reverse the designated polarity.
210.4	**Part I. General Provisions. Multiwire Branch Circuits:** (A) **General.**
	(B) **Disconnecting Means.**
210.5	**Identification for Branch Circuits:** (B) **Equipment Grounding Conductor.**
	(C) **Identification of Underground Conductors.**
210.6	**Branch-Circuit Voltage Limitations.**

Section	Highlight
210.8	**GFCI Protection for Personnel:** (A) **Dwelling Units.**
	(B) **Other Than Dwelling Units.**
210.12	**AFCI Protection:** (A) **Dwelling Units.**
	(B) **Dormitory Units.**
210.19	**Part II. Branch-Circuit Ratings - Conductors – Minimum Ampacity and Size.**
	(A) **Branch Circuits Not More Than 600 Volts.**
	(1) **General.** (a) Where a branch circuit supplies…load plus 125 percent of the continuous load.
	(3) **Household Ranges and Cooking Appliances.**
	(B) **Branch Circuits Over 600 Volts.**
210.20	**Overcurrent Protection:** (A) **Continuous and Noncontinuous Loads.**
210.21	**Outlet Devices:** (A) **Lampholders.**
	(B) **Receptacles.**
	(1) **Single Receptacle on an Individual Branch Circuit.**
	(2) **Total Cord-and-Plug-Connected Load.**
	(3) **Receptacle Ratings.**
210.23	**Permissible Loads, Multiple-Outlet Branch Circuits:** (A) **15- and 20-Ampere Branch Circuits.**
210.50	**Part III. Required Outlets – General.**
	(C) **Appliance Receptacle Outlets.** Appliance receptacle installed in a dwelling unit for specific appliances, such as laundry equipment, shall be installed within 1.8 m (6 ft) of the intended location of the appliance.
210.52	**Dwelling Unit Receptacle Outlets:** (A) **General Provisions.**
	(1) **Spacing.**
	(2) **Wall Space.** Highlight (1) – (3).
	(3) **Floor Receptacles.**
	(B) **Small Appliances.**
	(1) **Receptacle Outlets Served.**
	(2) **No Other Outlets.**
	(3) **Kitchen Receptacle Requirements.**
	(C) **Countertops and Work Surfaces.**

Section **Highlight**

(1) **Wall Countertop and Work Surface.**

(E) **Outdoor Outlets.**

(F) **Laundry Areas.**

(G) **Basements, Garages, and Accessory Buildings.**

(H) **Hallways.**

210.62 **Show Windows.**

210.63 **Heating, Air-Conditioning, and Refrigeration Equipment Outlet.**

210.70 **Lighting Outlets Required:** (A) **Dwelling Units.**

(3) **Storage or Equipment Spaces.**

215.2 **Article 215 Feeders - Minimum Rating and Size:** (A) **Feeders Not More Than 600 Volts.**

(1) **General.** (a)…the minimum feeder conductor size shall have an allowable ampacity not less than the noncontinuous load plus 125 percent of the continuous load.

(2) **Grounded Conductor.**

220.12 **Part II. Branch-Circuit Load Calculations - Lighting Load for Specified Occupancies.**

Exception No. 1: Highlight *(1)*, *(2)* and *(3)*.

220.14 **Other Loads – All Occupancies.**

(H) **Fixed Multioutlet Assemblies.** (1) …length shall be considered as one outlet of not less than 180 volt-amperes.

(I) **Receptacle Outlets.**

220.42 **Part III. Feeder and Service Load Calculations - General Lighting.**

220.43 **Show-Window and Track Lighting:** (A) **Show Windows.**

(B) **Track Lighting.**

Table 220.42 *Lighting Load Demand Factors*

220.52 **Small-Appliance and Laundry Loads – Dwelling Unit.**

(A) **Small-Appliance Circuit Load.** …the load shall be calculated at 1500 volt-amperes for each 2-wire small-appliance branch circuit.

220.54 **Electric Clothes Dryer – Dwelling Unit(s).** …shall be either 5000 watts (volt-amperes) or the nameplate rating, whichever is larger.

Table 220.54 *Demand Factors for Household Electric Clothes Dryer*

Table 220.55 *Demand Factors and Loads for…* Note 2. Over 8¾ kW through 27 kW ranges.

Note 3. Over 1¾ kW through 8¾ kW.

Section	Highlight
	Table 220.56 *Demand Factors for Kitchen Equipment – Other Than Dwelling Unit(s)*
220.84	**Part IV. Optional Feeder and Service Load Calculations - Multifamily Dwelling.**
	(B) **House Loads.**
	(C) **Calculated Loads.** (3) The nameplate rating of the following: Highlight a – d.
	Table 220.84 *Optional Calculations – Demand Factors for Three or More Multifamily Dwelling Units*
	Table 220.88 *Optional Method – Permitted Load Calculations for Service and Feeder Conductors for New Restaurants*
225.6	**Part I. General – Conductor Size and Support.**
	(A) **Overhead Spans.** (1) For 1000 volts, nominal or less, 10 AWG copper or 8 AWG aluminum …longer span unless supported by a messenger wire.
225.7	**Lighting Equipment Installed Outdoors:** (B) **Common Neutral.**
225.18	**Clearance for Overhead Conductors and Cables.** Overhead spans of open conductor cables of not over 1000 volts, nominal, shall have a clearance of not less than the following:
	(1) 3.0 m (10 ft) (4) 5.5 m (18 ft)
225.51	**Part III. Over 1000 Volts - Isolating Switches.** Where oil switches or air, oil, vacuum, or sulfur …building disconnecting means.
230.2	**Part I. General – Number of Services:** (B) **Special Occupancies.** By special permission, additional services shall be permitted for either of the following: Highlight (1) – (2).
230.6	**Conductors Considered Outside the Building.** Under any of the following conditions:(1) – (5).
230.24	**Part II. Overhead Service Conductors – Clearances.**
	(A) **Above Roofs.** …not less than 2.5 m (8 ft) above the roof surface.
	(B) **Vertical Clearance for Overhead Service Conductors.**
	(1) 3.0 m (10 ft) at the electrical service entrance…does not exceed 150 volts to ground. (2) 3.7 m (12 ft)…does not exceed 300 volts to ground. (4) 5.5 m (18 ft)…such as cultivated, grazing, forest, and orchard.
230.50	**Part IV. Service-Entrance Conductors – Protection Against Physical Damage.**
	(A) **Underground Service-Entrance Conductors.**
230.51	**Mounting Supports:** (A) **Service-Entrance Cables.** …within 300 mm (12 in.) of every service …and at intervals not exceeding 750 mm (30 in.).
230.53	**Raceways to Drain.** shall be listed or approved.

Section	Highlight
230.71	**Part VI. Service Equipment – Disconnecting Means - Maximum Number of Disconnects:** (A) **General.** Highlight (1) – (4).
230.72	**Grouping of Disconnects:** (A) **General.** The two to six disconnects as permitted in 230.71 shall be grouped.
230.75	**Disconnection of Grounded Conductor.** Where the service disconnecting means does not disconnect the ground conductor from the premises wiring, other means shall be provided for this purpose in the service equipment.
230.82	**Equipment Connected to the Supply Side of Service Disconnect.** (5) Taps used only to supply …equipment and installed in accordance with requirements for service-entrance conductors.
230.91	**Part VII. Service Equipment – Overcurrent Protection - Location.** Where fuses are used as the service overcurrent device, the disconnecting means shall be located ahead of the supply side of the fuses.
230.95	**Ground-Fault Protection of Equipment.** …of more than 150 volts to ground not exceeding 1000 volts phase-to-phase for each service disconnector rated 1000 amperes or more.
230.202	**Part VIII. Services Exceeding 1000 Volts, Nominal - Service-Entrance Conductor.**
	(A) **Conductor Size.** Service-entrance conductors shall not be smaller than 6 AWG unless in multiconductor cable.
240.5	**Part I. General – Protection of Flexible Cords, Flexible Cables and Fixture Wires.**
	(A) **Ampacities.**
	(B) **Branch-Circuit Overcurrent Device.**
	(2) **Fixture Wire.** Highlight (1) – (6).
	(4) **Field Assembled Extension Cord Sets.** 20-ampere circuits – 16 AWG and larger
240.6	**Standard Ampere Ratings:** (A) **Fuses and Fixed-Tripped Circuit Breakers.**
	Table 240.6 (A) *Standard Ampere Ratings for Fuses and Inverse Time Circuit Breakers*
240.8	**Fuses or Circuit Breakers in Parallel.** Individual fuses, circuit breakers, or combinations thereof shall not otherwise be connected in parallel.
240.21	**Part II. Location - Location in Circuit:** (B) **Feeder Taps.**
	(2) **Taps Not over 7.5 m (25 ft) Long.**
	(3) **Taps Supplying a Transformer [Primary Plus Secondary Not over 7.5 m (25 ft) Long].**
240.24	**Location in or on Premises:** (A) **Accessibility.**
	(D) **Not in Vicinity of Easily Ignitable Material.**
240.51	**Part V. Plug Fuses, Fuseholders, and Adapters - Edison-Base Fuses:** (A) **Classification.**
	(B) **Replacement Only.**

Section	Highlight
240.83	**Part VII. Circuit Breakers - Marking:** (C) **Interrupting Rating.** …other than 5000 amperes.
	(D) **Used as Switches.**
240.100	**Part IX. Overcurrent Protection over 1000 Volts, Nominal - Feeders and Branch Circuits.**
	(1) **Overcurrent Relays and Current Transformers.** …a minimum of three overcurrent relay elements operated from three current transformers.
250.20	**Part II. System Grounding - Alternating-Current System to Be Grounded.**
	(A) **Alternating-Current Systems of Less Than 50 Volts.** Highlight (1) – (3).
250.21	**Alternating-Current Systems of 50 Volts to 1000 Volts Not Required to Be Grounded.**
250.22	**Circuits Not to Be Grounded.** The following circuits shall not be grounded: (1) – (6).
250.24	**Grounding Service-Supplied Alternating-Current Systems.**
	(A) **System Grounding Connections.**
250.28	**Main Bonding Jumper and System Bonding Jumper:** (D) **Size.**
250.52	**Part III. Grounding Electrode System and Grounding Electrode Conductor - Grounding Electrodes.**
	(A) **Electrodes Permitted for Grounding.**
	(1) **Metal Underground Water Pipe.**
	(2) **Metal In-ground Support Structure(s).**
	(3) **Concrete-Encased Electrode.**
	(4) **Ground Ring.**
	(B) **Not Permitted for Use as Grounding Electrodes.**
250.53	**Grounding Electrode System Installation:** (B) **Electrode Spacing.**
250.58	**Common Grounding Electrode.**
250.64	**Grounding Electrode Conductor Installation.**
	(A) **Aluminum or Copper-Clad Aluminum Conductors.**
	(B) **Securing and Protection from Physical Damage.**
250.66	**Size of Alternating-Current Grounding Electrode Conductor.** The size of the grounding…of a grounded or ungrounded ac system shall not be less than given in Table 250.66….
	Table 250.66 *Grounding Electrode Conductor for Alternating-Current Systems*
250.70	**Methods of Grounding and Bonding Conductor Connection to Electrodes.**

<u>Section</u>	<u>Highlight</u>
250.86	**Part IV. Enclosure, Raceways, and Service Cable Connections - Other Conductor Enclosures and Raceways.**
250.92	**Part V. Bonding – Services.** (A) **Bonding of Equipment for Services.**
250.96	**Bonding Other Enclosures:** (A) **General.**
250.102	**Grounding Conductor, Bonding Conductors, and Jumpers.**
250.104	**Bonding of Piping Systems and Exposed Structural Metal.**
250.114	**Part VI. Equipment Grounding and Equipment Grounding Conductors - Equipment Connected by Cord and Plug.** (3) In residential occupancies: a – e.
250.118	**Types of Equipment Grounding Conductors.**
250.119	**Identification of Equipment Grounding Conductors.**
250.120	**Equipment Grounding Conductor Installation.**
	(A) **Raceway, Cable Trays, Cable Armor, Cablebus, or Cable Sheaths.**
	(C) **Equipment Grounding Conductors Smaller Than 6 AWG.**
250.122	**Size of Equipment Grounding Conductors.**
	Table 250.122 *Minimum Size equipment Grounding Conductors for Grounding Raceways and Equipment*
250.124	**Equipment Grounding Conductor Continuity.**
250.126	**Identification of Wiring Device Terminals.** (3) A green pressure wire connector. If the…area adjacent to the terminal shall be similarly marked.
250.136	**Part VII. Methods of Equipment Grounding - Equipment Considered Grounded.**
	(A) **Equipment Secured to Grounded Metal Supports.**
250.138	**Cord-and-Plug Connected Equipment:** (A) **By Means of an Equipment Grounding Conductor.**
250.140	**Frames and Ranges and Clothes Dryers.**
	Exception: (2) The grounded conductor is not smaller than 10 AWG copper or 8 AWG aluminum.
250.148	**Continuity and Attachment of Equipment Grounding Conductors to Boxes.**
250.166	**Part VIII. Direct-Current Systems - Size of Direct Current Grounding Electrode Conductor:** (A) **Not Smaller Than the Neutral Conductor.**
250.174	**Part IX. Instruments, Meters, and Relays - Cases of Instruments, Meters, and Relays Operating at 1000 Volts or Less.**
280.4	**Part I. General - Surge Arrester Selection:** (A) **Rating.**
	(1) **Solidly Grounded System.**

Section	Highlight
280.12	**Part II. Installation - Uses Not Permitted.**
280.21	**Part III. Connecting Surge Arresters - Connection.** Highlight (1) – (4).
300.3	**Part I. General Requirements – Conductors:** (B) **Conductors of the Same Circuit.**
	(1) **Parallel Installations.**
300.4	**Protection Against Physical Damage:** (A) **Cables and Raceways Through Wood Members.**
	(1) **Bored Holes.**
	(2) **Notches in Wood.**
	(B) **Nonmetallic-Sheathed cables and Electrical Nonmetallic Tubing Through Metal Framing Members.**
	(2) **Nonmetallic-Sheathed Cable and electrical Nonmetallic Tubing.**
	(F) **Cables and Raceways Installed in Shallow Grooves.**
300.5	**Underground Installations:** (D) **Protection from Damage.**
	(1) **Emerging from Grade.**
	(H) **Bushing.**
	Table 300.5 *Minimum Cover Requirements, 0 to 1000 volts, Nominal, Burial in…(Inches)*
300.6	**Protection Against Corrosion and Deterioration:** (A) **Ferrous Metal Equipment.**
300.11	**Securing and Supporting:** (A) **Secured in Place.**
	(C) **Raceways Used as Means of Support.**
300.13	**Mechanical and Electrical Continuity – Conductors:** (B) **Device Removal.**
300.14	**Length of Free Conductors at Outlets, Junctions, and Switch Points.**
300.15	**Boxes, Conduit Bodies, or Fittings – Where Required.**
300.16	**Raceway or Cable to Open or Concealed Wiring:** (A) **Box, Conduit Body, or Fitting.**
	(B) **Bushing.**
300.19	**Supporting Conductors in Vertical Raceways:** (A) **Spacing Intervals – Maximum.**
300.20	**Induced Currents in Ferrous Metal Enclosures or Ferrous Metal Raceways.**
	(A) **Conductors Grouped Together.**
	(B) **Individual Conductors.**
300.21	**Spread of Fire or Products of Combustion.**

Section	Highlight
300.22	**Wiring in Ducts Not Used for Air Handling, Fabricated Ducts for Environmental Air…**
	(B) **Ducts Specifically Fabricated for Environmental Air.**
	(C) **Other Spaces Used for Environmental Air (Plenums).**
	Table 300.50 *Minimum Cover[a] Requirements*
310.15	**Part II. Installation - Ampacities for Conductors Rated 0-2000 Volts.**
	Table 310.15(B)(2)(a) ***Ambient Temperature Correction Based on 30°C (86°F)***
	Table 310.15(B)(16) *Allowable Ampacities of Insulated Conductors Rated Up to and Including 2000 Volts 60°C through 90°C…Based on Ambient Temperature of 30°C (86°F)**
	Table 310.15(B)(17) *Allowable Ampacities of Single-Insulated Conductors Rated Up to and Including 2000 Volts in Free Air, Based on Ambient Temperature of 30°C (86°F)**
312.2	**Part I. Scope and Installation - Damp and Wet Locations.**
312.6	**Deflection of Conductors:** (B) **Wire-Bending Space at Terminals.**
	(2) **Conductors Entering or Leaving Opposite Wall.**
	Table 312.6(A) *Minimum Wire-Bending Space at Terminals and Minimum Width of Wiring Gutters*
	Table 312.6(B) *Minimum Wire-Bending Space at Terminals*
314.2	**Part I. Scope and General - Round Boxes.**
314.3	**Nonmetallic Boxes:** *Exception No. 2.*
314.16	**Part II. Installation - Number of Conductors in Outlet, Device, and Junction Boxes, and Conduit Bodies.**
	(A) **Box Volume Calculations.**
	(B) **Box Fill Calculations.**
	Table 314.16(A) *Metal Boxes*
	Table 314.16(B) *Volume Allowance Required Per Conductor*
314.20	**Flush-Mounted Installations.**
314.21	**Repairing Noncombustible Surfaces.**
314.23	**Supports:** (D) **Suspended Ceilings.**
	(1) **Framing Members.**
314.27	**Outlet Boxes:** (B) **Floor Boxes.**

Section	Highlight
314.28	**Pull and Junction Boxes and Conduit Bodies:** (A) **Minimum Size.**
	(1) **Straight Pulls.**
320.30	**Part II. Installation - Securing and Supporting:** (B) **Securing.**
322.10	**Part II. Installation - Uses Permitted:** (1) As branch circuits…shall not exceed 30 amperes.
322.120	**Part III. Construction Specifications - Marking.** (A) **Temperature Rating.**
324.2	**Part I. General - Definitions: Bottom Shield.**
324.12	**Part II. Installation - Uses Not Permitted:** Highlight (1) – (5).
324.100	**Part III. Construction Specifications - Construction:** (A) **Type FCC Cable.**
326.24	**Part II. Installation - Bending Radius.**
326.112	**Part III. Construction Specifications - Insulation.**
330.24	**Part II. Installation - Bending Radius.**
	(A) **Smooth Sheath.** (2) Twelve times the external diameter of…(1½ in.) in external diameter.
334.2	**Part I. General - Definitions: Type NM.**
334.15	**Part II. Installation - Exposed Work:** (A) **To Follow Surface.**
	(B) **Protection from Physical Damage.**
	(C) **In Unfinished Basements and Crawl Spaces.**
334.23	**In Accessible Attics.**
334.24	**Bending Radius.**
334.30	**Securing and Supporting.**
334.80	**Ampacity.**
334.104	**Part III. Construction Specifications - Conductors.**
334.112	**Insulation.**
336.100	**Part III. Construction Specifications - Construction.**
336.104	**Conductors.**
342.30	**Part II. Installation -Securing and Supporting:** (A) **Securely Fastened.**
344.20	**Part II. Installation - Size:** (A) **Minimum.**
344.30	**Securing and Supporting.**
	Table 344.30(B)(2) *Supports for Rigid Metal Conduit*

Section	Highlight
348.12	**Part II. Installation - Uses Not Permitted:** Highlight (1) – (7).
	Table 348.22 *Maximum Number of Insulated Conductors in Metric Designator 12…*
350.30	**Part II. Installation - Securing and Supporting:** (A) **Securely Fastened.**
352.26	**Part II. Installation - Bends – Number in One Run.**
352.30	**Securing and Supporting:** (B) **Supports.**
352.44	**Expansion Fittings.**
	Table 352.30 *Support of Rigid Polyvinyl Chloride Conduit (PVC)*
356.12	**Part II. Installation - Uses Not Permitted.** (3) In lengths longer than 1.8 m (6 ft), except as…or where a longer length is approved as essential for a required degree of flexibility.
358.10	**Part II. Installation - Uses Permitted.**
358.12	**Uses Not Permitted.** (2) For the support of luminaires or…the largest trade size of the tubing.
358.20	**Size:** (A) **Minimum.**
	(B) **Maximum.**
358.26	**Bends – Number in One Run.**
358.28	**Reaming and Threading:** (B) **Threading.**
358.30	**Securing and Supporting:** (A) **Securely Fastened.**
362.12	**Part II. Installation - Uses Not Permitted.**
366.6	**Part I. General - Listing Requirements.**
366.22	**Part II. Installation - Number of Conductors:** (A) **Sheet Metal Auxiliary Gutters.**
366.30	**Securing and Supporting:** (A) **Sheet Metal Auxiliary Gutters.**
370.12	**Part II. Installation - Uses Not Permitted.**
374.12	**Part II. Installation - Uses Not Permitted.** Highlight (1) – (3).
374.20	**Size of Conductors.**
376.10	**Part II. Installation - Uses Permitted:** (1) For exposed work.
376.22	**Number of Conductors and Ampacity.**
376.56	**Splices, Taps, and Power Distribution Blocks.** (A) **Splices and Taps.**
378.30	**Part II. Installation - Securing and Supporting.** (A) **Horizontal Support.**
386.56	**Part II. Installation - Splices and Taps.**
390.3	**Use.** (B) **Not Permitted.**

Section	**Highlight**
390.6	**Maximum Number of Conductors in a Raceway.**
392.10	**Part II. Installation - Uses Permitted.** (A) **Wiring Methods.**
394.30	**Part II. Installation - Securing and Supporting.** (A) **Supporting.**
398.10	**Part II. Installation - Uses Permitted.** Highlight (1) – (4).
400.4	**Part I. General - Types.**
400.5	**Ampacities For Flexible Cords and Flexible Cables:** (A) **Ampacity Tables.**
400.10	**Uses Permitted:** (A) **Uses.** Highlight (1) – (11).
400.12	**Uses Not Permitted.**
400.31	**Part III. Portable Cables Over 600 Volts, Nominal - Construction:** (A) **Conductors.**
402.5	**Allowable Ampacities for Fixture Wires.**
	Table 402.5 *Allowable Ampacity for Fixture Wires*
404.2	**Part I. Installation - Switch Connections:** (A) **Three-way and Four-Way Switches.**
404.8	**Accessibility and Grouping:** (A) **Location.**
404.14	**Rating and Use of Switches.**
	(B) **Alternating-Current or Direct-Current General-Use Snap Switch.**
	(C) **CO/ALR Snap Switches.**
404.20	**Part II. Construction Specifications - Marking:** (A) **Ratings.**
406.3	**Receptacles, Cord Connectors, & Attachment Plugs (Caps) – Receptacle Rating and Type.**
	(B) **Rating.**
	(D) **Isolated Ground Receptacles.**
406.9	**Receptacles in Damp or Wet Locations:** (B) **Wet Locations.**
408.18	**Part II. Switchboards and Switchgear - Clearances:** (A) **From Ceiling.**
410.54	**Part VI. Wiring of Luminaries - Pendant Conductors for Incandescent Filament Lamps.**
	(A) **Support.**
422.10	**Part II. Installation - Branch-Circuit Rating:** (A) **Individual Circuits.**
422.12	**Central Heating Equipment.**
422.16	**Flexible Cords:** (B) **Specific Appliances.**
	(1) **Electrically Operated In-Sink Waste Disposers.**
	Exception: (2) The length of the cord shall not be less than (18 in.) and not over (36 in.).

Section	Highlight
424.3	**Part I. General - Branch Circuits:** (B) **Branch-Circuit Sizing.**
424.34	**Part V. Electric Space-Heating Cables - Heating Cable Construction.**
424.35	**Marking of Heating Cables.**
424.36	**Clearances of Wiring in Ceilings.**
430.6	**Part I. General - Ampacity and Motor Rating Determination.**
	(A) **General Motor Applications.**
	(B) **Torque Motors.**
430.9	**Terminals.**
430.10	**Wiring Space in Enclosures.**
430.13	**Bushing.**
430.22	**Part II. Motor Circuit Conductors - Single Motor.**
	(A) **Direct-Current Motor-Rectifier Supplied.**
430.24	**Several Motors or a Motor(s) and Other Load(s).**
430.32	**Part III. Motor and Branch-Circuit Overload Protection - Continuous-Duty Motors.**
430.52	**Part IV. Motor Branch-Circuit Short-Circuit and Ground-Fault Protection - Rating or Setting for Individual Motor Circuit.**
430.53	**Several Motors or Loads on One Branch Circuit:** (A) **Not Over 1 Horsepower.**
430.82	**Part VII. Motor Controllers - Controller Design:** (A) **Starting and Stopping.**
430.83	**Ratings:** (A) **General.**
	(2) **Circuit Breaker.**
	(C) **Stationary Motors of 2 Horsepower or Less.**
	Table 430.248 *Full-Load Currents in Amperes, Single-Phase Alternating-Current Motors*
	Table 430.250 *Full-Load Current, Three-Phase Alternating-Current Motors*
440.12	**Part II. Disconnecting Means - Rating and Interrupting Capacity.**
	(A) **Hermetic Refrigerant Motor-Compressor.**
	(1) **Ampere Rating.**
440.22	**Part III. Branch-Circuit Short-Circuit and Ground-Fault Protection - Application and Selection:** (A) **Rating or Setting for Individual Motor-Compressor.**
440.63	**Part VII. Provisions for Room Air Conditioners - Disconnecting Means.**

Section	Highlight
440.64	**Supply Cords.**
445.13	**Ampacity of Conductors.**
445.14	**Protection of Live Parts.**
450.3	**Part I. General Provisions - Overcurrent Protection.**
450.11	**Marking: (A) General:** Highlight: (1) – (8).
450.21	**Part II. Specific Provisions Applicable to Different Types of Transformers - Dry-Type Transformers Installed Indoors:** (A) **Not Over 112½ kVA.**
	(B) **Over 112½ kVA.**
450.47	**Part III. Transformer Vaults - Water Pipes and Accessories.**
455.7	**Part I. General - Overcurrent Protection.**
460.6	**Part I. 1000 Volts, Nominal, and Under - Discharge of Stored Energy.**
	(A) **Time of Discharge.**
	(B) **Means of Discharge.**
460.8	**Conductors.**
460.24	**Part II. Over 1000 Volts, Nominal - Switching:** (A) **Load Current.**
500.5	**Classification of Locations:** (B) **Class I Locations.**
	(1) **Class I, Division 1.**
	(C) **Class II Locations.**
	(2) **Class II, Division 2.**
	(D) **Class III Locations.**
500.6	**Material Groups:** (B) **Class II Group Classifications.**
500.7	**Protection Techniques.**
500.8	**Equipment.**
501.5	**Part I. General - Zone Equipment.**
501.10	**Part II. Wiring - Wiring Methods:** (A) **Class I, Division 1.**
	(1) **General.**
	(B) **Class I, Division 2.**
	(1) **General.** Highlight (1) – (8).

Section	Highlight
501.15	**Sealing and Drainage:** (A) **Conduit Seals, Class I, Division 1.**
	(B) **Conduit Seals, Class I, Division 2.**
	(C) **Class I, Division 1 and 2.**
502.15	**Part II. Wiring - Sealing, Class II, Division 1 and 2.**
502.100	**Part III. Equipment - Transformers and Capacitors.**
503.30	**Part II. Wiring - Grounding and Bonding – Class III, Divisions 1 and 2.**
511.3	**Area Classification, General.**
511.12	**Ground-Fault Circuit-Interrupter Protection for Personnel.**
514.3	**Classification of Locations.**
514.8	**Underground Wiring.** *Exception No. 2.*
514.11	**Circuit Disconnects.**
517.13	**Part II. Wiring and Protection - Grounding of Receptacles and Fixed Electrical Equipment in Patient Care Spaces.**
	(B) **Insulated Equipment Grounding Conductors and Insulated Equipment Bonding Jumpers.**
517.18	**General Care (Category 2) Spaces:** (A) **Patient Bed Location.**
	(B) **Patient Bed Location Receptacles.**
550.10	**Part II. Mobile and Manufactured Homes - Power Supply.**
550.18	**Calculations:** (A) **Lighting, Small-Appliance, and Laundry Load.**
	(1) **Lighting Volt-Amperes.**
550.31	**Part III. Services and Feeders - Allowable Demand Factors.**
551.71	**Part VI. Recreational Vehicle Parks - Type Receptacles Provided.**
555.15	**Grounding.**
555.19	**Receptacles.**
	(4) **Ratings.** (a) Receptacles rated 30 amperes and 50 amperes shall be of the locking and grounding type.
590.3	**Time Constraints:** (B) **90 Days.**
590.4	**General:** (D) **Receptacles.**
600.5	**Part I. General - Branch Circuits.**
600.6	**Disconnects.**

Section	Highlight
600.21	**Ballasts, Transformers, and Electronic Power Supplies and Class 2 Power Sources.**
645.5	**Supply Circuits and Interconnecting Cables:** (A) **Branch-Circuit Conductors.**
	(D) **Physical Protection.**
645.10	**Disconnecting Means.**
645.15	**Equipment Grounding and Bonding.**
680.2	**Part I. General - Definitions: Wet-Niche Luminaire.**
680.6	**Grounding.** Highlight (1) – (7).
	Table 680.9(A) *Overhead Conductor Clearances*
680.21	**Part II. Permanently Installed Pools - Motors:** (A) **Wiring Methods.**
	(3) **Cord-and-Plug Connections.**
680.22	**Lighting, Receptacles, and Equipment.**
680.23	**Underwater Luminaries.**
680.24	**Junction Boxes and Electrical Enclosures for Transformers or Ground-Fault Circuit Interrupters:** (A) **Junction Boxes.**
680.26	**Equipotential Bonding:** (B) **Bonded Parts.**
680.41	**Part IV. Spas and Hot Tubs - Emergency Switch for Spas and Hot Tubs.**
680.42	**Outdoor Installations.**
680.43	**Indoor Installations.**
700.2	**Part I. General - Definitions: Relay, Automatic Load Control.**
720.5	**Lampholders.** Standard lampholders that have a rating of not less than 660 watts shall be used.
720.6	**Receptacle Rating.** Receptacles shall have a rating of not less than 15 amperes.
725.1	**Part I. General - Scope.**
725.2	**Definitions:**
	Abandoned Class 2, Class 3, and PLTC Cable.
	Circuit Integrity (CI) Cable.
	Class 1 Circuit.
	Class 2 Circuit.
	Class 3 Circuit.

Section	Highlight
725.41	**Part II. Class I Circuits - Class 1 Circuit Classifications and Power Source Requirements.**
	(A) **Class 1 Power-Limited Circuits.** These circuits shall be supplied from a source that has a rated output of not more than 320 volts and 1000 volt-amperes.
	(1) **Class 1 Transformers.**
	(2) **Other Class 1 Power Sources.** Power sources other than transformers shall be protected by overcurrent devices rated at not more than 167 percent of the volt-ampere rating of the source divided by the rated voltage.
	(B) **Class I Remote-Control and Signaling Circuits.** These circuits shall not exceed 600 volts.
725.43	**Class 1 Circuit Overcurrent Protection**
725.45	**Class 1 Circuit Overcurrent Device Location:** (C) **Branch-Circuit Taps.**
725.49	**Class 1 Circuit Conductors.**
	(A) **Sizes and Use.** Conductors of sizes 18 AWG and 16 AWG shall be permitted to be used.
770.1	**Part I. General - Scope.**
800.1	**Part I. General - Scope.**
800.44	**Part II. Wires and Cables Outside and Entering Buildings - Overhead (Aerial) Communication Wires and Cables:** (A) **On Poles and In-Span.**
800.47	**Underground Communication Wires and Cables:** (B) **Underground Block Distribution.**
800.50	**Circuits Requiring Primary Protectors:** (A) **Insulation, Wires, and Cables.**
	(B) **On Buildings.**
800.53	**Lighting Conductors.**
800.90	**Part III. Protection - Protection Devices:** (A) **Application.**
800.93	**Grounding or Interruption of Non-Current-Carrying Metallic Sheath Members of Communications Cables.**
800.100	**Part IV. Grounding Methods - Cable and Primary Protector Bonding and Grounding.**
	(A) **Bonding Conductor or Grounding Electrode Conductor.**
	(3) **Size.**
800.133	**Part V. Installation Methods Within Buildings - Installation of Communications Wires, Cables, and Equipment.**
	(A) **Separation from Other Conductors.**
	Table 800.154(a) *Applications of Listed Communications Wires and Cables in Buildings*

Section	Highlight
800.179	**Communications Wires and Cables:** (A) **Type CMP.**
	(E) **Type CMX.**
810.13	**Part II. Receiving Equipment – Antenna Systems - Avoidance of Contacts with Conductors of Other Systems.**
810.16	**Size of Wire-Strung Antenna – Receiving Station:** (B) **Self-Supporting Antennas.**
810.18	**Clearances – Receiving Stations:** (A) **Outside Buildings.**
810.21	**Bonding, Conductors, and Grounding Electrode Conductors – Receiving Stations.**
	(H) **Size.**
	(J) **Bonding of Electrodes.**
820.100	**Part IV. Grounding Materials - Cable Bonding and Grounding.**
820.133	**Part V. Installation Methods Within Buildings - Installation of Coaxial Cables and Equipment:** (A) **Separation from Other Conductors.**
Chapter 9	**Table 4: Dimensions and Percent Area of Conduit and Tubing**
	Table 8: Conductor Properties
Annex C	**Table C.1** *Maximum Number of Conductors or Fixture Wires in Electrical Metallic Tubing (EMT) (Based on Chapter 9: Table 1, Table 4, Table 5)*

NRCA Roofing Manual: Membrane Roof Systems 2023
Tabs and Highlights

These 1 Exam Prep Tabs are based on the National Roofing Contractors Association (NRCA) manual listed below: *Membrane Roof Systems – 2023.*

Each Tabs sheet has five rows of tabs. Start with the first tab at the first row at the top of the page, and proceed down that row placing the tabs at the locations listed below. Place each tab in your book setting it down one notch until you get to the bottom of the page, and then start back at the top again. After you have completed tabbing your book (the last tab is usually the glossary, appendix, or index), then you may start highlighting your book.

******This concludes the tabs for this bookPlease continue with the highlights on the following page.******

Page # **Highlight**

12 **Roof assembly:** An assembly of interacting roof components including the roof deck, air or vapor retarder (if present), insulation and membrane or primary roof covering designed to weather proof a structure

12-13 **Roof systems:** A system of interacting roof components generally consisting of membrane or primary roof covering and roof insulation (not including the roof deck) designed to weatherproof the sometimes to improve the building's thermal resistance.

13 **Low-slope roof systems:** A category of roof systems that generally includes weatherproof membrane types of roof systems installed on slopes at or less than 3:12

Steep-slope roof systems: A category of roof systems that generally includes water-shedding types of roof coverings installed on slopes greater than 3:12

15 **CHAPTER 1 – ROOF ASSEMBLY CONFIGURATIONS:** Roof assembly configurations are designated in the following order: project type, roof covering type, number of plies or layers (if applicable) attachment method (if applicable) and substrate type. Following is a description of these categories and the options listed under each category. *Highlight all of the following and become familiar with each one.*

- **Project Type:** There are three project types: new construction or roof replacement, roof re-cover and temporary roof, new construction or roof replacement and roof re-cover are included for every roof covering type.

16

- **Roof Covering Type**
- **Number of Plies or Layers**
- **Attachment Method**
- **Substrate Type:**

  - Nonnailable deck
  - Insulated deck
  - Nailable deck
  - Steel deck

81 **CHAPTER 2 – ROOF DECKS:** The following types of roof decks are addressed in this manual: *Highlight six (6) bullet points and become familiar with* **Cementitious wood fiber panels, Lightweight insulating concrete, Steel, Structural concrete (cast-in-place, post-tensioned and precast-prestressed), Wood panels (plywood, oriented strand board)** *and* **Wood planks and wood boards**

2.1 – Guidelines Applicable to All Roof Deck Types

82 **Structural Support:** A roof deck transfers live and dead loads to supporting framing members (e.g. joists, purlins, subpurlins). Live loads include environmental loads, such as wind, snow, rain and ice, and other nonstationary loads such as workers and mobile installation equipment.

Dead loads include stationary loads, such as topside and underside mechanical equipment, weight of the deck, any sheathing overlayment, roof membrane, insulation and ballast.

Page # **Highlight**

Roof Expansion Joints: Roof expansion joints are used to minimize the elects of stresses and movements of a building's components and to limit the effects of and potential for theses stresses to cause splitting, buckling/ridging or damage to a roof system. *Highlight four (4) bullet points and become familiar with* **The building's thermal movement characteristic, The structural supports and roof deck, The roof system selected** *and* **The climatic conditions**

83 **Slope and Drainage:** For new construction projects, *The International Building Code, 2021 Edition* indicates a design minimum slope of 1/4:12 is required for membrane roof systems, except for coal tar built-up roof systems where a design minimum slope of 1/8:12 is permitted.

84 The criterion for judging proper slope for drainage is that there be no ponding water on the roof 48 hours after a rain during conditions conducive to drying.

Slope generally is provided by: *Highlight four (4) bullet points and become familiar with* **Sloping the structural framing or roof deck, Designing a tapered insulation system, Proper location of roof drains, scuppers and gutters** *and* **A combination of the above**

Drains should be located at low points in a roof (points of maximum deck deflection), not a column or bearing walls (points of minimum deflection).

85 **Electrical Conduits and Other Piping:** If metallic conduit or wiring needs to be placed near the roof assembly, NRCA recommends it be positioned and supported at least 1½ inches from the bottom side of the roof deck or substrate to which the roof system is applied.

86 **Additional Insulation and Consideration for a Vapor Retarder:** Based on the dew-point calculation and to limit possible condensation and premature degradation of materials, a designer should consider provisions for a vapor retarder.

2.2 – Cementitious Wood Fiber Panels: Cementitious wood fiber panels intended as roof decks provide for structural support of the roof system and can provide for a finished interior ceiling surface that has acoustical properties.

87 **Vertical Alignment:** Elevation differences in excess of 1/8 of an inch between panels are considered unacceptable. Uneven joints of 1/8 of an inch or more should be grouted with the grout feathered to a slope of 1/8 of an inch per foot.

Attachment of Roof System Components: NRCA does not recommend directly adhering a base sheet, rigid board insulation or roof membrane to cementitious wood fiber panels without installing a mechanically fastened base sheet or other separator layer.

88 **2.3 – Lightweight Insulating Concrete:** Lightweight-aggregate insulating concrete and lightweight-cellular insulating concrete are used as a fill material, usually to add slope to drain or as a topping over another substrate, such as a corrugated metal form deck, structural concrete deck, wood deck or other structural components.

89 **Design:** NRCA recommends lightweight insulating concrete roof decks be a minimum of 2 inches thick, not including the thickness of any form board or other underlying substrate.

91 **Attachment of Roof System Components:** NRCA does not recommend the use of seam-fastened, mechanically attached single-ply membranes over lightweight insulating concrete roof decks because of the potential for fastener holes to reduce a lightweight insulating concrete roof deck's structural integrity and alignment of fastener penetrations, likely resulting in significant loss of the roof deck's structural integrity.

Page #	Highlight
92	**2.4 – Steel:** Steel roof decks are constructed of cold-rolled steel sheets or panels with ribs formed in each panel to provide strength and rigidity. The panels are available in several gauges, rib depths, flute spacings and yield strengths.
	Narrow-rib Steel Deck (Type A): A steel deck panel with a rib-width opening of 1inch maximum. See Figure 2-2.
	Intermediate-rib Steel Deck (Type F): A steel deck panel with a rib-width opening of 1 inch to 1¾ inch. See Figure 2-3.
	Wide-rib Steel Deck (Type B): A steel deck panel with a rib-width opening of 1¾ inches to 2 5/8 inches. See Figure 2-4.
	Deep-rib Steel Deck (Type 3DR): A steel deck panel with rib-width opening of 1½ inch to 2¾ inches and a rib depth of 3 inches minimum. See Figure 2-5.
93	**Design:** Most conventional steel deck panels are fabricated from steel with a minimum yield strength of 33 ksi or Grade 33 steel.
94	NRCA recommends steel roof decks be 22-gauge or heavier and have a minimum G-90 galvanized coating complying with ASTM A653.
	End Laps and Side Laps: Deck panel end laps should not be less than 2 inches and should be centered over structural supports. All side laps should be mechanically fastened. Side-lap fastener spacing should not exceed 3 feet.
	Deck Attachment:
97	SDI permits powder-actuated fasteners, pneumatically driven fasteners or screws instead of welding to fasten steel decks to supporting framing if fasteners meet project strength and service requirements.
98	Also, ANSI/SDI RD-2010 specifies the following dimensional tolerances for steel roof deck panels: *Highlight five (5) bullet points and become familiar with each one.*
99	**Attachment of Roof System Components:** Rigid board insulation should be applied in a minimum of two layers to minimize gaps and thermal breaks at board joints.
100	NRCA does not recommend the use of low-rise foam or liquid-applied adhesive as the primary means of attaching rigid board insulation to steel roof decks.
	2.5 – Structural Concrete: There are two general types of structural concrete used in roof decks: normal- weight structural concrete and light-weight structural concrete. • **Normal-weight Structural Concrete:** Steel reinforcing bars and/or steel wire mesh are used to reinforce the concrete. The density of reinforced, normal-weight structural concrete generally is about 150 pounds per cubic foot. • **Lightweight Structural Concrete:** Lightweight structural concretes have densities ranging from 95 to 120 pounds per square foot, about 80 percent of the density of normal-weight structural concrete.
	The most commonly used lightweight aggregate is expanded shale.

Page # **Highlight**

101 The three general installation types for structural concrete roof decks are cast-in-place, post-tensioned and precast-prestressed. *Highlight headings and become familiar with* **Cast-in-place Concrete, Post-tensioned Concrete** *and* **Precast-prestressed Concrete**

102 **Precast-prestressed Concrete:** The prestressing process generally results in upward deflection, also called "camber", which precast member at center of the span above the elevation of the supports. See Figure 2-9.

103 **Design:** Also, designers need to consider additional factors when using structural concrete roof decks, including drainage, curing and drying, high-humidity areas, roof openings, and weather and temperature.

Curing and Drying:

104 Normal-weight and lightweight structural concrete contain significant amounts of water when mixed, formed and poured, and finished. As concrete cures and hardens, it consumes large amount of this water through hydration and evaporation. For example, a 4-inch-thick concrete slab of normal weight concrete will release about 1 quart of water for each square foot of surface area.

105 Until recognized pass-fail criteria applicable for determining concrete's internal humidity is developed, NRCA suggests a maximum 75% relative humidity value be used; lower values may be necessary when using organic-based materials, such as wood fiberboard, perlite board and some insulation facer sheets - as roof system components.

Attachment of Roof System Components: Structural concrete roof decks are considered to be "nonnailable"; that is, mechanical fasteners such as screws and plates and nails are not used to attach rigid board insulation, base sheets or membrane components.

106 NRCA recommends designers specify a separator layer or rigid board insulation over a structural concrete roof deck before installing a single-ply membrane over the deck.

2.6 Wood Panels: There are two general types of wood panels used for roof decks: Plywood and oriented strand board (OSB).

Panels consists of a number of cross-laminated layers that vary in number according to the panel's thicknesses.

OSB panels are composed of layers of compressed, glued wood strands.

Design:

107 When plywood is used as a roof deck material, NRCA recommends the use of a minimum of four ply, 15/32-of-an-inch-thick or four-ply, nominal ½-of-an-inch-thick plywood for 16-inch joist or rafter spacings, and four-ply, nominal 5/8-of-an-inch-thick plywood for 24-inch joist or rafter spacings.

When OSB is used as a roof deck material, a minimum of 15/32-of-an-inch-thick OSB is recommended for 16-inch rafter spacings and nominal 5/8-of-an-inch-thicknesse OSB for 24-inch rafter spacings.

Generally, unless a panel manufacturer recommends otherwise, spacing between panel edges is recommended to be about 1/8 of an inch.

Page #	Highlight
108	**Fire-retardant-treated Panels:** NRCA does not recommend using FRT wood as a roof deck material.

Attachment of Roof System Components:

109 Built-up and polymer-modified bitumen membranes should not be adhered directly to wood panel roof decks.

NRCA does not recommend the torch application of polymer-modified bitumen membrane sheets directly to combustible substrates, such as wood panel roof decks.

Liquid-applied membrane roof systems should not be adhered directly to wood panel roof decks.

2.7 – Wood Planks and Wood Boards: Wood plank and wood board roof decks are composed of solid-sawn dimensional lumber. They are typically supported by wood beams, glue-laminated timber (glulams), and/or solid lumber joists or purlins.

113 **CHAPTER 3 – AIR AND VAPOR RETARDERS:** NRCA defines the terms "air retarder" and "vapor retarder" as follows:

Air retarder: A material or system in building construction designed and installed to reduce air leakage either into or through the opaque wall

Vapor retarder: A material or system that significantly impedes the transmission of water vapor under specified conditions

114 **3.1 – Air Retarders – Terminology:** The term "air barrier" often is used when referring to preventing or controlling air leakage through a building's envelope.

In building, in reality, it is virtually impossible to create an absolute barrier from all air leakage. For this reason, NRCA considers the term "air barrier" to be a misnomer. In this manual, NRCA has adopted and will use the term "air retarder" for what some will refer to as an "air barrier."

Following is additional terminology applicable to air retarders: *Highlight seven (7) bullet points and become familiar with* **Air leakage, Air infiltration, Air retarder, Air retarder system, Continuity, Air retarder accessary** *and* **Air leakage rate**

Fundamental concepts:

115 To be considered an effective air retarder material, the air permeance for that material has been established by some building and energy codes as no greater than 0.004 cubic foot per minute per square foot (cfm/ft^2) at a pressure difference of 0.3 inches of water.

116 **Roof Membrane Air Retarders:** For example, IECC and ASHRA 90.1 recognize the following types of roof systems as deemed-to-comply air retarder materials: *Highlight four (4) bullet points and become familiar with* **Built-up membranes, Polymer-modified bitumen membranes, Single-ply membranes** *and* **1.5 lbs./ft^3 density closed-cell spray foam, minimum 1½ inches thick**

The deemed-to-comply option's criteria for closed-cell spray foam, minimum 1.5 pcf density, minimum 1½ inches thick, can be interpreted to include spray polyurethane foam (SPF) roof systems.

NRCA Recommendations:

Page # **Highlight**

117 NRCA considers a continuous, air-impermeable roof membrane to function as an air retarder. Examples of continuous, air-impermeable roof membranes include built-up, polymer-modified bitumen and single-ply membrane roofing systems.

122 **3.2 – Vapor Retarders**

Vapor Retarder Design: The materials used to construct vapor retarders in roof assemblies using membrane roof systems may be classified into two broad categories: *Highlight two (2) bullet points and become familiar with* **Bituminous vapor retarders** *and* **Plastic sheet or film vapor retarders**

Bituminous Membrane Vapor Retarders: Bituminous membrane vapor retarders are the most commonly used type of vapor retarders.

Such a vapor retarder provides a perm rating that approaches 0 perms.

Plastic Sheet or Film Vapor Retarders: Depending on material type and thickness, permeance of these plastic sheets or film retarders ranges from approximately 0.04 to 0.50 perms.

127 **Selecting Vapor Retarder Materials:** The term "vapor retarder" refers to a broad range of materials used to control the flow of moisture vapor from the interior of building into the roof system. The following are important considerations when selecting a vapor retarder*: Highlight four (4) bullet points and become familiar with* **Roof deck type and possible puncture damage, Sandwich-type vapor retarder construction, Insulation type, Securement** *and* **Compliance with fire- and wind-resistance classifications**

129 **CHAPTER 4 – RIGID BOARD INSULATION:** The purpose of roof insulation is to provide a substrate for the application of a roof membrane and thermal resistance.

4.1 – Guidelines Applicable to All Insulation Types: Roof insulation that is properly manufactured, designed and installed serves several vital purposes: *Highlight six (6) bullet points and become familiar with.*

For example:

130

- While reducing the potential for interior moisture condensation, rigid roof insulation sandwiched between a roof deck and roof membrane can increase the probability of condensation occurring within the roof system.

Desirable Properties of Roof Insulation: An ideal roof insulation would have the following properties. *Highlight ten (10) bullet points and become familiar with* **Compatibility with bitumen and other adhesives, Component compatibility, Impact resistance, Fire resistance, Moisture resistance, Thermal resistance, Stable R-value, Attachment capability, Dimensional stability** *and* **Compressive strength**

132 **Principles of Thermal Insulation:** The primary function of insulation is to provide thermal resistance. Heat is a form of energy, and energy can be measured using a British thermal unit (Btu). A Btu is defined as the energy required to raise the temperature of 1 pound of water 1 degree Fahrenheit.

Page # **Highlight**

132-133 **Terminology:** *Highlight four (4) bullet points and become familiar with* **Thermal conductivity (k), Thermal conductance (C), Thermal resistance®** *and* **Thermal transmittance (U or U-factor)**

133 The following table provides a range of U-factor values and corresponding total assembly R-values.

Table with **U-factor values** *and* **corresponding total Assembly R-values**

137 **Multilayer Insulation:** In low-slope membrane roof system construction, use of two or more layers of continuous rigid board insulation with joints staggered between layers is an energy code requirement.

139 **4.2 – Cellular Glass:** The following properties of cellular-glass roof insulation make it an effective insulating material: *Highlight nine (9) bullet points and become familiar with these properties.*

140 **R-value:** Cellular-glass roof insulation has an R-value of 3.44 per inch thickness tested at a 75 F mean temperature. Cellular-glass roof insulation is recognized for having a stable R-value.

Combustibility: Cellular-glass roof insulation is noncombustible. It can be exposed directly to hot bitumen, torch flame or high temperatures, such as those produced by hot-air welders.

141 **4.3 – Expanded Polystyrene (EPS):** The following recognized properties of expanded polystyrene insulation make it an effective insulating material: *Highlight all seven (7) bullet points and become familiar with these properties.*

Typically, expanded polystyrene insulation is used in walls and roofs of commercial, industrial and residential buildings.

Product Standard: When expanded polystyrene insulation is used, NRCA recommends designers specify expanded polystyrene insulation with a compressive strength appropriate for specific project conditions.

143 **Compatibility:** Expanded polystyrene insulation is affected by exposure to the sun, organic solvents and some adhesives.

Application and Securement:

Nailable Roof Decks: NRCA does not recommend direct mechanical fastening for the attachment of expanded polystyrene roof insulation without the use of a cover board.

145 **4.4 – Extruded Polystyrene:** The following recognized properties of polystyrene board roof insulation make it an effective insulating material: *Highlight seven (7) bullet points and become familiar with these properties.*

Typically, extruded polystyrene insulation is used in buildings with low-temperature interior spaces, such as refrigeration rooms, and in walls and roofs of other commercial, industrial and residential buildings.

147 **Application and Securement**

Nailable Roof Decks: NRCA does not recommend direct mechanical fastening for the attachment of expanded polystyrene roof insulation without the use of a cover board.

Page # **Highlight**

149 **4.5 – Glass-faced Gypsum:** Although glass-faced gypsum is not typically classified as an insulating product, information about glass-faced gypsum is included here because glass-faced gypsum is used in roof assemblies as a thermal barrier to provide fire resistance, substrates for air and vapor retarders, and cover boards beneath roof membranes.

R-value: Glass-faced gypsum has R-values based upon thicknesses as follows.

Highlight Table **Glass-faced Gypsum**

150 **Combustibility:** Glass-faced gypsum boards are noncombustible. Gypsum boards are inherently fire-resistant because of gypsum calcination.

151 **4.6 – Fiber-reinforced Gypsum:**

R-value: Fiber-reinforced gypsum has R-values based upon thicknesses as follows. *Highlight Table* **Fiber-reinforced Gypsum**

153 **4.7 – Stone Wool:** Stone wool insulation intended for roofing purposes is manufactured as a rigid insulating material. It is manufactured using rock and slag as base ingredients. Natural mineral materials are combined, heated until molten and then spun into a fibrous material that is often referred to as stone wool. The stone wool fibers are bound together with a binding agent to form a rigid insulation board.

155 **4.8 – Perlite:** Perlite board insulation intended for roofing purposes is a rigid insulating material manufactured from expanded volcanic minerals combined with organic fivers and binders. The top surface of perlite board roof insulation is generally treated with an asphalt emulsion to minimize bitumen absorption. The common R-value used to calculate the total thermal resistance of a perlite board roof insulation system is 2.78 per inch of thickness.

157 **4.9 – Polyisocyanurate:**

158 **R-value:**

159 NRCA recommends designers specifying polyisocyanurate insulation determine roof system thermal resistance using an in-service R-value of 5.0 per inch.

163 **4.11 – Wood Fiberboard:** The common R-value used to calculate the total thermal resistance of a wood or cane fiberboard insulation system is about 2.78 per inch of thickness.

164 Wood-fiber "sheathing" boards generally do not possess sufficient physical properties to be suitable for use as roof insulation.

R-value: The common R-value used to calculate the total thermal resistance of a wood or cane fiberboard insulation system is about 2.78 per inch of thickness.

165 **4.12 – Cement Board**

166 **R-value:** Cement board does not contribute significant thermal resistance when used a part of roof assemblies.

172 **4.15 – Tapered Insulation:** Tapered insulation can be used to meet the requirements for slope in new construction and reroofing projects, as well as in cases where a roof deck will not provide adequate slope to drain water off a roof surface.

Page #	Highlight
	Although the primary reason for using tapered roof insulation is to improve slope and promote drainage, there are other advantages: *Highlight two (2) bullet points.*
173	**Thermal Insulation Value:** Minimum R-value: The minimum R-value approach establishes R-value for a tapered roof insulation system by determining the R-value of the tapered material at the thinnest point in the tapered system layout.
174	Average R-value: The average R-value approach establishes the R-value for a tapered roof insulation system by determining the R-value of the tapered material at the representative average thickness in the tapered system layout. • Arithmetic Average Thickness Method: Arithmetic average thickness is the thickness of tapered and flat stock insulation at the midpoint between the minimum thickness (i.e., low point) and the maximum thickness (i.e., high point) in a tapered insulation system. See Figure 4-5.
176	**Design:** Tapered insulation layouts should be designed to form a sump that measures the size of the drain bowl's diameter plus approximately 24 inches at roof drains, and crickets should be installed on the high sides of all roof curbs.
	Slope Pattern:
177	A general rule of thumb for designing sufficiently sloping saddles and crickets is the saddle/cricket material be twice the slope of the adjacent field of the roof, resulting in the final slope of the saddle/cricket being equal to that of the adjacent field of the roof. The maximum slope of saddle/cricket material is ½:12.
179	**Hips and Valleys:** When using performed tapered insulation boards of one consistent slope, all valley centerlines should be 45 degrees from the direction of slope, that is, the valley centerlines are 90 degrees apart.
185	**CHAPTER 5 – ROOF MEMBRANES:** Most low-slope roof membranes have two principal components: weatherproofing layer or layers and reinforcement.
	The weatherproofing component is the most important element within a roof membrane because it keeps water from entering a roof assembly.
	The reinforcement adds strength, puncture resistance and dimensional stability to a membrane.
	This chapter describes four types of common roof membranes: built-up membranes, polymer-modified bitumen sheet membranes, single-ply membranes, and liquid-applied membranes.
186	**5.1 – Guidelines Applicable to All Membrane Types - Slope and Drainage:** For new construction projects, *The International Building Code, 2021 Edition* indicates a design minimum slope of ¼:12 is required for membrane roof systems, except for coal tar built-up roof systems where a design minimum slope of ⅛:12 is permitted.
	Slope generally is provided by: *Highlight the five (5) bullet points.*
187	**Weather Conditions During Application:** When membrane roofing materials are applied, entrapment of moisture should be prevented. Moisture in or on materials may cause membrane blistering. If precipitation occurs before completely installing the roof membrane, the membrane surface in the immediate work area and the substrate should be dried or allowed to dry before work resumes.

Page # **Highlight**

5.2 – Built-up Roof Membranes: A built-up roof membrane, sometimes referred to as BUR, consists of multiple layers of saturated felts, coated felts, fabrics or mates assembled in place shingle fashion with alternate layers of bitumen and surfaced with mineral aggregate, bituminous materials, a liquid-applied coating or a granule-surfaced cap sheet.

188 The principal components used in constructing built-up roof membranes are: *Highlight four (4) bullet points and become familiar with* **Bitumens, Reinforcement layers, such as felts and ply sheets, Membrane flashings and Accessories.**

Bitumens: Asphalts have excellent resistance to moisture, good resistance to weathering and excellent cohesive and adhesive characteristics. These properties also make asphalts useful as adhesives for adhering rigid board insulation and applying surfacings.

Many coal tar built-up membranes remain in service, but coal tar is no longer widely used for built-up roof membrane construction.

Cold-applied Asphalt Adhesives: These liquid versions of asphalt are referred to as "cutbacks". Cutting the asphalt back with solvents makes it possible to apply the weatherproofing asphalt material with heating it in a kettle or tanker.

190 **Hot-applied Asphalt:** For most roof system applications, including the construction of built-up membrane roof systems, oxidized asphalt bitumens are used.

ASTM D312, "Standard Specification for Asphalt Used in Roofing," classifies asphalt into four different types based on the asphalt's softening point, penetration (hardness) and ductility. The following table lists the ranges of softening point values for the four types of asphalt defined by ASTM D312.

Highlight Table **Asphalt Softening Point**

An asphalt's penetration value is used as a measure of consistency (relative hardness).

An asphalt's ductility value provides one measure of an asphalt's tensile properties and can be used as a measure of ductility for specification requirements.

191 *Highlight Table* **Asphalt Penetration**

Highlight Table **Asphalt Ductility**

The 2015 edition of ASTM D312, designated as ASTM D312-15, revised the minimum FP temperature for asphalt used in roofing from 500 F to 575 F. As a result, ASTM D312 now indicates a maximum heating temperature for asphalt as 550 F.

For mechanical spreader application of asphalt, EVT has been established as the temperature at which the asphalt has a viscosity of 75 cP.

Highlight Table **Asphalt EVT Values**

192 NRCA recommends at the point of application asphalt be within a ±25 F range from an asphalt's initial EVT.

Asphalt complying with ASTM D312, Type III is generally appropriate for interplay moppings in built-up membrane application where the slope of the completed membrane is 1:12 or less. Use of asphalt complying with ASTM D312, Type V is suggested for slopes greater than 1:12.

Page # **Highlight**

Hot-Applied Polymer-modified Asphalt: This polymer-modified asphalt is made from standard roofing asphalt modified by the addition of styrene ethylene butadiene styrene. (SEBS)

ASTM D6152 specifies a 500 F minimum FP temperature; however, actual FP temperatures in excess of this value are desirable and common.

NRCA recommends kettle and tanker temperatures be maintained lower than 25 F below the asphalt's actual FP temperature and never heated to or above the actual FP temperature.

193 **Reinforcement Felts and Sheets:** Roll-roofing materials used as reinforcement inbuilt-up roof membrane construction fall into three categories: *Highlight the three (3) bullet points and become familiar with* **Base sheets, Ply sheets** *and* **Mineral-surfaced cap sheet**

Base Sheets: Base sheets work well to separate roof systems from substrates. When mechanically attached, a base sheet can serve as a separation layer or adhesive bond break between a roof deck and roof system so the roof system may move thermally, independently from the roof deck.

194 **Ply Sheets:** Ply sheets are installed directly over base sheets or over rigid board insulation as interplay sheets in built-up roof membranes. Historically, ply sheets have been either fiberglass-mat or organic-mat reinforced.

Asphalt-coated Polyester and Fiberglass-mat Sheets: Asphalt-coated polyester and fiberglass-mat sheets may be used as ply sheets, including flashing applications.

Ply sheets are produced in a standard width of 36 inches and metric width of about 1 meter (39⅜ in.).

196 **Membrane Flashings:** Membrane flashings are used to terminate a built-up roof membrane at a roof's perimeter and at roof penetrations. Membrane flashings typically consist of a base or backer layer or layers and a cap sheet.

SBS Polymer-modified Bitumen Base Sheets: Several types of bituminous roofing sheets are becoming more commonly used as multiple-ply membrane flashings in built-up roof systems and base plies in polymer-modified bitumen roof systems. Among the most common are several styrene butadiene styrene (SBS) polymer-modified asphalt base sheets.

197 **Liquid-applied flashings:** Liquid-applied flashings commonly are used in situations where penetrations or surfaces are irregularly shaped and difficult to flash using a membrane flashing.

Rosin-sized Sheathing Paper: One purpose of the rosin sheathing paper is to prevent the first ply of felt from adhering to wood decking. Another purpose is to prevent bitumen from dripping through some roof decks. Additionally, rosin sheathing paper will prevent contact between fresh wood resin and asphalt ply sheets, where the wood resin may act as a solvent to soften the asphalt and adhere to the wood deck.

198 **Application of Built-up Membrane Materials:** A complete built-up membrane roof system may include a slip sheet; air retarder or vapor retarder; rigid board roof insulation; cover board; interplay bitumen or adhesive; and layers of base sheet, ply sheet, cap sheet or other roof surfacing option.

Fasteners for Built-up Roof Membranes: Large-head, annular-threaded nails; barbed; ring-shank nails; or specifically approved mechanical fasteners should be used to fasten base sheets for built-up roof membranes to nailable decks, for back-nailing and to fasten base flashings in built-up roof membranes.

Page # **Highlight**

199 **Bitumen Heating:** The following guidelines apply to the heating of bitumen: *Highlight seven (7) bullet points and become familiar with each.*

Membrane Application: On low-slope roofs, roof membrane plies should be applied so the slow of water runoff will not be against the laps. When possible, all plies should be installed in shingle fashion. When slopes are greater than 2:12, consideration should be given to laying the felts parallel to the slope. This application method, consisting of plies laid parallel to the slope, is referred to as "strapping the plies" and also may be used on slopes less than 2:12.

200 **5.3 – Polymer-modified Bitumen Roof Membranes:** Polymer-modified roof membranes are composed of reinforcing fabrics, usually polyester, fiberglass or both, that serve as the carriers for the polymer- modified bitumen as it is manufactured into a roll material. The purposes for reinforcements in polymer-modified bitumen sheets essentially are the same as felts in built-up roof membranes. The reinforcements help keep the bitumen in place within the sheet, provide tensile strength and allow for varying degrees of sheet elongation.

201 Generally, APP polymers modify the asphalt to give the resultant material a "plasticized" nature. SBS polymers modify the asphalt to give the resultant material a "rubberized" nature.

The principal components used in constructing polymer-modified bitumen roof membranes are: *Highlight five (5) bullet points and become familiar with* **Adhesives, Base layer, such as a base sheet or interplay sheets, Polymer-modified bitumen cap sheet, Membrane flashings** *and* **Accessories**

205 **Interply Sheets:** In place of single-layer base sheets, the following sheets, sometimes referred to as "interply sheets", are often used in multiple layers beneath APP or SBS polymer-modified bitumen sheets.

205-207 *Highlight the four (4) bullet points and become familiar with* **Asphalt, Fiberglass Ply Sheet, APP Polymer-modified Interply Sheets, SBS Polymer-modified Bitumen Interply Sheets** *and* **Self- adhering Polymer-modified Bitumen Interply Sheets**

207 **Polymer-modified Bitumen Membrane Cap Sheet:** All polymer-modified bitumen-coated sheets are factory-coated on one or both sides with polymer-modified bitumen. Some sheets are surfaced on one or both sides with fine materials, such as sand, mica or talc, that serve as parting agents and prevent adhesion of the material while in roll form. Some manufacturers use liquid parting agents, and others use plastic films either removed by hand or intended to be burned off during the installation.

209 **Accessories:** Accessory products commonly used when constructing polymer-modified bitumen roof membranes include roof cements, adhesives and asphalt core board.

210 **Asphalt Core Board:** Asphalt core boards may be installed over structural substrates, rigid board insulation and existing roof membranes to provide substrates for torch-applied, hot mopped, cold adhesive applied and self-adhering asphalt-based membranes. Once the adhesive cures or cools to ambient temperature, the asphalt core boards become fused with the membrane.

210-211 Asphalt core board for roof system applications typically is available as 4- by 4-foot, 4- by 5-foot and 4- by 8-foot panels that are 1/8-of-an-inch, 3/16-of-an-inch, ¼-of-an-inch or ½-of-an-inch in thickness.

212 **Torch-applied Application:** NRCA recommends against specifying torch-applied polymer-modified bitumen membranes over combustible substrate roof decks, even where a thermal barrier insulation layer has been laid over the combustible roof deck. NRCA considers the potential fire risk associated with torch-applied application over combustible roof decks to outweigh any advantages torch application provides.

213 **Membrane Application:**

213-214 Blisters have been reported in some SBS polymer-modified bitumen membrane systems. Most have involved installation with hot asphalt and occurred between the cap sheet and base sheet or ply sheets. Application factors that can contribute to blistering include insufficient asphalt temperature at the point of application, long mop lead and lack of cap sheet embedment into the asphalt mopping.

215 **5.4 – Single-ply Roof Membranes:** There are two principal types of materials used in the construction of single-ply roof membranes: thermoset polymer sheets and thermoplastic polymer sheets. The terms describe the materials' different behaviors on heating that arise from their different molecular arrangements and chemical properties.

Currently, EPDM sheets are the only thermoset materials commonly used in construction of single-ply roof membranes in the North American market.

216 There are four common subcategories of thermoplastic membranes: *Highlight all four (4) bullet points and become familiar with* **PVC, PVC alloys, including copolymer alloy, ethylene interpolymer and nitrile alloy, Ketone ethylene ester,** *and* **TPO.**

Ethylene Propylene Diene Terpolymer (...; EPDM): EPDM is a synthetic rubber material that can be formulated with extensive flexibility for use as membrane roofing.

EPDM membranes exhibit good resistance to ozone, ultraviolet (UV) rays, weathering and abrasion. EPDM also has good low-temperature flexibility. EPDM is resistant to same acids; alkalis; and oxygenated solvents, such as ketones, esters and alcohols. On the other hand, exposure to aromatic, halogenated and aliphatic solvents, as well as animal and vegetable oils and petroleum-based products, should be avoided to prevent membrane swelling and distortion.

The most common thicknesses of EPDM single-ply roofing sheet materials are 45 mils and 60 mils.

217 **PVC:** PVC Sheets are resistant to bacterial growth, many industrial chemical atmospheres and plant-root penetration. Properly formulated, PVC sheets are fire-resistant and have hot-air welding seaming characteristics. PVC sheets are chemically incompatible with bituminous materials and as such, should be separated from asphalt products.

218 NRCA recommends designers specify PVC sheets with a minimum thickness of 45 mils for use in conventional single-ply roof systems.

PVC Alloys: PVC alloys compound various polymers with PVC. Sheets produced with PVC alloys are somewhat akin to PVC sheets in that they, too, are thermoplastic in nature; however, each has its own unique properties. PVC alloy materials manufactured for use as roof membranes typically are produced as reinforced sheets.

219 **Ketone Ethylene Ester:** KEE sheets generally are resistant to certain chemicals, air-conditioning coolants, jet fuels and restaurant grease, as well as UV radiation, airborne bacteria, acid rain and industrial pollutants.

Page # **Highlight**

They are compatible with asphalt and generally are white or light gray but also can be produced in custom colors.

220 **TPO:** TPO sheets are compounded from a blend of polypropylene and ethylene-propylene rubber polymers. Flame retardants, pigments, UV absorbers and other proprietary ingredients may be included in TPO sheet formulations.

Application of Single-ply Membranes: Single-ply membrane roof systems are typically designed and installed in three configuration types: loose-laid ballasted, mechanically attached and adhered.

Single-ply sheets should be unrolled and allowed time to relax and lie flat before application. Manufacturers commonly indicate a minimum period of 30 minutes for this.

221 **Loose-laid, Ballasted:** Loose-laid, ballasted systems seldom require field-membrane securement other than perimeter and base flashing attachment. As the system's name implies, the weight of the ballast and the force of gravity serve to secure the entire roof system.

The most common application rate for aggregate or stone ballast is 1,000 pounds to 1,200 pounds per 100 square feet for 1½ -inch to ¾-of-an-inch round, river-washed gravel designated as Size Number 4 in ASTM D7655.

221-222 **Mechanically Attached:** Mechanically attached systems use a variety of fasteners and fastening patterns to secure a membrane to a substrate. Among these methods are metal disks placed within a seam and attached through a membrane to a roof deck; metal or plastic bars placed within a seam and attached through a membrane to a roof deck; metal and plastic disks and/or bars placed over a membrane and covered with membrane stripping; polymer-coated metal disks used with fasteners to attach rigid board insulation to roof decks and heat welded to the underside of thermoplastic membranes using electromagnetic induction welding equipment; and other specialized proprietary securement systems.

224 **Heat Induction Welding:** An alternative method of attachment of single-ply roof membranes is heat welding a thermoplastic single-ply roof membrane to specially coated fastening plates using an electromagnetic heat-induction-welding tool.

227 Air Intrusion:

228 Air intrusion has significance for roof assembly performance for two primary reasons. It contributes to mechanical fatigue of roof assembly components, including field membrane, flashings, mechanical attachment components and roof deck. It also provides a mechanism for depositing excess moisture inside a roof assembly.

Adhered: Adhered membrane systems are generally applied using a liquid-applied contact adhesive. Some membranes are made with a factory-laminated fleece backing that allows adhesion with alternative types of adhesives, such as hot asphalt and low-rise polyurethane foam.

229 Depending on the liquid carrier(s) used, cold-applied single-ply roof membrane adhesives currently available can be placed into one of three categories: *Highlight all four (4) bullet points and become familiar with* **Volatile organic compound solvent- based adhesives, Low-VOC (also known as VOC-exempt solvent-based) adhesives, Water-based adhesives,** *and* **Self-adhering sheets.**

Page # **Highlight**

232 **5.5 – Liquid-applied Roof Membranes:** Liquid-applied roof membranes are constructed in place from a liquid resin and reinforcing material. The liquid resin is available as a one- or two-component product and is typically applied in two coats. Depending on the resin chemistry, a catalyst or hardener may be added to induce the curing process. In most instances, a primer is required.

234 **Application:** Liquid-applied roof membranes should be installed as continuously as possible. To do this, it is important wood nailers, curbs, drains and other penetrations be in place before roofing.

237 **CHAPTER 6 – ATTACHMENT - Design Considerations:** These characteristics are a function of the substrate type and strength and the fastener's size, shank, point or tip type, and thread design. The corrosion resistance of a fastener should also be considered, along with its desired service life, which should be equivalent to that of the roof system. A fastener should be compatible with the material being secured and the substrate into which it is embedded. The shear strength and tensile strength of a fastener also are important considerations.

238 **Fasteners and Preservative-treated Wood:** NRCA is of the opinion the corrosion-related concerns regarding the use of currently available preservative-treated wood possible outweigh the benefits that preservative-treated wood provides as a component in roof assemblies. In many instances, nontreated, construction-grade wood is suitable for use in roof assemblies as blocking or nailers provided reasonable measures are taken to ensure the nontreated wood remains reasonable dry when in service.

239 **6.1 – Base Sheet Fasteners – Material Types:** A majority of fasteners are fabricated from hardened carbon steel or stainless steel. Often, such designations as 1022 for carbon steel and 304 for stainless steel are included and refer to properties such as alloys, strength and corrosion resistance. Fasteners are often surfaced (or coated) with various corrosion-resistant coatings, such as zinc, epoxy, fluorocarbons or other proprietary materials. In some cases, fasteners are fabricated plastics, such as glass-reinforced nylon and other polymer materials. Fasteners made of metal are thermal bridges.

6.2 – Insulation Fasteners

241 **Fastener Spacing:** Because center-to-center metal rood deck rib spacing typically is 6 inches, the spacing for insulation fasteners typically is some multiple of 6 inches.

242 **6.3 – Membrane Fasteners**

247 **Fastener Spacing:** Spacing between the rows of fasteners and fastener spacing within the rows are two parameters that determine uplift resistance. Common fastener spacing with a row is 6 inches and 12 inches. See Figure 6-9 on page 248. Some common field-sheet row spacings are 6½ feet, 7 feet, 8 feet and 10 feet.

253 **CHAPTER 7 – SURFACINGS:** Membrane surfacing is the component that protects the weatherproofing component of some roof systems from the effects of direct sunlight, ultraviolet rays and weather exposure. Some surfacings provide other benefits, such as increased fire resistance, improved traffic and hail resistance, and aesthetic properties.

254 **7.1 – Guidelines Applicable to All Surfacing Types**

- Emittance, Thermal: The ratio of the radiant heat flux emitted by a sample to that emitted by a blackbody radiator at the same temperature.
- Reflectance, Solar: The ratio of the reflected solar flux to the incident solar flux.

Page # **Highlight**

- Solar Reflectance Index (SRI): A calculated value that combines solar reflectance and thermal emittance into a single metric as specified by ASTM E1980. Values typically range from 0 to 100, with especially dark or reflective products exceeding these bounds.

255 **7.2 – Aggregate:** When aggregate is used to surface a built-up roof system, it generally is for the following reasons: *Highlight all seven (7) bullet points.*

256 *Highlight Table* **Aggregate Gradation Amounts Finer than Sieve Specified, Mass Percent**

7.3 – Ballast: When single-ply membrane sheets are used in loose-laid, ballasted configurations, the surfacing commonly used are rounded aggregate or concrete roof pavers. Generally, ballasted roof systems are limited to roods with slopes of 2:12 or less.

258 **7.4 – Coatings:** A roof coating is a fluid material applied in the field as a film to the roof surface to provide weather protection to the original roof membrane. A coating protects the roof substrate from weather (solar radiation, heat and moisture) and determines its radiative properties.

260 **Roof Coating Characteristics:** When properly designed and installed, roof coatings can: *Highlight all eight (8) bullet points.*

Roof Coating Types: Most roof coatings consist of two general components:

- Primer
- Coating

Primer: Primers are intended to prepare a roof surface for accepting a coating and improve the overall adhesion of the coating to the substrate.

261 **Coatings:** The coating material itself is the topmost surface of the coating system application and the layer that provides the primary characteristic of the coating.

266 **Coating Application:** The three common application methods for roof coatings are:

- Airless Spray
- Roller
- Brush or broom

267 ***Figure 7-5: General guideline for primer and coating selection***

268 **Brush or Broom:** Most coatings should not be broom-applied.

Weather Conditions: Wind preferably should be less than 6 mph. Ambient temperatures should be moderate, with most coating applications specified to be conducted between 40 F and 100 F depending on manufacturers' recommendations.

271 **CHAPTER 8 – ROOF ACCESSORIES:** Examples of premanufactured accessories that may be encountered on a membrane roof system include. *Highlight five (5) bullet points.*

- Equipment curbs
- Expansion joint covers
- Skylights and roof/smoke hatches
- Prefabricated pipe flashings
- Pipe support systems

Page # **Highlight**

8.1 – Equipment Curbs

272 NRCA recommends a minimum of 24 inches of clearance between walls and curbs and minimum 12 inches of clearance between pipes and curbs.

For most membrane roof systems, equipment curbs should be detailed and constructed to a height of 8 inches above the finished roof membrane.

8.2 – Expansion Joint Covers: NRCA considers raised curb type expansion joints to be preferred, though for ballasted single-ply membrane roof systems, low-profile expansion joints in the same plane as the roof membrane are considered acceptable.

272-273 For most membrane roof systems, expansion joints should be detailed and constructed to a height of 8 inches above the finished roof membrane.

273 **8.3 – Skylights and Roof/Smoke Hatches:** Skylights and hatches should be installed with curbs tall enough to allow for an 8-inch vertical flashing height.

273-274 **8.4 – Prefabricated Pipe Flashings:** Pre-molded pipe flashings – commonly referred to as flashing boots or collars – are often used in single-ply membrane roof systems for sealing pipes or irregularly shaped penetrations.

274 NRCA recommends a minimum of 12 inches of clearance between pipes and a minimum 12 inches of clearance between pipes and curbs or walls.

For most membrane roof systems, pipe flashings should be detailed and constructed to a height of 8 inches above the finished roof membrane.

8.5 – Pipe Support Systems: It is common for the roofing contractor to be responsible for installation of pipe support systems in reroofing scenarios.

277 **CHAPTER 9 – REROOFING**

278 **9.1 – Definitions:** *Highlight five (5) bullet points and become familiar with* **Reroofing, Re-covering, Replacement, Roof assembly** *and* **Roof system.**

279

- **Low-slope roof systems:** A category of roof systems that generally includes weatherproof membranes types of roof systems installed on slopes of 3:12 or less
- **Steep-slope roof systems:** A category of roof systems that generally includes water-shedding types of roof coverings installed on slopes greater than 3:12

9.2 – Evaluation of Existing Roof Systems

279-280 **Interior Inspection:** An evaluation of an existing roof system for the purpose of determining whether to re-cover or replace it should include a visual inspection of the interior of the building in the area underneath the roof area being considered.

281 **Hidden Conditions**

282 NRCA does not recommend metallic conduit or wiring be embedded within roof assemblies or placed directly below roof decks. If metallic conduit or siring needs to be placed near the roof assembly, NRCA recommends it be positioned and supported at least 1½ inches from the bottom side of the roof deck or substrate to which the roof system is applied.

Page # **Highlight**

283 **Roof System Inspection:** Inspection of the roof system should include evaluation of installed materials, as well as design, and should take account of: *Highlight all seven (7) bullet points and become familiar with* **Perimeter edge-metal flashings, Penetrations, Roof surface condition, Drainage and slope, Roof system composition, Moisture with the existing roof assembly** *and* **Rooftop mechanical equipment**

284 **Moisture with the Existing Roof Assembly:** When evaluating moisture content of roof assemblies, nondestructive moisture evaluation techniques should be considered. Nondestructive moisture evaluation techniques include infrared thermography, neutron (nuclear) thermalization and electrical capacitance.

285 **Other Leak Sources:** There are many building components that may be sources for leakage, including: *Highlight all eleven (11) bullet points.*

286 Reuse of existing metal flashing materials only is permitted when the materials' remaining service life of the new roof system.

287 **Cementitious Wood Fiber Panels:**

Roof Replacement Considerations: When existing toggle bolts and auger-type fasteners are removed, NRCA recommends installation of a new structural roof deck because the structural capacity of the cementitious wood fiber roof deck can be reduced by the voids left by the removed fasteners.

288 **Vertical Alignment:** Elevation differences in excess of 1/8 of an inch between panels are considered unacceptable. Uneven joints of 1/8 inch or more should be grouted with the grout feathered to a slope of 1/8 of an inch per foot.

Lightweight Insulating Concrete:

Roof Replacement Considerations:

289 Securing a replacement roof system over an aged lightweight insulating concrete deck with new lightweight insulating concrete fasteners can be considered if the replacement roof system-specific pullout resistance can be achieved. NRCA suggests a minimum of four tests per continuous pour area be conducted when determining fastener withdrawal resistance for lightweight insulating concrete decks.

Steel:

Roof Replacement Considerations: NRCA is concerned with the structural capacity and potential fastener-holding power of steel roof decks lighter than 22 gauge (0.028 inches thick).

290 Installing new steel deck without removing the existing metal deck is called nesting. Nesting can be accomplished by using the same type and grade of steel or a steel roof deck with narrower flutes so the new deck fits into the existing deck.

291 **Lightweight Structural Concrete:**

Roof Replacement Considerations:

Page #	Highlight
292	For prestressed or post-tensioned concrete decks, drilling into the deck can be detrimental to the load-bearing capacity of the deck because to the possibility of severing a tension cable. NRCA does not recommend attaching the roof insulation or membrane to prestressed or pos-tensioned concrete decks with mechanical fasteners.
	Curing and Drying: Sealing the concrete's moisture into the deck by using a high-bond strength vapor retarder adhered directly to the deck followed by an adhered roof system is another option. A high-quality, 12- to 15- mil thick two-part epoxy has successfully been used as a vapor retarder in the flooring industry.
	Wood Panels:
	Roof Replacement Considerations:
293	NRCA does not recommend installing roof systems over structural wood panel roof decks, such as plywood and OSB, that re less than 15/32 of an inch thick.
294	Use of nominal 6-inch-wide wood boards is suggested for roof decks to prevent excessive movement and splitting. Boards thinner than nominal 1 inch are not considered strong enough to support roof loads.
	Roof Replacement Considerations: NRCA does not recommend installing roof systems over wood board roof decks with less than ¾ of an inch minimum thickness.
	Gypsum - Poured Gypsum:
295	Three general requirements are: *Highlight all three (3) bullet points.*
	Roof Replacement Considerations
296	If the existing roof system was sprinkle- or strip-mopped to the deck, the removal process may only cause minor damage to the deck. If the exiting roof was solid-mopped, the removal process may cause major damage to the deck. If major damage occurs, consideration should be given to replacing the roof deck or using a re-cover system.
	Thermal-setting Insulating Fill:
297	**Roof Replacement Considerations:** In a roof replacement situation, reusing thermal-setting insulating fill is generally not practical because a new roof system cannot be mechanically attached to it, and adequate adhesion typically cannot be achieved to provide for adequate uplift resistance of the new roof system.
298	**9.6 – Re-cover Guidelines for Membrane Roof Systems:** The following is a list of general recommendations for re-covering over an existing roof system with a new built-up, polymer-modified bitumen, single-ply or liquid-applied membrane roof system: *Highlight five (5) bullet points.*
299	**9.7 – Design Guidelines for Roof Replacement with New Membrane Roof Systems**
	Fire Resistance: An in-depth review of the code's criteria for classifying construction types is beyond the scope of this manual. The following brief descriptions provide a general idea of the classifications: *Highlight four (4) bullet points and become familiar with* **Type IA, IB, IIA, IIB, Types IIIA and IIIB, Type IV** *and* **Types VA and VB**

Page #	Highlight

300 **Condensation Control:** When designing a replacement roof system, one or more of the following considerations may need to be addressed with regard to its water vapor transport performance: *Highlight four (4) bullet points.*

301 **Perimeter Edge-metal Flashings:** Because of unknow attachment methods, NRCA suggests existing perimeter edge-metal flashings not be reused.

302 **Roof Curbs and Equipment Supports:** Figure 9-5 provides NRCA's guidelines for clearance for equipment support stands.

Figure 9-4: NRCA guidelines for clearance for equipment support stands

Pipe Penetrations: Different types of pipe penetrations require different methods of flashing during reroofing projects. *Highlight three (3) bullet points.*

305 **CHAPTER 10 – CONSTRUCTION DETAILS:** In this chapter, construction details are provided for the following membrane roof system types: *Highlight and become familiar with* **Built-up membrane, Polymer-modified bitumen membrane, EPDM membrane, Thermoplastic membrane** *and* **Liquid-applied membrane**

307 **Wood Nailers and Blocking:** Among other advantages, the nailers provide protection for the edges of rigid board insulation and provide a substrate for anchoring flashing materials. Wood nailers should be a minimum of 2 x 6 nominal-dimension lumber.

309 **Penetrations and Clearance:** The maximum amount of space should be provided between pipes, walls and curbs to facilitate proper installation of membranes and flashings. NRCA recommend a minimum of 12 inches of clearance between pipes, a minimum of 12 inches of clearance between pipes and curbs or walls, and a minimum of 24 inches of clearance between walls and curbs.

313 **Combustible Substrates:** Lumber and wood fiberboard cant strips are generally not considered to be noncombustible. NRCA suggest the use of noncombustible perlite, stone wool or other similar noncombustible material for cant strips.

317 **Independent Securement of Mechanically Attached Single-ply Roof Membranes:** For mechanically attached single-ply membrane roof systems, NRCA suggest the designer consider the inclusion of a mechanically fastened batten bar or plates approximately 6 inches to 12 inches away from the outside edge of the roof system, drain sumps, curbs and penetrations as independent membrane securement. This is commonly referred to as a peel-stop.

324 **Drains and Drain Sumps:** Drain sumps should be square or rectangular and typically are 4 feet or 8 feet per side where premanufactured sump insulation is used. NRCA suggest drain sump dimensions not be less than the drain bowl diameter plus 24 inches to allow for correct drain flashing installation.

325-326 **Crickets and Saddles:** To help reduce the amount of residual surface water between drains, behind curbs and along roof edges between scuppers, NRCA recommend installing crickets and saddles. Figure 10-13 and Figure 10-14 on pages 327-328 provide additional information regarding cricket and saddle slope and length-to-width ratios.

332 **EPDM Membrane Corner Flashings:** For flashing inside corners, it is suggested field membranes be used to bridge the roof-to-wall transition to provide a continuous wall flashing. Figure 10-17 on pages 337-339 illustrates the sequencing of steps for this technique.

NRCA Roofing Manual: Membrane Roof Systems 2019 Tabs and Highlights

These 1 Exam Prep Tabs are based on the National Roofing Contractors Association (NRCA) manual listed below: *Membrane Roof Systems – 2019.*

Each Tabs sheet has five rows of tabs. Start with the first tab at the first row at the top of the page, and proceed down that row placing the tabs at the locations listed below. Place each tab in your book setting it down one notch until you get to the bottom of the page, and then start back at the top again. After you have completed tabbing your book (the last tab is usually the glossary, appendix, or index), then you may start highlighting your book.

1 Exam Prep Tab	**Page #**
Table of Contents	7
Roof Assembly Configs	15
Roof Decks	77
Air & Vapor Retarders	109
Rigid Board Insulation	121
Roof Membranes	171
Polymer-modified Bitumen	185
Single-Ply Roof Membranes	201
Fasteners	219
Surfacings	233
Roof Accessories	251
Reroofing	257
Index of Construction Details	287
Appendix	545
Wind Uplift	547
Chemical Comp. of Roof Membranes	557
Temp. Roof Systems	561
Flood Testing	**563**
Bldg. Code Compliance	**563**

******This concludes the tabs for tis book. Please continue with the highlights on the following page.******

A.M. 03/25/2021

Page# **Highlight**

12 **Roof assembly:** An assembly of interacting roof components including the roof deck, air or vapor retarder (if present), insulation and membrane or primary roof covering designed to weather proof a structure

13 **Roof systems:** A system of interacting roof components generally consisting of membrane or primary roof covering and roof insulation (not including the roof deck) designed to weatherproof the sometimes to improve the building's thermal resistance

Low-slope roof systems: A category of roof systems that generally includes weatherproof membrane types of roof systems installed on slopes at or less than 3:12

Steep-slope roof systems: A category of roof systems that generally includes water-shedding types of roof coverings installed on slopes greater than 3:12

15 **CHAPTER 1 – ROOF ASSEMBLY CONFIGURATIONS:** Roof assembly configurations are designated in the following order: project type, roof covering type, number of plies or layers (if applicable) attachment method (if applicable) and substrate type. Following is a description of these categories and the options listed under each category. *Highlight all of the following and become familiar with each one.*

- **Project Type:** There are three project types: new construction or roof replacement, roof re-cover and temporary roof, new construction or roof replacement and roof re-cover are included
16 for every roof covering type.
- **Roof Covering Type**
- **Number of Plies or Layers**
- **Attachment Method**
- **Substrate Type:**

  - Nonnailable deck
  - Insulated deck
  - Nailable deck
  - Steel deck

77 **CHAPTER 2 – ROOF DECKS:** The following types of roof decks are addressed in this manual: *Highlight six (6) bullet points and become familiar with* **Cementitious wood fiber panels, Lightweight insulating concrete, Steel, Structural concrete (cast-in-place, post-tensioned and precast-prestressed), Wood panels (plywood, oriented strand board)** *and* **Wood planks and wood boards**

78 **2.1 – Guidelines Applicable to All Roof Deck Types - Structural Support:** A roof deck transfers live and dead loads to supporting framing members (e.g. joists, purlins, subpurlins). Live loads include environmental loads, such as wind, snow, rain and ice, and other nonstationary loads such as workers and mobile installation equipment.

Dead loads include stationary loads, such as topside and underside mechanical equipment, weight of the deck, any sheathing overlayment, roof membrane, insulation and ballast.

Roof Expansion Joints: Roof expansion joints are used to minimize the elects of stresses and movements of a building's components and to limit the effects of and potential for theses stresses to cause splitting, buckling/ridging or damage to a roof system. *Highlight four (4) bullet points and become familiar with* **The building's thermal movement characteristic, The structural supports and roof deck, The roof system selected** *and* **The climatic conditions**

Page# **Highlight**

79 **Slope and Drainage:** For new construction projects, *The International Building Code, 2018 Edition* indicates a design minimum slope of 1/4:12 is required for membrane roof systems, except for coal tar built-up roof systems where a design minimum slope of 1/8:12 is permitted.

80 The criterion for judging proper slope for drainage is that there be no ponding water on the roof 48 hours after a rain during conditions conducive to drying.

Slope generally is provided by: *Highlight four (4) bullet points and become familiar with* **Sloping the structural framing or roof deck, Designing a tapered insulation system, Proper location of roof drains, scuppers and gutters** *and* **A combination of the above**

Drains should be located at low points in a roof (points of maximum deck deflection), not a column or bearing walls (points of minimum deflection).

82 **Electrical Conduits and Other Piping:** If metallic conduit or wiring needs to be placed near the roof assembly, NRCA recommends it be positioned and supported at least 1½ inches from the bottom side of the roof deck or substrate to which the roof system is applied.

Additional Insulation and Consideration for a Vapor Retarder: Based on the dew-point calculation and to limit possible condensation and premature degradation of materials, a designer should consider provisions for a vapor retarder.

2.2 – Cementitious Wood Fiber Panels: Cementitious wood fiber panels intended as roof decks provide for structural support of the roof system and can provide for a finished interior ceiling surface that has acoustical properties.

83 **Vertical Alignment:** Elevation differences in excess of 1/8 of an inch between panels are considered unacceptable. Uneven joints of 1/8 of an inch or more should be grouted with the grout feathered to a slope of 1/8 of an inch per foot.

84 **Attachment of Roof System Components:** NRCA does not recommend the use of seam-fastened, mechanically attached single-ply membranes over cementitious wood fiber panel roof decks because of the potential for fastener holes to reduce a cementitious wood fiber panel roof deck's structural integrity and alignment of fastener penetrations likely resulting in significant loss of the roof deck's structural integrity.

2.3 – Lightweight Insulating Concrete: Lightweight-aggregate insulating concrete and lightweight-cellular insulating concrete are used as a fill material, usually to add slope to drain or as a topping over another substrate, such as a corrugated metal form deck, structural concrete deck, wood deck or other structural components.

85 **Design:** NRCA recommends lightweight insulating concrete roof decks be a minimum of 2 inches thick, not including the thickness of any form board or other underlying substrate.

87 **Attachment of Roof System Components:** NRCA does not recommend directly adhering base sheets, rigid board insulation or roof membrane to lightweight insulating concrete roof decks without installing a mechanically fastened venting base sheet or other coated base sheet separator.

88 **2.4 – Steel:** Steel roof decks are constructed of cold-rolled steel sheets or panels with ribs formed in each panel to provide strength and rigidity. The panels are available in several gauges, rib depths, flute spacings and yield strengths.

Narrow-rib Steel Deck (Type A): A steel deck panel with a rib-width opening of 1inch maximum. See **Figure 2-2**.

Page#	Highlight
	Intermediate-rib Steel Deck (Type F): A steel deck panel with a rib-width opening of 1 inch to 1¾ inch. See **Figure 2-3**.
	Wide-rib Steel Deck (Type B): A steel deck panel with a rib-width opening of 1¾ inches to 2 5/8 inches. See **Figure 2-4**.
	Deep-rib Steel Deck (Type 3DR): A steel deck panel with rib-width opening of 1½ inch to 2¾ inches and a rib depth of 3 inches minimum. See **Figure 2-5**.
89	**Design:** Most conventional steel deck panels are fabricated from steel with a minimum yield strength of 33 ksi or Grade 33 steel.
	NRCA recommends steel roof decks be 22-gauge or heavier and have a minimum G-90 galvanized coating complying with ASTM A653.
	End Laps and Side Laps: Deck panel end laps should not be less than 2 inches and should be centered over structural supports. All side laps should be mechanically fastened. Side-lap fastener spacing should not exceed 3 feet.
90	**Deck Attachment – SDI Guidelines:** SDI permits powder-actuated fasteners, pneumatically driven fasteners or screws instead of welding to fasten steel decks to supporting framing if fasteners meet project strength and service requirements.
94	Also, ANSI/SDI RD-2010 specifies the following dimensional tolerances for steel roof deck panels: *Highlight five (5) bullet points and become familiar with each one.*
95	**Attachment of Roof System Components:** Rigid board insulation should be applied in a minimum of two layers to minimize gaps and thermal breaks at board joints.
95 & 96	NRCA does not recommend the use of low-rise foam or liquid-applied adhesive as the primary means of attaching rigid board insulation to steel roof decks.
96	**2.5 – Structural Concrete:** There are two general types of structural concrete used in roof decks: normal- weight structural concrete and light-weight structural concrete. • **Normal-weight Structural Concrete:** Steel reinforcing bars and/or steel wire mesh are used to reinforce the concrete. The density of reinforced, normal-weight structural concrete generally is about 150 pounds per cubic foot (pcf). • **Lightweight Structural Concrete:** Lightweight structural concretes have densities ranging from 95 to 120 pounds per square foot, about 80 percent of the density of normal-weight structural concrete. The most commonly used lightweight aggregate is expanded shale.
97	The three general installation types for structural concrete roof decks are cast-in-place, post-tensioned and precast-prestressed. *Highlight headings and become familiar with* **Cast-in-place Concrete, Post-tensioned Concrete** *and* **Precast-prestressed Concrete**
98	**Precast-prestressed Concrete:** The prestressing process generally results in upward deflection, also called "camber", which precast member at center of the span above the elevation of the supports. See **Figure 2-9**.
99	**Design:** Also, designers need to consider additional factors when using structural concrete roof decks, including drainage, curing and drying, high-humidity areas, roof openings, and weather and temperature.

Curing and Drying: Normal-weight and lightweight structural concrete contain significant amounts of water when mixed, formed and poured, and finished. As concrete cures and hardens, it consumes large amount of this water through hydration and evaporation. For example, a 4-inch-thick concrete slab of normal weight concrete will release about 1 quart of water for each square foot of surface area.

101 Until recognized pass-fail criteria applicable for determining concrete's internal humidity is developed, NRCA suggests a maximum 75 percent relative humidity value be used; lower values may be necessary when using organic-based materials, such as wood fiberboard, perlite board and some insulation facer sheets, as roof system components.

Attachment of Roof System Components: Structural concrete roof decks are considered to be "nonnailable"; that is, mechanical fasteners such as screws and plates and nails are not used to attach rigid board insulation, base sheets or membrane components.

NRCA recommends designers specify a separator layer or rigid board insulation over a structural concrete roof deck before installing a single-ply membrane over the deck.

102 **2.6 Wood Panels:** There are two general types of wood panels used for roof decks: Plywood and oriented strand board (OSB).

Panels consists of a number of cross-laminated layers that vary in number according to the panel's thicknesses.

OSB panels are composed of layers of compressed, glued wood strands.

Design: When plywood is used as a roof deck material, NRCA recommends the use of a minimum of four ply, 15/32-of-an-inch-thick or four-ply, nominal ½-of-an-inch-thick plywood for 16-inch joist or rafter spacings, and four-ply, nominal 5/8-of-an-inch-thick plywood for 24-inch joist or rafter spacings.

103 When OSB is used as a roof deck material, a minimum of 15/32-of-an-inch-thick OSB is recommended for 16-inch rafter spacings and nominal 5/8-of-an-inch-thicknesse OSB for 24-inch rafter spacings.

Generally, unless a panel manufacturer recommends otherwise, spacing between panel edges is recommended to be about 1/8 of an inch.

104 **Fire-retardant-treated Panels:** NRCA does not recommend using FRT wood as a roof deck material.

Attachment of Roof System Components: Built-up and polymer-modified bitumen membranes should not be adhered directly to wood panel roof decks.

NRCA does not recommend the torch application of polymer-modified bitumen membrane sheets directly to combustible substrates, such as wood panel roof decks.

105 Liquid-applied membrane roof systems should not be adhered directly to wood panel roof decks.

2.7 – Wood Planks and Wood Boards: Wood plank and wood board roof decks are composed of solid-sawn dimensional lumber. They are typically supported by wood beams, glue-laminated timber (glulams), and/or solid lumber joists or purlins.

Page# **Highlight**

Use of nominal 6-inch-wide wood boards is suggested for roof decks to prevent excessive movement and splitting. Boards thinner than nominal 1 inch are not considered strong enough to support roof loads.

109 **CHAPTER 3 – AIR AND VAPOR RETARDERS:** NRCA defines the terms "air retarder" and "vapor retarder" as follows:

Air retarder: A material or system in building construction designed and installed to reduce air leakage either into or through the opaque wall

Vapor retarder: A material or system that significantly impedes the transmission of water vapor under specified conditions

110 **3.1 – Air Retarders – Terminology:** In this manual, NRCA has adopted and will use the term "air retarder" for what some will refer to as an "air barrier." Following is additional terminology applicable to air retarders: *Highlight seven (7) bullet points and become familiar with* **Air leakage, Air infiltration, Air retarder, Air retarder system, Continuity, Air retarder accessary** *and* **Air leakage rate**

111 **Fundamental concepts:** To be considered an effective air retarder material, the air permeance for that material has been established by some building and energy codes as no greater than 0.004 cubic foot per minute per square foot (cfm/ft^2) at a pressure difference of 0.3 inches of water.

112 **Roof Membrane Air Retarders:** For example, IECC and ASHRA 90.1 recognize the following types of roof systems as deemed-to-comply air retarder materials: *Highlight four (4) bullet points and become familiar with* **Built-up membranes, Polymer-modified bitumen membranes, Adhered single-ply membranes** *and* **1.5 pcf density closed-cell spray foam, minimum 1½ inches thick**

The deemed-to-comply option's criteria for closed-cell spray foam, minimum 1.5 pcf density, minimum 1½ inches thick, can be interpreted to include spray polyurethane foam (SPF) roof systems.

NRCA Recommendations: NRCA considers a continuous, air-impermeable roof membrane to function as an air retarder. Examples of continuous, air-impermeable roof membranes include built-up, polymer-modified bitumen and single-ply membrane roofing systems.

118 **3.2 – Vapor Retarders:** The materials used to construct vapor retarders in roof assemblies using membrane roof systems may be classified into two broad categories: *Highlight two (2) bullet points and become familiar with* **Bituminous vapor retarders** *and* **Plastic sheet or film vapor retarders**

Bituminous Membrane Vapor Retarders: Bituminous membrane vapor retarders are the most commonly used type of vapor retarders.

Such a vapor retarder provides a perm rating that approaches 0 perms.

Plastic Sheet or Film Vapor Retarders: Depending on material type and thickness, permeance of these plastic sheets or film retarders ranges from approximately 0.04 to 0.50 perms.

Selecting Vapor Retarder Materials: The term "vapor retarder" refers to a broad range of materials used to control the flow of moisture vapor from the interior of building into the roof system. The following are important considerations when selecting a vapor retarder*: Highlight four (4) bullet points and become familiar with* **Roof deck type and possible puncture damage, Sandwich-type vapor retarder construction, Insulation type, Securement** *and* **Compliance with fire- and wind-resistance classifications**

Page#	Highlight

121 **CHAPTER 4 – RIGID BOARD INSULATION:** The purpose of roof insulation is to provide a substrate for the application of a roof membrane and thermal resistance.

4.1 – Guidelines Applicable to All Insulation Types: Roof insulation that is properly manufactured, designed and installed serves several vital purposes: *Highlight six (6) bullet points and become familiar with*. For example:

122

- While reducing the potential for interior moisture condensation, rigid roof insulation sandwiched between a roof deck and roof membrane can increase the probability of condensation occurring within the roof system.

Desirable Properties of Roof Insulation: An ideal roof insulation would have the following properties. *Highlight ten (10) bullet points and become familiar with* **Compatibility with bitumen and other adhesives, Component compatibility, Impact resistance, Fire resistance, Moisture resistance, Thermal resistance, Stable R-value, Attachment capability, Dimensional stability** *and* **Compressive strength**

123 **Usage Guidelines:** In low-slope membrane roof system construction, use of two or more layers of rigid board insulation is preferred. (*4th Bullet*)

125 **Principles of Thermal Insulation:** The primary function of insulation is to provide thermal resistance. Heat is a form of energy, and energy can be measured using a British thermal unit (Btu). A Btu is defined as the energy required to raise the temperature of 1 pound of water 1 degree Fahrenheit.

125 & 126 **Terminology:** *Highlight four (4) bullet points and become familiar with* **Thermal conductivity (k), Thermal conductance (C), Thermal resistance®** *and* **Thermal transmittance (U or U-factor)**

126 The following table provides a range of U-factor values and corresponding total assembly R-values.

127 *Table with* **U-factor values** *and* **corresponding total Assembly R-values**

130 **4.2 – Cellular Glass:** The following properties of cellular-glass roof insulation make it an effective insulating material: *Highlight nine (9) bullet points and become familiar with these properties.*

R-value: Cellular-glass roof insulation has an R-value of 3.44 per inch thickness tested at a 75 F mean temperature. Cellular-glass roof insulation is recognized for having a stable R-value.

131 **Combustibility:** Cellular-glass roof insulation is noncombustible. It can be exposed directly to hot bitumen, torch flame or high temperatures, such as those produced by hot-air welders.

4.3 – Expanded Polystyrene (EPS): The following recognized properties of expanded polystyrene insulation make it an effective insulating material: *Highlight all seven (7) bullet points and become familiar with these properties.*

132 Typically, expanded polystyrene insulation is used in walls and roofs of commercial, industrial and residential buildings.

Product Standard: When expanded polystyrene insulation is used, NRCA recommends designers specify expanded polystyrene insulation with a compressive strength appropriate for specific project conditions.

133 **Compatibility:** Expanded polystyrene insulation is affected by exposure to the sun, organic solvents and some adhesives.

Page#	Highlight
134	**Application and Securement:** NRCA recommends designer specify a maximum 4-by-4-foot board size for expanded polystyrene insulation adhered to a substrate. The 4-by 8-foot board size is appropriate for loosely laid and mechanically attached membrane applications.
135	**4.4 – Extruded Polystyrene (XPS):** The following recognized properties of polystyrene board roof insulation make it an effective insulating material: *Highlight seven (7) bullet points and become familiar with these properties.* Typically, extruded polystyrene insulation is used in buildings with low-temperature interior spaces, such as refrigeration rooms, and in walls and roofs of other commercial, industrial and residential buildings.
138	**Application and Securement:** NRCA recommends designers specify a maximum 2-by 4-foot board size for extruded polystyrene insulation adhered to a substrate. The 2-by 8-foot board size is appropriate for loosely laid and mechanically attached membrane applications.
139	**4.5 – Glass-faced Gypsum:** Although glass-faced gypsum is not typically classified as an insulating product, information about glass-faced gypsum is included here because glass-faced gypsum is used in roof assemblies as a thermal barrier to provide fire resistance, substrates for air and vapor retarders, and cover boards beneath roof membranes. **R-value:** Glass-faced gypsum has R-values based upon thicknesses as follows. *Highlight Table* **Glass-faced Gypsum**
140	**Combustibility:** Glass-faced gypsum boards are noncombustible. Gypsum boards are inherently fire-resistant because of gypsum calcination.
141	**4.6 – Fiber-reinforced Gypsum - R-value:** Fiber-reinforced gypsum has R-values based upon thicknesses as follows. *Highlight Table* **Fiber-reinforced Gypsum**
143	**4.7 – Stone Wool:** Stone wool insulation intended for roofing purposes is manufactured as a rigid insulating material. It is manufactured using rock and slag as base ingredients. Natural mineral materials are combined, heated until molten and then spun into a fibrous material that is often referred to as stone wool. The stone wool fibers are bound together with a binding agent to form a rigid insulation board.
144	**4.8 – Perlite:** Perlite board insulation intended for roofing purposes is a rigid insulating material manufactured from expanded volcanic minerals combined with organic fivers and binders. The top surface of perlite board roof insulation is generally treated with an asphalt emulsion to minimize bitumen absorption. The common R-value used to calculate the total thermal resistance of a perlite board roof insulation system is 2.78 per inch of thickness.
148	**4.9 – Polyisocyanurate – R-value:** NRCA recommends designers specifying polyisocyanurate insulation determine roof system thermal resistance using an in-service R-value of 5.0 per inch.
152 & 153	**4.11 – Wood Fiberboard:** The common R-value used to calculate the total thermal resistance of a wood or cane fiberboard insulation system is about 2.78 per inch of thickness.
153	Wood-fiber "sheathing" boards generally do not possess sufficient physical proprties to be suitable for use as roof insulation. **R-value:** The common R-value used to calculate the total thermal resistance of a wood or cane fiberboard insulation system is about 2.78 per inch of thickness.

Page# **Highlight**

155 **4.12 – Cement Board - R-value:** Cement board does not contribute significant thermal resistance when used a part of roof assemblies.

158 **4.14 – Tapered Insulation:** Tapered insulation can be used to meet the requirements for slope in new construction and reroofing projects, as well as in cases where a roof deck will not provide adequate slope to drain water off a roof surface.

159 Although the primary reason for using tapered roof insulation is to improve slope and promote drainage, there are other advantages: *Highlight two (2) bullet points.*

161 **Thermal Insulation Value:** Minimum R-value: The minimum R-value approach establishes R-value for a tapered roof insulation system by determining the R-value of the tapered material at the thinnest point in the tapered system layout.

Average R-value: The average R-value approach establishes the R-value for a tapered roof insulation system by determining the R-value of the tapered material at the representative average thickness in the tapered system layout.

- Arithmetic Average Thickness Method: Arithmetic average thickness is the thickness of tapered and flat stock insulation at the midpoint between the minimum thickness (i.e., low point) and the maximum thickness (i.e., high point) in a tapered insulation system. See **Figure 4-5**.

164 **Design:** Tapered insulation layouts should be designed to form a sump that measures the size of the drain bowl's diameter plus approximately 24 inches at roof drains, and crickets should be installed on the high sides of all roof curbs.

165 **Slope Pattern:** A general rule of thumb for designing sufficiently sloping saddles and crickets is that they be twice the slope of the adjacent field of the roof. See **Figure 4-12** (on page 166).

166 **Hips and Valleys:** When using performed tapered insulation boards of one consistent slope, all valley centerlines should be 45 degrees from the direction of slope, that is, the valley centerlines are 90 degrees apart.

171 **CHAPTER 5 – ROOF MEMBRANES:** Most low-slope roof membranes have two principal components: weatherproofing layer or layers and reinforcement.

The weatherproofing component is the most important element within a roof membrane because it keeps water from entering a roof assembly.

The reinforcement adds strength, puncture resistance and dimensional stability to a membrane.

This chapter describes four types of common roof membranes: built-up membranes, polymer-modified bitumen sheet membranes, single-ply membranes, and liquid-applied membranes.

172 **5.1 – Guidelines Applicable to All Membrane Types - Slope and Drainage:** For new construction projects, *The International Building Code, 2018 Edition* indicates a design minimum slope of ¼:12 is required for membrane roof systems, except for coal tar built-up roof systems where a design minimum slope of ⅛:12 is permitted.

Slope generally is provided by: *Highlight the five (5) bullet points.*

Page# **Highlight**

173 **Weather Conditions During Application:** When membrane roofing materials are applied, entrapment of moisture should be prevented. Moisture in or on materials may cause membrane blistering. If precipitation occurs before completely installing the roof membrane, the membrane surface in the immediate work area and the substrate should be dried or allowed to dry before work resumes.

5.2 – Built-up Roof Membranes: A built-up roof membrane, sometimes referred to as BUR, consists of multiple layers of saturated felts, coated felts, fabrics or mates assembled in place shingle fashion with alternate layers of bitumen and surfaced with mineral aggregate, bituminous materials, a liquid-applied coating or a granule-surfaced cap sheet.

174 The principal components used in constructing built-up roof membranes are: *Highlight four (4) bullet points and become familiar with* **Bitumens, Reinforcement layers, such as felts and ply sheets, Membrane flashings and Accessories.**

Bitumens: Asphalts have excellent resistance to moisture, good resistance to weathering and excellent cohesive and adhesive characteristics. These properties also make asphalts useful as adhesives for adhering rigid board insulation and applying surfacings.

Many coal tar built-up membranes remain in service, but coal tar is no longer widely used for built-up roof membrane construction.

Cold-applied Asphalt Adhesives: These liquid versions of asphalt are referred to as "cutbacks". Cutting the asphalt back with solvents makes it possible to apply the weatherproofing asphalt material with heating it in a kettle or tanker.

176 **Hot-applied Asphalt:** For most roof system applications, including the construction of built-up membrane roof systems, oxidized asphalt bitumens are used.

classifies asphalt into four different types based on the asphalt's softening point, penetration (hardness) and ductility. The following table lists the ranges of softening point values for the four types of asphalt defined by ASTM D312.

Highlight Table **Asphalt Softening Point**

An asphalt's penetration value is used as a measure of consistency (relative hardness).

Highlight Table **Asphalt Penetration**

An asphalt's ductility value provides one measure of an asphalt's tensile properties and can be used as a measure of ductility for specification requirements.

Highlight Table **Asphalt Ductility**

177 Currently, asphalts complying with ASTM D312's, Type I or Type II are seldom used.

As a result, ASTM D312 now indicates a maximum heating temperature for asphalt as 550 F.

For mop application of asphalt, EVT is the temperature at which asphalt has a viscosity of 125 centipoise (cP). For mechanical spreader application of asphalt, EVT has been established as the temperature at which the asphalt has a viscosity of 75 cP.

Highlight Table **Asphalt EVT Values**

Page# **Highlight**

NRCA recommends at the point of application asphalt be within a ±25 F range from an asphalt's initial EVT.

178 Asphalt complying with ASTM D312, Type III is generally appropriate for interplay moppings in built-up membrane application where the slope of the completed membrane is 1:12 or less. Use of asphalt complying with ASTM D312, Type V is suggested for slopes greater than 1:12.

Hot-Applied Polymer-modified Asphalt: This polymer-modified asphalt is made from standard roofing asphalt modified by the addition of styrene ethylene butadiene styrene (SEBS).

ASTM D6152 specifies a 500 F minimum FP temperature; however, actual FP temperatures in excess of this value are desirable and common.

NRCA recommends kettle and tanker temperatures be maintained lower than 25 F below the asphalt's actual FP temperature and never heated to or above the actual FP temperature.

178 & 179 **Reinforcement Felts and Sheets:** Roll-roofing materials used as reinforcement inbuilt-up roof membrane construction fall into three categories as follows: *Highlight the three (3) bullet points and become familiar with* **Base sheets, Ply sheets** *and* **Mineral-surfaced cap sheet**

179 **Base Sheets:** Base sheets work well to separate roof systems from substrates. When mechanically attached, a base sheet can serve as a separation layer or adhesive bond break between a roof deck and roof system so the roof system may move thermally, independently from the roof deck.

Ply Sheets: Ply sheets are installed directly over base sheets or over rigid board insulation as interplay sheets in built-up roof membranes. Historically, ply sheets have been either fiberglass-mat or organic-mat reinforced.

180 **Asphalt-coated Polyester and Fiberglass-mat Sheets:** Asphalt-coated polyester and fiberglass-mat sheets may be used as ply sheets, including flashing applications.

Ply sheets are produced in a standard width of 36 inches and metric width of about 1 meter (39⅜ in.).

Membrane Flashings: Membrane flashings are used to terminate a built-up roof membrane at a roof's perimeter and at roof penetrations. Membrane flashings typically consist of a base or backer layer or layers and a cap sheet.

182 **SBS Polymer-modified Bitumen Base Sheets:** Several types of bituminous roofing sheets are becoming more commonly used as multiple-ply membrane flashings in built-up roof systems and base plies in polymer-modified bitumen roof systems. Among the most common are several styrene butadiene styrene (SBS) polymer-modified asphalt base sheets.

Liquid-applied flashings: Liquid-applied flashings commonly are used in situations where penetrations or surfaces are irregularly shaped and difficult to flash using a membrane flashing.

183 **Rosin-sized Sheathing Paper:** One purpose of the rosin-sized sheathing paper is to prevent the first ply of felt from adhering to wood decking. Another purpose is to prevent bitumen from dripping through some roof decks.

Application of Built-up Membrane Materials: A complete built-up membrane roof system may include a slip sheet; air retarder or vapor retarder; rigid board roof insulation; cover board; interplay bitumen or adhesive; and layers of base sheet, ply sheet, cap sheet or other roof surfacing option.

Page#	Highlight
184	**Fasteners for Built-up Roof Membranes:** Large-head, annular-threaded nails; barbed; ring-shank nails; or specifically approved mechanical fasteners should be used to fasten base sheets for built-up roof membranes to nailable decks, for back-nailing and to fasten base flashings in built-up roof membranes.
	Bitumen Heating: The following guidelines apply to the heating of bitumen: *Highlight seven (7) bullet points and become familiar with each.*
185	**Membrane Application:** On low-slope roofs, roof membrane plies should be applied so the slow of water runoff will not be against the laps. When possible, all plies should be installed in shingle fashion. When slopes are greater than 2:12, consideration should be given to laying the felts parallel to the slope. This application method, consisting of plies laid parallel to the slope, is referred to as "strapping the plies" and also may be used on slopes less than 2:12.
186	**5.3 – Polymer-modified Bitumen Roof Membranes:** Polymer-modified roof membranes are composed of reinforcing fabrics, usually polyester, fiberglass or both, that serve as the carriers for the polymer- modified bitumen as it is manufactured into a roll material. The purposes for reinforcements in polymer-modified bitumen sheets essentially are the same as felts in built-up roof membranes. The reinforcements help keep the bitumen in place within the sheet, provide tensile strength and allow for varying degrees of sheet elongation.
	Generally, APP polymers modify the asphalt to give the resultant material a "plasticized" nature. SBS polymers modify the asphalt to give the resultant material a "rubberized" nature.
	The principal components used in constructing polymer-modified bitumen roof membranes are: *Highlight five (5) bullet points and become familiar with* **Adhesives, Base layer, such as a base sheet or interplay sheets, Polymer-modified bitumen cap sheet, Membrane flashings** *and* **Accessories**
191 & 192	**Interply Sheets:** In place of single-layer base sheets, the following sheets, sometimes referred to as "interply sheets", are often used in multiple layers beneath APP or SBS polymer-modified bitumen sheets. *Highlight the four (4) bullet points and become familiar with* **Asphalt, Fiberglass Ply Sheet, APP Polymer-modified Interply Sheets, SBS Polymer-modified Bitumen Interply Sheets** *and* **Self- adhering (SA) Polymer-modified Bitumen Interply Sheets**
192	**Polymer-modified Bitumen Membrane Cap Sheet:** All polymer-modified bitumen-coated sheets are factor-coated on one or both sides with polymer-modified bitumen. Some sheets are surfaced on one or both sides with fine materials, such as sand, mica or talc, that serve as parting agents and prevent adhesion of the material while in roll form. Some manufacturers use liquid parting agents, and others use plastic films either removed by hand or intended to be burned off during the installation.
194	**Accessories:** Accessory products commonly used when constructing polymer-modified bitumen roof membranes include roof cements, adhesives and asphalt core board.
195	**Asphalt Core Board:** Asphalt core boards may be installed over structural substrates, rigid board insulation and existing roof membranes to provide substrates for torch-applied, hot mopped, cold adhesive applied and self-adhering asphalt-based membranes. Once the adhesive cures or cools to ambient temperature, the asphalt core boards become fused with the membrane.
196	Asphalt core board for roof system applications typically is available as 4- by 4-foot, 4- by 5-foot and 4- by 8-foot panels that are 1/8-of-an-inch, 3/16-of-an-inch, ¼-of-an-inch or ½-of-an-inch in thickness.

Page#	Highlight

197 & 198 **Torch-applied application:** Beginning with this edition of the NRCA Roofing Manual, NRCA no longer recommends designers specify torch-applied polymer-modified bitumen membranes over combustible substrate roof decks, even where a thermal barrier insulation layer has been laid over the combustible roof deck. NRCA considers the potential fire risk associated with torch-applied application over combustible roof decks to outweigh any advantages torch application provides.

199 **Membrane Application:** Blisters have been reported in some SBS polymer-modified bitumen membrane systems. Most have involved installation with hot asphalt and occurred between the cap sheet and base sheet or ply sheets. Application factors that can contribute to blistering include insufficient asphalt temperature at the point of application, long mop lead and lack of cap sheet embedment into the asphalt mopping.

200 **5.4 – Single-ply Roof Membranes:** There are two principal types of materials used in the construction of single-ply roof membranes: thermoset polymer sheets and thermoplastic polymer sheets. The terms describe the materials' different behaviors on heating that arise from their different molecular arrangements and chemical properties.

Currently, EPDM sheets are the only thermoset materials commonly used in construction of single-ply roof membranes in the North American market.

There are four common subcategories of thermoplastic membranes: *Highlight all three (3) bullet points and become familiar with* **Polyvinyl (PVC), PVC alloys, including copolymer alloy (CPA), ethylene interpolymer (EIP) and nitrile alloy (NBP)** *and* **Ketone ethylene ester (KEE)**

201 **Ethylene Propylene Diene Terpolymer (…; EPDM):** EPDM is a synthetic rubber material that can be formulated with extensive flexibility for use as membrane roofing.

EPDM membranes exhibit good resistance to ozone, ultraviolet (UV) rays, weathering and abrasion. EPDM also has good low-temperature flexibility. EPDM is resistant to same acids; alkalis; and oxygenated solvents, such as ketones, esters and alcohols. On the other hand, exposure to aromatic, halogenated and aliphatic solvents, as well as animal and vegetable oils and petroleum-based products, should be avoided to prevent membrane swelling and distortion.

The most common thicknesses of EPDM single-ply roofing sheet materials are 45 mils and 60 mils.

202 **Polyvinyl Chloride (PVC):** PVC Sheets are resistant to bacterial growth, many industrial chemical atmospheres and plant-root penetration. Properly formulated, PVC sheets are fire-resistant and have hot-air welding seaming characteristics. PVC sheets are chemically incompatible with bituminous materials and as such, should be separated from asphalt products.

NRCA recommends designers specify PVC sheets with a minimum thickness of 45 mils for use in conventional single-ply roof systems.

203 **PVC Alloys:** PVC alloys compound various polymers with PVC. Sheets produced with PVC alloys are somewhat akin to PVC sheets in that they, too, are thermoplastic in nature; however, each has its own unique properties. PVC alloy materials manufactured for use as roof membranes typically are produced as reinforced sheets.

204 **Ketone Ethylene Ester (KEE):** KEE Sheets are reported to be resistant to certain chemicals, air-conditioning coolants, jet fuels and restaurant grease, as well as UV radiation, airborne bacteria, acid rain and industrial pollutants.

KEE sheets are compatible with asphalt.

Page# **Highlight**

Thermoplastic Polyolefin (TPO): TPO sheets are compounded from a blend of polypropylene (PP) and ethylene-propylene rubber (EPR) polymers. Flame retardants, pigments, UV absorbers and other proprietary ingredients may be included in TPO sheet formulations.

205 **Application of Single-ply Membranes:** Single-ply membrane roof systems are typically designed and installed in three configuration types: loose-laid ballasted, mechanically attached and adhered.

Single-ply sheets should be unrolled and allowed time to relax and lie flat before application. Manufacturers commonly indicate a minimum period of 30 minutes for this.

206 **Loose-laid, Ballasted:** Loose-laid, ballasted systems seldom require field-membrane securement other than perimeter and base flashing attachment. As the system's name implies, the weight of the ballast and the force of gravity serve to secure the entire roof system.

The most common application rate for aggregate or stone ballast is 1,000 pounds to 1,200 pounds per 100 square feet for 1½ -inch to ¾-of-an-inch round, river-washed gravel designated as Size Number 4 in ASTM D7655.

Mechanically Attached: Mechanically attached systems use a variety of fasteners and fastening patterns to secure a membrane to a substrate. Among these methods are metal disks placed within a seam and attached through a membrane to a roof deck; metal or plastic bars placed within a seam and attached through a membrane to a roof deck; metal and plastic disks and/or bars placed over a membrane and covered with membrane stripping; polymer-coated metal disks used with fasteners to attach rigid board insulation to roof decks and heat welded to the underside of thermoplastic membranes using electromagnetic induction welding equipment; and other specialized proprietary securement systems.

207 **Heat Induction Welding:** An alternative method of attachment of single-ply roof membranes is heat welding a thermoplastic single-ply roof membrane to specially coated fastening plates using an electromagnetic heat-induction-welding tool.

211 Air Intrusion: Air intrusion has significance for roof assembly performance for two primary reasons. It contributes to mechanical fatigue of roof assembly components, including field membrane, flashings, mechanical attachment components and roof deck. It also provides a mechanism for depositing excess moisture inside a roof assembly.

Adhered: Adhered membrane systems are generally applied using a liquid-applied contact adhesive. Some membranes are made with a factory-laminated fleece backing that allows adhesion with alternative types of adhesives, such as hot asphalt and low-rise polyurethane foam.

212 Depending on the liquid carrier(s) used, cold-applied single-ply roof membrane adhesives currently available can be placed into one of three categories: *Highlight all three (3) bullet points and become familiar with* **Volatile organic compound (VOC) solvent- based adhesives, Low-VOC (also known as VOC-exempt solvent-based) adhesives** *and* **Water-based adhesives**

214 **5.5 – Liquid-applied Roof Membranes:** Liquid-applied roof membranes are constructed in place from a liquid resin and reinforcing material. The liquid resin is available as a one- or two-component product and is typically applied in two coats. Depending on the resin chemistry, a catalyst or hardener may be added to induce the curing process. In most instances, a primer is required.

217 **Application:** Liquid-applied roof membranes should be installed as continuously as possible. To do this, it is important wood nailers, curbs, drains and other penetrations be in place before roofing.

Page#	Highlight
219	**CHAPTER 6 – FASTENERS - Design Considerations:** These characteristics are a function of the substrate type and strength and the fastener's size, shank, point or tip type, and thread design. The corrosion resistance of a fastener should also be considered, along with its desired service life, which should be equivalent to that of the roof system. A fastener should be compatible with the material being secured and the substrate into which it is embedded. The shear strength and tensile strength of a fastener also are important considerations.
220	**Fasteners and Preservative-treated Wood:** NRCA is of the opinion the corrosion-related concerns regarding the use of currently available preservative-treated wood possible outweigh the benefits that preservative-treated wood provides as a component in roof assemblies. In many instances, nontreated, construction-grade wood is suitable for use in roof assemblies as blocking or nailers provided reasonable measures are taken to ensure the nontreated wood remains reasonable dry when in service.
221	**6.1 – Base Sheet Fasteners – Material Types:** A majority of fasteners are fabricated from hardened carbon steel or stainless steel. Often, such designations as 1022 for carbon steel and 304 for stainless steel are included and refer to properties such as alloys, strength and corrosion resistance. Fasteners are often surfaced (or coated) with various corrosion-resistant coatings, such as zinc, epoxy, fluorocarbons or other proprietary materials. In some cases, fasteners are fabricated plastics, such as glass-reinforced nylon and other polymer materials. Fasteners made of metal are thermal bridges.
223 & 224	**6.2 – Insulation Fasteners – Fastener Spacing:** Because center-to-center metal rood deck rib spacing typically is 6 inches, the spacing for insulation fasteners typically is some multiple of 6 in.
229	**6.3 – Membrane Fasteners – Fastener Spacing:** Spacing between the rows of fasteners and fastener spacing within the rows are two parameters that determine uplift resistance. Common fastener spacing with a row is 6 inches and 12 inches. See **Figure 6-9** (on page 230). Some common field-sheet row spacings are 6½ feet, 7 feet, 8 feet and 10 feet.
233	**CHAPTER 7 – SURFACINGS:** Membrane surfacing is the component that protects the weatherproofing component of some roof systems from the effects of direct sunlight, ultraviolet rays and weather exposure. Some surfacings provide other benefits, such as increased fire resistance, improved traffic and hail resistance, and aesthetic properties.
234	**7.1 – Guidelines Applicable to All Surfacing Types:** • Solar reflectance: The fraction of solar flux reflected by a surface expressed as a percent or within the range of 0.00 and 1.00 • Thermal emittance: The ratio of the radiant heat flux emitted by a sample to that emitted by a black-body radiator at the same temperature (total thermal emittance) **ENERGY STAR®:** for low-slope roof system products: • Initial solar reflectance must be greater than or equal to 0.65. • Solar reflectance three years after installation under normal conditions must be greater than or equal to 0.50 without cleaning prior to testing. For steep-slope roof systems: • Initial solar reflectance must be greater than or equal to 0.25. • Solar reflectance three years after installation under normal conditions must be greater than or equal to 0.15.
235	**7.2 – Aggregate:** When aggregate is used to surface a built-up roof system, it generally is for the following reasons: *Highlight all seven (7) bullet points.*

Page#	Highlight
	Highlight Table **Aggregate Gradation Amounts Finer than Sieve Specified, Mass Percent**

238 **7.3 – Ballast:** When single-ply membrane sheets are used in loose-laid, ballasted configurations, the surfacing commonly used are rounded aggregate or concrete roof pavers. Generally, ballasted roof systems are limited to roods with slopes of 2:12 or less.

239 **7.4 – Coatings:** A roof coating is a fluid material applied in the field as a film to the roof surface to provide weather protection to the original roof membrane. A coating protects the roof substrate from weather (solar radiation, heat and moisture) and determines its radiative properties.

241 **Roof Coating Characteristics:** When properly designed and installed, roof coatings can: *Highlight all eight (8) bullet points.*

Roof Coating Types: Most roof coatings consist of two general components:

- Primer
- Coating

Primer: Primers are intended to prepare a roof surface for accepting a coating and improve the overall adhesion of the coating to the substrate.

242 **Coatings:** The coating material itself is the topmost surface of the coating system application and the layer that provides the primary characteristic of the coating.

247 **Coating Application:** The three common application methods for roof coatings are:

- Airless Spray
- Roller
- Brush or broom

248 ***Figure 7-6: General guideline for primer and coating selection***

249 **Brush or Broom:** Most coatings should not be broom-applied.

Weather Conditions: Wind preferably should be less than 6 mph. Ambient temperatures should be moderate, with most coating applications specified to be conducted between 40 F and 100 F depending on manufacturers' recommendations.

251 **CHAPTER 8 – ROOF ACCESSORIES:** Examples of premanufactured accessories that may be encountered on a membrane roof system include. *Highlight five (5) bullet points.*

- Equipment curbs
- Expansion joint covers
- Skylights and roof/smoke hatches
- Prefabricated pipe flashings
- Pipe support systems

252 **8.1 – Equipment Curbs:** NRCA recommends a minimum of 24 inches of clearance between walls and curbs and minimum 12 inches of clearance between pipes and curbs.

For most membrane roof systems, equipment curbs should be detailed and constructed to a height of 8 inches above the finished roof membrane.

8.2 – Expansion Joint Covers: NRCA considers raised curb type expansion joints to be preferred, though for ballasted single-ply membrane roof systems, low-profile expansion joints in the same plane as the roof membrane are considered acceptable.

Page# **Highlight**

252 & 253 For most membrane roof systems, expansion joints should be detailed and constructed to a height of 8 inches above the finished roof membrane.

253 **8.3 – Skylights and Roof/Smoke Hatches:** Skylights and hatches should be installed with curbs tall enough to allow for an 8-inch vertical flashing height.

253 & 254 **8.4 – Prefabricated Pipe Flashings:** Pre-molded pipe flashings – commonly referred to as flashing boots or collars – are often used in single-ply membrane roof systems for sealing pipes or irregularly shaped penetrations.

254 NRCA recommends a minimum of 12 inches of clearance between pipes and a minimum 12 inches of clearance between pipes and curbs or walls.

For most membrane roof systems, pipe flashings should be detailed and constructed to a height of 8 inches above the finished roof membrane.

8.5 – Pipe Support Systems: It is common for the roofing contractor to be responsible for installation of pipe support systems in reroofing scenarios.

257 **CHAPTER 9 – REROOFING**

258 **9.1 – Definitions:** *Highlight five (5) bullet points and become familiar with* **Reroofing, Re-covering, Replacement, Roof assembly** *and* **Roof system**

259

- **Low-slope roof systems:** A category of roof systems that generally includes weatherproof membranes types of roof systems installed on slopes of 3:12 or less
- **Steep-slope roof systems:** A category of roof systems that generally includes water-shedding types of roof coverings installed on slopes greater than 3:12

9.2 – Evaluation of Existing Roof Systems – Interior Inspection: An evaluation of an existing roof system for the purpose of determining whether to re-cover or replace it should include a visual inspection of the interior of the building in the area underneath the roof area being considered.

262 **Hidden Conditions:** NRCA does not recommend metallic conduit or wiring be embedded within roof assemblies or placed directly below roof decks. If metallic conduit or siring needs to be placed near the roof assembly, NRCA recommends it be positioned and supported at least 1½ inches from the bottom side of the roof deck or substrate to which the roof system is applied.

263 **Roof System Inspection:** Inspection of the roof system should include evaluation of installed materials, as well as design, and should take account of: *Highlight all seven (7) bullet points and become familiar with* **Perimeter edge-metal flashings, Penetrations, Roof surface condition, Drainage and slope, Roof system composition, Moisture with the existing roof assembly** *and* **Rooftop mechanical equipment**

265 **Moisture with the Existing Roof Assembly:** When evaluating moisture content of roof assemblies, nondestructive moisture evaluation techniques should be considered. Nondestructive moisture evaluation techniques include infrared thermography, neutron (nuclear) thermalization and electrical capacitance.

Other Leak Sources: There are many building components that may be sources for leakage, including: *Highlight all eleven (11) bullet points.*

Page#	Highlight

268 **"1511.3.1.1 Exceptions.** A *roof recover* shall not be permitted where any of the following conditions occur:

1. Where the existing roof or roof covering is water soaked or has deteriorated to the point that the existing roof or roof covering is not adequate as a base for additional roofing.
2. Where the existing roof covering is slate, clay, cement or asbestos-cement tile.
3. Where the existing roof has two or more applications of any type of roof covering."

269 Reuse of existing metal flashing materials only is permitted when the materials' remaining service life of the new roof system.

270 **Roof Replacement Considerations:** When existing toggle bolts and auger-type fasteners are removed, NRCA recommends installation of a new structural roof deck because the structural capacity of the cementitious wood fiber roof deck can be reduced by the voids left by the removed fasteners.

271 **Vertical Alignment:** Elevation differences in excess of 1/8 of an inch between panels are considered unacceptable. Uneven joints of 1/8 inch or more should be grouted with the grout feathered to a slope of 1/8 of an inch per foot.

Roof Replacement Considerations: Securing a replacement roof system over an aged lightweight insulating concrete deck with new lightweight insulating concrete fasteners can be considered if the replacement roof system-specific pullout resistance can be achieved. NRCA suggests a minimum of four tests per continuous pour area be conducted when determining fastener withdrawal resistance for lightweight insulating concrete decks.

272 **Roof Replacement Considerations:** NRCA is concerned with the structural capacity and potential fastener-holding power of steel roof decks lighter than 22 gauge (0.028 inches thick).

Installing new steel deck without removing the existing metal deck is called nesting. Nesting can be accomplished by using the same type and grade of steel or a steel roof deck with narrower flutes so the new deck fits into the existing deck.

274 **Roof Replacement Considerations:** For prestressed or post-tensioned concrete decks, drilling into the deck can be detrimental to the load-bearing capacity of the deck because to the possibility of severing a tension cable. NRCA does not recommend attaching the roof insulation or membrane to prestressed or pos-tensioned concrete decks with mechanical fasteners.

275 **Curing and Drying:** Sealing the concrete's moisture into the deck by using a high-bond strength vapor retarder adhered directly to the deck followed by an adhered roof system is another option. A high-quality, 12- to 15- mil thick two-part epoxy has successfully been used as a vapor retarder in the flooring industry.

276 **Roof Replacement Considerations:** NRCA does not recommend installing roof systems over structural wood panel roof decks, such as plywood and OSB, that re less than 15/32 of an inch thick.

Roof Replacement Considerations: NRCA does not recommend installing roof systems over wood board roof decks with less than ¾ of an inch minimum thickness.

277 **Gypsum - Poured Gypsum:** Three general requirements are: *Highlight all three (3) bullet points.*

Page#	Highlight
278	**Roof Replacement Considerations:** If the existing roof system was sprinkle- or strip-mopped to the deck, the removal process may only cause minor damage to the deck. If the exiting roof was solid-mopped, the removal process may cause major damage to the deck. If major damage occurs, consideration should be given to replacing the roof deck or using a re-cover system.
280	**Roof Replacement Considerations:** In a roof replacement situation, reusing thermal-setting insulating fill is generally not practical because a new roof system cannot be mechanically attached to it, and adequate adhesion typically cannot be achieved to provide for adequate uplift resistance of the new roof system.
281	**9.6 – Re-cover Guidelines for Membrane Roof Systems:** The following is a list of general recommendations for re-covering over an existing roof system with a new built-up, polymer-modified bitumen, single-ply or liquid-applied membrane roof system: *Highlight five (5) bullet points.*
282	**9.7 – Design Guidelines for Roof Replacement with New Membrane Roof Systems – Fire Resistance:** An in-depth review of the code's criteria for classifying construction types is beyond the scope of this manual. The following brief descriptions provide a general idea of the classifications: *Highlight four (4) bullet points and become familiar with* **Type IA, IB, IIA, IIB, Types IIIA and IIIB, Type IV** *and* **Types VA and VB**
283	**Condensation Control:** When designing a replacement roof system, one or more of the following considerations may need to be addressed with regard to its water vapor transport performance: *Highlight four (4) bullet points.*
284	**Perimeter Edge-metal Flashings:** Because of unknow attachment methods, NRCA suggests existing perimeter edge-metal flashings not be reused.
285	**Roof Curbs and Equipment Supports:** Figure 9-5 provides NRCA's guidelines for clearance for equipment support stands. ***Figure 9-5: NRCA guidelines for clearance for equipment support stands*** **Pipe Penetrations:** Different types of pipe penetrations require different methods of flashing during reroofing projects. *Highlight three (3) bullet points.*
287	**CHAPER 10 – CONSTRUCTION DETAILS:** In this chapter, construction details are provided for the following membrane roof system types: *Highlight and become familiar with* **Built-up membrane, Polymer-modified bitumen membrane, EPDM membrane, Thermoplastic membrane** *and* **Liquid-applied membrane**
289	**Wood Nailers and Blocking:** Among other advantages, the nailers provide protection for the edges of rigid board insulation and provide a substrate for anchoring flashing materials. Wood nailers should be a minimum of 2 x 6 nominal-dimension lumber.
291	**Penetrations and Clearance:** The maximum amount of space should be provided between pipes, walls and curbs to facilitate proper installation of membranes and flashings. NRCA recommend a minimum of 12 inches of clearance between pipes, a minimum of 12 inches of clearance between pipes and curbs or walls, and a minimum of 24 inches of clearance between walls and curbs.
295	**Combustible Substrates:** Lumber and wood fiberboard cant strips are generally not considered to be noncombustible. NRCA suggest the use of noncombustible perlite, stone wool or other similar noncombustible material for cant strips.

Page#	Highlight
297	**Independent Securement of Mechanically Attached Single-ply Roof Membranes:** For mechanically attached single-ply membrane roof systems, NRCA suggest the designer consider the inclusion of a mechanically fastened batten bar or plates approximately 6 inches to 12 inches away from the outside edge of the roof system, drain sumps, curbs and penetrations as independent membrane securement. This is commonly referred to as a peel-stop.
306	**Drains and Drain Sumps:** Drain sumps should be square or rectangular and typically are 4 feet or 8 feet per side where premanufactured sump insulation is used. NRCA suggest drain sump dimensions not be less than the drain bowl diameter plus 24 inches to allow for correct drain flashing installation.
	Crickets and Saddles: To help reduce the amount of residual surface water between drains, behind curbs and along roof edges between scuppers, NRCA recommend installing crickets and saddles. **Figure 10-13** (on page 309) and **Figure 10-14** (on page 310) provide additional information regarding cricket and saddle slope and length-to-width (L:W) ratios.
308	**EPDM Membrane Corner Flashings:** For flashing inside corners, it is suggested field membranes be used to bridge the roof-to-wall transition to provide a continuous wall flashing. **Figure 10-17** (on pages 319-321) illustrates the sequencing of steps for this technique.

NRCA Roofing Manual: Steep-Slope Roof Systems 2021 Tabs and Highlights

These 1 Exam Prep Tabs are based on the National Roofing Contractors Association (NRCA) manual listed below: *Steep-Slope Roof Systems – 2021.*

Each Tabs sheet has five rows of tabs. Start with the first tab at the first row at the top of the page, and proceed down that row placing the tabs at the locations listed below. Place each tab in your book setting it down one notch until you get to the bottom of the page, and then start back at the top again. After you have completed tabbing your book (the last tab is usually the glossary, appendix, or index), then you may start highlighting your book.

******This concludes the tabs for this book. Please continue with the highlights on the following page.******

A.M. 03/25/2021

Page #	Highlight
26	**Ch.2: Roof Decks:** Asphalt shingle roof systems may be applied directly to the following roof deck substrates: (2 Bullets)
	2.1 – Wood Panels: Wood-panel roof decks can be subdivided into two general types: plywood roof decks and oriented strand board OSB roof decks.
27	When plywood is used as a roof deck material, NRCA recommends the use of a minimum of four-ply, nominal thickness of ½-of-an-inch-thick (actual thickness of 15/32-of-an-inch-thick) plywood for 16-inch rafter spacings, and four-ply, nominal thickness of 5/8-of-an-inch-thick (actual thickness of 19/32-of-an-inch-thick) plywood for 24-inch rafter spacings.
	When OSB is used as a roof deck material, a minimum nominal thickness of ½-of-an-inch-thick (actual thickness of 15/32-inch-thick) OSB is recommended for 16-inch rafter spacings and nominal thickness of 5/8-of-an-inch-thick (actual thickness of 19/32-of-an-inch-thick) OSB for 24-inch rafter spacings.
	Plywood and OSB sheathing panels should be installed with about 1/8-of-an-inch minimum gaps at panel edges to allow for expansion of the panels.
28	**2.2 – Wood Planks and Wood Boards:** Wood planks are long, relatively thick pieces of lumber. Specifications sometimes vary in thickness from 2 inches up to 5 inches with the width dimension in the plane of the roof deck.
	Wood boards are pieces of lumber that are less than 2 inches thick with square edges.
31	**Ch.3: Underlayments:** An underlayment performs several functions, it provides: (3 Bullets)
32	There are different underlayment configurations that can be used for asphalt roof systems. The following configurations are addressed in this manual: (2 Bullets)
35	**Roof Slope:** For roof substrates having slopes of 4:12 or more. NRCA recommends a minimum …D6757 asphalt felt underlayment be specified and applied horizontally in shingle fashion.
	When specifying asphalt shingle roof systems over roof substrates having slopes less than 4:12… NRCA recommends designers consider the following: (5 Bullets)
	Underlayment Configurations
	Single Layer of Mechanically Attached Underlayment: For single-layer applications, the underlayment should be applied horizontally in shingle fashion and lapped as recommended by… side laps of a minimum of 2 inches and the end laps of a minimum of 4 inches are recommended.
	Figure 3-2: Single layer underlayment
36	**Single-layer of Self-adhering Underlayment:** This configuration consists of one layer of self-adhering polymer-modified bitumen sheet applied over and entire roof deck.
	Typically, manufacturer's recommend side laps of a minimum of 3½ inches and end laps a minimum of 6 inches for self-adhering polymer-modified sheets installed as roof underlayments.
39	**Ch.4: Asphalt Shingles:** Asphalt shingles are designed for use as multilayered, water-shedding roof components that rely on the slope of a roof substrate to effectively shed water.
	Common dimensions for standard three-tab shingles are 12 inches by 36 inches.

Page #	Highlight
40	*Figure 4-1: Shapes and styles of asphalt shingles*
41	**Self-sealing Strip:** Commonly, asphalt strip shingles and laminated shingles contain adhesive, self-sealing strips.
42	**Asphalt Shingle Standards:** Asphalt shingles classified according to ASTM D7158 as Class D are said to pass at a basic wind speed up to and including 90 mph; those classified as Class G are said to pass at a basic wind speed up to and including 120 mph; and those classified as Class H are said to pass at a basic wind speed up to and including 150 mph.
	Figure 4-2: Asphalt shingles' wind-resistance classifications
48	**Fasteners:** Nails should be long enough to penetrate through all layers of roofing materials and achieve secure anchorage into a roof deck. Nails should extend a minimum of 1/8 inch through the underside of plywood or other acceptable wood panel decks less than 3/4 of an inch thick.
	Asphalt Roof Cement: There are two common types of asphalt roof dement: flashing cement and lap cement.
50	**Offset Patterns:** There are several offset or side-lap gauge patterns used with three-tab shingles, and the pattern used generally is selected based on manufacturer or installer preference, regional or climatic experience, or common practice.
51	**Shingle Attachment:** When attaching asphalt shingles, the intended location of fasteners depends on the particular shingle type.
51 & 52	**Attachment of three-tab strip shingles:** Fastening of full-length three-tab shingles requires a minimum of four roofing…positioned about 5/8 of an inch above the top of the shingle cutouts.
52	*Figure 4-10: Four-nail attachment locations for three-tab strip shingles*
	For areas considered to be high-wind regions, six-nail attachment of asphalt strip shingles may be required by the applicable building code.
	Figure 4-12: Six-nail attachment locations for three-tab strip shingles
	Attachment of laminated strip shingles: Fastening of full-length laminated strip shingles requires a minimum of four roofing nails per strip shingle.
53	*Figure 4-13: Four-nail attachment locations for laminated strip shingles*
	For areas considered to be high-wind regions, six-nail attachment of laminated shingles may be required by some building codes.
	Figure 4-14: Six-nail attachment locations for laminated strip shingles
54	**Hips and Ridges:** Asphalt shingles may be butted and nailed as work progresses up either side of a hip or a ridge.
55	**Drip Edge Metal:** Drip edge metal is most common for asphalt shingle roof systems. Drip edge metal is typically fabricated in two configurations, L-type or T-type.
	NRCA suggests fastening drip edge metal at about 12 inches on center, slightly staggered. Spacing may need to be closer in high-wind regions.

Page # **Highlight**

NRCA recommends drip edge metal for asphalt shingle roof systems be fabricated from one of the following metal types and minimum thicknesses: (9 Bullets)

Valleys: A valley is created at the downslope intersection of two sloping roof planes.

56 With asphalt shingle roof systems, there are four basic types of valleys: (4 Bullets)

Figure 4-19: Underlayment centered in valley to channel water runoff down the valley

56 & 57 Generally, fasteners should be kept back from the center of the valley a minimum of 8 inches.

57 **Open Valleys:** An open valley is constructed by installing typically 8-foot or 10-foot lengths of corrosion-resistant metal from the low point to the high point in the valley.

Figure 4-20: Open valley using metal valley flashing

A minimum 36-inch-wide layer of heavy weight felt, polymer-modified bitumen membrane or self-adhering underlayment is centered in the valley under the field underlayment.

NRCA suggests valley metal for asphalt shingle roof systems be fabricated from one of the following metal types and minimum thicknesses: (9 Bullets)

NRCA recommends valley metal for use with asphalt shingles be a minimum of 24 inches wide.

58 **Closed-cut Valleys:** In closed-cut valleys, shingles on one side of the valley are installed across the valley and shingles from the other side are cut about 2 inches short of the centerline of the valley.

59 **Woven Valleys:** NRCA does not recommend the use of woven valleys.

Flashings: Because roof systems are frequently interrupted by the intersection of adjoining roof sections, adjacent walls or penetrations such a s chimneys and vent pipes – all of which create opportunities for leakage – special provisions for weather protection must be made at these locations.

60 **Vertical Surface Flashings:** Four types of metal flashings commonly used at locations where an asphalt shingle roof system intersects a vertical surface are: apron flashing, step flashing, cricket or backer flashing, and counterflashing.

Figure 4-24: Sheet-metal Flashing components used at chimney

<u>Apron Flashings</u>**:** Apron flashings provide a weatherproofing transition material where a roof area intersects a head wall.

<u>Step Flashings</u>**:** Where a roof area intersects a vertical side wall, individual pieces of metal flashing are installed at the end of each shingle course.

61 NRCA recommends using metal step flashing that is 7 inches long by 8 inches wide for standard-size…extension is obtained onto each underlying shingle and 4 inches up the vertical surface.

<u>Cricket or Backer Flashing</u>**:** When a roof area intersects the upslope side of a chimney or curbed roof penetration. a cricket or backer flashing is installed.

Backer flashing is generally limited to penetrations that are 24 inches wide or less.

Page #	Highlight
62	Counterflashing: Apron, step, cricket and backer flashings require some form of counterflashing to cover and protect their top edges from water intrusion.
63	**Skylight Flashings:** Skylights, in terms of roof flashing, are much the same as other vertical surface flashings, particularly chimney flashings.
71 & 72	**6.1 – Definitions:** • **Reroofing** • **Re-covering** • **Replacement** • **Roof assembly** • **Roof system**
78	**6.4 – Roof Decks for Reroofing** **Wood Panels:** Plywood and OSB sheathing panels should be installed with about 1/8-of-an-inch minimum gaps at panel edges to allow for panel expansion.
79	*Figure 6-1: APA recommendations for wood structural panel attachment in the steep-slope applications*
80	**Roof Replacement Considerations:** NRCA does not recommend installing roof systems over structural wood panel roof decks that are less than nominal thickness of ½ of an inch (actual thickness of 15/32 of an inch).
83	**Drainage and Slope:** NRCA recommends installing a cricket on the upslope side of roof penetrations that are 24 inches wide or wider.
85	**Preparation of Existing Roof Surfaces:** Two items that should be verified when nesting new shingles over existing shingles are as follows: (2 Bullets)
96	Note and highlight the figure titled: **Eave**
97	Note and highlight the figure titled: **Eave with Gutter**
101	Note and highlight the information contained in the figure titled: **Rake**
104	Note and highlight the figure titled: **Ridge with Continuous Ridge Vent**
105	Note and highlight the figure titled: **Hip**
106	Note and highlight the figure titled: **Open Valley**
108	Note and highlight the figure titled: **Closed-Cut Valley**
114	Note and highlight the figure titled: **Chimney with Cricket Flashing**
115	Note and highlight the figure titled: **Chimney with Backer Flashing (24 inches wide or less)**
118	Note and highlight the figure titled: **Steep- to Low-Slope Roof System Transition**
194	**Ch.2: Roof Decks:** Clay and concrete tile may be fastened directly to the following substrates: (3 Bullets)

Page #	Highlight
	2.1 – Wood Panels: Wood panel roof decks can be subdivided into two general types: plywood roof decks and oriented strand board OSB roof decks.
196	**2.2 – Wood Planks and Wood Boards:** Wood plank and wood board roof decks are composed of solid-sawn dimensional lumber.
197	**2.3 – Batten Systems:** For some types of tile roofs, batten and counter-batten systems are used to hang tile that has head lugs.
198	If battens are not raised or kerfed to allow drainage, they should not be longer than 4 feet. Battens may be installed with aligned or staggered joints and about ½-of-an-inch separation between ends to help drain moisture that may migrate into a roof system.
202	**3.1 – Underlayment Materials**
	Asphalt Felts: Asphalt-saturated and asphalt impregnated felt underlayments traditionally have been the most are the most commonly used steep slope roof underlayments.
204	**Polymer-modified Bitumen Sheets:** Polymer-modified bitumen sheet membrane products are sometimes used an underlayments in tile roof systems.
205	**3.2 – Underlayment Design and Installation:** Clay and concrete tiles are designed for use as multilayered, water-shedding roof components that rely on the slope of the roof substrate to effectively shed water.
	Roof Slope: NRCA recommends designers specify the substrates for clay or concrete tile roof systems have slopes of 4:12 or more.
	Underlayment Configurations: There are different underlayment configurations that can be used for tile roof systems. There following configurations are addressed in this manual: (4 Bullets)
205 – 208	Note and highlight each section which describes the 4 categories.
213	**Ch. 4: Clay and Concrete Tile:** tile shapes commonly are categorized as follows: (4 Bullets)
214	*Figure 4-1: Clay and concrete roof tile classification by profile*
215	*Figure 4-2: Common clay tile profiles*
217	*Figure 4-6: S-tile dimensions*
218	**4.1 – Clay and Concrete Tile Materials**
	Clay Roof Tile: Clay tiles are fired in kilns at temperatures ranging from 1900 F to 2300 F.
	Roof Tile Physical Characteristics
	Water Absorption: Concrete tile absorption values range from 3% to 20%.
219	**Freeze-thaw Resistance:** Some types of tile are graded for their resistance to frost action. ASTM Standard C1167 provides grades of clay tile, and each has a different resistance to freeze-thaw cycles.
220	**Securement Methods:** Clay and concrete roof tile commonly is secured using the following means and methods: (6 Bullets)

Page #	Highlight
222	**Asphalt Roof Cement:** There are two common types of asphalt roof cement: flashing cement and lap cement.
224	**4.2 – Clay and Concrete Tile Roof System Design and Installation**
	Exposure and Appearance: Generally, a minimum 3-inch course-to-course overlap is recommended, unless precluded by roof tile product design.
225	**Hips and Ridges:** To weatherproof a roof at hips and ridges, special hip and ridge trim tiles are used as hip and ridge coverings.
	Rakes: To weatherproof a tile roof system along rake edges, specific details used depend on the tile type and profile, climate, and regional or area practices.
226	**Valleys:** A valley is created at the downslope intersection of two sloping roof planes.
	With tile roof systems, there are two basic types of valleys: (2 Bullets)
227	**Open Valleys:** NRCA suggests valley metal for tile roof systems be fabricated from one of the following metal types and minimum thicknesses: (6 Bullets)
228	NRCA recommends valley metal for use with tile be a minimum of 24 inches wide.
	Closed Valleys: In a closed valley, tiles on both sides are cut at an angle parallel to the centerline of the valley and butted together to form a mitered joint.
230	**Flashings:** Flashings are divided into the following categories: (4 Bullets)
	NRCA suggests metal flashings used in clay tile or concrete tile roof systems be fabricated from one of the following metal types and minimum thicknesses: (7 Bullets)
231	*Figure 4-18: Sheet-metal flashing components used at a chimney*
232	*Figure 4-19: Apron flashing at masonry chimney for pan and cover tile*
	Figure 4-20: Apron flashing at masonry chimney for interlocking or plain tile
	Figure 4-21: Step flashing at a masonry chimney for plain tile
	Figure 4-22: Channel flashing at a masonry chimney with pan and cover tile
232 & 233	NRCA suggests using metal step flashing pieces sized such that they match the tile in length, so a minimum step flashing head lap is achieved. The step flashing width should be sufficient to obtain a 4-inch extension onto each underlying tile and about a 4-inch vertical height over the exposed face of each overlying tile.
233	*Figure 4-23: Channel flashing at a vertical wall*
	Figure 4-25: Sheet-metal backer flashing at chimney
	Figure 4-25: Wood cricket built on upslope side of chimney
234	*Figure 4-27: Cricket flashing for upslope side of masonry chimney*
	Skylight Flashings: Skylights, in terms of roof flashing, are much the same as other vertical surface flashings, particularly chimney flashings.

Page # **Highlight**

243 **Ch. 6: Reroofing:** Reroofing also should be considered in other situations, including the following: (10 Bullets)

6.1 – Definitions:

- **Reroofing**
- **Re-covering**
- **Replacement**
- **Roof assembly**
- **Roof system**

244 **6.2 – Evaluation of Existing Roof Systems:** Clay and concrete tile roof systems cannot be re-covered.

248 **Base Flashings and Counterflashing:** When removing the existing roof system and installing new clay or concreate roof system, NRCA recommends the existing base flashings be removed and new base flashings be installed.

250 **6.4 – Roof Decks for Reroofing**

Wood Panels: NRCA does not recommend OSB panels to be used as a substrate for clay and concrete tile roof systems.

251 Wood sheathing panels should be installed with about 1/8-of-an-inch minimum gaps at panels edges to allow for panel expansion.

Roof Replacement Considerations: Roof decks should be continuous and without gaps. Gaps greater than ¼ of an inch should be covered or filled.

252 *Figure 6-1: APA recommendations for wood structural panel attachment in steep-slope applications*

NRCA does not recommend installation of clay or concrete tile roof systems over structural wood panel roof decks that are less than nominal thickness of 5/8 inches (…).

255 **Roof Slope:** For roof penetrations that are 24 inches wide or wider, NRCA recommends installing a cricket on the upslope side of the penetrations.

259 **Ch.7: Construction Details:** Construction details are provided for the following tile shapes: (4 Bullets)

262 *Figure 7-2: Sheet-metal counterflashing options*

Highlight: **A.** Through-wall Reglet and Counterflashing & **B.** Insert Reglet and Counterflashing

269 Note and highlight the figure titled: **Eave**

270 Note and highlight the figure titled: **Eave with Gutter**

274 Note and highlight the figure titled: **Eave/Rake**

275 Note and highlight the figure titled: **Ridge**

277 Note and highlight the figure titled: **HIP**

Page #	Highlight
279	Note and highlight the figure titled: **Open Valley**
280	Note and highlight the figure titled: **Headwall Flashing**
281	Note and highlight the figure titled: **Sidewall Flashing with Two-Piece Counterflashing**
282	Note and highlight the figure titled: **Sidewall Flashing with One-Piece Counterflashing**
287	Note and highlight the figure titled: **Chimney with Cricket Flashing**
288	Note and highlight the figure titled: **Chimney with Backer Flashing (24 Inches Wide or Less)**
289	Note and highlight the figure titled: **Curb-mounted Skylight**
291	Note and highlight the figure titled: **Steep- to Low-slop Roof System Transition**
293	Note and highlight the figure titled: **Eave**
294	Note and highlight the figure titled: **Eave with Gutter**
298	Note and highlight the figure titled: **Eave/Rake**
299	Note and highlight the figure titled: **Ridge**
301	Note and highlight the figure titled: **Hip**
303	Note and highlight the figure titled: **Open Valley**
304	Note and highlight the figure titled: **Headwall Flashing**
305	Note and highlight the figure titled: **Sidewall Flashing with Two-Piece Counterflashing**
306	Note and highlight the figure titled: **Sidewall Flashing with One-Piece Counterflashing**
311	Note and highlight the figure titled: **Chimney with Cricket Flashing**
312	Note and highlight the figure titled: **Chimney with Backer Flashing (24 Inches Wide or Less)**
313	Note and highlight the figure titled: **Curb-Mounted Skylight**
315	Note and highlight the figure titled: **Steep- to Low-slope Roof System Transition**
317	Note and highlight the figure titled: **Eave**
318	Note and highlight the figure titled: **Eave with Gutter**
322	Note and highlight the figure titled: **Eave/Rake**
323	Note and highlight the figure titled: **Ridge**
325	Note and highlight the figure titled: **Hip**
326	Note and highlight the figure titled: **Open Valley**
327	Note and highlight the figure titled: **Headwall Flashing**
328	Note and highlight the figure titled: **Sidewall Flashing with Two-Piece Counterflashing**

Page #	**Highlight**
329	Note and highlight the figure titled: **Sidewall Flashing with One-Piece Counterflashing**
333	Note and highlight the figure titled: **Chimney with Cricket Flashing**
334	Note and highlight the figure titled: **Chimney with Backer Flashing (24 Inches Wide or Less)**
335	Note and highlight the figure titled: **Curb-Mounted Skylight**
337	Note and highlight the figure titled: **Steep- to Low-slope Roof System Transition**
393	**2.3 – Batten Systems:** If battens are not raised or kerfed to allow drainage, they should not be longer than 4 feet. Battens may be installed with aligned or staggered joints and about ½-of-an-inch separation between ends to help drain moisture that may migrate into a roof system.
398	**3.1 – Underlayment Materials:** Materials used as underlayment for metal shingle roof systems generally consist of synthetic sheets, polymer-modified bitumen sheets and self-adhering polymer-modified bitumen sheets.
400	**Roof Slope:** NRCA recommends designers specify the substrate for metal shingle roof systems have slopes of 4:12 or more.
	Underlayment Configurations
406	**Naturally Weathering Metals:** For a metal to be appropriately considered a naturally weathering metal, the base metal itself must be able to oxidize sufficiently to form its own protective layer to withstand environmental exposures common to roof systems.
	The most common types of naturally weathering metals are: (4 Bullets)
411	**Paint Systems:** A wide variety of available factory-applied paint systems, and some manufacturers have their own formulations for each. Two common types of factory baked-on, paint-based systems are fluoropolymer and siliconized acrylic, or siliconized polyester.
416	**Securement Methods**
417	**Nail Application:** Nails should be long enough to penetrate through all layers of roofing materials …the underside of plywood or other acceptable wood panel decks less than ¾ of an inch thick.
423	**Valleys:** NRCA recommends valley metal for use with metal shingles be a minimum of 18 inches wide
435	Reroofing also should be considered in other situations, including the following: (10 Bullets)
435 & 436	**6.1 – Definitions:** • **Reroofing** • **Re-covering** • **Replacement** • **Roof assembly** • **Roof system**
440 & 441	**Roof Covering Condition:** The following conditions may adversely affect steep-slope roof coverings' water shedding function: (17 Bullets)

Page #	Highlight
442	**6.4 – Roof Decks for Reroofing**
443	**Wood Panels:** Plywood and OSB sheathing panels should be installed with about 1/8-of-an-inch minimum gaps at panels edges to allow for panel expansion.
444	*Figure 6-1: APA recommendations for wood structural panel attachment in steep-slope applications*
	Roof Replacement Considerations: NRCA does not recommend installing roof systems over structural wood panel roof decks that are less than nominal thickness of ½ of an inch (actual thickness of 15/32 of an inch).
448	**Drainage and Slope:** NRCA recommends installing a cricket on the upslope side of roof penetrations that are 24 inches or wider.
456	*Figure 7-2: Sheet-metal counterflashing options*
	A. Through-wall Reglet and Counterflashing & **B.** Insert Reglet and Counterflashing
460	Note and highlight the figure titled: **Eave**
461	Note and highlight the figure titled: **Eave with Gutter**
465	Note and highlight the figure titled: **Rake**
466	Note and highlight the figure titled: **Ridge**
468	Note and highlight the figure titled: **Hip**
469	Note and highlight the figure titled: **Valley**
470	Note and highlight the figure titled: **Headwall Flashing**
471	Note and highlight the figure titled: **Sidewall Flashing with Two-Piece Counterflashing**
472	Note and highlight the figure titled: **Sidewall Flashing with One-Piece Counterflashing**
475	Note and highlight the figure titled: **Chimney with Cricket Flashing**
476	Note and highlight the figure titled: **Chimney with Backer Flashing (24 Inches Wide or Less)**
477	Note and highlight the figure titled: **Curb-Mounted Skylight**
479	Note and highlight the figure titled: **Steep- to Low-slope Roof System Transition**
510	**Ch.2: Roof Decks:** NRCA recommends designers specify roof deck slopes intended for the application of slate roof systems at 4:12 or greater.
518	**3.2 – Underlayment Design and Installation**
	Roof Slope: NRCA recommends designers specify substrates for slate roof systems have roof slopes of 4:12 or more.
526	**4.1 – Slate Materials**
	Colors: The color of slate is determined by its chemical and mineral composition.

Page #	Highlight
	Weight: A square of slate on a roof system set at the standard 3-inch head lap will vary in weight from 700 pounds to 8,000 pounds depending on the thickness of each slate.
527	*Figure 4-1: Approximate weight of roofing slate at various thicknesses*
	Figure 4-2: Common Slate sizes, slates per square and exposures
528	*Figure 4-3: Physical Requirements for Roofing Slate*
532	**4.2 – Slate Roof System Design and Installation**
	Exposure and Appearance: Figure 4-7 shows the proper exposures for various length of slate if all are to be set with a 3-inch head lap.
	Figure 4-7: Slate exposures
551	**Ch. 6: Reroofing:** Reroofing should also be considered in other situations, including the following: (10 Bullets)
551 & 552	**6.1 – Definitions:** • **Reroofing** • **Re-covering** • **Replacement** • **Roof assembly** • **Roof system**
558	**6.4 – Roof Decks for Reroofing**
	Wood Panels: NRCA does not recommend OSB panels be used as a substrate for slate roof systems.
559	*Figure 6-1: APA recommendations for wood structural panel attachment in steep-slope roof system applications*
563	**Roof Slope:** For roof penetrations that are 24 inches wide or wider, NRCA recommends installing a cricket on the upslope side of penetrations.
568	*Figure 7-2: Sheet-metal counterflashing options*
	A. Through-wall Reglet and Counterflashing & **B.** Insert Reglet and Counterflashing
572	Note and highlight the figure titled: **Eave**
573	Note and highlight the figure titled: **Eave with Gutter**
577	Note and highlight the figure titled: **Rake**
578	Note and highlight the figure titled: **Ridge with Slate**
581	Note and highlight the figure titled: **Hip**
582	Note and highlight the figure titled: **Open Valley**
584	Note and highlight the figure titled: **Headwall Flashing**

Page #	Highlight
585	Note and highlight the figure titled: **Sidewall Flashing with Two-Piece Counterflashing**
586	Note and highlight the figure titled: **Sidewall Flashing with One-Piece Counterflashing**
589	Note and highlight the figure titled: **Chimney with Cricket Flashing**
590	Note and highlight the figure titled: **Chimney with Backer Flashing (24 Inches Wide or Less)**
593	Note and highlight the figure titled: **Steep- to Low-slop Roof System Transition**
620	**2.2 – Wood Planks and Wood Boards** When spaced sheathing is used, a roof deck may be composed of 1-inch nominal, 4-inch-wide boards for attaching wood shingles and 1-inch nominal, 6-inch-wide boards for attaching wood shakes.
627	**Roof Slope:** NRCA recommends designers specify the substrates for wood shake and wood shingle roof systems have slopes of 4:12 or more. NRCA recommends a minimum single layer of ASTM D4869, Type III, or Type IV asphalt felt underlayment be specified and applied horizontally in shingle fashion.
628	*Figure 3-2: Single-layer underlayment*
634	*Figure 4-1: Wood shakes*
635	*Figure 4-2: Wood shingles*
641	*Figure 4-5: Nails used with wood roofing*
643	*Figure 4-6: Wood shake coverage and exposure table*
644	**Field Application:** Joints in the first exposed course of wood shakes or wood shingles should be offset a minimum of 1½ inches from the joints in the underlying starter course. *Figure 4-7: Wood shingle coverage and exposure table*
649	**Open Valleys:** NRCA recommends valley metal for use with wood shakes or shingles be a minimum of 24-inches wide sheet metal.
661 & 662	**6.1 – Definitions:** • **Reroofing** • **Re-covering** • **Replacement** • **Roof assembly** • **Roof system**
668	**6.4 – Roof Decks for Reroofing** **Wood Panels:** Plywood and OSB sheathing panels should be installed with about 1/8-of-an-inch minimum gaps at panel edges to allow for panel expansion.
669	*Figure 6-1: APA recommendations for wood structural panel attachment in the steep-slope roof system applications*

Page #	Highlight
670	**Roof Replacement Considerations:** NRCA does not recommend installing roof systems over structural wood panel roof decks that are less than nominal thickness of ½ of an inch (…).
678	*Figure 7-2: Sheet-metal counterflashing options*
	A. Through-wall Reglet and Counterflashing & **B.** Insert Reglet and Counterflashing
684	Note and highlight the figure titled: **Eave**
685	Note and highlight the figure titled: **Eave with Gutter**
689	Note and highlight the figure titled: **Rake**
691	Note and highlight the figure titled: **Hip**
692	Note and highlight the figure titled: **Open Valley**
693	Note and highlight the figure titled: **Headwall Flashing**
694	Note and highlight the figure titled: **Sidewall Flashing with Two-Piece Counterflashing**
695	Note and highlight the figure titled: **Sidewall Flashing with One-Piece Counterflashing**
698	Note and highlight the figure titled: **Chimney with Cricket Flashing**
699	Note and highlight the figure titled: **Chimney with Backer Flashing (24 Inches Wide or Less)**
700	Note and highlight the figure titled: **Curb-Mounted Skylight**
703	Note and highlight the figure titled: **Eave**
704	Note and highlight the figure titled: **Eave with Gutter**
708	Note and highlight the figure titled: **Rake**
710	Note and highlight the figure titled: **Hip**
711	Note and highlight the figure titled: **Open Valley**
712	Note and highlight the figure titled: **Headwall Flashing**
713	Note and highlight the figure titled: **Sidewall Flashing with Two-Piece Counterflashing**
714	Note and highlight the figure titled: **Sidewall Flashing with One-Piece Counterflashing**
717	Note and highlight the figure titled: **Chimney with Cricket Flashing**
718	Note and highlight the figure titled: **Chimney with Backer Flashing (24 Inches Wide or Less)**
719	Note and highlight the figure titled: **Curb-Mounted Skylight**
721	Note and highlight the figure titled: **Steep- to Low-slop Roof System Transition**
722	Note and highlight the figure titled: **Eave**
723	Note and highlight the figure titled: **Eave with Gutter**

Page #	Highlight
727	Note and highlight the figure titled: **Rake**
729	Note and highlight the figure titled: **Hip**
730	Note and highlight the figure titled: **Open Valley**
731	Note and highlight the figure titled: **Headwall Flashing**
732	Note and highlight the figure titled: **Sidewall Flashing with Two-Piece Counterflashing**
733	Note and highlight the figure titled: **Sidewall Flashing with One-Piece Counterflashing**
736	Note and highlight the figure titled: **Chimney with Cricket Flashing**
737	Note and highlight the figure titled: **Chimney with Backer Flashing (24 Inches Wide or Less)**
738	Note and highlight the figure titled: **Curb-Mounted Skylight**
740	Note and highlight the figure titled: **Steep- to Low-slop Roof System Transition**
741	Note and highlight the figure titled: **Eave**
742	Note and highlight the figure titled: **Eave with Gutter**
746	Note and highlight the figure titled: **Rake**
748	Note and highlight the figure titled: **Hip**
749	Note and highlight the figure titled: **Open Valley**
750	Note and highlight the figure titled: **Headwall Flashing**
751	Note and highlight the figure titled: **Sidewall Flashing with Two-Piece Counterflashing**
752	Note and highlight the figure titled: **Sidewall Flashing with One-Piece Counterflashing**
755	Note and highlight the figure titled: **Chimney with Cricket Flashing**
756	Note and highlight the figure titled: **Chimney with Backer Flashing (24 Inches Wide or Less)**
757	Note and highlight the figure titled: **Curb-Mounted Skylight**
759	Note and highlight the figure titled: **Steep- to Low-Slope Roof System Transition**

NRCA Roofing Manual: Metal Panel and SPF Roof Systems 2020 Tabs and Highlights

These 1 Exam Prep Tabs are based on the National Roofing Contractors Association (NRCA) *Metal Panel and SPF Roof Systems – 2020.*

Each 1 Exam Prep tabs sheet has five rows of tabs. Start with the first tab at the first row at the top of the page; proceed down that row placing the tabs at the locations listed below. Place each tab in your book setting it down one notch until you get to the last tab. Then start with the highlights.

******This concludes the tabs for this book. Please continue with the highlights on the following page.******

A.M. 07/09/2020

Page #	Highlight
47	The following types of structural substrates are addressed in this manual: (6 Bullets)
48	**Deflection:** Structural substrate deflection should be limited to 1/240 of the structural substrate's total span to accommodate the stresses of concentrated or uniform loading.
49	**Slope and Drainage:**
50	The criterion for judging proper slope for drainage is that there be no ponding water on the roof 48 hours after a rainfall during conditions conducive to drying.
	Electrical Conduits and Other Piping
51	NRCA does not recommend metallic conduit or wiring be embedded within roof assemblies or be placed directly on the roof surface or directly below the roof deck.
52	**2.2 - Steel**
53	NRCA recommends steel decks be 22-gauge or heavier and have a minimum G-90 galvanized coating complying with ASTM A653.
71	**Naturally Weathering Metals**
	Metallic-coated Metals
71 & 72	Corrosion results from the steel reacting with oxygen…undesirable for two reasons: performance and appearance.
72	The primary purpose of metallic coatings is to protect…reduce change of rapid oxidation.
	Aluminum: Aluminum provides a lightweight, easily formed metal that does not require a protective coating for most exposures.
	It is not recommended aluminum be used as an in-wall flashing embedded in concrete or masonry.
73	**Aluminized Steel:** Aluminized steels rely almost solely on the aluminum's ability to act as a barrier for protecting the base steel.
74	**Copper:** Over time copper develops a bronze, brown, or blue-green color resulting from the formation of a protective layer of copper sulfate, referred to as patina.
75	**Copper-coated Stainless Steel (Copper Plus)**
	Copper-coated stainless steel was developed to provide a roofing or flashing material with the appearance, malleability and corrosion-resistance characteristics of copper but the strength of stainless steel.
	Figure 4-4: Metal thickness and weight information for copper-coated stainless steel sheets.
76	**Galvalume® (aluminum-zinc-coated steel):** This alloy coating is reported to be 55 percent aluminum and 45 percent zinc by weight.

Page # **Highlight**

Galvanized Steel: Galvanized steel is one of the oldest and most common metallic coated metals. Although the zinc coating extends the weatherability of the base steel, it is generally not considered adequate by itself for providing long-term service life in exposed applications.

77 **Lead:** Lead is used as a roofing accessory metal because of its workability.

Sheet lead has little structural strength and puncture resistance and therefore must be installed over solid substrates.

Weather and Corrosive Environments: A weight range of 2 pounds per square foot to 4 pounds per square foot is typical for roofing application, but heavier weights may be desirable for soldering purposes.

78 **Lead-coated Copper**: Lead coated copper has limited availability; however there still may be small regional manufacturer's that provide it.

The weight of lead coating should be at least 12 pounds and should not exceed 15 pounds.

Figure 4-8: Metal thickness and weight information for lead-coated copper sheets.

79 **Stainless Steel:** Stainless steel is a corrosion-resistant material.

For sheet metal flashings, 300-series stainless-steel material is preferred…Types 302 and 304 are the most common.

Stainless-steel sheets greater than 24-guage in thickness may be more difficult to work with because of the hardness of the metal.

Zinc: Zinc is a self-healing metal that weathers to a soft blue-gray patina.

80 The rate of patina formation varies with the environment and application.

Figure 4-10: Metal gauge, thickness and weight information for zinc sheets.

81 **Terne Metal:** Terne metal is a carbon-steel-based metal coated with a lead-tin alloy applied on both sides by the hot-dip process.

Zinc-tin-coated Steel (Terne II): The alloy coating was not applied solely to protect the steel but also to serve as a paintable surface and allow for ease of soldering.

89 **4.4 Oil-Canning:** Oil canning refers to physical distortions in the flatness of metal; however, this condition is only aesthetic in nature and does not have any adverse effect on the structural integrity or the weatherproofing capability of the metal.

4.5 - Joinery

95 **5.1 System Types: Architectural Metal Panel Roof Systems:** Architectural metal panel roof systems require continuous or closely spaced decking. Architectural metal panel roof systems are typically water-shedding roof systems.

96 Architectural metal panel roof systems perform well on slopes of 3:12 or greater.

Page #	**Highlight**

A minimum underlayment of an ASTM D4869 Type III or Type IV (No. 30) asphalt-saturated felt underlayment and separate slip sheet, such as rosin-sized sheathing paper or underlayment with slip-sheet capabilities is recommended beneath architectural metal roof panels.

Structural Metal Panel Roof Assemblies: Metal panel used in structural metal panel have the strength and capability of spanning structural members, such as joists or purlins, without being supported by a continuous or closely spaced roof deck…They are designed to resist the passage of water oat joints, laps and junctures under minimal hydrostatic pressure.

NRCA recommends 1/2 inch per foot as the minimum slope for structural metal panel roof assemblies even though numerous manufacturers will allow structural metal panel roof systems to be installed on slopes as low as 1/4 inch per foot.

98 **5.3 Seam Types and Configurations**

Flat Seam: Flat-seam metal panel roof systems are adaptable to many types of surfaces.

Flat Seam, Nonsoldered: A flat seam is created with individual flat-pan panels applied in an overlapped. interlocking shingle fashion. See Figure 5-2.

99 **Flat Seam, Soldered:** When the joints of flat-seam panels are joined together on low-slope roofs, the joints are soldered to make the system weatherproof. See Figure 5-3.

For those metals that require pre-tinning (e.g. copper), sheet edges should be pre-tinned to a minimum width of 1 1/2 inches before folding the edges.

Standing Seam: The term "standing seam" refers to almost any kind of metal roof panel with a raised vertical seam.

102 **5.4 - Seaming Methods:** There are four basic panel-to-panel seaming techniques: (4 bullets).

Mechanical Seam: A mechanical seam is completed by hand seamers, tongs, or electrical seaming devices.

Snap-lock Seam: In a snap-lock seam, male and female legs are adjoined to secure the seam in place…See figure 4-4 for an example of a snap-lock seam.

Snap-on Seam: A snap-on seam is typically simple to install. A separate cap or batten snaps onto a panel's rib and clip to complete the seam.

Hooked Seam: A hooked seam is a flat-lock, flat seam used in some types of architectural metal systems, such as Bermuda horizontal panels or metal shingles.

108 **5.12 - Thermal Movement Considerations:** The term “thermal movement" refers to a material’s dimensional changes resulting from changes in temperature…The net change in any one dimension is proportional to the net temperature change and is a material-specific property called the coefficient of See Figure 5-11.

113 Architectural metal panel roof systems typically are water-shedding roof systems.

Architectural metal roof panel systems perform well on slopes of 3:12 or greater.

A minimum underlayment of an ASTM D4869, Type III and IV (No. 30) asphalt-saturated felt underlayment…recommended beneath architectural metal roof panels.

Page # **Highlight**

114 Although metal panels classified as "structural panels" also can be used as architectural metal roof panels…See Chapter 7.

116 **Self-adhering Polymer-modified Bitumen:** Water and ice-dam protection membranes generally consist of a single layer of self-adhering polymer-modified bitumen sheet.

117 **Slip Sheets:** A slip sheet is a layer of rosin-sized or unsaturated building paper.

Before metal panel application, a rosin-sized slip sheet may be necessary to protect the underlayment from damage as panels can adhere to and tear the underlayment.

Single Layer of Underlayment: All sheets should have a minimum side lap of 2 inches over the preceding sheet, and end laps should be a minimum of 4 inches.

118 **Water and Ice-dam Protection Membranes**

119 **6.3 Insulation:** The primary purposed of roof insulation is to provide thermal resistance.

Rigid Board Insulation: Rigid board roof insulation can be installed over continuous or a closely spaced roof decking under an architectural metal panel roof system.

121 **6.5 Panel Profiles:** Panel profiles vary depending on the different methods used for forming panels.

Figure 6-7: Examples of seam types for common architectural metal roof panels

124 **6.7 Panel Attachment:** NRCA recommends a minimum of two fasteners per clip be installed.

126 **6.8 - Drainage:** An architectural metal panel roof system must provide localized positive drainage.

NRCA does not recommend internal drainage systems, including built-in gutters with drains.

6.9 Sheet-metal Flashing: Designers should consider the following factors for proper detailing of an architectural metal panel roof system and related sheet-metal flashings (9 Bullets)

133 **Support Penetrations**

139 Structural metal panel roof assemblies have the strength and capability of spanning structural members, such as joists or purlins, without being supported by a continuous or closely spaced roof deck. Structural metal panel roof assemblies are typically weatherproof roof systems. They are designed to resist the passage of water at joints, laps, and junctures under minimal hydrostatic pressure.

NRCA recommends ½ inch per foot as the minimum slope for structural panel roof assemblies.

Structural metal roof panel roof assemblies are used in architectural applications…continuous closely spaced substrates.

141 **7.4 - Panel Profiles**

142 There are three general panel profiles common to structural metal panels: (3 Bullets)

143 **Figure 673:** Example of structural metal roof panel profiles

Page #	Highlight
147	**7.7 - Drainage:** A structural metal panel roof system must provide positive drainage.
	NRCA does not recommend internal drainage systems, including built-in gutters with drains.
	7.8 - Sheet Metal Flashing: Designers should consider the following factors for proper detailing of a metal roof system and related sheet-metal flashings (9 Bullets)
152	**Support Penetrations:** Note and highlight the chart which lists Width of Equipment and Clearance.
157	**Design Considerations**
158	NRCA recommends a minimum of two fasteners per clip be installed.
159	**Figure 7-1:** Fasteners commonly used with sheet metal
160	**Figure 7-2:** Guidelines for the selection of fasteners based on galvanic action
165	**9.2 Skylights:** Skylight frames should overlap the curb a minimum of 3 inches to act as counterflashing, or a separate counterflashing could be installed.
167	When roof system maintenance and repair no longer can prevent recurrent leakage or extend a roof system's useful service life, consideration needs to be given to reroofing.
	Reroofing also should be considered in other situations, including when: (10 Bullets)
167-168	**10.1 Definitions:**

- **Reroofing**
- **Re-covering**
- **Replacement**
- **Roof assembly**
- **Roof system**

Page #	Highlight
180-181	**10.5 Re-cover Guidelines for Metal Panel Roof Systems:** The following design considerations apply to roof re-covers with new metal panel roof systems: (9 Bullets)
182	**Insulation:** Additional insulation may be added by installing rigid or blanket insulation over the existing roof system.
183	**Existing Flashings:** Re-covering an existing roof system with new metal panel roof system typically requires new metal flashings and counter flashings.
	Because of unknown attachment methods it is not recommended to use existing edge-metal flashings as cleats or forms of anchorage for new metal flashings.
184	**Drainage and Slope:** NRCA suggests design of metal framing systems provide for a minimum of ½:12 slope for structural metal panel roof systems in re-cover applications.
185	**Penetrations:** When re-cover structural metal panel systems are used, all existing penetrations need to be extended or raised through the new roof system and flashed in a watertight manner; additional framing may be required.
339	The following types of roof decks are addressed in this manual: (6 Bullets)

Page # **Highlight**

2.1 Guidelines Applicable to All Roof Deck Types

341 **Slope and Drainage:** The International Building Code 2018 Edition indicates a design minimum slope of ¼:12 is required for SPF roof systems.

344 **2.2 - Cementitous Wood Fiber Panels:** Cementitous wood fiber panels intended as roof decks provide for structural support of the roof system and can provide for a finished interior surface that has acoustical properties.

Design: It is recommended that the specifications require the joints between adjacent panels greater than ¼ of an inch be grouted with material recommended by the deck manufacturer.

345 **2.3 - Lightweight Insulating Concrete**

Design

346 NRCA recommends lightweight insulating concrete roof decks be a minimum of 2 inches thick…other underlying substrate.

347 **Structural Support:** Lightweight insulating concrete roof decks are designed for application over:

- Galvanized metal from decks
- Bulb-tee and form-board systems
- Structural or precast concrete substrates

348 **2.4 - Steel:** The most common steel roof deck panels are constructed in one of the following for configurations: narrow-rib steel deck (Type A); intermediate-rib steel deck (Type F); wide-rib steel deck (Type B) and deep-rib steel deck (type 3DR).

Design

349 NRCA recommends steel decks be 22-gauge or heavier and have a minimum G-90 galvanized coating complying with ASTM A653.

Structural Supports: Spacing of attachment points is recommended to be no more than 12 inches on center… under concentrated, moving loads.

356 **2.5 - Structural Concrete:** There are two general types of structural concrete used in roof decks: normal-weight structural concrete and light weight structural concrete.

361 **2.6 - Wood Panels:** There are two general types of wood panels used for roof decks: plywood and oriented strand board (OSB).

Design: When plywood is used as a roof deck material, NRCA recommends the use of a minimum of four-ply, 15/32-inch-thick plywood or four-ply, nominal 5/8-inch-thick plywood for 24-inch rafter spacings.

363 **2.7 - Wood Planks and Wood Boards**

367 & 368 **3.1 - Base Sheets:** Following are common varieties of base sheets that are used in SPF roof systems: (4 Bullets)

Page # **Highlight**

368 & 369 **3.2 - Rigid Board Insulation:** Following are the common types of rigid roof board insulation used with SPF roof systems (7 Bullets)

379 SPF roof systems are constructed by mixing and spraying a two-component liquid that forms the base of an adhered roof system. Isocyanate, referred to as component A, reacts chemically with the polyol resin, referred to as component B, immediately when mixed. This mixture expands 20 to 30 times its original liquid volume to form a closed-cell foam.

380 **Applicability and Restrictions:** The following are general applicability and restriction guidelines for the use of SPF roof systems. (7 Bullets)

381 **Weather Conditions During Application**

Temperature: The substrate temperature range for SPF application is between 50 F and 180 F. For temperatures below 50 F, low temperature, factory formulated materials and low temperature application techniques should be used.

This condition may develop when a roof deck temperature drops below 50 degrees Fahrenheit, depending on the SPF formulization and it may be necessary to stop SPF application until the condition is corrected.

Wind: Practical experience has shown that SPF should not be sprayed when wind speeds exceed 12 mph…at roof height unless some form of wind screen is used.

382 **Equipment:** Application of SPF required equipment designed to meter and spray the Isocyanate (Component A) and the resin (Component B) components at a 1-to-1 ratio.

Types of Primers:

383 Commonly used primers are categorized as follows: (6 Bullets)

Figure 5- 1: Primer application chart

385 **Thickness:** Optimum lift thickness should be from 1/2 inch to 1 1/2 inches.

385 & 386 **Surface Texture:** The following terms are used to describe SPF surface texture:

- Smooth
- Orange Peel
- Coarse orange peel
- Verge of popcorn
- Treebark

387 **SPF Application Guidelines**

388 & 389 **Lack of Isocyanate (Component A):** SPF that lacks isocyanate will exhibit one or more of the following characteristics: (6 Bullets)

389 **Lack of Polyol (Resin) (Component B):** SPF that lacks polyol is more difficult to discover unless the condition is extreme.

The more extreme condition of lack of polyol will exhibit one or more of the following characteristics: (6 Bullets)

Page #	Highlight
	Aged or Improper Components: An applicator cannot make equipment adjustments to improve the quality of the SPF. The obvious effects are one or more of the following: (11 Bullets)
	Ultraviolet Exposure/Degradation: The best way to prevent UV is to apply the first or base coat of the protective costing the same day the SPF is applied.
	Where there are larger areas of UV degradation…at least an additional 1 inch of new SPF must be applied.
391	**6.1 - Protective Surfacing Requirements:** Protective surfacing are part of SPF roof systems to provide weatherproofing, UV protection, mechanical damage protection and fire resistance.
392	**6.2 - Protective Coatings:** Protective coatings for use over SPF must: (5 Bullets)
394	**Protective Coating Types:** The following types of protective coatings: (6 Bullets)
399	**Figure 6-4:** Recommended minimum coating dry film thickness
405	Examples of pre-manufactured accessories that may be encountered on an SPF roof system include: (6 Bullets)
409	When roofing system maintenance and repair no longer can prevent recurrent leakage or extend a roof system's useful service life, consideration needs to be given to reroofing.
	Reroofing should also be considered in other situations, including the following (11 Bullets)
409 & 410	**8.1 Definitions:** ▪ **Reroofing** ▪ **Re-covering** ▪ **Replacement** ▪ **Roof assembly** ▪ **Roof system**
418	**Roof Replacement Considerations**
428 & 429	**8.5 – Preparation of Existing Roof Surfaces:** The following are brief guidelines for applying SPF over each of the common types of roof membranes. - **SPF Application over Existing Built-up Roof System** - **SPF Application over Existing Polymer-modified Bitumen Roof Systems** - **SPF Application over Existing Single-ply Roof Systems** - **SPF Application over Existing SPF Roof Systems**
429 & 430	**8.6 Re-cover Design Considerations:** The following is a list of general recommendations for re-covering an existing roof system with a new SPF roof system. (8 Bullets)

Code of Federal Regulations (OSHA) 29 CFR 1926
Questions and Answers

1. The minimum distance between side rails for all portable ladders shall not be less than ___________ inches.

   A. 11 ½
   B. 12
   C. 14
   D. 16

2. A stairway, ladder, ramp or other safe means of egress shall be located in trench excavations that are ___________ feet or more in depth so as to require no more than ___________ feet of lateral travel for employees.

   A. 4; 30
   B. 5; 30
   C. 4; 25
   D. 5; 25

3. Stairways that will not be a permanent part of the structure on which construction work is being performed shall have landings of not less than ___________ inches in the direction of travel.

   A. 22
   B. 30
   C. 36
   D. 24

4. Toeboards, when used as falling object protection, shall be a minimum of _________ inches in vertical height.

   A. 3 ½
   B. 4
   C. 6
   D. 8

5. Scaffold fabricated planks and platforms shall be designed for a working load of _________ pounds per square foot (psf), if considered light duty.

   A. 15
   B. 20
   C. 25
   D. 50

6. A scaffold designed for 75 pounds per square foot (psf) is classified as __________.

   A. Light-duty
   B. Medium-duty
   C. Heavy-duty
   D. One-person

7. An extra-heavy-duty type 1A metal or plastic ladder shall sustain at least __________ times the maximum intended load.

   A. 2
   B. 2.5
   C. 4
   D. 3.3

8. A bricklayer's square scaffold load shall not exceed __________ pounds per square feet.

   A. 25
   B. 50
   C. 75
   D. 100

9. OSHA requires an employer to provide a training program for each employee __________.

   A. Using ladders and stairways
   B. Working with toxic substances
   C. Working in excavations
   D. Using scaffolding

10. Cord sets and receptacles which are fixed and not exposed to damage shall be tested at intervals not exceeding __________ months.

    A. 2
    B. 3
    C. 4
    D. 6

11. When portable ladders are used for access to an upper landing surface, the ladder side rails shall extend at least __________ feet above the upper landing surface to which the ladder is used to gain access.

    A. 3
    B. 4
    C. 5
    D. 6

12. Personnel hoistway doors or gates shall be not less than __________ high.

    A. 4 feet 6 inches
    B. 6 feet 6 inches
    C. 8 feet 6 inches
    D. None of the above

13. The minimum illumination for indoor corridors during construction shall be __________ foot-candles.

A. 3
B. 5
C. 10
D. 30

14. The span between hangers for plank-type platforms shall not exceed __________ feet.

A. 6
B. 8
C. 10
D. 12

15. Bricklayers square scaffolds shall not exceed __________ tiers in height.

A. 2
B. 3
C. 4
D. 5

16. Where toeboards are used for falling object protection, the toeboard shall be capable of withstanding, without failure, a force of at least __________ pounds applied in any downward or horizontal direction.

A. 15
B. 25
C. 50
D. 100

17. Fixed ladders without cages or wells shall have a clear width to the nearest permanent object of at least __________ inches on each side of the centerline of the ladder.

A. 7
B. 12
C. 15
D. 18

18. Rungs, cleats and steps of portable ladders (except for special applications such as stepstools) shall be spaced not less than __________ inches apart, nor more than __________ inches.

A. 8; 11
B. 9; 14
C. 10; 14
D. 12; 16

19. Wire rope shall not be used for material handling if in any length of __________ diameter(s) the total number of visible broken wires exceeds 10% of the total number of wires.

A. 12
B. 18
C. 10
D. 8

20. The minimum illumination of general construction area lighting is __________ foot-candles.

A. 3
B. 5
C. 10
D. 30

21. All new safety nets shall meet accepted performance standards of __________.

A. 17,500 foot-pounds minimum impact resistance
B. 24,000 foot-pounds minimum impact resistance
C. Withstand five 200-pound sacks dropped simultaneously from a height of 25 feet
D. 10,000-pound rope tensile strength

22. The contents of the first aid kit shall be placed in a weatherproof container with individual sealed packages for each type of item, and shall be checked by the employer before being sent out on each job and at least __________ on each job to ensure that the expended items are replaced.

A. Daily
B. Weekly
C. Monthly
D. Annually

23. If the personnel hoist wire rope speed is 300 feet per minute, the minimum rope safety factor must be __________.

A. 9.20
B. 9.50
C. 9.75
D. 10.00

24. The use of non-self-supporting ladders shall be at such an angle that the horizontal distance from the top support to the foot of the ladder is approximately __________ of the working length of the ladder.

A. One-half
B. One-quarter
C. Three quarters
D. Seven eighths

25. Stairs shall be installed between __________ and __________ degrees horizontal.

A. 20; 40
B. 20; 50
C. 20; 30
D. 30; 50

26. Each employee on walking/working surfaces shall be protected from falling through holes, including skylights, by covers capable of supporting, without failure __________ that may be imposed on the cover at any one time.

A. At least twice the weight of employees, equipment and materials
B. An 800-pound load
C. A force of at least 200 pounds
D. A force of at least 150 pounds

27. Class II hazardous locations are those that are hazardous because of the presence of __________.

A. Combustible dust
B. Ignitable fibers
C. Flammable liquids
D. Explosives

28. Combustible materials shall be piled with regard to the stability of the piles and in no case shall be higher than __________ feet.

A. 12
B. 14
C. 16
D. 20

29. OSHA requires that for a structural steel assembly, at no time shall there be more than __________ feet or __________ floors, whichever is less, of unfinished bolting or welding above the foundation.

A. 20; 2
B. 24; 2
C. 30; 3
D. 48; 4

30. The term "ROPS" means __________.

A. Regional Operating Standards
B. Required Operating Steps
C. Rollover Protective Structures
D. None of the above

31. The maximum allowable slope for Type A soil for a simple slope in an excavation of 20 feet or less in depth is __________.

A. 1: 1
B. 2: 1
C. ½: 1
D. ¾: 1

32. When employees are required to be in trenches of __________ feet or more, an adequate means of egress such as a ladder, stairway or ramp shall be provided.

A. 3
B. 4
C. 5
D. 6

33. Openings are defined as a gap or void __________.

A. 12 inches or less in its least dimension in a floor
B. 30 inches or more high and 18 inches or more wide in a wall
C. Less than 12 inches but more than 1 inch in its least dimension in a floor
D. 12 inches or more in its greatest dimension in a floor

34. The top edge height of top rails, or equivalent guardrail system members, shall be __________ inches.

A. 30
B. 36
C. 42
D. 48

35. The use of spiral stairways that will not be a permanent part of the structure on which construction work is being performed is __________.

A. Permitted
B. Prohibited
C. Prohibited except with the permission of the building official
D. Permitted if the stairway is at least 7 feet in diameter

36. One toilet shall be provided at the construction jobsite for a maximum of __________ employees.

A. 5
B. 10
C. 15
D. 20

37. A Class C fire is a fire caused by __________.

A. Combustible metal
B. Flammable liquid
C. Trash
D. Electrical equipment

38. When materials are dropped more than __________ feet outside the exterior walls of a building, an enclosed chute shall be used.

A. 10
B. 15
C. 20
D. 25

39. Material shall not be stored indoors within __________ inches of a fire door opening.

A. 24
B. 30
C. 36
D. 48

40. Scaffold planking that is nominal two inches thick shall be used for a __________ psf workload at a maximum span of __________ feet.

A. 25; 10
B. 50; 8
C. 75; 6
D. 25; 8

41. OSHA requires that a safety factor based on load and speed be used in hoist cables. The safety factor for a cable with a speed of 200 feet per minute is __________.

A. 7.00
B. 6.65
C. 7.65
D. 8.60

42. Safety belt lanyards used for employee safeguarding shall have a minimum breaking strength of __________ pounds.

A. 1,000
B. 4,000
C. 5,000
D. 5,400

43. The proper maintenance for a carbon dioxide type fire extinguisher is to __________.

A. Discharge annually and recharge
B. Check pressure gauge monthly
C. Check pressure gauge annually
D. Weigh semi-annually

44. No more than __________ gallons of flammable or combustible liquids shall be stored in a room outside of an approved storage cabinet.

A. 10
B. 15
C. 20
D. 25

45. Exposure to impulsive or impact noise shall not exceed __________ dBA peak sound pressure level.

A. 92
B. 110
C. 140
D. 188

46. Simple slope-short-term excavations in Type A soil with a maximum depth of 12 feet shall have a maximum allowable slope of __________.

A. 1: 1
B. 2: 1
C. ¾: 1
D. ½: 1

47. The ratio of the ultimate breaking strength of a piece of material or equipment to the actual working stress when in use is known as the __________.

A. Occupational hazard
B. Unstructibility
C. Condition of protection
D. Safety factor

48. Wire, synthetic or fiber rope used for scaffold suspension shall be capable of supporting at least __________ times the rated load.

A. 6
B. 4
C. 3
D. 2

49. The proper maintenance for a multi-purpose ABC dry chemical stored pressure fire extinguisher is to __________.

A. Check pressure gauge monthly
B. Discharge annually and recharge
C. Weigh semi-annually
D. Check pressure gauge and condition of dry chemical annually

50. Metal tubular frame scaffolds, including components such as braces, brackets, trusses, screws legs, ladders, etc. shall be designed, constructed and erected to safely support its own weight and at least __________ times the maximum intended load applied.

A. 6
B. 2
C. 3
D. 4

51. The maximum span of 2" x 10" undressed lumber on a scaffold when loaded with 50 psf shall be __________ feet.

A. 5
B. 6
C. 10
D. 8

52. On construction sites, a fire extinguisher rated not less than 2A shall be provided for each __________ square feet of the protected building area, or major fraction thereof.

A. 1,000
B. 2,000
C. 3,000
D. 4,000

53. Potable drinking water, per OSHA, requires that __________.

A. If a container is used it shall be equipped with a tap
B. A common drinking cup is allowed if washed
C. Single serving cups do not have to be provided
D. Open containers can be used if single serving cups are provided

54. A safety belt lanyard shall provide for a fall not greater than __________ feet.

A. 3
B. 6
C. 12
D. 15

55. The maximum allowable height of a horse scaffold shall be two tiers or __________ feet.

A. 4
B. 8
C. 12
D. 10

56. When using carpenters' bracket scaffolds, the __________.

   A. Brackets shall be spaced a maximum of 8 feet
   B. Bolts used to attach shall be not less than 5/8 inches in diameter
   C. Tools and materials shall not exceed 75 pounds
   D. All of the above

57. When a material hoist tower is not enclosed, the hoist platform shall __________.

   A. Be caged on all sides
   B. Have ½-inch mesh number 16 U.S. gage wire covering
   C. Have a five-foot enclosure at ground level
   D. All of the above

58. Employees cannot be subjected to noise levels higher than __________ dBA for more than four hours per day.

   A. 95
   B. 97
   C. 102
   D. 105

59. The range of maximum intended working loads for light to heavy-duty Independent Wood Pole Scaffolds shall be __________ pounds per square foot (psf).

   A. 20 – 75
   B. 25 – 70
   C. 25 – 75
   D. 25 – 50

60. Safety nets shall be provided when workplaces are more than __________ feet above the ground or water surface.

   A. 6
   B. 8
   C. 10
   D. 25

61. No more than __________ employee(s) shall occupy any given eight feet of a form scaffold at any one time.

   A. 1
   B. 2
   C. 3
   D. 4

62. Given the following: 1 ½ hours noise exposure at 90 dBA
½ hour noise exposure at 100 dBA
¼ hour noise exposure at 110 dBA

If your employees are exposed to all of the above noise levels each workday, the "Equivalent Noise Exposure Factor __________.

A. Exceeds unity, therefore the noise exposure is within permissible levels
B. Exceeds unity, therefore the noise exposure is not within permissible levels
C. Does not exceed unity, therefore the noise exposure is within permissible limits
D. Does not exceed unity, therefore the noise exposure is not within permissible limits

63. A fire breaks out in a main electrical junction box at a construction site, an electrician is close by and asks you to get a fire extinguisher. According to OSHA, you should bring back a __________ extinguisher.

A. Soda acid
B. Foam
C. Stored pressure (water type)
D. CO_2

64. Oxygen cylinders, regulators and hoses shall be __________.

A. Stored only in approved containers
B. Prohibited in areas where fuel gasses other than acetylene are used
C. Unpainted
D. Kept away from oil or grease

65. A female employee complains that there are not separate toilets for the 20 women working on the site. She further states that all 160 employees use the same toilet. She said that the contractor is not complying with OSHA. According to the text, the employee __________.

A. Does not have a valid complaint since OSHA has no specific instructions as to male and female toilets. The project is only required to have four toilets and four urinals
B. Does not have a valid complaint since OSHA has no specific instructions as to male and female toilets. The project is only required to have five toilets and five urinals
C. Has a valid complaint since OSHA specifies that five toilets and five urinals for men and a separate toilet for women are required on a project of that size
D. Has a valid complaint since OSHA specifics four toilets and four urinals for men and a separate toilet for women are required on a project of that size

66. Employees shall not be exposed to noise levels exceeding __________ dBA for more than eight hours a day.

A. 90
B. 95
C. 102
D. 105

67. A Class A fire consists of burning __________.

A. Wood
B. Oil
C. Electrical equipment
D. Metals

68. Portable electric lighting used in wet and/or other conductive locations shall be operated at __________ volts or less.

A. 12
B. 32
C. 110
D. 220

69. __________ shall not be used if the rope shows other signs of excessive wear, corrosion, or defect.

A. Alloy steel chains
B. Synthetic fiber rope
C. Natural rope
D. Wire rope

70. According to OSHA, a sign lettered in legible red letters, not less than 6 inches high on a white field is used only as a/an __________ sign.

A. Danger
B. Exit
C. Caution
D. Safety Instructional

71. Material stored inside building under construction shall not be placed within __________ feet of any hoistway opening or inside floor openings.

A. 4
B. 5
C. 6
D. 10

72. Scaffold planks shall extend over the centerline of its supports at least __________ inches and not more than __________ inches.

A. 6; 12
B. 8; 12
C. 9; 12
D. 10; 16

73. A gap or void 2 inches or more in its least dimension in a floor, roof, or other walking/working surface is a __________.

A. Toeboard
B. Hole
C. Breech
D. Opening

74. Safety and health regulation for construction, the minimum diameter wire ropes used in personnel hoists shall be __________ inch.

A. ½
B. 5/8
C. ¾
D. 7/8

75. An electric power circular saw shall be __________.

A. Equipped with constant pressure switch
B. Equipped with a momentary on/off switch that may have a lock on control
C. Equipped with a positive on/off control
D. None of the above

76. For general cleaning operations, the compressed air shall be reduced to less than __________ psi.

A. 100
B. 20
C. 25
D. 30

77. For powder-actuated tools, fasteners shall be allowed to be driven into __________.

A. Face brick
B. Surface-hardened steel
C. Cast iron
D. None of the above

78. Sloping or benching for excavation more than __________ feet deep shall be designed by a registered professional engineer.

A. 10
B. 15
C. 20
D. 25

79. Stairway railings shall be capable of withstanding a minimum force of __________ pounds applied in any downward or outward direction at any point along the top edge.

A. 100
B. 150
C. 200
D. 250

80. Forms and shores in concrete shall not be removed until __________.

A. Directed by the architect or engineer
B. The removal time stated in the specifications has elapsed
C. The concrete has attained the specified compressive strength
D. The concrete has gained sufficient strength to support its weight and superimposed loads

81. When ropes are used to define controlled access zones, the rope shall have a minimum breaking strength of __________ pounds.

A. 75
B. 100
C. 200
D. 300

82. Excavations 8' or less in depth in Type A soil that have unsupported, vertically sided lower portions, shall have a maximum vertical side of __________ feet.

A. 3
B. 3.5
C. 4
D. 5

83. All the following are true concerning OSHA regulations about employees working over or near water except __________.

A. Ring buoys with at least 90 feet of line shall be provided and readily available
B. At least one lifesaving skiff shall be immediately available
C. Where the danger of drowning exists, provide employees with life jackets or buoyant work vests
D. At least one person certified in lifesaving swimming courses shall be employed at all times

84. __________ shall be located and determined prior to opening an excavation.

A. Dump site
B. Site entrances
C. Underground installations
D. Adjacent property elevations

85. The maximum intended load for a frame scaffold including its components is 1,000 pounds. The scaffold as described shall be designed to support a minimum of __________ ton(s).

A. 1.0
B. 1.5
C. 2.0
D. 4.0

86. Storing masonry blocks in stacks higher than 6 feet shall be permissible provided that __________.

A. Bracing is installed at the 6-foot level
B. Containment is provided every 4-foot
C. The stack is tapered back one-half block per tier above the 6-foot level
D. The stack is on a concrete floor

87. When hazardous waste cleanup and removal operations at any site take longer than __________ months to complete, the employer shall provide showers and changing rooms for employees exposed to such conditions.

A. 3
B. 6
C. 9
D. 12

88. No employee shall be exposed to lead at concentrations greater than __________ micrograms per cubic meter of air in an 8-hour period.

A. 30
B. 40
C. 50
D. 60

89. Training for Class II asbestos removal work requires hands-on training and shall take at least __________ hours.

A. 2
B. 8
C. 12
D. 16

90. Where oxygen deficiency (atmospheres containing less than 19.5 percent oxygen) or a hazardous atmosphere exists or could reasonably be expected to exist, such as in excavations in landfill areas or excavations in areas where hazardous substances are stored nearby, excavations deeper than __________ feet shall be tested before employees are allowed enter the excavation site.

A. 3
B. 4
C. 5
D. 6

91. Whenever a masonry wall is being constructed, a limited access zone shall be established. The access zone shall run the entire length of the wall, on the side of the wall that is not scaffolded and extend to the height of the wall to be __________.

A. Reconstructed
B. Reconstructed plus two feet
C. Reconstructed plus four feet
D. Reconstructed plus six feet

92. An employer shall ensure that no employee is exposed to an airborne concentration of asbestos in excess of __________ fiber(s) per cubic centimeter of air as averaged over a 30-minute sampling period.

A. 1.0
B. 2.0
C. 10.0
D. 20.0

93. A wire core manila rope is used as a lifeline where it may be subjected to cutting or abrasion. The required minimum size of the rope shall be __________ inch.

A. 1/2
B. 3/4
C. 7/8
D. 1

94. Routine inspection of open excavations shall be conducted by a competent person __________.

A. Daily
B. Weekly
C. Every two days
D. Every three days

95. Haulage vehicles, whose payload is loaded by means of cranes, power shovels, loaders, or similar equipment, shall have __________.

A. Pneumatic tires capable of supporting 1-1/2 times the payload capacity
B. Automatic dumping mechanisms capable of payload leveling
C. An automatic transmission and a cab shield on the load side of the operator station
D. A cab shield and/or canopy adequate to protect the operator from shifting or falling materials

96. When removing hazardous waste materials, personal protection equipment is divided into four categories based upon protection required. __________ has the highest level of respiratory protection but a lesser level of skin protection.

A. Level A
B. Level B
C. Level C
D. Level D

97. Fuel gas and oxygen manifolds shall NOT be placed __________.

A. Indirect sunlight
B. No closer than 15' of main electric
C. Elevated at least 6' off of a dirt floor
D. They shall not be located within enclosed areas

98. The term "point of operation" refers to the __________.

A. Starting point of a project
B. Specific operation of a project being performed
C. Area of a project where work is underway
D. Area on a machine where work is actually performed\

99. For excavation made in Type C soil, the minimum, above the top of the vertical side, that the support shield systems at the vertically sided lower portion of an excavation be shielded or supported shall be __________ inches.

A. 20
B. 18
C. 16
D. 14

100. The highest stack allowed when bricks are being stored shall be __________ feet.

A. 5
B. 7
C. 9
D. 10

101. Employees shall be provided with anti-laser eye protection devices when working in areas in which a potential exposure to reflected laser light is greater than __________ milliwatts.

A. 5
B. 4
C. 3
D. 2

102. The minimum illumination required for first aid stations shall be __________ foot-candles.

A. 30
B. 20
C. 5
D. 3

103. A job site having 90 employees with temporary restrooms shall have a minimum of __________ toilets and urinals.

A. One toilet and one urinal
B. Two toilets and two urinals
C. Three toilets and three urinals
D. Four toilets and four urinals

104. Employees shall be protected from excavated or other materials or equipment that could pose a hazard by falling or rolling into excavations. The minimum distance required from the edge of excavations for placing and keeping such materials or equipment is __________ feet.

A. 2
B. 3
C. 4
D. 5

105. Not more than __________ gallons of Category 4 flammable liquids shall be stored in any one storage cabinet.

A. 25
B. 60
C. 80
D. 120

106. A hand-held grinder with a 2-1/8" diameter wheel shall be equipped with only a __________.

A. Constant pressure switch
B. Momentary contact on/off switch
C. Positive percussion switch
D. Positive on/off switch

107. Each end of a scaffold platform, unless cleated or otherwise restrained, shall extend over the centerline of its support at least __________ inches.

A. 2
B. 4
C. 6
D. 12

108. Where scaffold platforms are overlapped to create a long platform, platforms shall be secured from movement or overlapped at least __________ inches unless the platforms are nailed together or otherwise restrained to prevent movement.

A. 2
B. 4
C. 6
D. 12

109. When lifting concrete slabs, operation of jacks shall be synchronized in such a manner as to insure even and uniform lifting of the slab. All points of the slab support shall be kept level within __________ inches.

A. 1/2
B. 1
C. 1-1/2
D. 2

110. A "Controlled Access Zone" is implemented to protect employees from access to an area where the erection of precast concrete members is being performed. The control lines in a "Controlled Access Zone" shall be erected not more than __________ feet from the unprotected or leading edge or half of the length of the member being erected, whichever is less.

A. 6
B. 15
C. 25
D. 60

111. Shoring for concrete shall be designed by a __________.

A. Contractor
B. Carpenter
C. Qualified designer
D. Lumber supplier

112. All masonry walls over __________ feet in height shall be adequately braced to prevent overturning and to prevent collapse unless the wall is adequately supported so that it will not overturn or collapse.

A. 8
B. 12
C. 16
D. 20

113. Self-supporting portable ladders shall be capable of supporting without failure at least __________ times the maximum intended load.

A. 3
B. 4
C. 5
D. 6

114. A non-self-supporting ladder has a working length of 20'. According to OSHA, the horizontal distance from the top support to the foot of the ladder is approximately __________ foot/feet.

A. 1/4 of a
B. 4
C. 5
D. 6

115. During asbestos removal, the asbestos disposal contractor shall erect __________ rooms in the decontamination area.

A. 2
B. 3
C. 4
D. 5

116. All pneumatic nailers, staplers and other similar equipment provided with automatic fastener feed shall have a safety device to prevent the tool from ejecting fasteners when operation pressures exceed __________ psi.

A. 75
B. 100
C. 125
D. 150

117. A portable ladder that is NOT self-supporting must be capable of supports at least __________ times the maximum intended load.

A. 2
B. 4
C. 6
D. 8

118. The common drinking cup is __________.

A. Prohibited
B. Not prohibited
C. Prohibited in areas where more than 3 workmen will use the cup
D. Prohibited in hazardous areas

119. Eye protection near dangerous working conditions __________.

A. Is required at the employee's cost
B. Is required at the employer's cost
C. Can only be required by union regulations
D. Is not required

120. During construction, the minimum illumination required for an indoor warehouse shall be __________ foot- candles.

A. 3
B. 5
C. 10
D. 30

121. When safety nets are required to be provided, such nets shall extend __________ feet beyond the edge of the work's surface.

A. 4
B. 6
C. 8
D. 10

122. The mesh size of safety nets shall not exceed __________.

A. 12" x 12"
B. 10" x 10"
C. 8" x 8"
D. 6" x 6"

123. When masonry blocks are stacked higher than __________ feet, the stack shall be tapered back one-half block per tier above the six-foot level.

A. 4
B. 6
C. 8
D. 10

124. Lumber that is handled manually shall not be stacked more than __________ feet high.

A. 14
B. 16
C. 18
D. 20

125. The components of a scaffold loaded with 500 pounds shall be capable of supporting its own weight and a load of at least ____________ ton(s) without failure.

A. 1
B. 2
C. 2.5
D. 4

126. All site clearing equipment shall be equipped with an overhead and rear canopy guard of at least 1/8" steel plate or __________ inch woven wire mesh with openings no greater than one inch, or equivalent.

A. 1/8
B. 1/4
C. 3/8
D. 1/2

127. Where doors or gates open directly on a stairway, a platform shall be provided, and the swing of the door shall not reduce the effective width of the platform to less than __________ inches.

A. 16
B. 18
C. 20
D. 24

128. Cohesive soil packed with an unconfined compressive strength of less than 1.5 tons per square foot but greater than .5 tons per square foot is defined as __________.

A. Type A
B. Type B
C. Type C
D. Type D

129. A six-foot deep trench excavated in Type C soil shall have the sides sloped at a maximum of __________.

A. ¾:1
B. 1:1
C. 1 ½ : 1
D. 1 ½: 1 ½

130. A simple slope excavation with a depth of 10 feet and which will be open for 20 hours shall have a maximum allowable slope of __________ in Type A soil.

A. 1: ¾
B. ¾ : 1
C. 1: ½
D. ½ : 1

131. When Type C soil is excavated over Type A soil, Type A soil shall be excavated to a maximum slope of __________ in layered soils.

A. 1: ¾
B. 1:1
C. ¾ : 1
D. 1 ½ : 1

132. Lifting inserts that are embedded, or otherwise attached to precast concrete members, other than the tilt-up members, shall be capable of supporting at least __________ times the intended maximum load.

A. 2
B. 3
C. 4
D. 5

133. The maximum number of manually controlled jacks allowed for lift-slab construction operations shall be limited to __________ on one slab.

A. 8
B. 10
C. 12
D. 14

134. The approximate angle of repose for sloping the sides of an excavation, less than 20' deep, in sand shall be __________.

A. 90°
B. 53°
C. 45°
D. 34°

135. When excavating in the proximity of adjoining buildings, a general contractor shall __________ for the safety and protection of workers.

A. Remove all loose soils and rocks
B. Compact adjacent soils and slope walls
C. Provide adequate shoring and bracing systems
D. Request a variance to move excavation farther away

136. When single post shores are tiered, they shall __________.

A. Never be spliced
B. Be vertically aligned
C. Be designed by a licensed engineer
D. Be adequately braced at top and bottom

137. When erecting systems-engineered metal buildings, during placing of rigid frame members, the load is not to be released from the hoisting equipment until __________.

A. The crane operator signals that is safe to proceed
B. All bolts have been installed and tightened to the specified torque
C. The members are secured with not less than 50% of the required bolts at each connection
D. Drift pins have driven into at least two bolt holes at each connection for the member

138. Prior to site layout, the contractor shall __________.

A. Obtain a certificate of occupancy and provide proof of occupancy
B. Alert subcontractors to the requirements of their scope
C. Start erecting structural steel and roof support members
D. Locate surface encumbrances that may pose a hazard to employees

139. Drawings or plans, including all revisions, for concrete formwork (including shoring equipment) shall be available at the __________.

A. Jobsite
B. Owner's office
C. Contractor's main office
D. Building department's office

140. Shoring for supported concrete slabs shall be removed only when the contractor __________.

A. Has had it inspected by the building inspector
B. Makes sure the concrete is dry to the touch
C. Determines that the concrete has gained sufficient strength to support its weight and superimposed loads
D. Has been told by the concrete supervisor that it is safe to strip the shoring

141. Where electrical transmission lines are energized and rated at least 50 kW or less, a minimum clearance distance of ___________ feet shall be maintained.

A. 5
B. 8
C. 10
D. 12

142. When debris is dropped through a hole in the floor without the use of chute, the drop area shall be enclosed with barricades measuring a minimum of __________ inches.

A. 30
B. 36
C. 42
D. 48

143. __________ require "point of operation guarding."

A. Hand chisels
B. Guillotine cutters
C. Powder-actuated tools
D. 1 ½ inch abrasive wheel grinder

144. A __________ scaffold has an adjustable platform mounted on an independent support frame and is equipped with a means to permit platform raising or lowering.

A. Multi-point adjustable suspension
B. Single-point adjustable suspension
C. Two-point adjustable suspension
D. Masons' adjustable supported

145. At more than __________ feet above a lower level, the tubular welded frame scaffolding shall have approved guardrails and toe boards at all open sides and ends.

A. 4
B. 6
C. 10
D. 12

146. A minimum of __________ bolts shall be in place at each structural steel beam connection during final placing of solid web members before the load is released.

A. One
B. Two
C. Three
D. Four

147. The maximum allowable height, without being retrained from tipping, for a free-standing mobile scaffold tower that has a base width of 4 feet is __________ feet.

A. 12
B. 16
C. 20
D. 24

148. The minimum plywood thickness required for an overhead protective covering above a material or personnel hoist cage is __________ inch(es).

A. 5/8
B. ¾
C. 7/8
D. ½

149. The maximum permissible span for a 2" x 9" full thickness undressed lumber scaffold plank, when used for a light duty rated load is __________ feet.

A. 6
B. 8
C. 9
D. 10

150. The maximum intended load on a float or ship scaffold shall be __________ lbs.

A. 250
B. 500
C. 750
D. 1,000

151. Which of the following is true about electric power-operated tools furnished by the contractor,

A. Each tool shall be cleaned daily after use
B. Each tool shall be checked daily before use
C. Each tool shall be tested daily before use
D. Each tool shall be double insulated or grounded

152. A __________ is an accidental failure of a cross brace in an excavation.

A. Kickout
B. Slip-in
C. Workout
D. Cave-in

153. The maximum permissible span for 1 ¼ x 9-inch full thickness wood plank having a maximum intended load of 50 pounds per square foot is __________ feet.

A. 4
B. 6
C. 8
D. 10

154. The minimum breaking strength for vertical lifelines used for fall protection shall be __________ pounds.

A. 3,000
B. 4,000
C. 5,000
D. 5,400

155. __________ gauge U.S. standard wire is used for the screen between the toe boards and top rails of an approved guardrail system.

A. No. 12
B. No. 14
C. No. 16
D. No. 18

156. A ground fault circuit interrupter, GFCI, which is not a part of the permanent wiring of the building on a construction site, protects the __________.

A. Cord sets
B. Power tools
C. Personnel
D. Wiring

157. The maximum opening size permitted in the ¼" woven wire mesh, used as a rear canopy guard on rider-operated equipment, when used for site clearing shall be __________ inch.

A. 1
B. ¾
C. ½
D. ¼

158. When a contractor discovers a piece of machinery on site which is not in compliance with OSHA requirements the contractor should __________.

A. Physically remove the machinery from the site
B. Identify the problem and inform anyone who operates it
C. Only operate the machinery on weekend or holidays
D. Schedule service to remedy the problem within 48 hours

159. A general contractor is building an apartment building with two exterior balconies. The general contractor and the carpentry subcontractor sign an agreement where the carpentry subcontractors will provide all temporary railings. There are 3 other subcontractors and their employees working on the site, using the balconies, when an OSHA inspector arrived and found the railing to be inadequate and unsafe. Which of the following represents the most likely outcome of this inspection visit?

A. The general contractor and all subcontractors on site will be fined the full amount
B. Only the carpentry subcontractor will be fined the full amount
C. Only the general contractor can be fined on the project
D. Only the general and the carpentry subcontractor will be fined

160. Of the following, which is not a true statement per OSHA regulations?

A. Jobsite first-aid kits shall be checked by the employer daily
B. Common drinking cups are prohibited for potable water
C. A jobsite with 50 employees must have 2 toilets and 2 urinals
D. The maximum duration of exposure to a sound level of 92 dba is 6 hours

161. According to OSHA, a hazardous atmosphere containing less than __________ percent oxygen may exist in deep excavations.

A. 100
B. 75
C. 50
D. 19.5

162. Which of the following is a true statement concerning OSHA regulations?

A. Manually stacked lumber piles shall not be more than 16 feet in height
B. Material stored inside building may not be placed within 2 feet of doors
C. Brick stacks shall not be more than 6 feet in height
D. Masonry blocks shall not be stacked more than 7 feet in height

163. Employers shall not issue or permit the use of unsafe hand tools. Which of the following tools is considered unsafe?

A. A drift pin with a mushroomed head
B. A splintered wooden handled shovel
C. A pipe wrench with a sprung jaw
D. All of the above are unsafe tools

164. Powder-actuated tools shall be tested __________ to insure proper working condition.

A. Every hour of each day in use
B. Each day before loading
C. One per week
D. After a malfunction occurs

165. "Asbestos containing material" is any material that contains __________ asbestos.

A. Up to one percent
B. More than one percent
C. Two percent or less
D. Between five and seven percent

166. Guarding for use with belts, gears, shafts, pulleys, drums, fly wheels or other power operated tools with reciprocating, rotating or moving parts should meet the requirements of __________.

A. OSHA Regulations
B. American National Standards Institute
C. Florida Building Code
D. U.S. Department of Labor

167. In excavations where a trench shield system is installed, the maximum depth of earth material that can be excavated below the bottom of the shield is __________ inches.

A. Zero
B. Not more than 6
C. Not more than 12
D. Not more than 24

168. In accordance with OSHA, the __________ has the responsibility of being safe, conducting activities safely and in accordance with all applicable laws and rules.

A. Individual
B. Employer
C. Building official
D. Foreman

169. The minimum number of sanitation facilities (chemical toilets) required for a 10-person mobile crew having transportation readily available to nearby toilet facilities is __________.

A. Not less than 1 toilet
B. 2
C. 3
D. Zero

170. __________ soil, which looks and feels damp, can easily be shaped into a ball and rolled into small diameter threads before crumbling.

A. Cohesive
B. Fissured
C. Moist
D. Granular

171. Inspections of alloy steel chains when used for rigging equipment for material handling shall occur __________.

A. Daily
B. Weekly
C. Monthly
D. Annually

172. Concrete mixers with __________ or larger loading skips shall be equipped with guardrails installed on each side of the skip.

A. One cubic foot
B. Ten cubic feet
C. One cubic yard
D. Ten cubic yards

173. A dry chemical, sodium or potassium bicarbonate-based fire extinguisher operated by cartridge is ranked as a type __________ extinguisher.

A. A
B. B
C. C
D. B and C only

174. When using control lines to demarcate controlled decking zones, non-mandatory guidelines require that each line be rigged and supported in such a way that its highest point is not more than __________ inches from the working surface.

A. 39
B. 40
C. 42
D. 45

175. A powder-operated tool shall be tested __________.

A. Each day before loading
B. Once a week
C. Once a month
D. At least semi-annually

176. A room used for storage of more than 60 gallons of flammable or combustible liquids shall have at least one portable fire extinguisher, having a rating of not less than 20-B units, shall be located outside of, but nor more than __________ feet from the door opening into the room.

A. 5
B. 7
C. 10
D. 12

177. The maximum number of people that can use a ladder jack scaffold at the same time is __________.

A. 1
B. 2
C. 3
D. 4

178. Guardrail systems shall be designed capable of withstanding a force of at least __________ pounds.

A. 100
B. 150
C. 200
D. 250

179. Toeboards are required on scaffolding more than __________ feet in height.

A. 6
B. 8
C. 10
D. 3

180. All pneumatically driven nailers provided with automatic fastener feed, which operate at more than 100 psi pressure at the tool shall have a __________.

A. Slight angle to the decking
B. Safety device installed at the muzzle
C. Regulated pressure to not exceed 110 psi
D. Regulated pressure not to have less than 90 psi

181. When using a hand-tool that is not grounded, the user should make sure the tool is __________.

A. Double insulated
B. Dust free
C. Newly painted
D. Serviced by a three-prong adapter

182. Each employee on a scaffold more than __________ feet above a lower level must be protected from falling to that lower level.

A. 6
B. 8
C. 10
D. 12

183. Scaffolding cannot be moved with employees still on it unless the surface on which it is moving is within __________ degrees of level.

A. 2
B. 3
C. 4
D. 5

184. Material chutes at an angle of more than 45° from the horizontal shall have openings not to exceed __________ inches in height.

A. 24
B. 48
C. 60
D. 72

185. When it is not practical to use nails to secure roof bracket scaffolds, brackets shall be secured in place with first-grade manila rope of at least __________ inch(es).

A. ½
B. ¾
C. 1
D. 1 ½

186. The warning line erected around all sides of the roof work area shall not be less than __________ feet from the roof edge when mechanical equipment is not being used.

A. 3
B. 4
C. 5
D. 6

187. On low-sloped roofs of __________ feet or less in width, the use of a safety monitoring system alone as a means of providing fall protection during roofing operation is permitted.

A. 40
B. 45
C. 50
D. 60

****** Please see Answer Key on the following page ******

OSHA Federal Safety and Health Regulations
Questions and Answers
Answer Key

Q	Answer	Section #
1.	A	1926.1053 (a)(4)(ii)
2.	C	1926.651 (c)(2)
3.	B	1926.1052 (a)(1)
4.	A	1926.502 (j)(3)
5.	C	Subpart L, Appendix A 1(c)
6.	C	Subpart L, Appendix A 1(c)
7.	D	1926.1053 (a)(1)(i)
8.	B	Subpart L, Appendix A 2(e)
9.	A	1926.1060 (a)
10.	D	1926.404 (b)(1)(iii)(E)(4)
11.	A	1926.1053 (b)(1)
12.	B	1926.552 (c)(4)
13.	B	1926.56, Table D-3
14.	C	Subpart L, Appendix A 2(p)(4)
15.	B	1926.452 (e)(4)
16.	C	1926.451(h)(4)(i)
17.	C	1926.1053 (a)(17)
18.	C	1926.1053 (a)(3)(i)
19.	D	1926.251 (c)(4)(iv)
20.	B	1926.56, Table D-3
21.	A	1926.105 (d)
22.	B	1926.50 (d)(2)
23.	A	1926.552 (c)(14)(iii)
24.	B	1926.1053 (b)(5)(i)
25.	D	1926.1052 (a)(2)
26.	A	1926.501 (b)(4)(ii) & 1926.502(i)(2)
27.	A	1926.449
28.	D	1926.151 (c)(1)

Q	Answer	Section #
29.	D	1926.754 (b)(2)
30.	C	1926.1002
31.	D	Subpart P, Appendix B, Table B-1 Maximum Allowable Slopes
32.	B	1926.651 (c)(2)
33.	B	See "Opening" in Glossary or 1926.500(b)
34.	C	1926.502 (b)(1)
35.	B	1926.1051 (a)(1)
36.	D	1926.51, Table D-1
37.	D	Subpart F, Table F-1 – Fire Extinguishers Data
38.	C	1926.252 (a)
39.	C	1926.151 (d)(7)
40.	D	Subpart L, Appendix A, Scaffold Specifications, (1)(b)(i), Table
41.	D	1926.552 (c)(14)(iii)
42.	D	1926.104 (d)
43.	D	Subpart F, Table F-1 – Fire Extinguishers Data
44.	D	1926.152 (b)(1)
45.	C	1926.52 (e)
46.	D	Subpart P, Appendix B, Table B-1 Maximum Allowable Slopes Figure B-1 Slope Configurations Figure B-1.1 Excavations made in Type A Soil
47.	D	See "Safety Factor" in Glossary or 1926.32(n)
48.	A	1926.451 (a)(4)
49.	D	Subpart F, Table F-1 – Fire Extinguishers Data
50.	D	1926.451 (a)(1)
51.	D	Subpart L, Appendix A (1)(b)(i), Table
52.	C	1926.150 (c)(1)(i)
53.	A	1926.51 (a)(2)
54.	B	1926.104 (d)
55.	D	1926.452 (f)(1)
56.	D	Subpart L, Appendix A, Scaffold Specifications, Paragraph (g)(2)(3)(4)
57.	A	1926.552 (b)(5)(ii)
58.	A	1926.52, Table D-2

Q	Answer	Section #
59.	C	Subpart L, Appendix A, Scaffold Specifications, 2. Specifications and Tables, (a) Pole Scaffolds, Table: Independent Wood Pole Scaffolds
60.	D	1926.105 (a)
61.	B	Subpart L, Appendix A, Scaffold Specifications, 2.Specific Guidelines and Tables (g)(4)
62.	C	1926.52 (d)(2)(iii) Fe = (T1 ÷ L1) + (T2 ÷ L2) + (Tn ÷ Ln) Fe = (1/4 ÷ ½) + (1/2 ÷ 2) + (1 ½ ÷ 8) Fe = 0.500 + 0.25 + 0.188 Fe = 0.938
63.	D	Subpart F, Table F-1 – Fire Extinguishers Data
64.	D	1926.350 (i)
65.	A	1926.51, Table D-1
66.	A	1926.52 (d)(1), Table D-2
67.	A	Subpart F, Table F-1 – Fire Extinguishers Data
68.	A	1926.405 (a)(2)(ii)(G)
69.	D	1926.251 (c)(4)(iv)
70.	B	1926.200 (d)
71.	C	1926.250 (b)(1)
72.	A	1926.451 (b)(4) & (5)
73.	B	See “Hole” in Glossary or 1926.500(b)
74.	A	1926.552 (c)(14)(ii)
75.	A	1926.300 (d)(3)
76.	D	1926.302 (b)(4)
77.	D	1926.302 (e)(7)
78.	C	Subpart P, Appendix B, Table B-1 Maximum Allowable Slopes (Note 3)
79.	C	1926.1052 (c)(5)
80.	D	1926.703 (e)(2)
81.	C	1926.502 (g)(3)(iii)
82.	B	1926.652, Subpart P Appendix B, Figure B-1 Slope Configurations B-1.1 Excavations made in Type A soil
83.	D	1926.106
84.	C	1926.651(b)(1)
85.	C	1926.451(a)(1) 1,000 x 4 = 4,000 4,000 ÷ 2,000 = 2 tons

Q	Answer	Section #
86.	C	1926.250(b)(7)
87.	B	1926.65 (n)(7)
88.	C	1926.62 (c)(1)
89.	B	1926.1101 (k)(9)(iv)(A)
90.	B	1926.651(g)(1)(i)
91.	C	1926.706(a)(2)
92.	A	1926.1101(c)(2)
93.	C	1926.104(c)
94.	A	1926.651(k)(1)
95.	D	1926.601(b)(6)
96.	B	1926.65 Appendix B, Part A, II
97.	D	1926.350(e)(2)
98.	D	1926.300(b)(4)(i)
99.	B	1926.652 Subpart P Appendix B, Figure B-1 Slope Configurations Figure B-1.3 Excavations Made in Type C Soil
100.	B	1926.250(b)(6)
101.	A	1926.54(c)
102.	A	1926.56, Table D-3 Minimum Illumination Intensities in Foot-Candles
103.	C	1926.51, Table D-1
104.	A	1926.651(j)(2)
105.	D	1926.152(b)(3)
106.	B	1926.300(d)(2)
107.	C	1926.451(b)(4)
108.	D	1926.451(b)(7)
109.	A	1926.705(g)
110.	D	1926.502(g)(1)(ii)
111.	C	1926.703 (b)(8)(i)
112.	A	1926.706(b)
113.	B	1926.1053(a)(1)(i)
114.	C	1926.1053(b)(5)(i) 20 feet ÷ 4 feet = 5 feet
115.	B	1926.1101(j)(1)(i)
116.	B	1926.302(b)(3)

Q	Answer	Section #
117.	B	1926.1053(a)(1)(ii)
118.	A	1926.51(a)(4)
119.	B	1926.102(a)(1)
120.	B	1926.56, Table D-3 Minimum Illumination Intensities in Foot-Candles
121.	C	1926.105(c)(1)
122.	D	1926.105(d)
123.	B	1926.250(b)(7)
124.	B	1926.250(b)(8)(iv)
125.	A	1926.451(a)(1)
		500 x 4 = 2,000 = 1 ton
126.	B	1926.604(a)(2)(i)
127.	C	1926.1052(a)(4)
128.	B	1926.652, Subpart P Appendix A (b)
129.	C	1926.652, Subpart P Appendix B, Table B-1 Maximum Allowable Slopes
130.	D	1926.652, Subpart P Appendix B, Figure B-1.1 Excavations made in Type A soil
131.	C	1926.652, Subpart P Appendix B, Figure B-1.4 Excavations Made in Layered Soils
132.	C	1926.704(c)
133.	D	1926.705(j)
134.	D	1926.652 Subpart P Appendix A (b) Note: "Sand" is classified as Type C soil 1926.652 Subpart P Appendix B, Table B-1 Maximum Allowable Slopes
135.	C	1926.651(i)(1)
136.	B	1926.703(b)(8)(ii)
137.	C	1926.758(c)
138.	D	1926.651(a)
139.	A	1926.703(a)(2)
140.	C	1926.703(e)(1)
141.	C	1926.1408, Table A
142.	C	1926.252 (b)
143.	B	1926.300(b)(4)(iv)(a)
144.	D	1926.450(b), See "Self-contained Adjustable Scaffold"
145.	C	1926.451(g)(1)
146.	B	1926.756(a)(1)

Q	Answer	Section #
147.	B	1926.451(c)(1) Note: Not more than 4:1 4 x 4 feet = 16 feet
148.	B	1926.552(b)(3), 1926.552(c)(7)
149.	D	1926.454, Subpart L Appendix A, Scaffold Specifications, General Guidelines and Tables, 1.(b)(i) – Table 1926.454, Subpart L Appendix A, Scaffold Specifications, General Guidelines and Tables, 1.(c) – Table
150.	C	1926.454, Subpart L Appendix A, Scaffold Specifications, 2. General Guidelines and Tables (s)(1)
151.	D	1926.302(a)(1)
152.	A	See "Kickout" in Glossary
153.	A	1926.454, Subpart L Appendix A, 1.(b)(ii)
154.	C	1926.502(d)(9)
155.	D	1926.454, Subpart L Appendix A, 1.(f)
156.	C	1926.404(b)(1)(ii)
157.	A	1926.604(2)(ii)
158.	A	1926.20(b)(3)
159.	A	1926.16(a) – (d)
160.	A	1926.50(d)(2), 1926.51(a)(4), 1926.51(c)(1), 1926.52, Table D-2
161.	D	1926.651(g)(1)(i)
162.	A	1926.250(b)(1), 1926.250(b)(6), 1926.250(b)(7), 1926.250(b)(8)(iv)
163.	D	1926.301(b) – (d)
164.	B	1926.302(e)(2)
165.	B	1926.1101(b), See "Asbestos-containing material" (ACM)
166.	B	1926.300(b)(2)
167.	D	1926.652(e)(2) or 1926.652(g)(2)
168.	B	1926.21(b)(1)
169.	D	1926.51(c)(4)
170.	C	1926.652, Subpart P Appendix A, (b), See "Moist Soil"
171.	D	1926.251(b)(6)(i)(D)
172.	C	1926.702(b)
173.	D	1926.150, Table F-1 – Fire Extinguishers Data
174.	D	1926.761, Subpart R Appendix D, (2)(i)

Q	Answer	Section #
175.	A	1926.302(e)(2)
176.	C	1926.152(d)(1)
177.	B	1926.454, Subpart L Appendix A, 2.(k)
178.	C	1926.502(b)(3)
179.	C	1926.451(h)(2)(ii)
180.	B	1926.302(b)(3)
181.	A	1926.302(a)
182.	C	1926.451(g)
183.	B	1926.452(w)(6)(i)
184.	B	1926.852(b)
185.	B	1926.452(h)(2)
186.	D	1926.502(f)(1)(i)
187.	C	1926.503, Subpart M Appendix A, (1)

Walker's Building Estimator's Reference Book, 32nd Edition
Questions and Answers
(Roofing Contractors)

1. The symbol for makeup water piping is __________.

   A. - - - - - - - - - - - - - -
   B. —··—··—··—··—··
   C. — — — — — — — — —
   D. —·—·—·—·—·—·—

2. A __________ bond is a bond furnished by the contractor that guarantees they will sign a contract in accordance with their bid and will provide performance and payment bonds.

   A. Surety
   B. Maintenance
   C. Bid
   D. Permit

3. In CPM scheduling, CPM stands for __________ and will calculate two sets of dates for each activity, the __________ finish and the Late Start-Late Finish.

   A. Computer program method, Early Start – Early Finish
   B. Contracts per month, Early Start – Early Finish
   C. Cost program method, Early Start – Early Finish
   D. Critical path method, Early Start – Early Finish

4. Plans and elevations are usually drawn at no less than __________.

   A. 1/16" = 1'-0"
   B. 1/8 " = 1'-0"
   C. 3/16 = 1'-0"
   D. 1/4" = 1'-0"

5. Under the Uniform System developed by the Construction Specifications Institute (CSI), Division 2 includes __________.

   A. General requirements
   B. Subsurface Investigation
   C. Concrete
   D. Finishes

6. The area of a roof measuring 100'-0" x 100'-0" with a ¼ pitch and a 12" or 1' overhanging cornice is __________ ft^2. Select the closest answer.

    A. 10,000
    B. 10,967
    C. 11,180
    D. 11,632

7. A __________ bond is a bond assuring that the contractor will complete a project in accordance with plans and specs identified in the contract documents.

    A. Performance
    B. Bid
    C. Maintenance
    D. Surety

8. An activity with zero float is called a __________.

    A. Burst activity
    B. Critical activity
    C. Merge activity
    D. None of the above

9. A __________ is a drawing in which all horizontal and vertical lines have true length and vertical lines are vertical but horizontal lines are set at 30 degrees or -30 degrees.

    A. Oblique
    B. Schematic
    C. Isometric
    D. Orthographic

10. Most working drawings for building construction are based on __________.

    A. Structural specifications
    B. Perspective
    C. Orthographic projection
    D. Isometrics

11. __________ work is usually publicly advertised.

    A. Commercial
    B. Private
    C. Competitive bidding
    D. Public

12. The typical dead weight of a ¾ inch piece of plywood is __________ pounds.

A. 71
B. 12.8
C. 38.4
D. 28

13. A __________ contract allows the owner control over the selection of his general contractor.

A. Lump-sum
B. Negotiated
C. Competitive
D. Cost plus fee

14. Once a loan is approved and accepted, __________ is/are NOT considered a closing cost(s).

A. Points
B. Interest
C. Origination fee
D. Discounts

15. Which of the following is *not* an advantage of renting or leasing construction equipment?

A. Eliminates personal property taxes on equipment
B. Offers flexibility in choosing equipment
C. Eliminates maintenance costs and the expense of training personnel to handle those tasks
D. Depreciation, insurance, repairs, taxes, and interest are deductible

16. A contractor can borrow money at 2 points above the current prime rate. This means that __________.

A. That the interest the contractor will be paying is 2% over treasury notes
B. That the interest the contractor will be paying is deposits are currently paying is 2 points above whatever certificates of deposits are currently paying
C. That the contractor is a preferred customer and the bank will charge him the prime rate of 2%
D. That the interest the contractor will be paying is 2% over the prime rate

17. __________ determine the quality requirements on a project during the process of bidding.

A. Specifications
B. Isometric drawings
C. Blueprints
D. Addendums

18. The __________ is NOT one of the three traditional methods of construction scheduling.

A. Project Schedule
B. Critical Path Method (CPM)
C. Bar (or Gant) Chart
D. Program Evaluation and Review Technique (PERT)

19. The maximum distance that can typically be spanned by a wood truss is __________ feet.

A. 25
B. 70
C. 150
D. 200

20. Any discrepancies on the plans or specifications or changes the architect or owner wish to make after the plans and specifications have been issued, but before bids are turned in, are incorporated in the __________.

A. Submittals
B. Change order
C. Construction change directive
D. Addenda

21. The type of cost estimate where the estimator starts an entirely new cost estimate based on the items of work identified in the contract specifications and drawings is called the __________ estimate.

A. Pre design
B. Conceptual
C. Construction Documents Milestone
D. Bid Cost

22. The average life expectancy of truck tires in construction work is __________ hours.

A. 2,000
B. 2,500
C. 3,000
D. 3,500

23. Money set aside to replace future equipment should be put into a separate fund know as a(an) __________.

A. Future fund
B. Escrow fund
C. Equipment depreciation fund
D. Sinking fund

24. The federal government, under the __________, requires that a contractor furnish two separate bonds, one for performance and one for the payment of labor and materials.

A. Copeland Act
B. Taft-Hartley Act
C. Miller Act
D. Davis-Bacon Act

25. A defect in workmanship is found 18 months after a project is completed. A __________ bond would cover this defect.

   A. Payment
   B. Performance
   C. Maintenance
   D. Bid

26. If a contractor regularly operates within an area that requires a permit bond, the cost of this bond should be expensed to __________.

   A. Job expense
   B. General ledger
   C. Office overhead
   D. Permit fees

27. An AIA form __________, the Contractors Qualification Statement, is used to furnish information needed to bid on public work.

   A. A305
   B. A101
   C. A201
   D. A701

28. Another reference name for a Bar Chart is a __________.

   A. Pert Chart
   B. Gantt Chart
   C. Precedence Diagram
   D. CPM Chart

29. The terms CPM and PERT pertain to __________.

   A. Specifications
   B. Scheduling
   C. Inventory
   D. Contract performance management

30. The principal objective of construction scheduling is to manage all of the following resources used in the construction process except for __________.

   A. Labor
   B. Materials
   C. Subcontractors
   D. Cash flow

31. The standard tool for resource control in project scheduling which calculates the project completion date and dates for completion of project activities and intermediate milestones is the __________.

A. Bar Chart
B. Gant Chart
C. Critical Path Method (CPM)
D. Master Network

32. There are __________ board feet in 2600 L.F. of 2 x 4's.

A. 1,734
B. 650
C. 144
D. 2,600

33. Equipment rental rates vary greatly throughout the country. It is standard practice to base rates on __________ hours per month.

A. 100
B. 150
C. 160
D. 176

34. When renting non-tractor equipment, the __________ is usually responsible for the cost of repairs due to normal wear and tear.

A. Leaser
B. Contractor
C. Lessee
D. Insurance company

35. The weight of 150' of 2-1/2" x 2-1/2" x 3/16" steel angles is __________ pounds.

A. 23
B. 3.07
C. 225
D. 460.5

36. An arch having horizontal or nearly horizontal upper and lower surfaces is referred to as a __________ arch.

A. Trimmer
B. Jack
C. Back
D. Minor

37. Construction drawings will generally depict details through the use of __________.

A. Notes, schedules, symbols, elevations
B. Architects notes and manufacturers reference
C. Written specifications and instruction to bidders
D. Addendum issued by the architect to the contractors

38. After acquiring a piece of construction equipment, the contractor should __________.

A. Divide the lease payments by the number of jobs in progress and charge each accordingly
B. Divide the annual depreciation by the number of estimated jobs for the year for a per-job charge
C. Develop an hourly rate charge, sufficient to cover interest charges and replacement costs
D. Develop a chargeable rate that is comparable to the local rental rates for similar equipment

39. A blueprint shows a rectangular building lot that scales out a 15.0" by 22.5". The scale given for the site plan is 1" = 12'. The area of the building lot is __________ ft^2.

A. 4.860
B. 33,750
C. 48,600
D. 53,460

40. __________ is the amount of time for an activity, obtained by subtracting its early start (ES) from its late start (LS) or early finish (EF) from its late finish (LF).

A. Total float
B. Forward scheduling
C. Backward scheduling
D. Mean flow time

41. Modifications issued after contract is signed are called a(n) __________.

A. Addenda
B. Letter
C. Change order
D. Oral or verbal directive

42. According to a set of plans, a contractor is to construct a residential structure that measures 40' x 60' with a hip slope sloped at 5/12 slope. The total area of the roof is __________ ft^2.

A. 2,000
B. 2,400
C. 2,600
D. 3,000

43. __________ is NOT a correct statement.

A. The total float is obtained by subtracting its' ES from its' LS time
B. The total float is obtained by subtracting its' EF from its' ES time
C. The use of total float for one activity will reduce it by a like amount in other items
D. The activities in a chain share total float

44. A minor arch with a maximum span of 6 feet and a load not exceeding 1000 lbs. per foot is typically referred to as a __________ arch.

A. Relieving
B. Jack
C. Trimmer
D. Back

45. A vertical plane represented by an orthographic projection of the outside building is a (an) __________.

A. Isometric drawing
B. Plan view
C. Section
D. Elevation

46. If the lap is 4" wide and only a single thickness of felt is used, add about __________% to allow for laps and the additional felt required at the top and bottom of wall.

A. 0
B. 10
C. 15
D. 20

47. A contractor is building a house with a hip roof. The slope of the roof is 5/12. The plan dimensions of the house are 40' x 60'. Assuming a 10% waster factor, the contractor must order __________ sheets of plywood. Select the closest answer.

A. 90
B. 80
C. 100
D. 70

48. A contractor is buying a bundle of 2" x 6" x 8' long. The cost of lumber is $0.25 per bf. If the cost of the bundle is $100, there are __________ pieces are in the bundle.

A. 100
B. 25
C. 50
D. 150

49. The principal objective of a construction schedule is to __________.

A. Support claims against the owner
B. Assist architect in planning project completion
C. Efficiently manage resources in order to complete within the estimated time and costs for the project
D. Track progress of all subcontractors on the project

50. A __________ arch is another name for a major arch

A. Gothic
B. Back
C. Segmental
D. Relieving

51. The late start of an activity is __________.

A. The latest it can finish without effecting the end of the date of the project
B. The latest it can start without effecting the end date of the project
C. The earliest date the activity can finish
D. The date that impacts the schedule finish date the most

52. A contractor needs to purchase 25 lengths of structural steel angle, 3 ½ x 2 ½ x 3/8. Each piece of 20' long. The total weight to be purchased is __________ pounds.

A. 3,300
B. 3,600
C. 3,750
D. 3,800

53. A contractor is estimating the amount of roofing material to buy for a project. According to Walker's, a waste factor of __________% would be used to estimate the quantity of asphalt shingles for a structure with hip roofs, including dormers and valleys.

A. 10
B. 15
C. 20
D. 25

54. Based on the house plan below, the total roof area is __________ square feet.

A. 3,670
B. 3,850
C. 4,297
D. 4,579

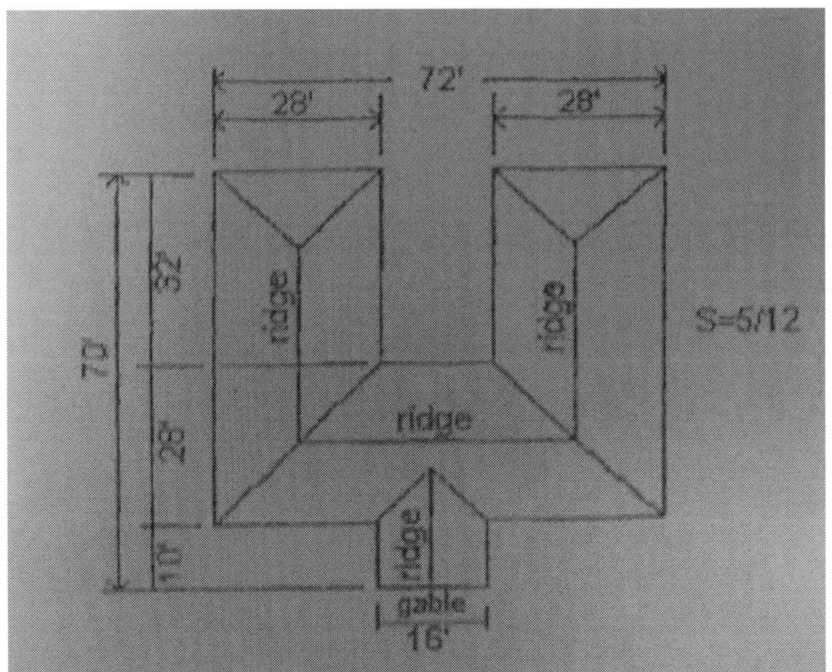

****Please see Answer Key on the following page*****

ABC 12/09/2021

Walker's Building Estimator's Reference Book, 32nd Edition
Questions and Answers
(Roofing Contractors)
Answer Key

	Answer	Page #
1.	D	31
2.	C	24
3.	D	65
4.	B	29
5.	B	81
6.	D	471 – 472 , Table: Sample Roof Factor Estimate Solution - Length x Width = (100' + 1'+ 1') x (100' + 1' + 1') = 10,404 ft^2 Flat or horizontal area – multiply by factor in Table with ¼ pitch = 1.118 Answer is 10,404 x 1.118 = 11,631.67 ft^2 Round up to 11,632
7.	A	24
8.	B	67
9.	C	27
10.	C	27
11.	D	15
12.	A	134, Table: Nominal Plywood Weights for Form Plywood
13.	B	25
14.	B	4
15.	D	25
16.	D	6
17.	A	15
18.	A	62
19.	D	389
20.	D	57
21.	D	9
22.	C	842
23.	D	25
24.	C	24
25.	C	24
26.	C	24

	Answer	Page #
27.	A	22
28.	B	64
29.	B	64
30.	D	64 – 65
31.	C	64
32.	A	825 Solution - 2 x 4 ÷ 2600 = 1733.33
33.	D	825
34.	C	825
35.	D	354, Table: Weights of Steel Angles Solution - 150 x 3.07 = 460.5 pounds
36.	B	883
37.	A	27
38.	C	825
39.	C	870 Solution = 15" x 12' = 180 feet 22.5" x 12' = 270 feet 180' x 270' = 48,600 ft^2
40.	A	66
41.	C	26, See "change order"
42.	C	471, Table: Sample Roof Factor Estimate Solution = roof area = L x W = 40' x 60' = 2400 ft^2 Table on page 788 – 5/12 slope – multiply flat area by 1.083 2400 ft^2 x 1.083 = 2599.2 ft^2– round up 2600 ft^2
43.	B	66
44.	B	883
45.	D	27
46.	D	457
47.	A	471 Solution – (40' x 60') x 1.083 from table x 1.10 ten percent waste factor = 2859.12 ft^2 2859.12 ft^2 ÷ (4 x 8) piece of plywood = 89.347 = round up to 90 sheets
48.	C	376 Solution – 2" x 6" x 8' /12 = 8 BF x $0.25/ BF= $2.00 $100 / $2 = 50
49.	C	62
50.	A	833, See "Arch – major arch"
51.	B	66, See "Late Start (LS)"

	Answer	Page #
52.	B	354, Table: Weights of Steel Angles Solution = 25 x 20’ x 7.20 from table = 3,600
53.	C	472
54.	C	471

Solution = Obtain area of the roof = divide into rectangles
(28’ x 60’) + (28’ x 60’) + (28’ x 16’) + (16’ x 10’) = 3,968 ft^2 flat or horizontal
Area - 3,968 ft^2 x 1.083 from Table on page 788 = 4,297 ft^2

Florida Building Code – Residential, 2020
Solar Contractor
Questions and Answers

1. A solar thermal system in which the gas or liquid in the solar collector loop is not separated from the load is a ______________ system.

   A. Drain-Back
   B. Closed Loop
   C. Direct
   D. Indirect

2. Thermal solar energy systems shall be equipped with means to limit the maximum water temperature of the system fluid entering or exchanging heat with any pressurized vessel inside the dwelling to _____°F.

   A. 104
   B. 130
   C. 150
   D. 180

3. In concealed locations, where piping, other than ________, is installed through holes or notches in studs, joists, rafters or similar members less than 1.5 inches from the nearest edge of the member, the pipe shall be protected by shield plates.

   A. copper and galvanized steel
   B. cast-iron and copper
   C. galvanized steel and cast-iron
   D. PVC and copper

4. Class A, B or C photovoltaic panel systems and modules shall be installed in jurisdictions designated by law
   as requiring their use or where the edge of the roof is less than ________ feet from a lot line.

   A. 2
   B. 3
   C. 4
   D. 5

5. According to Florida Residential Code, _________________ conforming to ASTM F656 shall be applied to PVC joints.

   A. approved solvent cement
   B. caulking ferrules
   C. purple primer
   D. elastomeric seals

6. The maximum water velocity in copper tubing shall not exceed _______ feet per second.

A. 5
B. 8
C. 10
D. 12

7. Photovoltaic panels and modules shall be listed and labeled in accordance with __________.

A. UL 1703
B. UL 1741
C. UL 9540
D. UL 723

8. When water heating equipment which is installed in a closed system has a valve between the appliance and the pool, a __________ valve shall be installed on the discharge side of the water heating equipment.

A. check
B. butterfly
C. pressure relief
D. globe

9. Solar collector sensor installation, sensor location and the protection of exposed wires from ultraviolet light shall be in accordance with ___________.

A. SRCC 300
B. IAPMO/ANSI Z124
C. FSEC Standard 101-15
D. ISO Standard 9806

10. A check or shutoff valve shall not be installed between _________________.

A. a relief valve and the termination point of the relief valve discharge pipe
B. a relief valve and a tank.
C. a relief valve and heating appliances or equipment
D. All of the above

11. For each roof plane with a photovoltaic array, a pathway not less than ______ inches wide shall be provided from the lowest roof edge to ridge on the same roof plane as the photovoltaic array, on an adjacent roof plane, or straddling the same and adjacent roof planes.

A. 24
B. 36
C. 42
D. 48

12. Where heated water is discharged from a solar thermal system to a hot water distribution system, a thermostatic mixing valve complying with ASSE 1017 shall be installed to temper the water to a temperature of not greater than _________°F.

A. 104
B. 120
C. 130
D. 140

13. Where a solar thermal system directly heats chemically treated water for a system other than a potable water distribution system, a potable water supply connected to such system shall be protected by a ____________________ complying with ASSE 1013.

A. backflow preventer with an intermediate atmospheric vent
B. double check valve assembly
C. reduced pressure principle backflow prevention assembly
D. None of the above

14. Which of the following most accurately describes a BTU?

A. The amount of heat required to raise 1 liter of water 1°C
B. The amount of heat required to raise 1 gallon of water 1°F
C. The amount of heat required to raise 1 pound of water 1°F
D. The amount of heat required to raise I pound of water 1°C

15. Where a pipe penetrates a roof, a flashing of ____________shall be installed in manner that prevents water entry into the building.

A. aluminum, lead, or copper
B. lead, copper, galvanized steel or an approved elastomeric material
C. anodized aluminum or galvanized steel
D. galvalume, copper, or steel

16. Joints in plastic piping shall be made with approved fittings by ____________.

A. solvent cementing, heat fusion, corrosion-resistant metal clamps with insert fittings or compression connections
B. compression connections, solvent cementing, or fiberglass wrap
C. heat fusion, hose clamps, solvent cementing, or compression connections
D. None of the above

17. What is the maximum horizontal hanger spacing for 2" PVC pipe?

A. 10'
B. 8'
C. 6'
D. 4'

18. Water supplies of any type shall not be connected to the solar heating loop of a/an _______ solar thermal hot water heating system.

A. Direct
B. Indirect
C. Drain-Back
D. Closed Loop

19. For photovoltaic arrays occupying not more than 33 percent of the plan view total roof area, not less than an ________inch clear setback is required on both sides of a horizontal ridge.

A. 18
B. 24
C. 30
D. 36

20. All pool water heating equipment shall be installed with ____________ adjacent to the heater.

A. a check valve
B. flanges or a union connection
C. backflow prevention
D. full-way (gate) valve

21. Expansion tanks in solar energy systems shall be designed in accordance with __________ to provide an expansion tank that is sized to withstand the maximum operating pressure of the system.

A. IAPMO/ANSI Z1157
B. FSEC Standard 104-10
C. ISO Standard 9806
D. SRCC 300

22. The flash point of the heat transfer fluids utilized in solar thermal systems shall be not less than _____°F above the design maximum nonoperating or no-flow temperature attained by the fluid in the collector.

A. 30
B. 35
C. 40
D. 50

23. Which of the following is not required for the labeling of solar thermal collectors and panels?

A. Trademark and warranty information
B. Model number and serial number
C. maximum allow temperatures and pressures
D. type of heat transfer fluids that are compatible

24. What is the maximum horizontal hanger spacing for copper pipe?

A. 12'
B. 10'
C. 8'
D. 6'

25. Solar thermal collectors and panels shall be listed and labeled in accordance with _______________.

A. SRCC 100 or SRCC 300
B. ISO Standard 9806
C. SRCC 100 or SRCC 600
D. FSEC Standard 104-10

Florida Building Code – Residential, 2020
Solar Contractor
Answers

1.	C	202, See "DIRECT SYSTEM"
2.	D	M2301.2.12
3.	C	P2603.2.1
4.	B	R902.4
5.	C	P2906.9.1.4
6.	B	R4501.6.3, Figure AP103.3(2) Note, Figure AP103.3(3) Note, AP103.3(4) Note
7.	A	R324.3.1
8.	C	R4501.14.5
9.	A	M2301.2.2.2
10.	D	P2804.6
11.	B	R324.6.1
12.	D	P2802.1
13.	C	P2902.5.5.3
14.	C	G2403, See "BTU"
15.	B	P2607.1
16.	A	P2906.9
17.	D	Table M2101.9
18.	A	P2902.5.5.1
19.	A	R324.6.2
20.	B	R4501.14.4
21.	D	M2301.2.8
22.	D	M2301.4
23.	A	M2301.3.1
24.	A	Table M2101.9
25.	C	M2301.3.1

Florida Building Code – Residential, 2017
Solar Contractor
Questions and Answers

1. A solar thermal system in which the gas or liquid in the solar collector loop is not separated from the load is a ______________ system.

    A. Drain-Back
    B. Closed Loop
    C. Direct
    D. Indirect

2. Thermal solar energy systems shall be equipped with means to limit the maximum water temperature of the system fluid entering or exchanging heat with any pressurized vessel inside the dwelling to _____°F.

    A. 104
    B. 130
    C. 150
    D. 180

3. In concealed locations, where piping, other than _________, is installed through holes or notches in studs, joists, rafters or similar members less than 1.5 inches from the nearest edge of the member, the pipe shall be protected by shield plates.

    A. copper and galvanized steel
    B. cast-iron and copper
    C. galvanized steel and cast-iron
    D. PVC and copper

4. Class A, B or C photovoltaic panel systems and modules shall be installed in jurisdictions designated by law as requiring their use or where the edge of the roof is less than ________ feet from a lot line.

    A. 2
    B. 3
    C. 4
    D. 5

5. According to Florida Residential Code, _________________ conforming to ASTM F656 shall be applied to PVC joints.

    A. approved solvent cement
    B. caulking ferrules
    C. purple primer
    D. elastomeric seals

6. The maximum water velocity in copper tubing shall not exceed _______ feet per second.

A. 5
B. 8
C. 10
D. 12

7. Photovoltaic panels and modules shall be listed and labeled in accordance with __________.

A. UL 1703
B. UL 1741
C. UL 9540
D. UL 723

8. When water heating equipment which is installed in a closed system has a valve between the appliance and the pool, a __________ valve shall be installed on the discharge side of the water heating equipment.

A. check
B. butterfly
C. pressure relief
D. globe

9. Solar collector sensor installation, sensor location and the protection of exposed wires from ultraviolet light shall be in accordance with ___________.

A. SRCC 300
B. IAPMO/ANSI Z124
C. FSEC Standard 101-15
D. ISO Standard 9806

10. A check or shutoff valve shall not be installed between ________________.

A. a relief valve and the termination point of the relief valve discharge pipe
B. a relief valve and a tank.
C. a relief valve and heating appliances or equipment
D. All of the above

11. _____________in the plumbing system shall be gas tight and water-tight for the intended use or required test pressure.

A. Joints
B. Connections
C. Both A and B
D. neither

12. Where heated water is discharged from a solar thermal system to a hot water distribution system, a thermostatic mixing valve complying with ASSE 1017 shall be installed to temper the water to a temperature of not greater than _________°F.

A. 104
B. 120
C. 130
D. 140

13. Where a solar thermal system directly heats chemically treated water for a system other than a potable water distribution system, a potable water supply connected to such system shall be protected by a ______________________ complying with ASSE 1013.

A. backflow preventer with an intermediate atmospheric vent
B. double check valve assembly
C. reduced pressure principle backflow prevention assembly
D. None of the above

14. Which of the following most accurately describes a BTU?

A. The amount of heat required to raise 1 liter of water 1°C
B. The amount of heat required to raise 1 gallon of water 1°F
C. The amount of heat required to raise 1 pound of water 1°F
D. The amount of heat required to raise I pound of water 1°C

15. Where a pipe penetrates a roof, a flashing of _____________shall be installed in manner that prevents water entry into the building.

A. aluminum, lead, or copper
B. lead, copper, galvanized steel or an approved elastomeric material
C. anodized aluminum or galvanized steel
D. galvalume, copper, or steel

16. Joints in plastic piping shall be made with approved fittings by _____________.

A. solvent cementing, heat fusion, corrosion-resistant metal clamps with insert fittings or compression connections
B. compression connections, solvent cementing, or fiberglass wrap
C. heat fusion, hose clamps, solvent cementing, or compression connections
D. None of the above

17. What is the maximum horizontal hanger spacing for 2" PVC pipe?

A. 10'
B. 8'
C. 6'
D. 4'

18. Water supplies of any type shall not be connected to the solar heating loop of a/an _______ solar thermal hot water heating system.

A. Direct
B. Indirect
C. Drain-Back
D. Closed Loop

19. Hydronic piping systems shall be tested hydrostatically at a pressure of not less than _______ pounds per square inch for a duration of not less than 15 minutes and not more than 20 minutes.

A. 25
B. 50
C. 75
D. 100

20. All pool water heating equipment shall be installed with ____________ adjacent to the heater.

A. a check valve
B. flanges or a union connection
C. backflow prevention
D. full-way (gate) valve

21. Expansion tanks in solar energy systems shall be designed in accordance with ___________ to provide an expansion tank that is sized to withstand the maximum operating pressure of the system.

A. IAPMO/ANSI Z1157
B. FSEC Standard 104-10
C. ISO Standard 9806
D. SRCC 300

22. The flash point of the heat transfer fluids utilized in solar thermal systems shall be not less than _____°F above the design maximum nonoperating or no-flow temperature attained by the fluid in the collector.

A. 30
B. 35
C. 40
D. 50

23. Which of the following is not required for the labeling of solar thermal collectors and panels?

A. Trademark and warranty information
B. Model number and serial number
C. maximum allow temperatures and pressures
D. type of heat transfer fluids that are compatible

24. What is the maximum horizontal hanger spacing for copper pipe?

A. 12'
B. 10'
C. 8'
D. 6'

25. Solar thermal collectors and panels shall be listed and labeled in accordance with ________________.

A. SRCC 100 or SRCC 300
B. ISO Standard 9806
C. SRCC 100 or SRCC 600
D. FSEC Standard 104-10

Florida Building Code – Residential, 2017
Solar Contractor
Answers

1.	C	202, See "DIRECT SYSTEM"
2.	D	M2301.2.12
3.	C	P2603.2.1
4.	B	R902.1
5.	C	P2906.9.1.4
6.	B	R4501.6.3, Figure AP103.3(2) Note, Figure AP103.3(3) Note, AP103.3(4) Note
7.	A	R324.3.1
8.	C	R4501.14.5
9.	A	M2301.2.2.2
10.	D	P2804.6
11.	C	P2906.8
12.	D	P2802.1
13.	C	P2902.5.5.3
14.	C	G2403, See "BTU"
15.	B	P2607.1
16.	A	P2906.9
17.	D	Table M2101.9
18.	A	P2902.5.5.1
19.	D	M2101.10
20.	B	R4501.14.4
21.	D	M2301.2.8
22.	D	M2301.4
23.	A	M2301.3.1
24.	A	Table M2101.9
25.	C	M2301.3.1

Florida Building Code - Plumbing, 2020
Solar Contractor
Questions and Answers

1. According to Florida Plumbing Code, ____________ is prohibited for use in the water distribution piping.

   A. compression fitting
   B. saddle-type fitting
   C. threaded joint
   D. soldered joint

2. According to Florida Plumbing Code copper vent pipe flashing shall weigh not less than_______________ per square foot.

   A. 8 ounces
   B. 10 ounces
   C. 12 ounces
   D. 16 ounces

3. A 2" diameter galvanized steel water service pipe is installed vertically in a building that has twelve floors, 15 feet floor -to-floor. According to code, the minimum number of supports required for a section of pipe passing through eight floors would be________________.

   A. 8
   B. 10
   C. 12
   D. 13

4. A combination of approved bends that makes 2 changes in direction bringing one section of the pipe out of line but into a line parallel with the other section is called a/an______________.

   A. offset
   B. tee-wye
   C. jumper
   D. parallel pipe

5. According to Florida Plumbing Code, a 150' length of 4" diameter existing galvanized steel water pipe, with a 200 gpm flow rate, will have a pressure drop of approximately____ psi.

   A. 2.6
   B. 3.9
   C. 5.2
   D. 8.0

6. According to Florida Plumbing Code, vertical cast iron pipe shall be supported at intervals not exceeding ________________.

A. 10 feet
B. 12feet
C. 15 feet
D. 20 feet

7. According to Florida Plumbing Code, the minimum size Type L copper tubing required to convey 10 gallons of water per minute a distance of 100 feet with a maximum pressure drop of 1 psi is____________. Assume new tubing.

A. 1" diameter tubing
B. 1-1/4" diameter tubing
C. 1-1/2" diameter tubing
D. 2" diameter tubing

8. According to Florida Plumbing Code, an underground water service pipe and a building sewer shall be separated horizontally by at least__________ of undisturbed or compacted earth.

A. 2 feet
B. 5 feet
C. 10 feet
D. 12 feet

9. According to Florida Plumbing Code, wherever water pressure from the street main supply is insufficient to provide flow pressures at fixture outlets as required, then______________.

A. a water pressure booster system shall be installed
B. the building will be vacated until pressure resumes
C. a new water main will need to be installed
D. gauges to monitor pressure shall be installed

10. According to Florida Plumbing Code, _________is an approved material for underground water distribution pipe.

A. black steel piping
B. ABS plastic pipe
C. asbestos cement pipe
D. type M copper tubing

11. The code does not permit a crown vent to be installed within_____of a 4" trap weir.

A. 14 inches
B. 12 inches
C. 10 inches
D. 8 inches

12. A maximum of ____________ fixtures connected to a horizontal branch can be circuit vented.

A. 12
B. 8
C. 4
D. 2

13. According to Florida Plumbing Code, the pressure loss through a 1-1/4" tap at a flow rate of 90 gpm is_________.

A. 2.94 psi
B. 4.90 psi
C. 6.21 psi
D. 6.94 psi

14. According to Florida Plumbing Code, ____________joints in drainage piping may be used within the trap seal.

A. slip
B. flanged
C. brazed
D. welded

15. The backflow of potentially contaminated water into the potable water system as a result of the pressure in the potable water system failing below atmospheric pressure of the plumbing fixtures, pools, tanks or vats connected to the potable water distribution piping is called____________________.

A. Backflow
B. Air gap
C. Backsiphonage
D. Back pressure

16. According to Florida Plumbing Code, a combination plumbing fixture is permitted to be installed on one trap provided the waste outlets are not more than_____________ apart.

A. 24 inches
B. 30 inches
C. 36 inches
D. 48 inches

17. According to Florida Plumbing Code, the developed length of a pipe is its length______________________.

A. from inlet to outlet measured in a straight line
B. before installation in a plumbing system
C. measured from its highest to its lowest invert elevation
D. measured along the centerline of the pipe and fittings

18. According to Florida Plumbing Code, field constructed sheet lead vent pipe flashing shall weigh_________________ psf.

A. not less than 2 pounds
B. not less than 2 1/2 pounds
C. not less than 3 pounds
D. not less than 4 pounds

19. According to Florida Plumbing Code, soldering bushings for 4" pipe shall weigh at least_________ ounces.

A. 32
B. 38
C. 48
D. 56

20. The code permits a crown vent to be installed_______from the trap weir on a 3" pipe.

A. 2"
B. 3"
C. 4"
D. more than 6"

21. According to Florida Plumbing Code, trenches installed parallel to footings shall not extend______.

A. above the 45 degree bearing plane of the footing
B. below the 45 degree bearing plane of the footing
C. unless protected by a sleeve two pipe sizes larger
D. within 12 inches of the 45 degree bearing plane

22. According to Florida Plumbing Code, sheet copper for general applications shall weigh not less than_________________.

A. 8 ounces per square foot
B. 12 ounces per square foot
C. 16 ounces per square foot
D. 32 ounces per square foot

23. According to Florida Plumbing Code, water heaters having an ignition source, installed in garages, shall be elevated such that the source of ignition is not less than__________ above the garage floor.

A. 12 inches
B. 15 inches
C. that specified in the Mechanical and Fuel Gas Codes
D. 24 inches

24. According to Florida Plumbing Code, unfired hot water storage tanks shall be insulated to a minimum of___________.

A. R-5
B. R-10
C. R-11
D. R-12.5

25. Water service pipe shall be not less than _______ in diameter.

A. 1-1/2"
B. 3/4"
C. 1"
D. 1-1/4"

26. Water service pipe, installed underground and outside of the structure, shall have a minimum working pressure rating of________at 73.4 degrees F.

A. 160 psi
B. 120 psi
C. 100 psi
D. 80 psi

27. All vent terminals shall extend at least 6" above the roof, and at least________above the roof, when the roof is used for any purpose other than weather protection.

A. 2 feet
B. 5 feet
C. 6 feet
D. 7 feet

28. An open vent terminal from a drainage system shall not terminate beneath a window, and any such vent terminal shall not be within 10 feet horizontally of such an opening______________________________.

A. unless it is at least 12" above the top of the opening
B. unless it is at least 18" above the top of the opening
C. unless it is at least 24" above the top of the opening
D. unless it is at least 36" above the top of the opening

29. Using Type K copper tubing 2 inches in diameter, what would the pressure drop be at a 60 gallon per minute flow rate?

A. 1 psi per 100 feet
B. 3 psi per 100 feet
C. 7 psi per 100 feet
D. 12 psi per 100 feet

30. Where wastewater from a swimming pool discharges to the sanitary drainage system, discharge shall be through___________________.

A. an approved strainer
B. indirect waste piping with an air gap
C. a drain pipe one pipe size larger
D. not permitted by code

****See answer key on the following page****

Florida Building Code - Plumbing, 2020
Solar Contractor
Answers

1. B 605.9(4)
2. A 705.16.1
3. A Table 308.5
   8 x 15'=120'/15' max = 8
4. A 202 See "Offset"
5. B E103.3(7) Friction loss per 100 feet
   2.6 psi per 100' x 1.5 = 3.9 psi
   150' / 100' = 1.5 units of 100
6. C Table 305.4
7. C Figure E103.3(3)
   10 GPM 1 psi per 100 feet
   Intersect the lines at 10 gpm and 1 psi per 100', note, just above 1-1/4"
   Answer: 1-1/2" new Type "L" copper tubing
8. B 603.2
9. A 604.6
10. D Table 605.4
11. D 909.3
    2 pipe diameters 4" x 2 = 8 inches
12. B 914.1
13. C Table E103.3(4)
14. A 405.8
15. C 202 See "Backflow; Backsiphonage"
16. B 1002.1(2)
17. D 202 See "Developed length"
18. C 902.3
19. D Table 705.19
    16 oz. x 3 = 48 oz.
    16 oz + 8 oz = 56 oz.

20 D 909.3
   not within two pipe diameters, 2 x 3" = 6"

21. B 307.5
22. B 402.3

23.	C	502.1.1
24.	D	505.1
25.	B	603.1
26.	A	605.3
27.	D	903.1
28.	D	903.5
29.	B	Figure E103.3(2)
30.	B	802.1.4

Florida Building Code -Plumbing, 2017
Questions and Answers
(Solar Contractor)

1. According to code, a___________ fitting is prohibited for use in the water distribution piping.

a) compression
b) saddle-type
c) threaded joint
d) soldered joint

2. According to code, copper vent pipe flashing shall weigh not less than______ per square foot.

a) 8 ounces
b) 10 ounces
c) 12 ounces
d) 16 ounces

3. A 2" diameter galvanized steel water service pipe is installed vertically in a building that has twelve floors, 15 feet floor -to-floor. According to code, the minimum number of supports required for a section of pipe passing through eight floors would be________________

a) 8
b) 10
c) 12
d) 13

4. A combination of approved bends that makes 2 changes in direction bringing one section of the pipe out of line but into a line parallel with the other section is called a/an______________

a) offset
b) tee-wye
c) jumper
d) parallel pipe

5. According to code, a 150' length of 4" diameter existing galvanized steel water pipe, with a 200 gpm flow rate, will have a pressure drop of approximately ____ psi.

a) 2.6
b) 3.9
c) 5.2
d) 8.0

6. According to code, vertical cast iron pipe shall be supported at intervals not exceeding___________

a) 10 feet
b) 12feet
c) 15 feet
d) 20 feet

7. According to code, the minimum size Type L copper tubing required to convey 10 gallons of water per minute a distance of 100 feet with a maximum pressure drop of 1 psi is_________ . Assume new tubing.

a) 1" diameter tubing
b) 1-1/4" diameter tubing
c) 1-1/2" diameter tubing
d) 2" diameter tubing

8. According to code, an underground water service pipe and a building sewer shall be separated horizontally by at least ____________of undisturbed or compacted earth.

a) 2 feet
b) 5 feet
c) 10 feet
d) 12 feet

9. According to code, wherever water pressure from the street main supply is insufficient to provide flow pressures at fixture outlets as required, then_____________________________.

a) a water pressure booster system shall be installed
b) the building will be vacated until pressure resumes
c) a new water main will need to be installed
d) gauges to monitor pressure shall be installed

10. According to code, __________________is an approved material for underground water distribution pipe.

a) black steel piping
b) ABS plastic pipe
c) asbestos cement pipe
d) type M copper tubing

11. The code does not permit a crown vent to be installed within______of a 4" trap weir.

a) 2 inches
b) 4 inches
c) 6 inches
d) 8 inches

12. A maximum of ____________ fixtures connected to a horizontal branch can be circuit vented.

a) 12
b) 8
c) 4
d) 2

13. According to code, the pressure loss through a 1-1/4" tap at a flow rate of 90 gpm is_________

a) 2.94 psi
b) 4.90 psi
c) 6.21 psi
d) 6.94 psi

14. According to code, ____________joints in drainage piping may be used within the trap seal.

a) slip
b) flanged
c) brazed
d) welded

15. According to code, each fixture directly connected to a drainage system shall have____________
.

a) a vacuum breaker
b) a back-flow valve
c) a trap primer valve
d) a water seal trap

16. According to the code, a combination plumbing fixture is permitted to be installed on one trap provided the waste outlets are not more than___________apart.

a) 24 inches
b) 30 inches
c) 36 inches
d) 48 inches

17. According to code, the developed length of a pipe is its length____________________________

a) from inlet to outlet measured in a straight line
b) before installation in a plumbing system
c) measured from its highest to its lowest invert elevation
d) measured along the centerline of the pipe and fittings

18. According to code, field constructed sheet lead vent pipe flashing shall weigh_____psf.

a) not less than 2 pounds
b) not less than 2 1/2 pounds
c) not less than 3 pounds
d) not less than 4 pounds

19. According to code, soldering bushings for 4" pipe shall weigh at least__________ounces.

a) 32
b) 38
c) 48
d) 56

20. The code permits a crown vent to be installed_______from the trap weir on a 3" pipe.

a) 2"
b) 3"
c) 4"
d) more than 6"

21. According to code, trenches installed parallel to footings shall not extend___________ .

a) above the 45 degree bearing plane of the footing
b) below the 45 degree bearing plane of the footing
c) unless protected by a sleeve two pipe sizes larger
d) within 12 inches of the 45 degree bearing plane

22. According to code, sheet copper for general applications shall weigh not less than_______.

a) 8 ounces per square foot
b) 12 ounces per square foot
c) 16 ounces per square foot
d) 32 ounces per square foot

23. According to the code, water heaters having an ignition source, installed in garages, shall be elevated such that the source of ignition is not less than______________above the garage floor.

a) 12 inches
b) 15 inches
c) 18 inches
d) 24 inches

24. According to the code, unfired hot water storage tanks shall be insulated to a minimum of_______

a) R-5
b) R-10
c) R-11
d) R-12.5

25. The minimum diameter of a water service pipe shall be________, to comply with the code.

a) 112"
b) 3/4"
c) 1"
d) 1-1/4"

26. Water service pipe, installed underground and outside of the structure, shall have a minimum working pressure rating of________at 73.4 degrees F.

a) 160 psi
b) 120psi
c) 100 psi
d) 80 psi

27. All vent terminals shall extend at least 6" above the roof, and at least________above the roof, when the roof is used for any purpose other than weather protection.

a) 2 feet
b) 5 feet
c) 6 feet
d) 7 feet

28. An open vent terminal from a drainage system shall not terminate beneath a window, and any such vent terminal shall not be within 10 feet horizontally of such an opening______________________________.

a) unless it is at least 12" above the top of the opening
b) unless it is at least 18" above the top of the opening
c) unless it is at least 24" above the top of the opening
d) unless it is at least 30" above the top of the opening

29. Using Type K copper tubing 2 inches in diameter, what would the pressure drop be at a 60 gallon per minute flow rate?

a) 1 psi per 100 feet
b) 3 psi per 100 feet
c) 7 psi per 100 feet
d) 12 psi per 100 feet

30. Where wastewater from a swimming pool discharges to the sanitary drainage system, discharge shall be through____________

a) an approved strainer
b) indirect waste piping with an air gap
c) a drain pipe one pipe size larger
d) not permitted by code

Florida Building Code -Plumbing, 2017
Questions and Answers
(Solar Contractor)

1	B	605.9 (4)
2	A	902.2
3	A	Table 308.5 ; 8 x 15’=120’/15’ max = 8
4	A	202
5	B	Figure E103.3 (7)
6	C	Table 308.5
7	C	Figure E103.3 (3)
8	B	603.2
9	A	604.7
10	D	Table 605.4
11	D	906.3
12	B	914.1
13	C	Table E103.3 (4)
14	A	405.8
15	D	P3201.6
16	B	1002.1 (2)
17	D	202
18	C	902.3
19	D	Table 705.19
20	D	909.3
21	B	307.5
22	B	402.3
23	C	304.3
24	D	505.1
25	B	603.1
26	A	605.3
27	D	903.1
28	C	903.5
29	B	Figure E103.3 (2)
30	B	802.1.4

NRCA Membrane Roof Systems, 2023
Questions and Answers

1. NRCA recommends __________ as the preferred method of installing rigid insulation board to cementitious wood-fiber roof decks.

    A. Spot mopping
    B. Blind nailing
    C. Hot mopping
    D. Installing a mechanically fastened base sheet or other separator layer prior

2. Steel roof decks are recommended to be __________ gauge or heavier.

    A. 22
    B. 20
    C. 26
    D. 18

3. Special attention to manufacturer recommended specifications should be observed when installing roofing materials below __________°F.

    A. 40
    B. 50
    C. 32
    D. 90

4. Moisture in or on materials may cause membrane __________.

    A. Slippage
    B. Fishmouths
    C. Blistering
    D. Skipping

5. NRCA recommends that asphalt be applied in the field within a __________ range from the asphalt's indicated EVT.

    A. ± 15° F
    B. ± 25° F
    C. ± 35° F
    D. ± 45° F

6. Roll-roofing materials used as reinforcement in built-up roof membrane construction fall into all of the following categories except for __________.

   A. Mineral-surfaced cap sheet
   B. Base sheets
   C. Ply sheets
   D. Adhesive sheets

7. NRCA does not recommend that __________ conduit be embedded with roof assemblies or placed below roof decks.

   A. Metallic
   B. PVC
   C. CPVC
   D. PEX

8. When installing perlite insulation as the primary insulation, NRCA recommends __________ layer(s) usage to allow for offsetting and staggering board joints.

   A. One
   B. Two
   C. Two and one half
   D. Three

9. The equiviscous temperature (EVT) range measures and identifies an asphalt's __________ and preferred application temperature.

   A. Melting point
   B. Elasticity
   C. Viscosity
   D. Flash point

10. Bitumen can be __________.

   A. Heated to or above the actual flash point
   B. Maintained at high temperatures for prolonged periods
   C. Allowed to stand in luggers for long periods of time
   D. Circulated while heating

11. When using concrete pavers as ballast, pavers should have a minimum compressive strength of __________ psi.

   A. 2,200
   B. 2,300
   C. 2,400
   D. 2,600

12. The materials used to construct vapor retarders can be categorized as __________ and plastic or film.

A. Asphalt
B. Bitumen
C. Perlite
D. Insulation

13. With use of EPDM Membrane materials, exposure to __________ should be avoided to prevent swelling.

A. Ketones
B. Esters
C. Hypalon Coatings
D. Aliphatic Solvents

14. Reinforced EPDM roof sheets require that __________ be applied at exposed cut edges of the sheet to prevent moisture intrusion.

A. Contact Solvents
B. Silica Sand
C. Sealant
D. Cut sheets

15. Rosin sheets are used to __________.

A. Prevent drippage of bitumen
B. Separate roof membranes
C. Provide adhesion
D. Provide vapor migration

16. All of the following are common application methods for roof coatings except for __________.

A. Airless spray
B. Roller
C. Brush or broom
D. Pressure spray

17. The criterion for judging proper slope for drainage is that there be no ponding water on the roof __________ hours after a rain during conditions conducive to drying.

A. 8
B. 24
C. 12
D. 48

18. When installing BUR roof drains, copper must be __________ inches square minimum.

A. 6
B. 24
C. 30
D. 48

19. Excessive, prolonged heating of bitumen can cause __________.

A. Poor adhesion
B. Flash hazards
C. Slippage
D. Decreased strength

20. In a built-up roof system, base flashing at a parapet wall with metal coping shall be a minimum height of __________ inches.

A. 8
B. 6
C. 10
D. 5

21. In a built-up roof system, a plumbing vent stack shall be flashed a minimum of __________ inches high.

A. 8
B. 10
C. 12
D. 14

22. Cement board has all the following properties that make it well-suited for use in roof assemblies except for __________.

A. Compressive strength
B. Tensile strength
C. Moisture resistance
D. Adhesive compatibility

23. The minimum R-value/minimum thickness is determined at the __________ of the roof insulation assembly.

A. Ridge
B. Valley
C. Low point
D. Curb

24. Side-lap fastener spacing should not exceed __________ feet.

A. 1
B. 2
C. 3
D. 4

25. An intermediate rib deck is a steel panel with a rib opening of __________.

A. 1 in to 1 in
B. 1 in to 1 ¼ in
C. 1 in to 1 ½ in
D. 1 in to 1 ¾ in

26. Deck panel end laps should not be less than __________ inches and should be centered over structural supports.

A. 2
B. 3
C. 4
D. 5

27. Faced cellular-glass roof insulation is typically available in __________ board sizes.

A. 1 ft x 1 ft
B. 1 ft x 1 ½ ft
C. 2 ft x 2 ft
D. 2 ft x 4 ft

28. A low-slope roof system that generally includes weatherproof membrane types of roof systems installed on slopes at or less than __________.

A. 2:12
B. 3:12
C. 4:12
D. 5:12

29. A coal tar built-up roof system has a design minimum slope of __________.

A. 1/8:12
B. 1/4:12
C. ½:12
D. 1:12

30. For steel roof decks with spans greater than __________ feet, side laps shall be fastened at 36 inches on center maximum.

A. 2
B. 4
C. 5
D. 10

31. Skylights and hatches should be installed with curbs tall enough to allow for an __________ inches of vertical flashing height.

A. 4
B. 6
C. 8
D. 10

32. __________ is the time rate of steady-state heat flow through a unit area of material or construction induced by a unit temperature difference between the body surfaces.

A. Thermal conductance
B. Thermal conductivity
C. Thermal resistance
D. Thermal transmittance

33. According to the NRCA manual, asphalt shall be applied at a temperature within plus or minus __________ degrees of the equiviscous temperature.

A. 10
B. 15
C. 20
D. 25

34. There are __________ subcategories of common Thermoplastic membranes.

A. 4
B. 6
C. 7
D. 2

35. Field lap seams when installing EPDM are typically constructed with __________.

A. Durable locks
B. Snap caps
C. Seam tape
D. Heat seams

36. A four-way slope, high point of 12 and low point of 3 can provide uniform perimeter __________.

A. Depth
B. Width
C. Temperature
D. Thickness

37. __________ are the fasteners to be used to secure insulation to cementitious wood fiber roof decks.

A. Two-piece tube nails
B. Self-locking with fasteners with caps
C. Twin-lock fasteners with round plates
D. All of the above

38. A minimum of __________ layer(s) reduces the thermal loss that occurs through the joints between single-layer insulation boards.

A. One
B. Two
C. Three
D. Four

39. The maximum mop application temperature for Type IV asphalt is __________°F.

A. 350
B. 425
C. 450
D. 470

40. Currently, asphalts conforming to ASTM D312's Type __________ and Type __________ are seldom used for built-up membrane construction.

A. I, II
B. I, III
C. I, IV
D. II, III

41. This application method, consisting of plies laid parallel to the slope, is referred to as "strapping the plies" and also may be used on slopes less than __________.

A. 1:12
B. 2:12
C. 3:12
D. 4:12

42. Substituting adhesives in thermoset single-ply roofing is __________.

A. Suggested
B. Not recommended
C. Always acceptable
D. Recommended

43. The following are types of sheets that may be classifies as PVC alloys except for __________.

A. Copolymer Alloy (CPA)
B. Ethylene Interpolymer (EIP)
C. Nitrile Alloys (NBP)
D. Polyestene (PYT)

44. Irregularities, such as __________, should be cut and patched and a thin squeegee coat of hot bitumen be applied before workers leave the work area for the night.

A. Blisters
B. Fishmouths
C. Ridges
D. Buckles

45. For example, a 4-inch-thick concrete slab of normal-weight concrete will release about __________ quart(s) of water for each square foot of surface area.

A. ½
B. 1
C. 1 ½
D. 2

46. Base flashing height at a prefabricated metal curb should not be lower than __________ inches.

A. 8
B. 6
C. 10
D. 5

47. Number 2 aggregate ballast is typically applied at a coverage rate of about __________ pounds per 100 square feet for loose-laid ballasted membrane roof systems.

A. 1,000
B. 1,300
C. 1,500
D. 1,750

48. When using nails with cementitious wood-fiber, NRCA suggests using __________.

A. Barbed clip fasteners
B. Two-piece tube nails
C. Three-piece tube nails
D. Toggle bolts

49. A narrow-rib steel deck (Type A) is a steel deck panel with a rib-width opening of __________ inch(es) maximum.

A. 1
B. 1 ¾
C. 2
D. 2 ½

50. When a design requires steel decks be welded, it is recommended that "puddle welds" of __________ of an inch or larger be welded into steel washers.

A. ¼
B. ½
C. 5/8
D. ¾

51. A typical roof coating can cure by all of the following mechanism except for __________.

A. Solvent evaporation
B. Air drying
C. Oxidation or reaction with moisture
D. Two-component chemical reaction

52. Mineral surfaced cap sheets should be unrolled and allowed to relax __________.

A. For eight hours
B. Until soft and pliable
C. For four hours
D. Until flat

53. The two general categories of membrane roofing systems are __________ and __________.

A. Water shedding and water repellant
B. Architectural and field engineered
C. Waterproof and water-resistant
D. Water shedding and weatherproof

54. A thermal transmittance (U or U-factor) of 0.14 is equivalent to an assembly R-value of __________.

A. 8.33
B. 7.69
C. 7.14
D. 6.67

55. When installing insulation board for cement-wood fiber decks, the maximum elevation difference allowed is __________ inch.

A. 1/8
B. ½
C. 5/8
D. ¾

56. A/an __________ deck is a where roof system components are installed directly over rigid board insulation.

A. Nonnailable
B. Insulated
C. Nailable
D. Steel

57. Vapor retarders should be used to __________.

A. Control the flow of moisture vapor from the interior of the building into the roof system
B. Control the flow of moisture vapor from the exterior of the building into the roof system
C. Remove the moisture vapor from the interior of the building
D. Remove the moisture vapor from the exterior of the building

58. All of the following are types of rigid roof insulation except for __________.

A. Perlite
B. Vermiculite
C. Expanded Polystyrene
D. Composite board

Please see Answer Key on the following page

2/23/22

NRCA Membrane Roof Systems, 2023
Questions and Answers
Answer Key

	Answer	Page
1.	D	87
2.	A	94
3.	A	187
4.	C	187
5.	B	192
6.	D	193
7.	A	85
8.	B	156
9.	C	191
10.	D	199
11.	D	257
12.	B	122
13.	D	216
14.	C	217
15.	A	197
16.	D	266
17.	D	84
18.	C	398
19.	B	199
20.	A	358-359
21.	A	388
22.	B	166
23.	C	173
24.	C	94
25.	D	92
26.	A	94
27.	D	140
28.	B	13
29.	A	83
30.	C	97

	Answer	Page
31.	C	273
32.	A	132
33.	D	192
34.	A	216
35.	C	217
36.	D	176
37.	C	241
38.	B	138
39.	D	191
40.	A	190
41.	B	199
42.	B	215
43.	D	218
44.	B	200
45.	B	104
46.	A	375
47.	B	257
48.	B	239
49.	A	92
50.	B	94
51.	B	259
52.	D	200
53.	D	13
54.	C	133
55.	A	83
56.	B	16
57.	A	127
58.	B	131

NRCA Membrane Roof Systems, 2019
Questions and Answers

1. NRCA recommends __________ as the preferred method of installing rigid insulation board to cementitious wood-fiber roof decks.

    A. Spot mopping
    B. Blind nailing
    C. Hot mopping
    D. Installing a mechanically fastened base sheet or other separator layer prior

2. Steel roof decks are recommended to be __________ gauge or heavier.

    A. 22
    B. 20
    C. 26
    D. 18

3. Special attention to manufacturer recommended specifications should be observed when installing roofing materials below __________°F.

    A. 40
    B. 50
    C. 32
    D. 90

4. Moisture in or on materials may cause membrane __________.

    A. Slippage
    B. Fishmouths
    C. Blistering
    D. Skipping

5. NRCA recommends that asphalt be applied in the field within a __________ range from the asphalt's indicated EVT.

    A. $\pm 15^0$ F
    B. $\pm 25^0$ F
    C. $\pm 35^0$ F
    D. $\pm 45^0$ F

6. Roll-roofing materials used as reinforcement in built-up roof membrane construction fall into all of the following categories except for __________.

   A. Mineral-surfaced cap sheet
   B. Base sheets
   C. Ply sheets
   D. Adhesive sheets

7. NRCA does not recommend that __________ conduit be embedded with roof assemblies or placed below roof decks.

   A. Metallic
   B. PVC
   C. CPVC
   D. PEX

8. NRCA recommends that designers specify cellular-glass insulation as multiply layers when the total required thickness of the cellular-glass insulation is __________ inch(es) or greater.

   A. 3
   B. 2
   C. 1 ½
   D. 1

9. When installing perlite insulation as the primary insulation, NRCA recommends __________ layer(s) usage to allow for offsetting and staggering board joints.

   A. One
   B. Two
   C. Two and one half
   D. Three

10. When the total required thickness of the insulation is greater than __________ inches, multiple-layer insulation of wood fiberboard is recommended.

    A. 1 ½
    B. 1 1/3
    C. 1 ¾
    D. 2

11. The equiviscous temperature (EVT) range measures and identifies an asphalt's __________ and preferred application temperature.

    A. Melting point
    B. Elasticity
    C. Viscosity
    D. Flash point

12. Bitumen can be __________.

   A. Heated to or above the actual flash point
   B. Maintained at high temperatures for prolonged periods
   C. Allowed to stand in luggers for long periods of time
   D. Circulated while heating

13. When using concrete pavers as ballast, pavers should have a minimum compressive strength of __________ psi.

   A. 2,200
   B. 2,300
   C. 2,400
   D. 2,600

14. The materials used to construct vapor retarders can be categorized as __________ and plastic or film.

   A. Asphalt
   B. Bitumen
   C. Perlite
   D. Insulation

15. With use of EPDM Membrane materials, exposure to __________ should be avoided to prevent swelling.

   A. Ketones
   B. Esters
   C. Hypalon Coatings
   D. Aliphatic Solvents

16. Reinforced EPDM roof sheets require that __________ be applied at exposed cut edges of the sheet to prevent moisture intrusion.

   A. Contact Solvents
   B. Silica Sand
   C. Sealant
   D. Cut sheets

17. Rosin sheets are used to __________.

   A. Prevent drippage of bitumen
   B. Separate roof membranes
   C. Provide adhesion
   D. Provide vapor migration

18. All of the following are common application methods for roof coatings except for __________.

   A. Airless spray
   B. Roller
   C. Brush or broom
   D. Pressure spray

19. The criterion for judging proper slope for drainage is that there be no ponding water on the roof __________ hours after a rain during conditions conducive to drying.

A. 8
B. 24
C. 12
D. 48

20. When installing BUR roof drains, copper must be __________ inches square minimum.

A. 6
B. 24
C. 30
D. 48

21. Excessive, prolonged heating of bitumen can cause __________.

A. Poor adhesion
B. Flash hazards
C. Slippage
D. Decreased strength

22. In a built-up roof system, base flashing at a parapet wall with metal coping shall be a minimum height of __________ inches.

A. 8
B. 6
C. 10
D. 5

23. In a built-up roof system, a plumbing vent stack shall be flashed a minimum of __________ inches high.

A. 8
B. 10
C. 12
D. 14

24. Cement board has all the following properties that make it well-suited for use in roof assemblies except for __________.

A. Compressive strength
B. Tensile strength
C. Moisture resistance
D. Adhesive compatibility

25. The minimum R-value/minimum thickness is determined at the __________ of the roof insulation assembly.

A. Ridge
B. Valley
C. Low point
D. Curb

26. Side-lap fastener spacing should not exceed __________ feet.

A. 1
B. 2
C. 3
D. 4

27. An intermediate rib deck is a steel panel with a rib opening of __________.

A. 1 in to 1 in
B. 1 in to 1 ¼ in
C. 1 in to 1 ½ in
D. 1 in to 1 ¾ in

28. Deck panel end laps should not be less than __________ inches and should be centered over structural supports.

A. 2
B. 3
C. 4
D. 5

29. It is required that steel roof decks be designed to resist uplift forces not less than __________ psf at eave overhangs and __________ psf for all other roof areas.

A. 20, 40
B. 30, 60
C. 40, 30
D. 45, 30

30. Faced cellular-glass roof insulation is typically available in __________ board sizes.

A. 1 ft x 1 ft
B. 1 ft x 1 ½ ft
C. 2 ft x 2 ft
D. 2 ft x 4 ft

31. A low-slope roof system that generally includes weatherproof membrane types of roof systems installed on slopes at or less than __________.

A. 2:12
B. 3:12
C. 4:12
D. 5:12

32. A coal tar built-up roof system has a design minimum slope of __________.

A. 1/8:12
B. 1/4:12
C. ½:12
D. 1:12

33. For steel roof decks with spans greater than __________ feet, side laps shall be fastened at 36 inches on center maximum.

A. 2
B. 4
C. 5
D. 10

34. Skylights and hatches should be installed with curbs tall enough to allow for an __________ inches of vertical flashing height.

A. 4
B. 6
C. 8
D. 10

35. __________ is the time rate of steady-state heat flow through a unit area of material or construction induced by a unit temperature difference between the body surfaces.

A. Thermal conductance
B. Thermal conductivity
C. Thermal resistance
D. Thermal transmittance

36. According to the NRCA manual, asphalt shall be applied at a temperature within plus or minus __________ degrees of the equiviscous temperature.

A. 10
B. 15
C. 20
D. 25

37. There are __________ subcategories of common Thermoplastic membranes.

A. 4
B. 6
C. 7
D. 2

38. Field lap seams when installing EPDM are typically constructed with __________.

A. Durable locks
B. Snap caps
C. Seam tape
D. Heat seams

39. A four-way slope, high point of 12 and low point of 3 can provide uniform perimeter __________.

A. Depth
B. Width
C. Temperature
D. Thickness

40. __________ are the fasteners to be used to secure insulation to cementitious wood fiber roof decks.

A. Two-piece tube nails
B. Self-locking with fasteners with caps
C. Twin-lock fasteners with round plates
D. All of the above

41. A minimum of __________ layer(s) reduces the thermal loss that occurs through the joints between single-layer insulation boards.

A. One
B. Two
C. Three
D. Four

42. The maximum mop application temperature for Type IV asphalt is __________°F.

A. 350
B. 425
C. 450
D. 470

43. Currently, asphalts conforming to ASTM D312's Type __________ and Type __________ are seldom used for built-up membrane construction.

A. I, II
B. I, III
C. I, IV
D. II, III

44. This application method, consisting of plies laid parallel to the slope, is referred to as "strapping the plies" and also may be used on slopes less than __________.

A. 1:12
B. 2:12
C. 3:12
D. 4:12

45. Substituting adhesives in thermoset single-ply roofing is __________.

A. Suggested
B. Not recommended
C. Always acceptable
D. Recommended

46. The following are types of sheets that may be classifies as PVC alloys except for __________.

A. Copolymer Alloy (CPA)
B. Ethylene Interpolymer (EIP)
C. Nitrile Alloys (NBP)
D. Polyestene (PYT)

47. Irregularities, such as __________, should be cut and patched and a thin squeegee coat of hot bitumen be applied before workers leave the work area for the night.

A. Blisters
B. Fishmouths
C. Ridges
D. Buckles

48. For example, a 4-inch-thick concrete slab of normal-weight concrete will release about __________ quart(s) of water for each square foot of surface area.

A. ½
B. 1
C. 1 ½
D. 2

49. Base flashing height at a prefabricated metal curb should not be lower than __________ inches.

A. 8
B. 6
C. 10
D. 5

50. The building is located in a 90 mph basic wind speed region in Exposure "B". The maximum allowable height of the building if using aggregate on the roof is __________ feet.

A. 100
B. 110
C. 120
D. 90

51. Number 2 aggregate ballast is typically applied at a coverage rate of about __________ pounds per 100 square feet for loose-laid ballasted membrane roof systems.

A. 1,000
B. 1,300
C. 1,500
D. 1,750

52. When using nails with cementitious wood-fiber, NRCA suggests using __________.

A. Barbed clip fasteners
B. Two-piece tube nails
C. Three-piece tube nails
D. Toggle bolts

53. A narrow-rib steel deck (Type A) is a steel deck panel with a rib-width opening of __________ inch(es) maximum.

A. 1
B. 1 ¾
C. 2
D. 2 ½

54. When a design requires steel decks be welded, it is recommended that "puddle welds" of __________ of an inch or larger be welded into steel washers.

A. ¼
B. ½
C. 5/8
D. ¾

55. A typical roof coating can cure by all of the following mechanism except for __________.

A. Solvent evaporation
B. Air drying
C. Oxidation or reaction with moisture
D. Two-component chemical reaction

56. Mineral surfaced cap sheets should be unrolled and allowed to relax __________.

A. For eight hours
B. Until soft and pliable
C. For four hours
D. Until flat

57. The two general categories of membrane roofing systems are __________ and __________.

A. Water shedding and water repellant
B. Architectural and field engineered
C. Waterproof and water-resistant
D. Water shedding and weatherproof

58. A thermal transmittance (U or U-factor) of 0.14 is equivalent to an assembly R-value of __________.

A. 8.33
B. 7.69
C. 7.14
D. 6.67

59. When installing insulation board for cement-wood fiber decks, the maximum elevation difference allowed is __________ inch.

A. 1/8
B. ½
C. 5/8
D. ¾

60. A __________ deck is a where roof system components are installed directly over rigid board insulation.

A. Nonnailable
B. Insulated
C. Nailable
D. Steel

61. Vapor retarders should be used to __________.

A. Control the flow of moisture vapor from the interior of the building into the roof system
B. Control the flow of moisture vapor from the exterior of the building into the roof system
C. Remove the moisture vapor from the interior of the building
D. Remove the moisture vapor from the exterior of the building

62. All of the following are types of rigid roof insulation except for __________.

A. Perlite
B. Vermiculite
C. Expanded Polystyrene
D. Composite board

Please see Answer Key on the following page

NRCA Membrane Roof Systems, 2019
Questions and Answers
Answer Key

	Answer	Page
1.	D	83
2.	A	89
3.	A	173
4.	C	173
5.	B	177
6.	D	179
7.	A	82
8.	A	131
9.	B	145
10.	A	153
11.	C	177
12.	D	184
13.	D	238
14.	B	118
15.	D	201
16.	C	201
17.	A	183
18.	D	247
19.	D	80
20.	C	380
21.	B	184
22.	A	387
23.	A	370
24.	B	154 – 155
25.	C	161
26.	C	89
27.	D	88
28.	A	89
29.	D	90
30.	D	130

	Answer	Page
31.	B	13
32.	A	79
33.	C	93
34.	C	253
35.	A	126
36.	D	177
37.	A	200
38.	C	201
39.	D	160 – 161
40.	C	223
41.	B	124
42.	D	177
43.	A	177
44.	B	185
45.	B	200
46.	D	203
47.	B	185
48.	B	99
49.	A	459
50.	B	236
51.	B	238
52.	B	221
53.	A	88
54.	B	89
55.	B	239, 240
56.	D	185
57.	D	13
58.	C	127
59.	A	83
60.	B	16
61.	A	118
62.	B	123

1 Exam Prep

NRCA Membrane Roof Systems Questions

1. The preferred method of installing rigid insulation board to cementitious wood-fiber roof decks is?

A Spot mopping
B Blind nailing
C Loose laid
D Adhesion to the base sheet

2. The recommended steel panel roof deck gauge is________ or heavier.

A 22
B 20
C 26
D 18

3. Roofing materials normally should not be applied below what temperature?

A 40 degrees
B 50 degrees
C 32 degrees
D 90 degrees

4. Moisture in or on materials can cause?

A Slippage
B Fishmouths
C Blistering
D Skipping

5. The maximum mop application of Type IV asphalt is?

A 450 degrees
B 475 degrees
C 500 degrees
D 525 degrees

6. The minimum temperature for the application of Type I coal tar pitch is?

A 360 degrees
B 335 degrees
C 330 degrees
D 385 degrees

7. NRCA recommends steel decks be_________ gauge or heavier?

A 22
B 24
C 26
D 20

8 .When installing cellular-glass, multiple-layer insulation is required when the total thickness of the insulation is greater than?

A 3"
B 2"
C 1 1/2"
D 1"

9. When using perlite insulation as the primary insulation NRCA recommends________ layers.

A 2
B 2 1/2
C 1
D 3

10. Multiple-layer insulation of wood fiberboard is recommended when the total required thickness of the insulation is greater than how many inches?

A 1 1/2
B 1 1/3
C 13/4
D 2

11. The equiviscous temperature is?

A Proper melting point
B Minimum melting temperature
C Proper viscosity for application
D Flash point

12. Bitumen can be heated and held at the high temperatures for__________

A Long periods
B 1 hour
C 4 hours
D Short periods

13. The EVT range must be within___________ degrees of viscosity at 125 centistokes.

A 10° F
B 15° F
C 20° F
D 25° F

14. Coal-tar Type I Bitumen has an application temperature of___________. (2011 Only)

A 375°F
B 360°F
C 350°F
D 450°F

15. When using EPDM Membrane materials,__________ should be avoided to prevent swelling.

A Glues
B Sand
C Hypalon Coatings
D Aliphatic Solvents

16. EPDM single-ply requires the use of___________ to prevent wicking at exposed cut edges.

A Contact Solvents
B Silica Sand
C Sealant
D Cut sheets

17. Rosin sheets work well to___________

A Prevent drippage
B Divorce roof membranes
C Provide adhesion
D Provide vapor migration

18. Correctly designed penetration pockets should have compatible____________

A Projections
B Sealant
C Dripholes
D Sealing

19. NRCA recommends for slope and drainage that there be no ponding on the roof_________

A 8 hours after raining
B 24 hours after raining
C 12 hours after raining
D 48 hours after raining

20. When installing BUR roof drains, copper must be___________ inches square.

A 28
B 30
C 6
D 48

21. Overheating bitumens can cause__________

A Poor Adhesion
B Flash hazards
C Slippage
D Yellow smoke

22. Base flashing height for Atatic smooth surface roofing should not be lower than__________

A 8 inches
B 6 inches
C 10 inches
D 5 inches

23. Raised curbs using BUR roofing should be flashed a minimum of__________

A 8"
B 10"
C 12"
D 14"

24. There should be no evidence of standing water on the deck_______ hours after it stops raining.

A 24
B 48
C 72
D 86

25. When determining the thermal resistance of a tapered insulation system a common industry approach is___________

A Average thickness
B C value
C Minimum R value
D Maximum R value

26. Cold rolled ribs lighter than__________ gauge have little strength.

A 18
B 20
C 22
D 24

27. Intermediate rib decking has a maximum rib opening of how many inches?

A 1
B 1 3/4
C 2
D 2 ½

28. Spacing between side lap fasteners should not exceed how many feet?

A 3
B 4
C 6
D 21

29. The weld spacing along the perimeter should be__________ inches.

A 18
B 12
C 6
D 3

30. Cellular glass board is approved at__________ inches minimum thickness.

A 1
B 1 1/2
C 1 3/4
D 6

31. There should be no evidence of water on the roof__________ hours after it stops raining.

A 24
B 48
C 36
D 12

32. According to the NRCA manual, the Equiviscous Temperature range is defined as__________

A 125 centistokes
B 125 centistokes plus 25 degrees Fahrenheit
C 125 centistokes plus or minus 25 degrees Fahrenheit
D 125 centistokes minus 25 degrees Fahrenheit

33. According to the NRCA manual, the roofing contractor should take special precautions when the temperature is below how many degrees?

A 60
B 50
C 40
D 55

34. Loose-laid **EPDM** single-ply systems require the use of___________ to provide resistance against wind-uplift forces.

A Screw fasteners
B Special adhesives
C Heat applied seams
D Ballast

35. One of the more common types of insulation layers is_________________

A 15 pound asphalt felt
B 30 pound fiberglass
C Fiberglass insulation
D Board insulation

36. According to the NRCA manual, asphalt shall be applied at a temperature within __________ degrees of the equiviscous temperature.

A 10
B 15
C 20
D 25

37. There are how many subcategories of common Thermoplastic membranes?

A 4
B 6
C 7
D 2

38. Field lap seams when installing EPDM are typically constructed with_____________

A Durable locks
B Snap caps
C Seam tape
D Heat seams

39. A four-way slope, high point of 12 and low point of 3 can provide uniform perimeter________

A Depth
B Width
C Temperature
D Thickness

40. When installing cementitious wood fiber decks,___________ type fasteners should be used.

A Auger
B One Piece Tube nails
C Three Piece Tube nails
D Nylon expansion fasteners

41. For added benefit NRCA recommends insulation be applied a minimum of __________layers?

A 1
B 2
C 3
D 9

42. Mop Temperature for Type IV asphalt is____________

A 350°F
B 425°F
C 450°F
D 475°F

43. Type II ASTM D312 is ____________ asphalt?

A Deadlevel
B Flat
C Steep
D Special

44. The Equiviscous Temperature range must be plus or minus____________

A 10°F
B 15°F
C 20°F
D 25°F

45. Substituting adhesives in thermoset single-ply roofing is______________

A Good
B Bad
C Ugly
D Recommended

46. When using EPDM Membrane materials, which of the following will prevent wicking?

A Seam sealant
B Corn oil
C Lard
D Solvents

47. Fishmouths in thermoset roofing should be____________

A Cut
B Spliced
C Bonded
D Hot mopped

48. The minimum square inches for the lead sheet when installing roof drains is_____________

A 18
B 22
C 24
D 30

49. Base flashing height should not be lower than ___________ inches.

A 8
B 6
C 10
D 5

50. The building is located in a 90 mph basic wind speed region in Exposure "B". The maximum allowable height of the building if using gravel is_______________

A 100 feet
B 110 feet
C 120 feet
D 90 feet

51. Number 4 aggregate ballast is typically applied at a coverage rate of about __________ pounds per 100 square feet for loose-laid ballasted membrane roof systems.

A 2,000
B 1,300
C 1,500
D 2,500

52. When using nails with cementitious wood-fiber, NRCA suggests using____________

A Barbed clip fasteners
B Two-piece tube nails
C Three-piece tube nails
D Toggle bolts

53. Intermediate rib decking has a maximum nominal rib opening of ___________ inches.

A 1
B 13/4
C 2
D 2 ½

54. A metal roof deck should be welded no more than how many inches on center?

A 6
B 8
C 12
D 16

55. Ballast systems should be designed using______________

A Patterns
B Thickness
C Porosity
D Weight calculations

56. Mineral surfaced cap sheets should be unrolled and allowed to relax for how long?

A Eight hours
B Until soft and pliable
C Four hours
D Until flat

57. The two general categories of metal roofing systems are_________ and __________

A Water shedding and water repellant
B Architectural and field engineered
C Waterproof and water-resistant
D Cold-rolled and panel

58. The tanker temperature should always be less than how many degrees below the actual flash point of coal tar bitumen?

A 25
B 50
C 75
D 10

59. When installing insulation board for cement-wood fiber decks, the maximum elevation difference allowed is__________

A 2"
B 1"
C 1/2"
D 1/8"

60. Type **"F"** decking has flute spacing of___________

A 1 inch maximum
B 1 to 1 3/4 inches
C 1 3/4 to 2 5/8 inches
D 1 1/2 to 2 3/4 inches

61. Vapor retarders should be used to___________

A Control the flow of moisture vapor from the interior of the building into the roof system
B Control the flow of moisture vapor from the exterior of the building into the roof system
C Remove the moisture vapor from the interior of the building
D Remove the moisture vapor from the exterior of the building

62. Which of the following is not a type of rigid roof insulation?

A Perlite
B Vermiculite
C Polystyrene
D Mineral fiber

63. Asphalt with a maximum softening point of 225 degrees is___________

A Type I
B Type II
C Type III
D Type IV

64. Moisture in or on materials can cause membrane_____________

A Deterioration
B Softening
C Blistering
D Buckling

65. Type III asphalt is for slopes up to___________

A 1/4:12
B 1/2:12
C 1:12
D 3:12

66. Type IV asphalt is suggested for slopes greater than______________

A 1/4:12
B 1/2:12
C 1:12
D 3:12

67. The **NRCA** states lightweight structural concrete has a density of not less than _______ pcf?

A 60
B 85
C 90
D 120

68. Which of the following is not a type of rigid roof insulation?

A Cellular glass
B Spun glass modules
C Wood fiberboard
D Gypsum board

69. Type I asphalt requires a minimum mop application temperature of how many degrees?

A 350
B 325
C 375
D 400

70. According to the NRCA, 24 inch by 24 inch roof mounted equipment requires support height of __________ inches.

A 14
B 30
C 36
D 48

71. NRCA recommends the height of a base flashing be no lower than how many inches?

A 8
B 10
C 12
D 16

72. A typical Type **F** deck panel should have a minimum rib width of _________ inches?

A 1
B 1 1/2
C 1 3/4
D ½

73. A rigid board made from crushing glass and mixing it with hydrosulfide gas is ____________

A Roof covering
B Decking
C Cellular-glass
D A vapor barrier

74. The maximum slope required for low slope roofing is ____________

A 1:12
B 2:12
C 4:12
D 3:12

75. The temperature of the hot asphalt should be measured _____________

A At the kettle
B On the roof
C At the pipe
D After installation

76. TPO is available in all except ____________ mils?

A 40
B 72
C 45
D 90

77. Based on dew-point calculation and to limit possible condensation and premature degradation of materials, a designer should consider _____________

A Installing more than normal insulation
B Provisions for a vapor retarder
C An extra layer of hot mop or cold process depending upon the roof style
D The use of a deck sealer

78. Type 1 low-softening point asphalt cement is governed by ____________

A ASTM D 312
B ASTM D 4586
C DBPR D 6977
D ASTM D 3019

79. Which is not an advantage of Ethylene Propylene Diene Monomer roofing?

A Resistance to ozone
B Weathering
C Abrasion
D Resistance to vegetable oils

80. According to the NRCA, the softening point for Type I asphalt is how many degrees Fahrenheit?

A 210 to 235
B 210 to 225
C 185 to 176
D 135 to 151

81. Which is not property of a rigid board roof insulation system?

A Moisture resistance
B R-value
C Compressive strength
D Tactile compatibility

82. Which of the following is not a common subcategory of thermoplastic membranes?

A PVC
B CPA
C EIP
D DIP

83. The ASTM standard governing polyisocyanurate foam board roof insulation is ____________

A D1289
B D6163
C C578
D C1289

84. The minimum R-value approach establishes the thermal resistance for a tapered roof insulation system by determining the R-value of the tapered material at the ____________

A Thickest point in the tapered system layout
B Thinnest point in the tapered system layout
C Average point in the tapered system layout
D Any point in the tapered system layout

85. Which is not a common subcategory of thermoplastic membranes?

A EPDM
B KEE
C TPO
D PVC

86. The tapered systems is 6 inches at the thickest point and 2 inches at the thinnest point. Using the Average R-Value approach, the R-value of the tapered system is Valued at how many inches of thickness?

A 8
B 6
C 4
D 2

87. Caution should be used when applying roofing materials below what temperature?

A 40 degrees Centigrade
B 50 degrees Fahrenheit
C 50 degrees Centigrade
D 40 degrees Fahrenheit

88. EVT is defined as the temperature at which the viscosity of roofing asphalt is ____________

A Explosive
B At flash point
C Emits yellow smoke
D 125 Cs

89. Type III asphalt may be used on roof slopes __________ or less?

A 1/4 inch per foot
B 1/2 inch per foot
C 3/4 inch per foot
D 1 inch per foot

90. When applying polymer-modified asphalt roofing, the contractor should use ________

A Low kettle temperatures
B Detailed torch kits
C Coal tar roof cements
D Asphalt roof cements

91. Kettle temperature should be maintained at less than how many degrees below flash point?

A 100
B 75
C 50
D 25

92. When applying modified bitumen membrane sheets directly to combustible substrates such as wood decks, NRCA recommends ______________

A Not using a torch
B Using a torch
C Nailing the rosin paper
D Not using rosin paper

93. The maximum temperature for the application of Type 2 asphalt for mop applications Is ____________

A 350 degrees F
B 375 degrees F
C 400 degrees F
D 425 degrees F

94. The two types of vapor retarders are?

A Hydrostatic and hydrokinetic
B Bitumen and plastic sheet or film vapor retarders (non-bitumen)
C Semi-permeable and permeable
D Type 1 and Type 2

ANSWER KEY

0

		2011	2015
1.	D	17	124
2.	A	22	129
3.	A	78	198
4.	C	79	199
5.	B	81	202
6.	B	82	203
7.	A	22	129
8.	A	49	161
9.	A	61	174
10.	A	66	181
11.	C	80	202
12.	D	87	209
13.	D	80	202
14.	B	82	N/A
15.	D	98	224
16.	C	98	224
17.	A	86	208
18.	B	344	410
19.	D	15	122
20.	B	300	363
21.	B	87	209
22.	A	305	369
23.	A	282	342
24.	B	15	122
25.	C	69	187
26.	C	22	129
27.	B	21	128
28.	A	22	129
29.	B	22	129
30.	B	49	161

31.	B	15	122
32.	C	80	202
33.	C	78	200
34.	D	122	255
35.	D	42	155
36.	D	80	202
37.	A	97/98	223
38.	C	98	224
39.	D	68	187-188
40.	A	110	242
41.	B	43	155
42.	C	81	203
43.	B	81	203
44.	D	80	202
45.	B	97	223
46.	A	121	254
47.	C	97	223
48.	D	300/349	363/418
49.	A	400	440
50.	B	121	254
51.	B	122	255
52.	D	109	241
53.	B	21	128
54.	C	22	129
55.	D	122	255
56.	D	88	210
57.	D	21	128
58.	A	81	203
59.	D	17	124
60.	B	21	128
61.	A	39	151
62.	B	42	155
63.	D	80	202

64.	C	79	201
65.	C	81	203
66.	C	81	203
67.	B	18	125
68.	B	42	155
69.	B	81	203
70.	A	276/279	384/388
71.	A	392/400	469/477
72.	D	21	128
73.	C	48	161
74.	D	11	12
75.	B	81	203
76.	A	101	226
77.	B	38	150
78.	A	80	202
79.	D	98	224
80.	D	80	202
81.	D	42	154
82.	D	97/98	223
83.	D	72	192
84.	B	69	187
85.	A	97	223
86.	C	69	187
87.	D	78	200
88.	D	80	202
89.	D	81	203
90.	D	94	208
91.	D	81	203
92.	A	33	124
93.	D	98	224
94.	B	38	150

NRCA Steep-Slope Roof Systems, 2021
Questions and Answers

1. For single layer application mechanically attached on an asphalt shingle roof system, the underlayment should be applied horizontally in shingle fashion with side laps of a minimum of ____________ inches

A. 1
B. 2
C. 3 ½
D. 4

2. Fastening of full-length three-tab strip shingles requires a minimum of _________ roofing nails per strip shingle.

A. 4
B. 6
C. 8
D. 32

3. With asphalt shingle roof systems, a/an __________ valley is NOT one of the basic types of valleys.

A. Open
B. California-cut
C. Woven
D. Closed-cut

4. In closed-cut valleys, shingles on one side of the valley are installed across the valley and shingles from the other side are cut about _________ inches short of the centerline of the valley.

A. 2
B. 4
C. 6
D. 5

5. Drip edge metal is most common for asphalt shingle roof systems and mechanically attached underlayment should be installed _________ drip edge metal at eaves.

A. Over
B. Under
C. With bull membrane
D. Using fasteners every 6 inches

6. With tile roof systems, the two basic valleys are____________ valleys.

A. Open and woven
B. Closed and woven
C. No-cut and closed
D Open and closed

7. A minimum of ______________ inches of clearance is recommended between walls and curbs.

A. 12
B. 16
C. 18
D. 24

8. Generally, asphalt shingle fasteners should be kept back a minimum of _______ inches from the center of the valley.

A. 6
B. 8
C. 10
D. 12

9. Metal flashings used in wood shake or shingle systems may be fabricated from any of the following EXCEPT ______________.

A. 26-gauge prefinished galvanized steel
B. 3-pound lead
C. 26-gauge stainless steel
D. 16-ounce copper

10. A minimum _____ inch-wide layer of polymer-modified bitumen underlayment, base sheet or self-adhering underlayment is centered in the valley under the field underlayment

A. 19
B. 36
C. 18
D. 6

11. Hip and ridge cover fasteners should extend a minimum of an _________ inch through the underside of roof decks less than ¾ of an inch thick.

A. 1/8
B. 3/4
C. 1/2
D. 1/4

12. A minimum distance of __________ inches is recommended between a penetration and valley center.

A. 6
B. 12
C. 16
D. 18

13. The minimum length of 5d box nails to be used on 24-inch taper-split shakes is ___________ inches.

A. 1 1/4
B. 1 3/4
C. 2
D. 6

14. Crickets shall be installed at the upslope side of chimneys or curbed roof penetrations when the chimney or curb is more than _________ inches wide.

A. 24
B. 18
C. 16
D. 12

15. There are _________ 22 x 12 slates in a square of roofing.

A. 98
B. 114
C. 108
D. 126

16. In clay and concrete tile roof systems, drip edge should be nailed at about _____________ inches on centers, slightly staggered.

A. 6
B. 12
C. 10
D. 8

17. Metal shingle roof systems may be secured using ______________.

A. Staples, screws or nails
B. Staples, nails or clips and tabs
C. Screws, nails or clips and tabs
D. Staples, screws or clips and tabs

18. If a starter course of shakes consists of two layers, joints should be offset between neighboring units in the adjacent courses a minimum of ____________ inches.

A. 3/4
B. 1
C. 1 1/4
D. 1 1/2

19. ______________ is a natural, self-healing metal that weathers to a soft blue-gray patina.

A. Stainless steel
B. Aluminum
C. Zinc
D. Copper

20. For steep – to low-slope transitions, it is recommended that asphalt shingles be held back a minimum of ________inches above the transition.

A. 8
B. 10
C. 12
D. 14

21. It is suggested that ________ be used when installing slate roofing.

A. Galvanized nails
B. Stainless steel nails
C. Electroplated nails
D. Copper-slating nails

22. When tapering a 16- foot open valley, the bottom of the valley will be ___________inches greater than at the top of the valley.

A. 4
B. 1
C. 2
D. 3

23. Water and ice-dam underlayment protection should be applied starting at a roof system's eaves and extend upslope to a point corresponding to a minimum _______ inches inside the exterior wall line of a building.

A. 22
B. 12
C. 24
D. 36

24. The common dimensions for standard three-tab shingles are ______________ .

A. 12” x 36”
B. 12” x 40”
C. 11” x 36”
D. 11” x 40”

25. It is recommended that valley metal for use with wood shakes or shingles be a minimum of _______inches wide.

A. 12
B. 14
C. 18
D. 24

26. _____________ flashings provide a weatherproof transition material where a roof area intersects a head wall.

A. Step
B. Apron
C. Backer
D. Counter

27. Counter-battens should be spaced not more than ___________on center when used with nominal 2-by-2 wood battens.

A. 12
B. 16
C. 18
D. 24

28. A type ___________ clay or concrete tile has a rise-to-width ratio greater than 1:5.

A. I
B. II
C. III
D. IV

29. ____________ is NOT recommended to be used as a valley underlayment.

A. Heavy weight felt
B. Full-width sheet of polymer-modified bitumen
C. Base sheet
D. Self-adhering polymer-modified bitumen sheet

30. The minimum nominal thickness recommended for ___________roof shingles is 0.024 inches.

A. Asphalt
B. Aluminum
C. Copper
D. Zinc

31. Where wall cladding counterflashes wall flashing metal, the cladding material and water-resistive barrier should extend past and cover the top edge of the flashing metal a minimum of ____________ inches.

A. 2
B. 4
C. 6
D. 8

32. _____________ is the most common method of fastening tile.

A. Nailing
B. Screwing
C. Clipping
D. Wire ties and strapping

33. Each wood shingle should be fastened with ___________ fastener (s) located approximately ¾ of an inch to 1 inch from the side edges.

A. 1
B. 2
C. 3
D. 4

34. No. 30 asphalt felt is commonly designated Type __________ by ASTM D4869 standards.

A. I
B. II
C. III
D. IV

35. Asphalt shingles classified according to ASTM D7158 as Class ______ are said to pass at a basic wind speed up to and including 150 mph.

A. D
B. F
C. G
D. H

Please See Answer Key on following page

1 Exam Prep
NRCA Steep-Slope Roof Systems, 2021
Answers

	Answer	Section/Page#
1.	B	35
2.	A	52
3.	B	56
4.	A	58
5.	A	55
6.	D	226
7.	D	90,261, 432, 454, 548
8.	B	56-57
9.	B	650-651
10.	B	57
11.	A	54
12.	D	91
13.	B	644, Fig. 4-3
14.	A	61
15.	D	530, Fig. 4-2
16.	B	225
17.	C	416
18.	D	644
19.	C	408
20.	B	63
21.	D	528-529
22.	A	58
23.	C	36-37
24.	A	39
25.	D	649
26.	B	60
27.	D	197
28.	A	214, Fig. 4-1
29.	A	56
30.	B	406
31.	A	62
32.	A	220
33.	B	645
34.	D	33, Fig. 3-1
35.	D	42

NRCA Steep-slope Roof Systems, 2017
Questions and Answers

1. For single layer application mechanically attached on an asphalt shingle roof system, the underlayment should be applied horizontally in shingle fashion with side laps of a minimum of ____________ inches

A. 1
B. 2
C. 3 ½
D. 4

2. Fastening of full-length three-tab strip shingles requires a minimum of _________ roofing nails per strip shingle.

A. 4
B. 6
C. 8
D. 32

3. With asphalt shingle roof systems, a/an __________ valley is NOT one of the basic types of valleys.

A. Open
B. California-cut
C. Woven
D. Closed-cut

4. In closed-cut valleys, shingles on one side of the valley are installed across the valley and shingles from the other side are cut about _________ inches short of the centerline of the valley.

A. 2
B. 4
C. 6
D. 5

5. Drip edge metal is most common for asphalt shingle roof systems and mechanically attached underlayment should be installed _________ drip edge metal at eaves.

A. Over
B. Under
C. With bull membrane
D. Using fasteners every 6 inches

6. With tile roof systems, the two basic valleys are____________ valleys.

A. Open and woven
B. Closed and woven
C. No-cut and closed
D Open and closed

7. A minimum of ______________ inches of clearance is recommended between walls and curbs.

A. 12
B. 16
C. 18
D. 24

8. Asphalt shingle fasteners should be kept back a minimum of _______ inches from the center of the valley.

A. 6
B. 8
C. 10
D. 12

9. Metal flashings used in wood shake or shingle systems may be fabricated from any of the following EXCEPT ______________.

A. 26-gauge prefinished galvanized steel
B. 3-pound lead
C. 26-gauge stainless steel
D. 16-ounce copper

10. A minimum ______ inch-wide layer of polymer-modified bitumen underlayment, base sheet or self-adhering underlayment is centered in the valley under the field underlayment

A. 19
B. 36
C. 18
D. 6

11. Hip and ridge cover fasteners should extend a minimum of an _________ inch through the underside of roof decks less than ¾ of an inch thick.

A. 1/8
B. 3/4
C. 1/2
D. 1/4

12. A minimum distance of __________ inches is recommended between a penetration and valley center.

A. 6
B. 12
C. 16
D. 18

13. The minimum length of 5d box nails to be used on 24-inch taper-split shakes is ___________ inches.

A. 1 1/4
B. 1 3/4
C. 2
D. 6

14. Crickets shall be installed at the upslope side of chimneys or curbed roof penetrations when the chimney or curb is more than _________ inches wide.

A. 24
B. 18
C. 16
D. 12

15. There are _________ 22 x 12 slates in a square of roofing.

A. 98
B. 114
C. 108
D. 126

16. In clay and concrete tile roof systems, drip edge should be nailed at about _____________ inches on centers, slightly staggered

A. 6
B. 12
C. 10
D. 8

17. Metal shingle roof systems may be secured using ______________.

A. Staples, screws or nails
B. Staples, nails or clips and tabs
C. Screws, nails or clips and tabs
D. Staples, screws or clips and tabs

18. If a starter course of shakes consists of two layers, joints should be offset between neighboring units in the adjacent courses a minimum of ____________ inches.

A. 3/4
B. 1
C. 1 1/4
D. 1 1/2

19. ______________ is a natural, self-healing metal that weathers to a soft blue-gray patina.

A. Stainless steel
B. Aluminum
C. Zinc
D. Copper

20. For steep – to low-slope transitions, it is recommended that asphalt shingles be held back a minimum of ________inches above the transition.

A. 8
B. 10
C. 12
D. 14

21. It is suggested that ________ be used when installing slate roofing.

A. Galvanized nails
B. Stainless steel nails
C. Electroplated nails
D. Copper-slating nails

22. When tapering a 16- foot open valley, the bottom of the valley will be ___________inches greater than at the top of the valley.

A. 4
B. 1
C. 2
D. 3

23. Water and ice-dam underlayment protection should be applied starting at a roof system's eaves and extend upslope to a point corresponding to a minimum _______ inches inside the exterior wall line of a building.

A. 22
B. 12
C. 24
D. 36

24. The common dimensions for standard three-tab shingles are ______________ .

A. 12" x 36"
B. 12" x 40"
C. 11" x 36"
D. 11" x 40"

25. It is recommended that valley metal for use with wood shakes or shingles be a minimum of _______inches wide.

A. 12
B. 14
C. 18
D. 24

26. _____________ flashings provide a weatherproof transition material where a roof area intersects a head wall.

A. Step
B. Apron
C. Backer
D. Counter

27. Counter-battens should be spaced not more than ___________on center when used with nominal 2-by-2 wood battens.

A. 12
B. 16
C. 18
D. 24

28. A type ___________ clay or concrete tile has a rise-to-width ratio greater than 1:5.

A. I
B. II
C. III
D. IV

29. ____________ is NOT recommended to be used as a valley underlayment.

A. Heavy weight felt
B. Full-width sheet of polymer-modified bitumen
C. Base sheet
D. Self-adhering polymer-modified bitumen sheet

30. The minimum nominal thickness recommended for ____________roof shingles is 0.024 inches.

A. Asphalt
B. Aluminum
C. Copper
D. Zinc

31. Where wall cladding counterflashes wall flashing metal, the cladding material and water-resistive barrier should extend past and cover the top edge of the flashing metal a minimum of _____________ inches.

A. 2
B. 4
C. 6
D. 8

32. ______________ is the most common method of fastening tile.

A. Nailing
B. Screwing
C. Clipping
D. Wire ties and strapping

33. Each wood shingle should be fastened with ___________ fastener (s) located approximately ¾ of an inch to 1 inch from the side edges.

A. 1
B. 2
C. 3
D. 4

34. No. 30 asphalt felt is commonly designated Type __________ by ASTM D4869 standards.

A. I
B. II
C. III
D. IV

35. Asphalt shingles classified according to ASTM D7158 as Class ______ are said to pass at a basic wind speed up to and including 150 mph.

A. D
B. F
C. G
D. H

******Please See Answer Key on following page******

ALH 01/30/2020

1 Exam Prep
NRCA Steep-slope Roof Systems, 2017
Questions and Answers

ANSWER KEY

	Answer	Section/Page#
1.	B	53
2.	A	68
3.	B	72
4.	A	74
5.	A	71
6.	D	211
7.	D	104,241,404,506,611
8.	B	72
9.	B	586
10.	B	73
11.	A	70
12.	D	104
13.	B	576, Fig. 4-3
14.	A	77
15.	D	471
16.	B	210
17.	C	372
18.	D	578
19.	C	363
20.	B	78
21.	D	472
22.	A	74
23.	C	55
24.	A	57
25.	D	584
26.	B	76
27.	D	187
28.	A	200, Fig. 4-1
29.	A	72
30.	B	362
31.	A	78
32.	A	206
33.	B	580
34.	D	50, Fig. 3-1
35.	D	60

NRCA Metal Panel and SPF Roof Systems, 2020
Questions and Answers

1. One of the advantages of heavier gauge galvanized steel is that if thick enough, a panel will not exhibit an objectionable amount of __________.

    A. Oil canning
    B. Surface defects
    C. Glare
    D. Rusting

2. According to NRCA, architectural metal panel roof systems perform well on slopes of __________ inch(es) or greater.

    A. 14
    B. 3
    C. ½
    D. 1/8

3. The height of a mechanical equipment stands supporting 12-inch-wide equipment is __________ inches.

    A. 14
    B. 18
    C. 24
    D. 30

4. The nominal thickness of 16-ounce copper is __________ inches.

    A. .0270
    B. .0216
    C. .0418
    D. .0340

5. Sixteen-ounce copper weighs __________ per square foot.

    A. 16 pounds
    B. 16 ounces
    C. 3/4 pounds
    D. 14 ounces

6. During a reroof pipe penetrations require __________.

   A. Same type of flashing regardless of use
   B. Different methods of flashing
   C. Stacks to have an unlimited height
   D. None of the above

7. If unsatisfactory or questionable roof deck conditions are observed, the roofing contractor should __________.

   A. Install new roofing system over existing deck
   B. Replace and repair damaged area of roof deck
   C. Promptly inform the building owner or other responsible parties
   D. Place tarp over the area and continue working in order to avoid wasting time

8. The __________ is responsible for installing pipe support systems in reroofing.

   A. Plumbing contractor
   B. Mechanical contractor
   C. Roofing contractor
   D. At the discretion of the owner/property manager

9. Expansion joints be located __________ in a roof assembly.

   A. Expansion joints are never needed in a roof assembly
   B. At the center of a commercial building
   C. Every 12 feet
   D. In the same location as the building's structural expansion joint

10. Why would a recoat be needed for an SPF system?

    A. Thin coat becoming slightly translucent
    B. Extensive physical damage
    C. Damage caused by hail, wind, or hurricane
    D. All of the above

11. All stored materials should be stored according to __________.

    A. International Building Code
    B. Per NRCA guidelines
    C. Within temperature range and guidelines required by the system manufacturer
    D. All of the above

12. The standard time for testing and evaluating concrete's compressive strength and its dryness or suitability to be covered by a roofing system is __________ days.

    A. 7
    B. 15
    C. 30
    D. 28

13. Metal panel roof systems are fabricated at __________.

A. Contractor's facility or jobsite
B. Manufacturing facilities
C. Both A and B
D. None of the above

14. There are __________ different commonly used sheet metal fasteners.

A. 8
B. 12
C. 13
D. 18

15. __________ can be used as underlayment.

A. Asphalt felt
B. Synthetic sheets
C. Self-adhering polymer-modified bitumen sheets
D. All of the above

Please see Answer Key on the following page

NRCA Metal Panel and SPF Roof Systems, 2020
Questions and Answers
Answer Key

	Answer	Page #
1.	A	89
2.	B	96
3.	A	152
4.	B	75
5.	B	75
6.	B	192
7.	C	417
8.	C	165
9.	D	406
10.	D	401
11.	C	380
12.	D	359
13.	C	104
14.	C	159
15.	D	115 – 116

NRCA Metal Panel and SPF Roof Systems, 2016

Questions and Answers

1. One of the advantages of heavier gauge galvanized steel is that if thick enough, a panel will not exhibit an objectionable amount of____________

A Oil canning
B Surface defects
C Glare
D Rusting

2. According to NRCA, architectural metal panel roof systems perform well on slopes of _______ in 12 or greater.

A 14
B 3
C 1/2
D 1/8

3. The height of a mechanical equipment stand supporting 12 inch wide equipment is________

A 14"
B 18"
C 24"
D 30"

4. The nominal thickness of 16-ounce copper is how many inches?

A .0270
B .0216
C .0418
D .0340

5. Sixteen ounce copper weighs how much per square foot?

A 16 pounds
B 16 ounces
C 3/4 pounds
D 14 ounces

6. During a reroof pipe penetrations require?

A Same type of flashing regardless of use
B Different type of flashing
C Stacks to have an unlimited height
D None of the above

7. If unsatisfactory or questionable roof deck conditions are observed, the roofing contractor should___________?

A Install new roofing system over existing deck
B Replace and repair damaged area of roof deck
C Promptly inform the building owner or other responsible parties
D Place tarp over the area and continue working in order to avoid wasting time

8. Who is responsible for installing pipe support systems in reroofing?

A Plumbing contractor
B Mechanical contractor
C Roofing contractor
D At the discretion of the owner/property manager

9. Where should expansion joints be located in a roof assembly?

A Expansion joints are never needed in a roof assembly
B At the center of a commercial building
C Every 12 ft
D In the same location as the buildings structural expansion joint

10. Why would a recoat be needed for an SPF system?

A Thin coat becoming slightly translucent
B Extensive physical damage
C Damage caused by hail, wind, or hurricane
D All of the above

11. All stored materials should be stored according to__________?

A International Building Code
B Per NRCA guidelines
C Within temperature range and guidelines required by the system manufacturer
D All of the above

12. What is the standard time for testing and evaluating concrete's compressive strength and its dryness or suitability to be covered by a roofing system?

A 7 days
B 15 days
C 30 days
D 28 days

13. Where are metal panel roof systems fabricated?

A contractor's facility or jobsite
B manufacturing facilities
C Both A and B
D None of the above

14. How many different commonly used sheet metal fasteners are there?

A 8
B 12
C 13
D 18

15. What kind of material can be used as underlayment?

A asphalt felt
B synthetic sheets
C self-adhering polymer-modified bitumen sheets
D All of the above

Please See Answer Key on following page

ALH 02/24/2020

1 Exam Prep

NRCA Metal Panel and SPF Roof Systems, 2016

Questions and Answers

ANSWER KEY

	Answer	Section/Page#
1.	A	Page 83
2.	B	Page 88
3.	A	Page 141
4.	B	Page 501
5.	B	Page 71
6.	B	Page 409
7.	C	Page 394
8.	C	Page 379
9.	D	Page 378
10.	D	Page 375
11.	C	Page 354
12.	D	Page 340
13.	C	Page 95
14.	C	Page 147
15.	D	Page 106

NFPA 70 National Electrical Code, 2017
Practice Exam 1
Questions and Answers

1. Solar photovoltaic system dc circuits on or in one- and two-family dwellings shall be permitted to have a MAXIMUM voltage of _____ or less.

A. 125 volts
B. 250 volts
C. 300 volts
D. 600 volts

2. What is the MINIMUM height allowed for a fence enclosing an outdoor installation of 2,400-volt electrical equipment?

A. 6 feet
B. 7 feet
C. 8 feet
D. 9 feet

3. Where power for equipment is directly associated with the radio frequency distribution system is carried by the coaxial cable, and the power source is a power limiting transformer, what is the MAXIMUM voltage this coaxial cable may carry?

A. 50 volts
B. 60 volts
C. 120 volts
D. 150 volts

4. Where a 15-ampere rated general-use ac snap switch is used as a disconnecting means for an ac motor of 2 HP or less, the NEC® requires the MAXIMUM full-load current rating of the motor to be NO more than _____.

A. 7.5 amperes
B. 10 amperes
C. 12 amperes
D. 15 amperes

5. Determine the MAXIMUM number of 125-volt, general-purpose receptacles the NEC® permits to be protected by a 20-ampere, 120-volt, single-pole inverse time circuit breaker in a commercial occupancy.

A. 18
B. 15
C. 13
D. 10

6. Which of the following statements, if any, is/are true regarding illumination for service equipment installed in electrical equipment rooms?

I. The illumination shall not be controlled by means of three way switches.
II. The illumination shall not be controlled by automatic means only.

A. I only
B. II only
C. both I and II
D. neither I nor II

7. In regard to the tenant spaces in a retail shopping mall; each occupant shall have access to the main disconnecting means, EXCEPT:

A. where the service and maintenance are provided by the building management and are under continuous building management supervision
B. where there are more than six disconnecting means provided.
C. where the primary feeder transformer does not exceed 600 volts.
D. where the secondary of the service transformer does not exceed 240-volts to ground.

E. Determine the conductor allowable ampacity given the following conditions:

* ambient temperature of 44 deg. C
* 250 kcmil THWN copper conductors
* four (4) current-carrying conductors are in the raceway
* length of raceway is 25 feet

A. 160 amperes
B. 167 amperes
C. 200 amperes
D. 209 amperes

9. Determine the MAXIMUM overcurrent protection permitted for size 14 THWN copper motor control circuit conductors tapped from the load side of a motor overcurrent protection device. Given: the conductors require short-circuit protection and do not extend beyond the motor control equipment enclosure.

A. 20 amperes
B. 25 amperes
C. 30 amperes
D. 100 amperes

10. Circuit breakers rated ______ or less and 1000 volts or less shall have the ampere rating molded, stamped, etched or similarly marked into their handles or escutcheon areas.

A. 600 amperes
B. 200 amperes
C. 400 amperes
D. 100 amperes

11. In the kitchen of a dwelling unit where a single-phase, 125-volt, 15-or 20-ampere rated receptacle outlet is installed for a refrigerator and is located within 6 feet from the top inside edge of the bowl of the kitchen sink, the receptacle outlet shall be provided with ______.

A. GFCI protection only
B. AFCI protection only
C. both GFCI and AFCI protection
D. neither GFCI nor AFCI protection

12. Where a rooftop mounted air-conditioning unit is supplied with three (3) size 8 AWG THWN copper conductors, enclosed in an electrical metallic tubing (EMT) within three (3) inches of the rooftop, and exposed to direct sunlight and an ambient temperature of 100 degrees F, the allowable ampacity of the conductors is ______ .

A. 50 amperes
B. 44 amperes
C. 29 amperes
D. 25 amperes

13. Which of the following listed conductor insulations is oil resistant?

A. TW
B. TFE
C. THWN
D. MTW

14. All exposed non-current-carrying metal parts of an information technology system shall _____ or shall be double insulated.

A. be bonded to the equipment grounding conductor
B. not be bonded to the equipment grounding conductor
C. be bonded to the grounded conductor
D. be isolated

15. Determine the MINIMUM number of 15-ampere, 120-volt general lighting branch circuits required for 12,000 square feet multifamily condo where each dwelling unit has cooking facilities provided.

A. 15
B. 20
C. 24
D. 30

16. Storage batteries used as a source of power for emergency systems shall be of a suitable rating and capacity to supply and maintain the total load for at LEAST _____.

A. 1/2 hour
B. 1 hour
C. 1½ hours
D. 2 hours

17. When a conduit containing service-entrance conductors runs beneath a building, what is the MINIMUM depth of concrete required to cover the conduit for it to be considered "outside" the building?

A. 2 inches
B. 6 inches
C. 12 inches
D. 18 inches

18. The entire area of an aircraft hangar, including any adjacent and communicating areas not suitably cut off from the hangar, shall be classified as a Class I, Division 2 or Zone 2 location up to a level _____ above the floor.

A. 12 inches
B. 18 inches
C. 24 inches
D. 30 inches

19. Where a 240-volt, single-phase 90 ampere load is located 225 feet from a panelboard and supplied with size 3 THWN copper conductors; what does the approximate voltage drop on this circuit? (K = 12.9)

A. 6 volts
B. 4 volts
C. 8 volts
D. 10 volts

20. The continuity of the equipment grounding conductor system for portable electrical carnival equipment shall be verified _____.

A. and recorded on an annual basis
B. and recorded on a quarterly basis
C. and recorded on a monthly basis
D. each time the equipment is connected

21. Electrical services and feeders for recreational vehicle parks shall be calculated based on NOT less than _____ per RV site equipped with both 20-ampere and 30-ampere supply facilities.

A. 2400 volt-amperes
B. 9600 volt-amperes
C. 4800 volt-amperes
D. 3600 volt-amperes

22. In a commercial garage work area, which of the following 125-volt, single-phase receptacles, if any, are required to have GFCI protection?

I. 15-ampere general-purpose receptacles for hand tools and portable lighting equipment.
II. 20-ampere receptacles serving electrical diagnostic equipment only.

A. I only
B. II only
C. both I and II
D. neither I nor II

23. When sizing time-delay Class CC fuses for motor branch-circuit, short-circuit and ground-fault protection, they are to be sized at the same value as _____.

A. inverse-time circuit breakers
B. nontime-delay fuses
C. instantaneous trip circuit breakers
D. adjustable trip circuit breakers

24. The MINIMUM spacing required between the bottom of a 600 volt rated switchboard and the noninsulated busbars mounted in the switchboard cabinet is _____.

A. 6 inches
B. 8 inches
C. 10 inches
D. 12 inches

25. Given: A rigid metal conduit (RMC) to be installed will contain only the following three (3) circuits on the load side of the service overcurrent protective devices:

* two - 150 ampere, 3-phase circuits
* one - 300 ampere, single-phase circuit

The load side equipment bonding jumper for this conduit must be a MINIMUM size of _____ copper.

A. 1 AWG
B. 2 AWG
C. 4 AWG
D. 6 AWG

Please See Answer Key on following page

1 Exam Prep
NFPA 70 National Electrical Code
Practice Exam 1
Questions and Answers

ANSWER KEY

Answer	Section/Page#
1. D	690.7
2. B	110.31
3. B	820.15
4. C	430.109(C)(2)

15 amperes x 80% = 12 amperes

5. C	220.14(I)

120 volts x 20 amps = 2,400 VA (circuit)
2,400 VA (circuit) ÷ 180 VA (one receptacle) = 13 outlets

6. B	110.26(D)
7. A	240.24(B)(1)
8. B	310.15(B)(2) Table 310.15(B)(16) Table 310.15(B)(2)(a) Table 310.15(B)(3)(a)

Size 250 kcmil THWN copper ampacity before derating = 255 amperes
255 amps x .82 (temp. correction) x .8 (adjustment factor) = 167.28 amperes

9. D	Table 430.72(B)
10. D	240.83(B)
11. C	210.8(A)(7) 210.12(A)

Answer	Section/Page#
12. B	310.15(B)(2) Table 310.15(B)(2)(a) Table 310.15(B)(16)

outdoor ambient temperature = 100 deg. F
Note - A temperature correction factor of .88 must be applied.

Size 8 AWG THWN ampacity (before derating) = 50 amperes
50 amperes x .88 (temp. correction) = 44 amperes

13. D	Table 310.104(A)
14. A	645.15
15. B	Table 220.12 and 220.14(J)

12,000 sq. ft. x 3 VA = 36,000 VA (building)
120 volts x 15 amps = 1,800 VA (1 circuit)

$$\frac{36{,}000 \text{ VA (building)}}{1{,}800 \text{ VA (1 circuit)}} = 20 \text{ circuits}$$

16. C	700.12(A)
17. A	230.6(1)
18. B	513.3(B)
19. D	Chapter 9, Table 8 Voltage-drop formula

$$VD = \frac{2KID}{CM} \quad VD = \frac{2 \times 12.9 \times 90 \text{ amps} \times 225 \text{ ft.}}{52{,}620 \text{ CM}} = 9.92 \text{ volts dropped}$$

20. D	525.32
21. D	551.73
22. C	511.12
23. B	Table 430.52, Note 1
24. C	Table 408.5
25. C	250.102(D) 250.122(C) Table 250.122

NFPA 70 National Electrical Code, 2017
Practice Exam 2

1. Where conduits enter a floor-standing switchboard, switchgear or, panelboard at the bottom, the conduits, including their end fittings, shall NOT rise more than _____ above the bottom of the enclosure.

A. 6 inches
B. 4 inches
C. 2 inches
D. 3 inches

2. For emergency systems where internal combustion engines are used as the prime mover, an on-site fuel supply shall be provided with an on-site fuel supply sufficient for NOT less than _____ full-demand operation of the system.

A. 2 hours
B. 3 hours
C. 4 hours
D. 6 hours

3. Conductors supplying outlets for arc and xenon motion picture projectors of the professional type shall be a MINIMUM size of _____.

A. 12 AWG
B. 10 AWG
C. 8 AWG
D. 6 AWG

4. Thermostatically controlled switching devices serving as both controllers and disconnecting means for fixed electric space heating equipment shall _____.

A. be prohibited
B. be located not more than 5 feet above the floor level
C. directly open all grounded conductors when manually placed in the *OFF* position
D. be designed so that the circuit cannot be energized automatically after the device has been manually placed in the *OFF* position

5. A bonding jumper connected between the communications grounding electrode and power grounding electrode system at the building or structure service where separate electrodes are used shall NOT be smaller than size _____ copper.

A. 8 AWG
B. 6 AWG
C. 12 AWG
D. 10 AWG

6. Given: A straight pull of size 4 AWG and larger conductors is to made in a junction box that will have a trade size 3 in. conduit and two (2) trade size 2 in. conduits entering on the same side and exiting on the opposite wall. No splices or terminations will be made in the box. Which of the following listed junction boxes is the MINIMUM required for this installation?

A. 18 in. x 12 in.
B. 20 in. x 18 in.
C. 20 in. x 12 in.
D. 24 in. x 24 in.

7. Given: A dairy farm with a 120/240-volt, single phase electrical system will have the following three loads supplied from a common service; one – 18,000 VA, one - 16,000 VA, and one –10,000 VA. What is the demand load, in amperes, on the ungrounded service-entrance conductors?

A. 183 amperes
B. 152 amperes
C. 304 amperes
D. 114 amperes

8. All 15- or 20-ampere, single-phase, 125-volt receptacles located within at LEAST _____ of the edge of a decorative fountain shall be provided with GFCI protection for personnel.

A. 10 feet
B. 15 feet
C. 20 feet
D. 25 feet

9. The emergency electrical disconnects for attended self-service gasoline stations or convenience stores with motor fuel dispensing facilities must be located NOT more than _____ from the motor fuel dispensers that they serve.

A. 20 feet
B. 50 feet
C. 75 feet
D. 100 feet

10. Given: A dry-type transformer is fed with four (4) parallel size 500 kcmil conductors per phase. The conductors enter the enclosure on the opposite wall of the terminals. What is the MINIMUM wire-bending space required for the conductors at each terminal?

A. 16 inches
B. 14 inches
C. 12 inches
D. 10 inches

11. What MINIMUM size THWN copper conductors are required to supply a continuous-duty, 25 hp, 208-volt, 3-phase motor, where the motor is on the end of a short conduit run that contains only three (3) conductors, at an ambient temperature of 115 deg. F?

A. 6 AWG
B. 3 AWG
C. 2 AWG
D. 1 AWG

12. Where time-delay (dual-element) fuses are used for short-circuit and ground-fault protection for both windings of a part-winding start induction motor, the fuses shall be permitted to have a rating NOT exceeding _____ of the full-load current of the motor.

A. 200 percent
B. 150 percent
C. 175 percent
D. 225 percent

13. Where a conductor is marked *RHW-2* on the insulation, what does the *-2* represent?

A. The cable has 2 conductors.
B. The conductor is double insulated.
C. The conductor has a nylon outer jacket.
D. The conductor has a maximum operating temperature of 90ºC.

14. Apply the general method of calculation for dwellings and determine the demand load, in kW, on the ungrounded service-entrance conductors for four (4) household electric ranges rated 19 kW each.

A. 34 kW
B. 17 kW
C. 38 kW
D. 23 kW

15. In movie theaters, all switches for controlling the emergency lighting systems shall be located _____.

A. on the stage
B. in the lobby
C. in the manager's office
D. in the projection booth

16. Single-conductor cable Type _____ shall be permitted in exposed outdoor locations in photovoltaic source circuits for photovoltaic module interconnections within the photovoltaic array.

A. UF
B. THHN
C. USE-2
D. THWN

17. What percent of electrical supplied spaces in a recreational vehicle park must be equipped with at least one (1) 30-ampere 125-volt receptacle outlet?

A. 60 percent
B. 70 percent
C. 90 percent
D. 100 percent

18. Each operating room of a health care facility shall be provided with a MINIMUM of _____ listed "hospital grade" receptacles.

A. 12
B. 24
C. 30
D. 36

19. Where a 3-phase, 25 kVA rated transformer with a 480-volt primary and a 208Y/120-volt secondary is to be installed where both primary and secondary protection is required to be provided, determine the MAXIMUM standard ampere rating of the secondary overcurrent protection as permitted by the NEC®.

A. 80 amperes
B. 90 amperes
C. 100 amperes
D. 110 amperes

20. Where ungrounded conductors are run in parallel in multiple raceways, the equipment grounding conductor, where used, shall be _____.

A. omitted
B. run in parallel in each raceway
C. installed in one raceway only
D. bare

21. Where track lighting is installed in a continuous row, each individual section of NOT more than _____ in length shall have one additional support.

A. 2 feet
B. 4 feet
C. 6 feet
D. 8 feet

22. Determine the MINIMUM size THWN copper feeder conductors required by the NEC® to supply the following 480-volt, continuous duty, 3-phase, induction-type, Design C, motors.

* one - 40 hp
* one - 50 hp
* one - 60 hp

A. 2/0 AWG
B. 3/0 AWG
C. 4/0 AWG
D. 250 kcmil

23. In health care facilities, essential electrical systems shall have a MINIMUM _____.

A. of one (1) hour back-up time
B. capacity of 200 gallons of fuel for the auxiliary generator
C. of two (2) independent sources of power
D. capacity of 150 kVA

24. Where compressed natural gas vehicles are repaired in a commercial major repair garage, the area within _____ of the ceiling shall be considered unclassified where adequate ventilation is provided.

A. 18 inches
B. 24 inches
C. 30 inches
D. 36 inches

25. Where a 3-phase, 480-volt, 100 ampere demand load is located 390 feet from a panelboard, what MINIMUM size THWN aluminum conductors are required to supply the load where the voltage drop is required to be limited to 3 percent? (K = 21.2)

A. 2 AWG
B. 1 AWG
C. 1/0 AWG
D. 2/0 AWG

Please See Answer Key on following page

1 Exam Prep
NFPA 70 National Electrical Code, 2017
Practice Exam 2
Questions and Answers

ANSWER KEY

Answer	Section/Page#
1. D	408.5
2. A	700.12(B)(2)
3. C	540.13
4. D	424.20(A)(3)
5. B	800.100(D)
6. D	314.28(A)(1)

3 in. (largest conduit) x 8 = 24 inches

7. B	220.103 Table 220.103 Single-phase current formula

18,000 VA x 100% = 18,000 VA
16,000 VA x 75% = 12,000 VA
10,000 VA x 65% = 6,500 VA
Demand = 36,500 VA ÷ 240 volts = 152 amperes

8. C	680.58
9. D	514.11(B)
10. A	312.6(B)(2) Table 312.6(B)

Answer	Section/Page#
11. D	Table 430.250 430.22 Table 310.15(B)(2)(a) Table 310.15(B)(16)

25 hp motor FLC = 74.8 amperes x 125% = 93.5 amperes
93.5 amps /.75 (temperature correction) = 124.6 amperes
*NOTE: The wire size needs to be increased because of the elevated ambient temperature. Size 1 AWG THWN conductors with an allowable ampacity of 130 amperes should be selected.

12. B	430.4, Exception
13. D	Table 310.104(A)
14. D	Table 220.55 & Note 1

19 kW – 12 kW = 7 kW x 5% = 35% increase in Column C
17 kW (4 appliances in Col. C) x 135% = 22.95 kW demand

15. B	700.21 / 520.8
16. C	690.31(C)(1)
17. B	551.71(B)
18. D	517.19(C)(1)
19. B	3-Phase Current Formula Table 450.3(B) Note 1 Table 240.6(A)

$I = \frac{kVA \times 1000}{208 \times 1.732}$ $\quad I = \frac{25 \times 1,000}{208 \times 1.732} = \frac{25,000}{360.25} = 69.3$ amperes

69.3 amperes x 125% = 86.62 amperes

*NOTE: You are permitted to go up to the next standard size OCP device which has a rating of 90 amperes.

20. B	250.122(F)(b)
21. B	410.154

Answer	**Section/Page#**
22. C	Table 430.250 430.24(1) & (2) Table 310.15(B)(16)

40 hp FLC = 52 amps x 100% = 52 amperes
50 hp FLC = 65 amps x 100% = 65 amperes
60 hp FLC = 77 amps x 125% = 96 amperes
Total = 213 amperes

Size 4/0 AWG THWN conductors with an ampacity of 230 amperes should be selected.

23. C	517.41(A)
24. A	511.3(D) Table 511.3(C)
25. C	Chapter 9, Table 8 3-phase voltage drop formula

*NOTE: 3% of 480 volts = .03 x 480 = 14.4 (voltage drop permitted)

$$CM = \frac{1.732 \times K \times I \times D}{\text{VD permitted}}$$

$$CM = \frac{1.732 \times 21.2 \times 100 \text{ amps} \times 390 \text{ ft.}}{14.4 \text{ volts}} = 99{,}446 \text{ CM}$$

Size 1/0 AWG conductors with a CMA of 105,600 should be selected.

NFPA 70 National Electrical Code, 2017
Final Exam 1

1. Given: After all demand factors have been taken into consideration for an office building, the demand load is determined to be 90,000 VA; the building has a 120/240-volt, single-phase electrical system. What MINIMUM size copper conductors with THHN/THWN insulation are required for the ungrounded service-lateral conductors?

A. 400 kcmil
B. 350 kcmil
C. 300 kcmil
D. 500 kcmil

2. Given: A commercial building is to be supplied from a transformer having a 480Y/277-volt, 3-phase primary and a 208Y/120-volt, 3-phase secondary. The secondary will have a balanced computed demand load of 416 amperes per phase. The transformer is required to have a MINIMUM kVA rating of _____.

A. 100 kVA
B. 150 kVA
C. 86 kVA
D. 200 kVA

3. Manhole covers shall be OVER _____ or otherwise require the use of tools to open.

A. 25 lbs.
B. 50 lbs.
C. 75 lbs.
D. 100 lbs.

4. The branch circuit conductors supplying one or more units of information technology equipment shall have an ampacity of NOT less than _____ of the connected load.

A. 80 percent
B. 100 percent
C. 115 percent
D. 125 percent

5. In regard to a 7½ hp, 480-volt, 3-phase ac motor with an 80 percent power factor and a full-load ampere rating of 19 amperes indicated on the nameplate, and a service factor of 1.15; when the initial setting of the overload device you have selected is not sufficient to carry the load, what is the MAXIMUM setting permitted for the overload protection?

A. 21.85 amperes
B. 23.75 amperes
C. 24.70 amperes
D. 26.60 amperes

6. Electrical services and feeders for recreational vehicle parks shall be calculated on the basis of NOT less than ______ per RV site equipped with both 20-ampere and 30-ampere supply facilities.

A. 9600 volt-amperes
B. 4800 volt-amperes
C. 3600 volt-amperes
D. 2400 volt-amperes

7. What MINIMUM voltage is required after 1½ hours to serve emergency lighting from a storage battery, when the normal source voltage of 120 volts is interrupted?

A. 60 volts
B. 90 volts
C. 105 volts
D. 120 volts

8. Determine the absolute MAXIMUM ampere setting permitted for an overload protective device responsive to motor current, where used to protect a 20 hp, 240-volt, 3-phase, induction type ac motor with a temperature rise of 48 deg. C and a FLA of 54 amperes indicated on the nameplate.

A. 54.0 amperes
B. 70.2 amperes
C. 62.1 amperes
D. 75.6 amperes

9. Where Type SRD multiconductor cable consist of size 8 AWG conductors and only two (2) conductors in the cable are current-carrying, what is the allowable ampacity of the conductors?

A. 20 amperes
B. 30 amperes
C. 40 amperes
D. 50 amperes

10. Aluminum or steel cable trays shall be permitted to be used as equipment grounding conductors, provided ______.

I. the cable tray sections and fittings are identified as an equipment grounding conductor
II. the cable tray sections and fittings are durably marked to show the cross-sectional area of the metal

A. I only
B. II only
C. neither I nor II
D. both I and II

11. When intermediate metal conduit (IMC) is threaded in the field, a standard cutting die with a ______ taper per ft. shall be used.

A. 3/8 in.
B. 1/2 in.
C. 3/4 in.
D. 1 in.

12. In regard to emergency systems, where internal combustion engines are used as the prime movers, they shall NOT be solely dependent on a public utility gas system for their fuel supply, unless ______.

A. it is acceptable to the authority having jurisdiction
B. the gas system is listed and approved
C. the gas system and electrical utility are jointly owned and maintained
D. none of these apply

13. When a motor controller enclosure is installed outdoors and is subject to be exposed to sleet, it shall have a MINIMUM rating of ______, where the controller mechanism is required to be operable when ice covered.

A. Type 3
B. Type 3S
C. Type 3R
D. Type 3SX

14. Each operating room of a health care facility shall be provided with a MINIMUM of ______ "hospital grade" receptacles.

A. 12
B. 24
C. 36
D. 18

15. Ceiling-suspended luminaires (lighting fixtures) or paddle fans located ______ or more above the maximum water level of an indoor installed spa or hot tub shall NOT require GFCI protection.

A. 10 feet
B. 7½ feet
C. 8 feet
D. 12 feet

16. When flat conductor cable (FCC) is used for general-purpose branch circuits, the MAXIMUM rating of the circuits shall be ______.

A. 20 amperes
B. 30 amperes
C. 15 amperes
D. 10 amperes

17. When sizing overcurrent protection for fire pump motors, the device(s) shall be selected or set to carry indefinitely the _____ of the motor.

A. starting current
B. full-load running current
C. locked-rotor current
D. full-load amperage as indicated on the nameplate

18. Under which, if any, of the following conditions is the neutral conductor to be counted as a current-carrying conductor?

I. When it is only carrying the unbalanced current.
II. When it is the neutral conductor of a 3-phase, wye-connected system that consist of nonlinear loads.

A. I only
B. II only
C. neither I nor II
D. both I and II

19. In general, all mechanical elements used to terminate a grounding electrode conductor or bonding jumper to a grounding electrode shall be accessible. Which of the following, if any, is/are an exception(s) to this rule?

I. A connection to a concrete encased electrode.
II. A compression connection to fire-proofed structural metal.

20. I only
21. II only
22. neither I nor II
23. both I and II

20. For other than listed low-voltage luminaires not requiring grounding, all electrical equipment within a fountain or within _____ of the inside wall of a fountain shall be grounded.

A. 5 feet
B. 6 feet
C. 8 feet
D. 10 feet

21. Fuses shall NOT be permitted to be connected in parallel where ______.

I. they are factory assembled and listed as a unit
II. they are installed by a technician on the jobsite

A. I only
B. II only
C. neither I nor II
D. both I and II

22. Each multiwire branch circuit shall be provided with a means that will _____ at the point where the branch circuit originates.

A. simultaneously disconnect all ungrounded conductors
B. not simultaneously disconnect all ungrounded conductors
C. simultaneously disconnect all grounded and ungrounded conductors
D. simultaneously disconnect all grounded, ungrounded and grounding conductors

23. When calculating the total load for a mobile home park before demand factors are taken into consideration, each individual mobile home lot shall be calculated at a MINIMMUM of _____.

A. 20,000 VA
B. 15,000 VA
C. 24,000 VA
D. 16,000 VA

24. A single electrode consisting of a ground rod, pipe, or plate that does not have a resistance to ground of 25 ohms or less, shall be supplemented by one (1) additional electrode. Which of the following listed is/are approved for this purpose?

A. a concrete-encased electrode
B. a ground ring
C. the metal frame of the building
D. all of these

25. It shall be permissible to compute the feeder and service loads for dwellings using the optional method of calculations for dwellings instead of the general method of calculations for dwellings, if the dwelling unit is supplied with a single-phase, 120/240-volt service and the load is at LEAST _____ or greater.

A. 100 amperes
B. 125 amperes
C. 200 amperes
D. 150 amperes

26. In the critical care (Category 1) spaces of a health care facility, each patient bed location shall be provided with a MINIMUM of ______" hospital grade" receptacles.

A. fourteen
B. twelve
C. ten
D. eight

27. Nonmetallic surface extensions shall be permitted to be run in any direction from an existing outlet, but NOT within ______ of the floor level.

A. 1 foot
B. 1½ feet
C. 2 feet
D. 2 inches

28. The NEC® permits a building to have more than one service when:

I. the load requirements of the building are at least in excess of 800 amperes.
II. the building is separated by firewalls with a four-hour rating.

A. I only
B. II only
C. either I or II
D. neither I nor II

29. In the garage of a dwelling unit, a 125-volt, single-phase, 15 amperes, receptacle installed in the ceiling provided for the garage door opener must be ______.

I. a single receptacle
II. GFCI protected for personnel

30. I only
31. II only
32. either I or II
33. neither I nor II

30. Underground installed service conductors that are not encased in concrete and buried 18 inches or more below grade level, shall have their location identified by a warning ribbon placed at LEAST ____ above the underground installation.

A. 6 inches
B. 8 inches
C. 12 inches
D. 18 inches

31. Outlets supplying permanently installed swimming pool pump motors from single-phase, 15- or 20-ampere, 120- or 240-volt branch circuits, shall
be provided with GFCI protection _____.

A. where installed outdoors
B. when cord-and-plug connected
C. when direct (hard-wired) connected
D. where any of the above conditions exist

32. The branch circuit conductors supplying a 240-volt, single-phase, 15 kW rated fixed electric space heater provided with a 10-ampere blower motor are required to have an ampacity of at LEAST _____.

A. 63 amperes
B. 78 amperes
C. 91 amperes
D. 109 amperes

33. A commercial kitchen is to contain the following listed cooking related equipment:

* one - 14 kW range
* one - 5.0 kW water heater
* one - 0.75 kW mixer
* one - 2.5 kW dishwasher
* one - 2.0 kW booster heater
* one - 2.0 kW broiler

Determine the demand load, in kW, after applying the demand factors for the kitchen equipment.

A. 19.00 kW
B. 26.25 kW
C. 18.38 kW
D. 17.06 kW

34. When two (2) ground rods are used to form the entire grounding electrode system of a building, the grounding conductor that bonds the two rods together shall NOT be required to be larger than size _____ copper, regardless of the size of the service-entrance conductors.

A. 8 AWG
B. 6 AWG
C. 4 AWG
D. 2 AWG

35. A kitchen with a total demand load of 54,000 VA is to be added to an existing church. The electrical system is 208Y/120-volts, 3-phase. What MINIMUM size THWN copper feeder conductors are required for the kitchen addition?

A. 1 AWG
B. 1/0 AWG
C. 2/0 AWG
D. 3/0 AWG

36. A feeder at a school welding shop is to supply the following listed transformer arc welders all with a 50 percent duty cycle.

* two (2) with 60 amperes rated primary current
* two (2) with 50 amperes rated primary current
* two (2) with 40 amperes rated primary current

The feeder is required to have an ampacity of at LEAST _____.

A. 213 amperes
B. 196 amperes
C. 182 amperes
D. 176 amperes

37. The National Electrical Code® requires ventilation of a battery room where batteries are being charged to prevent:

A. battery corrosion.
B. electrostatic charge.
C. deterioration of the building steel.
D. an accumulation of an explosive mixture.

38. What is the MAXIMUM balanced demand load, in VA, permitted to be connected to a new service of a commercial building, given the following conditions?

I. The service is 208Y/120 volts, 3-phase, with a 600-ampere rated main circuit breaker.
II. The maximum load must not exceed 80 percent of the ampere rating of the main circuit breaker.

A. 57,600 VA
B. 99,840 VA
C. 172,923 VA
D. 178,692 VA

39. Determine the MAXIMUM standard size overcurrent protection required for the primary and secondary side of a transformer, when primary and secondary overcurrent protection is to be provided, given the following related information.

* 150 kVA rating
* Primary - 480 volt, 3-phase, 3-wire
* Secondary - 208Y/120 volt, 3-phase, 4-wire

A. Primary - 500 amperes, Secondary - 500 amperes
B. Primary - 450 amperes, Secondary - 600 amperes
C. Primary - 500 amperes, Secondary - 450 amperes
D. Primary - 450 amperes, Secondary - 500 amperes

40. Openings around electrical penetrations of a wall of a designated information technology room are required to be _____.

A. insulated
B. airtight
C. firestopped
D. soundproof

41. When buried raceways pass under streets, roads or driveways, the MINIMUM cover requirements _____.

A. decrease if installed in rigid metal conduit (RMC)
B. do not change in regard to wiring methods used
C. shall be increased for direct burial cables
D. can be increased, decreased, or remain the same, depending on the wiring method used

42. For capacitors over 1000 volts, a means shall be provided to reduce the residual voltage to _____ after the capacitor is disconnected from the source of power.

A. 50 volts or less within 1 minute
B. 50 volts or less within 5 minutes
C. 24 volts or less within 5 minutes
D. 12 volts or less within 1 minute

43. Where used outside of a, building, aluminum or copper-clad aluminum grounding electrode conductors shall not be terminated WITHIN_____ of the earth.

A. 18 inches
B. 24 inches
C. 3 feet
D. 6 feet

44. Where installed for a commercial occupancy, determine the MINIMUM size THWN copper conductors required from the terminals of a 3-phase, 277/480-volt, 4-wire, 200 kW generator to the first distribution device(s) containing overcurrent protection. Assume the design and operation of the generator does NOT prevent overloading.

A. 250 kcmil
B. 300 kcmil
C. 400 kcmil
D. 500 kcmil

45. Enclosures containing circuit breakers, switches and motor controllers located in Class II, Division 2 locations, shall be _____ or otherwise identified for the location.

A. gastight
B. vapor-proof
C. dusttight
D. stainless steel

46. Information technology equipment is permitted to be connected to a branch circuit by flexible cord-and-attachment plug cap, if the cord does NOT exceed _____ in length.

A. 6 feet
B. 8 feet
C. 10 feet
D. 15 feet

47. Where required, conduit seals installed in Class I, Division 1 & 2 locations shall have the minimum thickness of the sealing compound not less than the trade size of the sealing fitting and, in no case less than _____.

A. 1/2 in.
B. 5/8 in.
C. 3/4 in.
D. 1 in.

48. Given: A one-family dwelling to be built will have 4,000 sq. ft. of livable space, a 600 sq. ft. garage, a 400 sq. ft. open porch, a 2,000 sq. ft. unfinished basement (adaptable for future use), three (3) small-appliance branch-circuits and a branch circuit for the laundry room. Determine the demand load, in VA, on the ungrounded service-entrance conductors for the general lighting and receptacle loads using the standard method of calculation for a one-family dwelling.

A. 10,350 VA
B. 9,825 VA
C. 7,350 VA
D. 24,000 VA

49. Determine the MINIMUM size Type SOW flexible cord that may be used to supply a 30 hp, 3-phase, 480-volt, continuous-duty, ac motor from the motor controller to the motor terminations. Assume voltage-drop and elevated ambient temperature are not considerations.

A. 4 AWG
B. 6 AWG
C. 8 AWG
D. 10 AWG

50. Portable structures for fairs, carnivals and similar events shall not be located under or within _____ horizontally of conductors operating in excess of 600 volts.

A. 22½ feet
B. 15 feet
C. 10 feet
D. 12 feet

51. Flexible cord and cables shall be permitted to be attached to building surfaces ______.

A. under no circumstances
B. where concealed
C. where used as a substitute for the fixed wiring of a structure
D. where the length of the cord or cable from a busway plug-in device to a suitable tension "take-up" support device does not exceed 6 feet

52. In regard to outside branch circuits of overhead spans of open individual conductors for 1000 volts or less up to 50 feet in length, the NEC® mandates the conductors to be NOT less than ______ copper in size.

A. 12 AWG
B. 10 AWG
C. 8 AWG
D. 6 AWG

53. The ampacity requirements for a disconnecting means of x-ray equipment shall be based on at LEAST ______ of the input required for the momentary rating of the equipment, if greater than the long-term rating.

A. 125 percent
B. 115 percent
C. 80 percent
D. 50 percent

54. The MINIMUM spacing required between live bare metal parts in feeder circuits of 480-volt industrial control panels and bare metal parts of the enclosure is ______.

A. 1/2 in.
B. 3/4 in.
C. 1 in.
D. 1¼ in.

55. AFCI protection is required for all 15- and 20-ampere, 120-volt branch circuits supplying outlets located in ______.

A. boat houses
B. recreational vehicles
C. all guest rooms and suites of hotels
D. residential garages

56. All swimming pool electric water heaters shall have the heating elements subdivided into loads not exceeding 48 amperes and protected at NOT over _____ .

A. 45 amperes
B. 50 amperes
C. 55 amperes
D. 60 amperes

57. In regard to emergency and legally required standby systems, transfer switches shall be _____ and approved by the authority having jurisdiction.

A. manual
B. automatic
C. nonautomatic
D. red in color

58. Where Type SE service-entrance cable with ungrounded conductors' sizes 10 AWG or smaller, is used for interior wiring as a substitute for Type NM cable, is installed in thermal insulation, the ampacity shall be in accordance with the _____ conductor temperature rating.

A. 40ºC
B. 60ºC
C. 75ºC
D. 90ºC

59. Power distribution blocks shall be permitted in pull and junction boxes having a volume over _____ for connections of conductors where installed in boxes, provided the power distribution blocks do not have uninsulated live parts exposed within the box, whether or not the box cover is exposed.

A. 50 cu. in.
B. 75 cu. in.
C. 100 cu. in.
D. 1650 cu. in.

60. Where a receptacle outlet is removed from an underfloor raceway, the conductors supplying the outlet shall be _____.

A. capped with an approved insulating material
B. taped off with red colored tape
C. marked and identified
D. removed from the raceway

61. What is the MINIMUM dimension required by the NEC® for a working space containing live parts on both sides of the equipment that will require examination and maintenance of the equipment when energized and operating at 480-volts between conductors?

A. 4 feet
B. 3 feet
C. 6 feet
D. 5 feet

62. Where a mobile home park has 25 mobile home lots calculated at 15,000 VA for each mobile home, determine the MINIMUM required ampacity required for the ungrounded service-entrance conductors.

A. 400 amperes
B. 380 amperes
C. 820 amperes
D. 782 amperes

63. A 3-phase, 150 kVA transformer with a 208Y/120-volt secondary has an existing load of 212 amperes on each of the ungrounded phases. What is the MAXIMUM load, in amperes, that may be added to each of the ungrounded secondary phases?

A. 416 amperes
B. 180 amperes
C. 204 amperes
D. 250 amperes

64. In regard to an isolated grounding type receptacle, the reason the insulated isolated grounding conductor is not bonded to the outlet box is _____.

A. for the reduction of electrical noise
B. to insure the circuit breaker will trip in the event of a ground-fault
C. to prevent the circuit breaker from tripping in the event of a ground-fault
D. for the reduction of voltage-drop

65. Where a central vacuum assembly is located in a storage closet adjacent to the laundry room of a dwelling, accessible non-current-carrying metal parts of the assembly likely to be energized shall be _____.

A. isolated
B. insulated
C. GFCI protected
D. connected to an equipment grounding conductor

66. Type CMP communications cable of NOT more than ____ in length shall be permitted in ducts used for environmental air if they are directly associated with the air distribution system.

A. 8 feet
B. 6 feet
C. 4 feet
D. 2 feet

67. The disconnecting switch or circuit breaker for electric signs and outline lighting systems shall open all _____ conductors simultaneously on multi-wire branch circuits supplying the sign or outline lighting system.

A. grounded and ungrounded
B. grounded, ungrounded and grounding
C. grounding, ungrounded and bonding
D. ungrounded

68. In an industrial establishment, what is the MAXIMUM length of 200 ampere rated busway that may be tapped to a 600-ampere rated busway, without additional overcurrent protection?

A. 10 feet
B. 25 feet
C. 50 feet
D. 75 feet

69. For circuits of OVER _____ to ground, the electrical continuity of rigid metal conduit (RMC) or intermediate metal conduit (IMC) that contain any conductor other than service conductors shall be insured with two (2) locknuts, one inside and one outside the box or cabinet.

A. 480 volts
B. 300 volts
C. 250 volts
D. 125 volts

70. In general, the NEC® does not mandate the maximum number of circuit breakers a panelboard may contain. An exception to this rule is _______, which is limited to no more than 42 overcurrent protection devices.

A. a delta-connected panelboard
B. a split-bus panelboard
C. a 3-phase panelboard
D. panelboards containing overcurrent protection devices rated only 30 amperes or less

71. When water reaches the height of the established electrical datum plane for an irrigation pond, the service equipment must _______.

A. be installed in a NEMA 6 enclosure
B. float
C. be installed in a NEMA 6P enclosure
D. disconnect

72. In health care facilities, essential electrical systems shall have a MINIMUM _______.

A. capacity of 200 gallons of fuel for the auxiliary generator
B. of two independent sources of power
C. of 1-hour back-up time
D. capacity of 150 kVA

73. Lampholders shall be constructed, installed, or equipped with shades or guards so that combustible material is not subjected to temperatures in EXCESS of _______.

A. 130 degrees F
B. 140 degrees F
C. 162 degrees F
D. 194 degrees F

74. Pendant conductors having a length of at LEAST _______ or more, shall be twisted together where not cabled in a listed assembly.

A. 3 feet
B. 4 feet
C. 5 feet
D. 6 feet

75. For nonshielded conductors of over 1000 volts, the conductors shall NOT be bent to a radius of less than ______ times the overall conductor material.

A. six
B. eight
C. ten
D. twelve

76. At least one structural support member of a building or structure that is direct contact with the earth for at LEAST ______ or more, with or without concrete encasement shall be permitted to be used as a grounding electrode.

A. 20 feet
B. 8 feet
C. 10 feet
D. 6 feet

77. The circuit supplying an autotransformer-type dimmer installed in theaters and similar places shall NOT exceed ______ between conductors.

A. 480 volts
B. 277 volts
C. 250 volts
D. 150 volts

78. At least one 125-volt, single-phase 15- or 20-ampere rated receptacle outlet shall be installed within 18 inches of the top of a show window of a retail store for each ______ of show window area measured horizontally.

A. 8 linear ft.
B. 10 linear ft.
C. 12 linear ft.
D. 15 linear ft.

79. Each luminaire installed in Class III, Divisions 1 and 2 locations shall be clearly marked to show the maximum wattage of the lamps that shall be permitted without exceeding an exposed surface temperature of ______ under normal conditions of use.

A. 329º F
B. 165º F
C. 144º F
D. 125º F

80. Conductors supplying a continuous-rated, varying-duty motor shall have an ampacity of NOT less than _____ of the motor nameplate current rating.

A. 125 percent
B. 140 percent
C. 150 percent
D. 200 percent

81. Where located in Class I, Division 1 locations, transformers containing oil or a liquid that will burn shall be _____.

A. enclosed in a fence
B. installed in vaults only
C. identified for use in Class I locations
D. installed in a fire-resistant room

82. Where a lighting track is installed with two (2), four (4) ft. sections, mounted end-to-end, how many supports are required?

A. five
B. four
C. three
D. two

83. What is the MAXIMUM standard size circuit breaker that may be used for overcurrent protection of size 4/0 AWG THWN copper conductors that are not serving a motor load?

A. 200 amperes
B. 225 amperes
C. 230 amperes
D. 250 amperes

84. Motor fuel dispensing systems shall be provided with one or more identified emergency shutoff devices or electrical disconnects. Such devices or disconnects shall NOT be more than _____ from the fuel dispensing units that they serve.

A. 30 feet
B. 50 feet
C. 75 feet
D. 100 feet

85. The depth of the working space in front of a 120-volt, single-phase, fire alarm control panel (FACP) is required to be at LEAST _____.

A. 2½ feet
B. 3 feet
C. 3½ feet
D. 4 feet

86. Where an air conditioning unit is supplied with size 6 AWG CU conductors and protected by a 60-ampere circuit breaker, the MINIMUM size CU equipment grounding conductor permitted for this installation is _____.

A. 12 AWG
B. 10 AWG
C. 8 AWG
D. 6 AWG

87. Which of the following is NOT required to be marked on the nameplate of a transformer?

A. overcurrent protection
B. manufacturer
C. kVA rating
D. voltage

88. When combination surface nonmetallic raceways are used for both signaling and for power and lighting circuits, the different systems shall be _____.

A. prohibited
B. run in the same compartment
C. run in separate compartments
D. maintain a spacing of at least ½ in.

89. Where explosionproof equipment is provided with metric threaded entries, which of the following methods is approved to adapt the entries from metric threads to NPT threads?

A. Approved adapters from metric threads to NPT threads shall be used.
B. Tap the metric threaded entries to NPT threads.
C. Thread the conduit with metric threads.
D. All of these are approved methods.

90. Where installed outdoors, dry-type transformers exceeding 112½ kVA shall NOT be located within _____ of combustible materials of buildings, unless the transformer has Class 155 insulation systems or higher and completely enclosed except for ventilating openings.

A. 6 inches
B. 10 inches
C. 12 inches
D. 18 inches

91. A clearance of NOT less than _____ must be maintained from the maximum water level of a permanently installed swimming pool and messenger-supported *tri-plex* service-drop conductors of 0-750 volts.

A. 10 feet
B. 14½ feet
C. 19 feet
D. 22½ feet

92. Where an apartment complex has a calculated connected lighting load of 205.4 kVA, what is the DEMAND load, in kVA, on the ungrounded service-entrance conductors where applying the standard (general) method of calculation? Given: Each dwelling unit in the complex has cooking facilities provided.

A. 58.9 kVA
B. 60.2 kVA
C. 16.5 kVA
D. 65.3 kVA

93. What is the MINIMUM permitted sill height of a transformer vault doorway?

A. 2 inches
B. 4 inches
C. 6 inches
D. 8 inches

94. For the purpose of sizing branch circuits for fixed storage-type water heaters with a capacity of 120 gallons or less, the water heater shall be considered ____.

A. a continuous load
B. an intermittent load
C. a noncontinuous load
D. a short-time load

95. When supplying a 36,000 VA, 240-volt, single-phase load in an area where the ambient temperature reaches 119º F, determine the MINIMUM size 75ºC rated copper conductors required to supply the load.

A. 1/0 AWG
B. 2/0 AWG
C. 3/0 AWG
D. 4/0 AWG

96. Color coding shall be permitted to identify intrinsically safe conductors where they are colored _____ and where no other conductors of the same color are used.

A. light blue
B. orange
C. yellow
D. purple

97. What is the MINIMUM bend radius of trade size 4 in. rigid metal conduit (RMC) where the bend is not made with a one-shot or full-shoe bender?

A. 16 inches
B. 18 inches
C. 24 inches
D. 30 inches

98. Where exceptions are not to be applied, determine the MINIMUM required length of a junction box that has a trade size 3½ in. conduit containing four (4) size 250 kcmil conductors, pulled through the box for a 90º angle pull.

A. 21 inches
B. 24 inches
C. 28 inches
D. 34 inches

99. An approved method of protection for equipment installed in Class I, Zone 0, hazardous locations are ______.

A. purged and pressurized
B. encapsulation
C. powder filling
D. oil immersion

100. Cables operating at over 1000 volts and those operating at 1000 volts or less, are permitted to be installed in a common cable tray without a fixed barrier, where the cables operating at over 1000 volts are _____.

A. Type MI
B. Type AC
C. Type CT
D. Type MC

Please See Answer Key on following page

ALH 04/03/2019

1Exam Prep
NFPA 70 National Electrical Code, 2017
Final Exam 1
Questions and Answers

ANSWER KEY

Answer	Section/Page#
1. D	300.5(B) Table 310.104(A) Table 310.15(B)(16) Single-phase Current Formula

I = P ÷ E I = 90,000 VA ÷ 240 volts = 375 amperes

Size 500 kcmil THHN/THWN conductors with an ampacity of 380 amperes should be selected from Table 310.15(B)(16).

2. B	3-phase Power Formula VA = I x E x 1.732

VA = 416 amperes x 208 volts x 1.732 = 149,866 VA
149,866 VA ÷ 1,000 = 149.8 kVA

3. D	110.75(D)
4. D	645.5(A)
5. D	430.6(A)(2) 430.32(A)(1) 430.32(C)

19 amperes x 140% = 26.60 amperes

6. C	551.73(A)
7. C	700.12(A)

120 volts x 87.5% = 105 volts

8. B	430.6(A)(2) 430.32(C)

54 amperes x 130% = 70.2 amperes

Answer	Section/Page#
9. C	Table 440.5(A)(1), Column B
10. D	392.60(B)(1) & (3)
11. C	342.28
12. A	700.12(B)(3), Exception
13. B	Table 110.28
14. C	517.19(C)(1)
15. D	680.43(B)(1)(a)
16. A	324.10(B)(2)
17. C	695.5(B)
18. B	310.15(B)(5)(a) &(c)
19. D	250.68(A), Exceptions 1 & 2
20. A	680.54(1)
21. B	240.8
22. A	210.4(B)
23. D	550.31(1)
24. D	250.53(A)(2) 250.52(A)(2) -(A)(8)
25. A	220.82(A)
26. A	517.19(B)(1)
27. D	382.15(A)
28. D	230.2(A), (B), &(C)
29. B	210.8(A)(2)
30. C	300.5(D)(3)
31. D	680.21(C)

Answer	**Section/Page#**
32. C	424.3(B) 210.19(A)(1)(a) Single-Phase Current Formula

$$I = \frac{kW \times 1{,}000}{volts} \quad I = \frac{15 \times 1{,}000}{240} = \frac{15{,}000}{240} = 62.5 \text{ amperes (heater)}$$

62.5 amperes (heater)
+10.0 amperes (blower)
72.5 amperes x 125% = 91 amperes

33. A	220.56 Table 220.56

14.00 kW - range
5.00 kW - water heater
0.75 kW - mixer
2.50 kW - dishwasher
2.00 kW - booster heater
2.00 kW - broiler
26.25 kW - total connected load x 65% = 17.06 kW

*NOTE: However, the NEC® states the demand shall not be less than the two largest pieces of equipment. 14.00 kW + 5.00 kW = 19 kW demand

34. B	250.66(A)
35. B	3-phase current formula Table 310.15(B)(16)

$$I = \frac{54{,}000 \text{ VA}}{208 \times 1.732} = \frac{54{,}000}{360.25} = 149.89 \text{ amperes}$$

Size 1/0 THWN conductors with an ampacity of 150 amperes should be selected from Table 310.15(B)(16).

36. D	Table 630.11(A) 630.11(B)

60 amperes x .71 = 43 amperes x 100% = 43 amperes
60 amperes x .71 = 43 amperes x 100% = 43 amperes
50 amperes x .71 = 36 amperes x 85% = 31 amperes
50 amperes x .71 = 36 amperes x 70% = 25 amperes
40 amperes x .71 = 28 amperes x 60% = 17 amperes
40 amperes x .71 = 28 amperes x 60% = 17 amperes
TOTAL = 176 amperes

Answer	**Section/Page#**
37. D	480.10(A)
38. C	3-phase Power Formula P = I x E x 1.732

P = 600 amperes x 208 volts x 1.732 x 80% = 172,923 VA

39. B	3-phase Current Formula 450.3(B) Table 450.3(B) Table 240.6(A)

(Primary)

$$I = \frac{kVA \times 1{,}000}{E \times 1.732} \quad I = \frac{150 \times 1{,}000}{480 \times 1.732} = \frac{150{,}000}{831.36} = 180 \text{ amps} \times 250\% = 450 \text{ amps}$$

(Secondary)

$$I = \frac{kVA \times 1{,}000}{E \times 1.732} \quad I = \frac{150 \times 1{,}000}{208 \times 1.732} = \frac{150{,}000}{360.25} = 416 \text{ amps} \times 125\% = 520 \text{ amps}$$

*NOTE: For the secondary you are permitted to go up to the next standard size overcurrent device which has a rating of 600 amperes.

40. C	645.3(A) 300.21
41. B	Table 300.5
42. B	460.28(A)
43. A	250.64(A)
44. B	3-phase Current Formula 445.13(A) Table 310.15(B)(16)

$$I = \frac{kW \times 1{,}000}{volts \times 1.732} \quad I = \frac{200 \times 1{,}000}{480 \times 1.732} = \frac{200{,}000}{831.36} = 240.56 \text{ amperes (FLC)}$$

241 amperes x 115% = 277 amperes (required ampacity of conductors)

Size 300 kcmil THWN conductors with an allowable ampacity of 285 amperes should be selected.

45. C	502.115(B)
46. D	645.5(B)(1)

Answer	**Section/Page#**
47. B	501.15(C)(3)
48. A	220.12 Table 220.12 220.52(A) & (B) Table 220.42

4,000 sq. ft. + 2,000 sq. ft. = 6,000 sq. ft. x 3 VA = 18,000 VA
three small appliance circuits @ 1,500 VA each = 4,500 VA
one laundry circuit @ 1,500 VA = 1,500 VA
Total connected load = 24,000 VA

1st 3,000 VA @ 100% 3,000 VA
24,000 VA - 3,000 VA = 21,000 VA (remainder) @ 35% = 7,350 VA
Total demand load = 10,350 VA

49. A	430.6 & .6(A)(1) 430.22 Table 430.250 Table 400.5(A)(1), Column A

FLC of 30 HP motor = 40 amperes x 125% = 50 amperes

Size 4 AWG SOW cord with an allowable ampacity of 60 amperes should be selected from Table 400.5(A)(1).

50. B	525.5(B)(2)
51. D	400.12(4), Exception 368.56(B)(2)
52. B	225.6(A)(1)
53. D	517.72(A)
54. C	409.106 Table 430.97(D)
55. C	210.12(A) 210.12(C)
56. D	680.10
57. B	700.5(A) 701.5(A)
58. B	338.10(B)(4)(a)

Answer	Section/Page#
59. C	314.28(E)
60. D	390.8
61. A	Table 110.26(A)(1), Condition 3
62. A	550.30 & .31(1) Table 550.31 Single-phase current formula

25 lots x 16,000 VA (minimum) = 400,000 VA
X .24 (demand factor)
96,000 VA (demand load)

$I = \frac{\text{power}}{\text{Volts}}$ $I = \frac{96,000 \text{ VA}}{240 \text{ volts}} = 400$ amperes

Answer	Section/Page#
63. C	3-phase current formula

$I = \frac{\text{kVA} \times 1000}{E \times 1.732}$ $I = \frac{150 \times 1000}{208 \times 1.732} = \frac{150,000}{360.25} =$ 416 amperes (FLA)
- 212 amperes (existing load)
= 204 amperes (additional load)

Answer	Section/Page#
64. A	250.146(D)
65. D	422.15(C)
66. C	800.113(B)(1)
67. D	600.6
68. C	368.17(B), Exception
69. C	250.97(2)
70. B	408.36, Exception 2
71. D	682.11
72. B	517.30(A)
73. D	410.97
74. A	410.54(C)
75. B	300.34
76. C	250.52(A)(2)

Answer	Section/Page#
77. D	520.25(C)
78. C	210.62
79. A	503.130(A)
80. D	430.22(E) Table 430.22(E)
81. B	501.100(A)(1)
82. C	410.154
83. D	Table 310.15(B)(16) 240.4(B)(2) & (3) Table 240.6(A)
84. D	514.11(A)
85. B	Table 110.26(A)(1)
86. B	Table 250.122
87. A	450.11(A)
88. C	388.70
89. A	500.8(E)(2)
90. C	450.22(A)
91. D	Table 680.9(A)
92. D	Table 220.42

205.4 kVA x 1,000 = 205,400 VA

first 3,000 VA @ 100% = 3,000 VA
3,001 to 120,000 VA @ 35% = 117,000 VA @ 35% = 40,950 VA
Remainder 205,400 VA – 120,000 VA = 85,400 VA @ 25% = 21,350 VA
Demand = 65,300 VA

$\frac{65,300 \text{ VA}}{1,000} = 65.3 \text{ kVA}$

93. B	450.43(B)
94. A	422.13

Answer	Section/Page#
95. C	Single-phase current formula Table 310.15(B)(16) Table 310.15(B)(2)(a)

$$I = \frac{\text{power}}{\text{volts}} \quad I = \frac{36{,}000\ \text{VA}}{240\ \text{volts}} = 150 \text{ amperes load}$$

$$\text{required ampacity} = \frac{150\ \text{amperes}}{.75\ (\text{temp. cor.})} = 200 \text{ amperes}$$

96. A	504.80(C)
97. C	Chapter 9, Table 2
98. A	314.28(A)(2)
	3.5 inches (conduit) x 6 = 21 inches
99. B	505.8(G)
100. D	392.20(B)(1)

1 Exam Prep
Photovoltaic Systems, 3rd Ed.
Questions and Answers

1. A solar energy technology that uses unique properties of semiconductors to directly convert solar radiation into electricity is?

A Solar Array
B Photovoltaics
C Solar Cell
D Photodiodes

2. A device that converts AC power to DC power is a?

A Transformer
B Converter
C Maximum power point tracker
D Rectifier

3. The array tilt angle is the?

A Vertical angle between the azimuth and the incidence
B The vertical angle between horizontal and the array surface
C The horizontal angle between vertical and the array surface
D The azimuth and the incidence angle

4. The battery system must include a disconnect when more than how many volts?

A 6
B 12
C 24
D 48

5. If the PV system uses net metering, the utility electricity meter runs?

A Forward
B Backward
C Forward and backward
D At a constant speed

6. The overcurrent protection device has a rating of 60. The conductor size should be?

A 14
B 12
C 10
D 8

7. A PV output circuit composed of four source circuits, each with a rated short-circuit current of 8 A will have a maximum current of the output circuit of?

A 32 A
B 40 A
C 48 A
D 64 A

8. The required working space for less than 150 V is at least how many feet deep?

A 1.5
B 2
C 3
D 5

9. To charge a nominal 12V battery, the array must be at least?

A 12 V
B 14.5 V
C 18 V
D 24 V

10. A 20 foot plastic collector may expand and contract as much as _______ inches in length.

A 1
B 2
C 3
D 4

11. The conducting medium allowing the transfer of ions between battery cell plates is?

A Electrolysis
B Hydrochloric acid
C Electrolyte
D Array

12. Modules are typically connected together with?

A Copper tightening bands
B CPVC of PEX tubing
C Internal enclosed connectors
D External exposed connectors

13. The gas burner is usually located?

A At the mid-point of the system
B At the bottom of the tank
C At the top of the tank
D Inside the tank

14. The term panel typically refers to?

A A group of judges usually consisting of at least one building official and one representative from the electric authority
B A larger group of modules in array usually three physically connected together as an installation unit
C An assembly of 2 or more modules mechanically and electrically intergrated into a unit
D Usually three physically connected considered an installation unit

15. If the average solar irradiance is 800 W/m2 over 7 hours, what is the total solar irradiation over this period?

A 8,700 Wh/m2 or 8.7 kWh/m2
B 5,600 Wh/m2 or 5.6 kWh/m2 I
C 4,800 Wh/m2 or 48.0 kWh/m2
D 5,600 Wh/m2 or 56.0 kWh/m2

16. The condition where essentially no electrical or chemical changes are occurring is known as?

A Dead level state
B Plus/minus voltage conditions
C Roaming
D Steady state

17. The decomposition of water into hydrogen and oxygen gasses as the battery charges is known as?

A Gassing
B Phasing
C Powering
D Charging

18. The incidence angle is the angle between the direction of?

A Radiation and a line exactly perpendicular to the azimuth surface
B Radiation and a line exactly perpendicular to the array surface
C Radiation and a line exactly vertical to the array surface I
D Declination and the perpendicular tilt

19. Sizing PV systems for stand-alone operation involves how many sets of calculations?

A 2
B 3
C 4
D 6

20. A 5,420 W inverter outputting 220 V will have a listed continuous output rating of approximately _________amps.

A 24
B 25.53 I
C 25
D 24.63

21. Voltage unbalance should not be more than ________ percent.

A 3
B 2
C 1
D 10

22. The vertical angle between the sun and the horizon is called the?

A Solar azimuth angle
B Solar elevation angle
C Solar zenith angle
D Solar altitude angle

23. ____________ control and condition the DC power from the array and either direct it to DC I loads or convert it to AC power for use by AC loads.

A Loads
B Utilities
C Arrays
D Electrical components

24. If the average solar irradiance is 550 W/m2 over 6 hours, the total solar irradiation over this period in Wh/m2 and kWh/m2 is?

A 2,300 or 2.3
B 2,000
C 3,300 or 3.3 I
D 3,000

25. The size of an interactive system is essentially limited by the?

A Azimuth
B Tilt
C Angle of incidence
D Space

26. Connecting all of the positive terminals together and all of the negative terminals together placing the battery in ______________ condition.

A Parallel
B Series
C Steady state
D Charge

27. The purpose of a battery is to?

A Store energy for a later use
B Convert DC current to AC current
C Provide inexpensive voltage at the proper time
D Convert electrical energy into chemical energy during the charging cycle

28. Thyristors have ___________ leads.

A 1
B 2
C 3
D 4

29. In southern coastal climates corrosion rates may be as much as ________ times higher than in the arid desert areas.

A 100
B 200
C 300
D 400

30. To charge the batteries the array voltage must be?

A At or equal to the battery-bank voltage
B No more than 15 percent below the battery-bank voltage
C No more than 15 percent above the battery-bank voltage
D Higher than the battery-bank voltage

31. A PV output circuit composed of four source circuits, each with a rated short-circuit current of 6 A will have a maximum current of the output circuit of?

A 24
B 25
C 30
D 26

32. A problem that should be considered when installing modules directly on the roof is?

A Hurricane frequency
B Angle and dangle
C Array alignment
D Heat transfer

33. Long-term high temperatures can also lead to premature degradation of?

A Photovoltaic cell alignment
B Module encapsulation
C Array distortion
D Panel complacence

34. Most of the daily solar radiation occurs between?

A Dawn and dusk
B 10:30 am to 5 pm EST
C 9:00 am and 3 pm
D 8:30 am and 4:30 pm

35. The solar energy reaching the earth's surface is?

A Ultra-violet rays
B Sunrays
C Heat
D Terrestrial solar radiation

36. A semiconductor device that converts solar radiation into direct current electricity is a/an?

A Inverter
B Converter
C Array
D Photovoltaic cell

37. A solar energy collector that absorbs solar energy on a flat surface without concentrating it and can utilize solar radiation directly from the sun as well as radiation that is reflected or scattered by clouds and other surfaces is?

A Solar energy collector
B Concentrating collector
C Flat-plate collector
D Geothermal collector

38. The maximum current of the output circuit is 26 A. The required overcurrent protection device rating is?

A 32
B 32.5
C 22
D 22.5

39. The operation point at which a PV device produces its maximum power output lies between the?

A Short-circuit condition and the open-circuit
B Array controller and the battery inverter
C Photovoltaic cell and the maximum power point
D Discharge focal point and the intake upload

40. A 4,500 W inverter outputting 240 V will have a listed continuous output rating of approximately?

A 18.7 A
B 20.8 A
C 22.9 A
D 240 A

41. Output circuit wiring applications should use which of the following?

A USE-2
B THNN
C USE
D TC

42. An important consideration in array mechanical design is?

A Temperature
B Weather
C Location
D Roof design

43. Given 2 therms, the number of BTU's is?

A 200,000
B 20,000
C 2,000
D 200

44. The maximum current of the output circuit is 34 A. The required overcurrent protection device rating is?

A 34 A
B 42.5 A
C 51 A
D 68 A

45. The average solar radiation for a flat-plate collector facing south at a fixed tilt in Tampa, Florida at latitude plus 15 degrees in January is?

A 4.8
B 3.5
C 3.3
D 4.5

46. A collection of cells that are contained in the same case and connected together electrically to produce a desired voltage is a/an?

A Array
B Photovoltaic system
C Battery
D Charge controller

47. A charge controller that limits charging current to a battery system by short-circuiting the array is a/an?

A Shunt charge controller
B Array charge diverter
C Panel controller
D Photovoltaic cell controller

48.A solar energy collector that enhances solar energy by focusing it on a smaller area I through reflective surfaces or lenses is?

A Concentrating collector
B Biomass energy collector
C Flat-plate collector
D Solar energy collector

49. The width of working space in front of any electrical equipment shall be at least?

A 24 inches
B 30 inches
C 3 feet
D 4 feet

50. An electrical system consisting of an array of one or more PV modules, conductors, electrical components and one or more loads is?

A Photovoltaic system
B Hybrid system
C Grid-Tied system
D Standalone system

51. The level of the electrolyte must not be allowed to?

A Spill over
B Fall below the halfway mark
C Rise above the top of the battery plates
D Fall below the top of the battery plates

52. To minimize voltage drop, the charge controller should be installed?

A No more than 12 feet from the batteries
B No more than 10 feet from the batteries
C No more than 5 feet from the batteries
D Close to the batteries

53. Nearly every PV systems that uses a battery requires a/an?

A Charge controller
B Inverter
C Converter
D Acid flow

54. A charge controller limiting the charging current to a battery system by open-circuiting the array is a/an?

A Shunt controller
B Series charge controller
C Parallel charge controller
D Array controller

55. PV devices are connected in __________ to achieve a desired voltage.

A Series
B Parallel
C Passive phase
D Active phase

56. A dynamic structural load resulting in downward lateral or lifting forces is?

A Nascent force
B Atomical depression
C Wind load
D Pressure dynamics

1 Exam Prep
Photovoltaic Systems
Answers

1	B	4	
2	D	224	
3	B	49	
4	D	345	
5	B	113	
6	C	341	
7	B	312	
		Solution: 4 X 8 + 25 % is 40	
8	C	388	
9	B	268	
10	A	Photovoltaic Systems, 3rd Edition	40
11	C	Photovoltaic Systems, 3rd Edition	160
12	D	Photovoltaic Systems, 3rd Edition	144
13	B	Solar Water & Pool Heating Manual, 2006	Sys. Corn. 2-5
14	C	Photovoltaic Systems, 3rd Edition	143
15	B	Photovoltaic Systems, 3rd Edition	32
		800 X 7 = 5,600	
		800 X 7 ÷ 1,000 = 5.6	
16	D	Photovoltaic Systems, 3rd Edition	161
17	A	Photovoltaic Systems, 3rd Edition	166
18	B	Photovoltaic Systems, 3rd Edition	50
19	C	Photovoltaic Systems, 3rd Edition	250
20	D	Photovoltaic Systems, 3rd Edition	479
		5,420 ÷ 220 = 24.63	
21	C	Photovoltaic Systems, 3rd Edition	222
22	D	Photovoltaic Systems, 3rd Edition	58
23	D	Photovoltaic Systems, 3rd Edition	4
24	C	Photovoltaic Systems, 3rd Edition	32
		550 X 6 = 3,300 Wh/m2 OR 3.3 kWh/m2	
25	D	Photovoltaic Systems, 3rd Edition	248
26	A	Photovoltaic Systems, 3rd Edition	177
27	D	Photovoltaic Systems, 3rd Edition	99
28	C	Photovoltaic Systems, 3rd Edition	230
29	D	Photovoltaic Systems, 3rd Edition	288
30	D	Photovoltaic Systems, 3rd Edition	266
31	C	Photovoltaic Systems, 3rd Edition	312

		4 X 6 X 125% is 30	
32	D	Photovoltaic Systems, 3rd Edition	278
33	B	Photovoltaic Systems, 3rd Edition	139
34	C	Photovoltaic Systems, 3rd Edition	76
35	D	Photovoltaic Systems, 3rd Edition	37
36	D	Photovoltaic Systems, 3rd Edition	489
37	C	Photovoltaic Systems, 3rd Edition 21	
38	B	Photovoltaic Systems, 3rd Edition	332
		26 X 1.25 = 32.5	
39	A	Photovoltaic Systems, 3rd Edition	134
40	A	Photovoltaic Systems, 3rd Edition	479
		4,500 ÷ 240 = 18.7	
41	A	Photovoltaic Systems, 3rd Edition	319
42	A	Photovoltaic Systems, 3rd Edition	277
43	A	Trade knowledge - A therm is 100,000 btu's	
44	B	Photovoltaic Systems, 3rd Edition	332
		34 + 25 % is 42.5	
45	A	Photovoltaic Systems, 3rd Edition	467
46	C	Photovoltaic Systems, 3rd Edition	160
47	A	Photovoltaic Systems, 3rd Edition	193
48	A	Photovoltaic Systems, 3rd Edition	22
49	B	Photovoltaic Systems, 3rd Edition	388
50	A	Photovoltaic Systems, 3rd Edition	4
51	D	Photovoltaic Systems, 3rd Edition	409
52	D	Photovoltaic Systems, 3rd Edition	206
53	A	Photovoltaic Systems, 3rd Edition	102
54	B	Photovoltaic Systems, 3rd Edition	194
55	A	Photovoltaic Systems, 3rd Edition	144
56	C	Photovoltaic Systems, 3rd Edition	492

1 Exam Prep
National Electrical Code (Solar Contractor)
Questions and Answers

1 According to the NEC, the maximum distance from the point of entrance to the building that the water pipe maybe used as a grounding electrode interconnect is:

A. 3'
B. 4'
C. 5'
D. 6'

2 The purpose of NEC is to provide:

A. requirements for safe electrical installations
B. an instruction manual for apprentice electricians
C. design spec for electrical installations
D. installations that are adequate for good service

3 The purpose of the NEC is to:

A. provide a minimum design specific
B. to provide a concise instruction manual for untrained individuals
C. to provide a manual of common electrical procedures
D. the safe guarding of persons from electrical hazards

4 According to the NEC, mandatory wording is characterized by:

A. FPM
B. the word "shall"
C. the word "may"
D. the word "would"

5 According to the NEC, that portion of the circuit between the final over-current protection device prior to the load is:

A. main circuit
B. feeder circuit
C. branch circuit
D. motor circuit

6 A __________box may be weatherproof.

A. watertight
B. rain tight
C. rainproof
D. all of the above

7 What is the maximum number of unused raceway openings permitted to remain open for a service enclosure? (370-18)

A. none
B. two if located on the bottom box
C. two if located in a dry location
D. two if service size is less than 100 AMPS

8 According to the NEC, electrical equipment may NOT be mounted on concrete, cinder block, or brick walls with _____________ .

A. lead plugs
B. wooden plugs
C. lag bolts
D. toggle bolts

9 Any connection device between aluminum and copper shall be identified ________.

A. for the purpose and conditions
B. and color coded
C. and copper clad
D. if less than 600 volts

10 What is the maximum size of solid conductor that is permitted by the Code to be connected by means of terminal parts having screws?

A. #6 AWG
B. #8 AWG
C. #10 AWG
D. #12 AWG

11 A heating and air-conditioning unit is located on the roof of a residence. For service, a 125 volt receptacle is required on the same level at a maximum of ___________ feet from the unit.

A. 20
B. 25
C. 30
D. 35

12 What is the minimum vertical clearance distance for a service-drop over an extended porch roof of a dwelling where the voltage does not exceed 300 volts and the pitch is not less than 4" vertically and 12" horizontally?

A. 3'
B. 6' in all directions from the edge of the roof.
C. 8'
D. 10' except when the voltage is 110

13 The electric service mast head is located above the roof. Disregarding exception, what is the minimum vertical clearance required between the roof and service conductors?

A. 6'
B. 8'
C. 10'
D. 12'

14 According to the NEC, service drop conductors above roofs (porches) shall have a vertical clearance of no less than ___________ feet above the roof surface.

A. 6
B. 7
C. 8
D. 9

15 3 size 10 THW copper conductors in a conduit are installed above ceiling without insulation between the ceiling and roof shall be rated at ___________ amps.

A. 35.0
B. 28.2
C. 26.25
D. 23.45

16 Three size 8 THHW copper conductors are installed in conduit 2" above a heated ceiling which has 2" of insulation between the ceiling and the roof. The conductors rated ampacity is ___________ amps.

A. 50
B. 55
C. 41.25
D. 39.75

17 When routing general purpose communications cabling across a roof, it must clear the roof by at least __________ feet.

A. 2
B. 4
C. 6
D. 8

18 Communications cable which are installed above roofs, must have a vertical clearance of not less than __________ feet from all points on the roof above which they pass.

A. 6'
B. 7'
C. 8'
D. 10'

19 A self supporting satellite dish antennae is being installed on the roof of a multi-story apartment building. The roof is crossed by overhead power and communication conductors. The dish is unprotected from the weather. This dish must be:

A. sized not less than specified when using Table 810-116 (a)
B. strong enough to withstand ice and wind blowing
C. kept away from overhead power lines of 120 volts or less
D. at least 12' from light circuits

20 The maximum resistance to ground permitted by Code when the grounding electrode system is made up of two or more ground rods that are bonded together is _________ Ohms.

A. 10
B. 25
C. 35
D. none

1 Exam Prep
National Electrical Code (Solar Contractor)
Answers

1.	C	NEC 250.52 (A)(1)
2.	A	NEC 90.1 (A)
3.	D	NEC 90.1 (A)
4.	B	NEC 90.5 (A)
5.	C	NEC 100 Definitions – Branch Circuit
6.	C	NEC 100 Definitions - Weatherproof
7.	A	NEC 110.12 (A)
8.	B	NEC 110.13 (A)
9.	A	NEC 110.14
10.	C	NEC 110.14 (A)
11.	B	NEC 210.63
12.	A	NEC 230.24 (A) exception 2
13.	B	NEC 230.24 (A)
14.	C	NEC 230.24 (A)
15.	C	NEC 424.36 and Table 310.16
16.	B	NEC 424.36 and Table 310.16
17.	D	NEC 800.44 (B)
18.	C	NEC 800.44 (B)
19.	B	NEC 810.16 (B)
20.	B	NEC 250.56

1 Exam Prep
Photovoltaic System Design
Questions and Answers

1. All of the following are major elements to consider when properly designing PV system EXCEPT?

   A. energy use
   B. energy storage
   C. energy conservation
   D. energy distribution

2. Design and sizing procedures are developed for 3 major types of systems. Which is not one of these system types?

   A. stand-alone systems without battery storage
   B. water pumping without battery storage
   C. hybrid systems which use a combination of a photovoltaic array and an engine generator set
   D. stand-alone systems with battery storage

3. A collection of PV modules electrically wired together and mechanically installed in their working environment describes what?

   A. alternating current
   B. array
   C. diode
   D. panel

4. A semiconductor that allows current to flow in only one direction is what?

   A. diode
   B. fuse
   C. circuit breaker
   D. arrestor

5. _____ diodes prevent reverse current flow through the modules.

   A. shunt
   B. bypass
   C. blocking
   D. none of the above

6. What is a fault also known as a/an?

   A. short-circuit
   B. block
   C. charge controller
   D. harmonic distortion

7. What is the most simple series regulator?

A. shunt-linear
B. shunt-interrupting
C. series-linear
D. series-interrupting type

8. The rate at which water is delivered by a pump is called what?

A. dynamic head
B. flow rate
C. velocity head
D. discharge rate

9. What are bypass diodes also known as?

A. shunt
B. bypass
C. blocking
D. none of the above

10. Low voltage or self-regulating PV modules ________________.

A. have a an electronic charge regulator built-in
B. can allow a system to operate without battery charge regulation
C. can require the need for a charge eliminator
D. all of the above

11. For grounded systems, the insulation on grounded conductors must be what color?

I. Grey
II. White
III. Green

A. I
B. II
C. I and II
D. I and III

12. The current handling capability of a conductor is also known as what?

A. ampacity
B. voltage capacity
C. cut-off voltage
D. current-voltage

13. Rack mounted arrays are above and tilted at a _____ angle to the roof.

A. 15 degree
B. Non-zero
C. slope of 2 in 12 or less
D. none of the above

14. When troubleshooting loads, if the load does not operate at all what could be the cause?

A. load is too large for the system
B. inadequate sun
C. load is in poor condition
D. all of the above

15. When troubleshooting inverters, the motor is running hot, what could be a cause?

A. square wave inverter was used
B. the capacitor is bad
C. inverter not equipped with frequency control
D. surge current is too high

16. A number of modules wired together is known as what?

A. electrolyte
B. array
C. diode
D. panel

17. The equivalent feet of water that a pump must supply to move the water or liquid at a given velocity is known as what?

A. dynamic head
B. flow rate
C. velocity head
D. discharge rate

18. Light rays that pass from one medium to another are said to be _____.

A. deflected
B. refracted
C. transmitted
D. absorped

19. What is/are common lamp types used in a PV system?

A. standard fluorescents
B. compact fluorescents
C. low pressure sodium
D. all of the above

20. All of the following are important functions of battery charge regulators and controls in PV system EXCEPT?

A. serves as a wiring center
B. prevents battery over discharge
C. provides load control functions
D. self-charges the battery

21. A series–linear, constant voltage regulator can be used on all types of batteries.

A. True
B. False

22. What is not a type of PV Systems?

A. Stand-alone with battery storage
B. Utility-interactive
C. Stand-alone engine generator systems
D. None of the above

23. The method of measuring and recording electricity that is produced, consumed or sold is called?

A. metering
B. grounding
C. resonance
D. consumption assessment

24. Telecommunications is one of the largest and most suitable fields for PV.

A. True
B. False

25. The optimal selection of voltage regulation __________will ensure the battery is maintained at the highest possible state of charge without overcharging.

A. discharge rate
B. set point
C. shunt
D. load

26. _______________ are defined as the end-use appliances, devices, or equipment that require electricity to operate.

A. arrays
B. diodes
C. machines
D. electrical loads

27. A measure of how well an ac signal compares with a pure sine wave is known as what?

A. wattage
B. power quality
C. ionic transfer
D. load quality

28. A stand alone system operates _______________ of electric utility grid.

A. independently
B. autonomously
C. both A and B
D. none of the above

29. What are utilty-interactive systems also referred to as?

A. grid connected
B. grid dependent
C. grid-interactive
D. all of the above

30. What is BOS short for?

A. battery operated system
B. balance of system
C. block of system
D. none of the above

31. The basic electrochemical unit in a battery is known as what?

A. electrolyte
B. array
C. diode
D. cell

32. Which National Electric Code (NEC) article is not applicable to PV systems.

A. switchboards and panels
B. transformers and transformer vaults
C. phase convertors
D. recreation vehicles, Parks

33. Which of the following tools you should NOT bring with you to troubleshoot and inspect PV system.

A. rubber gloves
B. flashlight
C. safety goggles
D. chalk

34. What does a luminance meter measure?

A. light distribution on surfaces in the field
B. light reflected or emitted from a surface
C. lamp lumen depreciation
D. luminaire dirt depreciation

35. What is NOT a common lamp types used in a PV system?

A. standard fluorescents
B. compact fluorescents
C. low pressure sodium
D. mercury vapor

36. Which of the following tools you should bring with you to troubleshoot and inspect PV system.

A. ammeter
B. volt-ohm meter
C. insolation meter
D. all of the above

37. Array cooling helps extend its lifetime.

A. True
B. False

38. What is a grounding electrode also known as?

A. grounding rod
B. grounding diode
C. charge controller
D. terminal

39. What is an electrolyte?

A. lead alloy framework supporting the active material on the battery plate
B. a conducting medium that allows the flow of current through ionic transfer
C. an electrical component which converts dc power to ac power
D. none of the above

40. Nickel-cadmium batteries are _________batteries.

A. rechargeable
B. secondary
C. both A and C
D. none of the above

41. An instrument used to measure the specific gravity of a solution is called what?

A. ammeter
B. volt-ohm meter
C. insolation meter
D. hydrometer

42. A method of connection in which positive terminals are connected together and negative terminals are connected together and the voltage remains the same is called _______.

A. parallel connected
B. double pole connected
C. double
D. balance of system

43. What is a voltage regulation hysteresis?

A. the voltage at which the array is connected
B. the maximum voltage the charge regulator allows the battery to reach while limiting overcharge
C. the voltage span or difference between the voltage regulation set point and the array reconnect voltage
D. another name for low voltage load disconnect

44. ______ refers to the test data which describes characteristics of a luminaries light output.

A. photometry
B. illuminace
C. luminance
D. lumens

45. An irregular or unsteady flow of current is called what?

A. flicker
B. blocking
C. harmonic ditortion

46. What is sulfation?

A. A process allowing the flow of current through a sulfate crystal plate
B. A process occurring in a lead-acid battery resulting from prolonged operation at partial states of charge and involving the growth of lead sulfate crystal on positive plate
C. A condition when the concentration or specific gravity of the electrolyte increases from the bottom to the top of the cell
D. A characteristic of batteries that dictates voltage change

47. In the U.S. The common frequency for alternating currents is ______________ .

A. 40 hertz
B. 50 hertz
C. 60 hertz
D. 70 hertz

48. What is Ohm's Law?

A. the algebraic sum of currents in all wires that meet at a point is zero
B. the total change of potential or voltage around any closed circuit is zero
C. for a steady-state current, the current in an electrical circuit is directly proportional to the voltage across the circuit
D. None of the above

49. ______ is a measure of undesirable electrical signals in a circuit.

A. load disturbance
B. photometry
C. electrical distortion
D. harmonic distortion

50. The ratio of the density of a solution to the density of water is ______________ .

A. specific gravity
B. buoyancy
C. water to electrolyte ratio
D. conductor density ratio

1 Exam Prep
Photovoltaic System Design
Answers

1.	C	1-1	
2.	A	1-3	
3.	B	G-1	
4.	A	G-3	
5.	C	7-19	
6.	A	7-14	
7.	D	5-42	
8.	B	G-5	
9.	A	4-7	
10	B	5-57	
11.	C	7-6	
12.	A	7-7	
13.	B	8-7	
14.	D	9-7	Table 9.2
15.	A	9-13	Table 9.7
16.	D	G-8	
17.	C	G-13	
18.	B	10a-3	
19.	D	10a-6	
20.	D	5-30	
21.	A	5-43	
22.	D	1-6/1-8	
23.	A	G-7	
24.	A	1-6	
25.	B	5-53	
26.	D	5-5	
27.	B	G-9	
28.	C	5-2	
29.	A	5-9	

30.	B	5-5
31.	D	5-7
32.	C	7-4
33.	D	9-15
34.	B	10a-5
35.	D	10a-6
36.	D	9-15
37.	A	8-5
38.	A	7-15
39.	B	5-9
40.	C	5-21
41.	D	5-27
42.	A	G-8
43.	C	5-35
44.	A	10a-9
45.	B	G-5
46.	B	5-12
47.	C	2a-2
48.	C	2a-3
49.	D	G-5
50.	A	5-11

Photovoltaic System Design- Course Manual Questions

1. What are 5 major elements to consider when properly designing PV system?
2. Design and sizing procedures are developed for 3 major types of systems. What are they?
3. A collection of PV modules electrically wired together and mechanically installed in their working environment describes what?
4. A semiconductor that allows current to flow in only one direction is what?
5. _____ diodes prevent reverse current flow through the modules.
6. What is a fault also known as?
7. In a series –linear, constant voltage regulator design, the regulator maintains the battery voltage at a regulation _____.
8. What is the most simple series regulator?
9. What are 2 types of PV systems?
10. ______ is one of the largest and most suitable fields for PV.
11. The rate at which water is delivered by a pump is called what?
12. The method of measuring and recording electricity that is produced, consumed or sold is called?
13. PV arrays are designed to meet an _____ need.
14. What are bypass diodes also known as?
15. How should you select a PV array?
16. The optimal selection of voltage regulation set point will ensure the battery is maintained at the highest possible state of charge without_______
17. Low voltage or ______ PV modules can allow system to operate without battery charge regulation.
18. What NEC articles are applicable to PV systems?
19. For grounded systems, the insulation on grounded conductors must be what color?
20. The current handling capability of a conductor is also known as what?
21. Rack mounted arrays are above and tilted at a ____ angle to the roof.
22. What are the 2 types of weather sealing for PV system?
23. When troubleshooting system wiring, if the load does not operate at all what could be the cause?
24. When troubleshooting inverters, the motor is running hot, what could be a cause?
25. A number of modules wired together is known as what?
26. A measure of how well an ac signal compares with a pure sine wave is known as what?
27. The equivalent feet of water that a pump must supply to move the water or liquid at a given velocity is known as what?
28. _____ loads are defined as the end-use appliances, devices, or equipment that require electricity to operate.
29. A stand alone system operates ____ or independently of electric utility grid.
30. What are utilty-interactive systems also referred to as?
31. What is BOS short for?
32. The basic electrochemical unit in a battery is known as what?
33. Light rays that pass from one medium to another are said to be ____

34. What does a luminance meter measure?
35. What are some common lamp types used in a PV system?
36. List the tools you should bring with you to troubleshoot and inspect PV system.
37. True or false. Array cooling helps extend its lifetime.
38. What is a grounding electrode also known as?
39. What is an electrolyte?
40. Nickel-cadmium batteries are _____ or rechargeable batteries.
41. An instrument used to measure the specific gravity of a solution is called what?
42. What are 7 most important functions of battery charge regulators and controls in PV system?
43. What is a voltage regulation hysteresis?
44. ______ refers to the test data which describes characteristics of a luminaries light output.
45. An irregular or unsteady flow of current is called what?
46. What is sulfation?
47. The number of alternating current cycles per second.
48. What is Ohm's Law?
49. ______ is a measure of undesirable electrical signals in a circuit.
50. Define specific gravity.

Photovoltaic System Design-Course Manual Answers

1. Answer page 1-1
2. Answer page 1-3
3. An array G-1
4. Diode G-3
5. Blocking 7-19
6. Short circuit 7-14
7. Set point 5-43
8. Series-interrupting type 5-42
9. Stand alone and utility-interactive 1-5
10. Telecommunications 1-6
11. Flow rate G-5
12. Metering G-7
13. Electrical 4-4
14. Shunt diodes 4-7
15. Answer page 4-10
16. Overcharging 5-53
17. Self-regulating 5-57
18. Answer Table7.1 7-4
19. Grey or white 7-6
20. Ampacity 7-7
21. Non-zero 8-7
22. Dry and wet 8-12
23. Answer table9.1 page 9-6
24. Table 9.7 page 9-13
25. Panel G-8
26. Power quality G-9
27. Velocity head G-13
28. Electrical 5-5
29. Autonomously 5-2
30. Grid-connected 5-1
31. Balance of system 5-5
32. Cell 5-7
33. Refracted 10a-3
34. Answer 10a-5
35. Standard and compact fluorescent. And low pressure sodium lamos 10a-6
36. List on 9-15
37. True 8-5
38. Grounding rod 7-15
39. Answer page 5-9
40. Secondary 5-21

41. Hydrometer 5-27
42. Answer page 5-30
43. Answer bottom of 5-35
44. Photometry 10a-9
45. Flicker G-5
46. Answer page 5-12
47. Frequency 2a-2
48. Answer 2a-3
49. Harmonic distortion G-5
50. Answer page 5-11

1 Exam Prep
Solar Construction Safety by
Oregon Solar Energy Industries Association
Questions and Answers

1. Why is it important to use a proper tool belt?

2. Employers must have employees on hand who are trained in basic first aid and CPR unless a hospital or clinic is in near proximity. (T or F)

3. If 911 is not available in the jobsite area, what should be done before on-site work begins?

4. Back belts are considered personal protective equipment (PPE) by OR-OSHA. (T or F)

5. It is easier and safer to lift from an elevated surface. (T or F)

6. Can a step ladder be used to access the roof?

7. How can you tell if the ladder is set up at the proper angle?

8. When using a ladder during construction work, under what conditions is it required to be secure against tipping?

9. How many points of contact should you have when working from a ladder?

10. The body should be centered between the rails of a ladder while climbing or working from the ladder. (T or F)

11. When should ladders be inspected?

12. An aluminum ladder should not be used when?

13. Falls are the leading cause of work-related deaths among construction workers. (T or F)

14. What is the purpose of identifying roof and fall safety hazards?

15. What factors can increase the risk of falls?

    A. Tasks exposing workers to overhead power lines
    B. Using scaffolds, ladders, or aerial lifts on unstable or uneven ground
    C. Working during hot, cold, or windy weather
    D. Working extended shifts that could contribute to fatigue
    E. All of the above

16. What is fall protection?

    A. Eliminating fall hazards
    B. Preventing falls
    C. Safety equipment designed to prevent or reduce the impact of falls
    D. Ensuring that workers who may fall aren't injured
    E. All of the above

17. What does a personal fall-arrest system do?

18. What does a personal fall-restraint system do?

19. What plumbing activity is unique to solar contractors?

20. Solar collectors remain cool until fluid is added. (T or F)

21. Covering a solar collector with opaque material prevents sunlight from heating the elements inside. (T or F)

22. When choosing a fire extinguisher, a good option for most situations in solar plumbing is what type?

23. When soldering joints above eye level, what are three ways to reduce risk of injury?

24. Solar collectors that are exposed to direct sunlight cool down quickly when they are covered. (T or F)

25. What are the three things to know the location of to be prepared for an emergency?

26. Overhead power lines are dangerous and can kill. (T or F)

27. Solar PV panels can product electric current with very little sunlight or other light source. (T or F)

28. What is the minimum distance to stay away from overhead power lines?

29. AC current is more dangerous than DC. (T or F)

30. GFCI is required for contractors unless you are using extension cords. (T or F)

1 Exam Prep
Solar Construction Safety by
Oregon Solar Energy Industries Association
Answers

1. Using a proper tool belt will save many trips up and down the ladder. A tool belt will leave your hands free to hold onto the ladder. Prevents jobsite trip hazards.
2. True
3. The telephone numbers of physicians, hospitals, or ambulances must be conspicuously posted.
4. False
5. True
6. No.
7. 4-1 rule or stand straight and reach rule.
8. All
9. Three
10. True
11. Prior to use/after dropping
12. When any electrical lines or energized equipment are present.
13. True
14. To determine how to eliminate or control them before they cause injuries.
15. E. is the correct answer
16. E. is the correct answer
17. Arrests a fall.
18. Prevents a fall.
19. Working from rooftops and heat from solar collectors.
20. False

21. True

22. ABC11

23. Try to position yourself above the joint, use eye protection gear, wear long-sleeved shirts and gloves.

24. False

25. Electrical shut off location, First aid supplies, telephone.

26. True

27. True

28. 10 ft.

29. False

30. False

SOLAR CONSTRUCTION SAFETY REVIEW QUESTIONS

Review Quiz: General jobsite safety

The following questions and true or false statements help ensure that you understand the material presented in this module.

1. Oregon OSHA requires employees to be trained in the work that they do?

2. Why is it important to identify potential safety hazards at a jobsite?

3. Why is it important to use a proper tool belt?

4. It is important to plan for workplace accidents to increase your ability to act properly to avoid further injury. (T or F)

5. Effective emergency-response plans need to be elaborate. (T or F)

6. 911 is available in all areas. (T or F)

7. Not every jobsite needs first-aid supplies. (T or F)

8. Employers must have employees on hand who are trained in basic first aid and CPR unless a hospital or clinic is in near proximity. (T or F)

9. If 911 is not available in the jobsite area, what should be done before on-site work begins?

Demonstrate the following to the trainer:

- An employee is injured on the job (a fall or other injury). What are the steps taken to address the injury?

- Describe personal protective equipment and provide examples of when it would apply to the work you are doing.

Review Quiz: Lifting safety

The following questions and true or false statements help ensure you understand the material presented in this module.

1. Back injuries account for one of every five workplace injuries or illnesses. (T or F)

2. Most back injuries are the result of a single factor. (T or F)

3. Back belts are considered personal protective equipment (PPE) by OR-OSHA. (T or F)

4. Name three points of proper lifting technique.

5. How many natural curves are in your back?

6. It is easier and safer to lift from an elevated surface. (T or F)

7. Stretching should be done once at the end of the day. (T or F)

Demonstrate the following to the trainer:

- Demonstrate your neutral strong back position.

- Properly lifting an object from the floor, moving it a short distance and placing it back down.

Review Quiz: Ladder safety

The following questions and true or false statements help to ensure that you understand thematerial presented in this module.

1. Can a step ladder be used to access the roof?

2. How can you tell if the ladder is set up at the proper angle?

3. When using a ladder during construction work, under what conditions is it required to be secure against tipping?

4. How many points of contact should you have when working from a ladder?

5. The body should be centered between the rails of a ladder while climbing or working from the ladder. (T or F)

6. Ladders are safe in windy conditions. (T or F)

7. When should ladders be inspected?

8. You can safely carry objects while climbing a ladder. (T or F)

9. An aluminum ladder should not be used when?

Demonstrate the following to the trainer:

- Properly lifting and carrying a ladder.

- Proper ladder setup.

- Properly climbing a ladder.

Review Quiz: Fall protection and jobsite trip hazards

The following questions and true or false statements help to ensure you understand the material presented in this module.

1. Falls are the leading cause of work-related deaths among construction workers. (T or F)

2. A fall hazard is anything in the workplace that could cause an unintended loss of balance or bodily support and result in a fall. (T or F)

3. What is the purpose of identifying roof and fall safety hazards?

4. What factors can increase the risk of falls?
    a. Tasks exposing workers to overhead power lines
    b. Using scaffolds, ladders, or aerial lifts on unstable or uneven ground
    c. Working during hot, cold, or windy weather
    d. Working extended shifts that could contribute to fatigue
    e. All of the above

5. What is fall protection?
    a. Eliminating fall hazards
    b. Preventing falls
    c. Safety equipment designed to prevent or reduce the impact of falls
    d. Ensuring that workers who may fall aren't injured
    e. All of the above

6. What does a personal fall-arrest system do?

7. What does a personal fall-restraint system do?

8. What does "prompt rescue" mean?

9. What can happen to a worker suspended in a harness after a fall?

Review Quiz: Fall protection and jobsite trip hazards cont'd

Demonstrate the following to the trainer:

•Properly donning a fall-protection harness

• Properly hooking into an anchor point (located at ground level for training)

•The proper use of fall-protection gear

• Describe the conditions when fall protection is required

Review Quiz: Solar plumbing safety

The following questions and true or false statements will help to ensure you understand the material presented in this module.

1. What plumbing activity is unique to solar contractors?

2. Solar collectors remain cool until fluid is added. (T or F)

3. Covering a solar collector with opaque material prevents sunlight from heating the elements inside. (T or F)

4. When choosing a fire extinguisher, a good option for most situations in solar plumbing is what type?

5. What are the most common plumbing hazards?

6. The direct application of ice is not recommended for burns. (T or F)

7. When soldering joints above eye level, what are three ways to reduce risk of injury?

8. Solar collectors that are exposed to direct sunlight cool down quickly when they are covered. (T or F)

Demonstrate the following to the trainer:

- Explain how to check a fire extinguisher and how it is supposed to be used when putting out a fire.

Review Quiz: Solar electrical safety

The following questions and true or false statements will help to ensure you understand the material presented in this module.

1. What are the three things to know the location of to be prepared for an emergency?

2. Overhead power lines are dangerous and can kill. (T or F)

3. Solar PV panels can product electric current with very little sunlight or other light source. (T or F)

4. What is the minimum distance to stay away from overhead power lines?

5. AC current is more dangerous than DC. (T or F)

6. DC current is more dangerous than AC. (T or F)

7. GFCI is required for contractors unless you are using extension cords. (T or F)

8. Working around electrical circuits when wet is more dangerous than when dry. (T or F)

Demonstrate the following to the trainer:

• Describe the company's GFCI policy

• Describe the company's lock out / tag out policy

• Properly use a multi-meter and current clamp to check a circuit prior to working on it

SOLAR CONSTRUCTION SAFETY REVIEW ANSWERS

Answers-General jobsite safety

1. Oregon OSHA requires employees to be trained in the work that they do?
True

2. Why is it important to identify potential safety hazards at a jobsite?
Knowing how to identify potential safety hazards is critical to understanding potential injuries, preventing accidents, and recovering from accidents.

3. Why is it important to use a proper tool belt?
Using a proper tool belt will save many trips up and down the ladder. A tool belt will leave your hands free to hold onto the ladder. Prevents jobsite trip hazards.

4. It is important to plan for workplace accidents to increase your ability to act properly to avoid further injury.
True

5. Effective emergency-response plans need to be elaborate.
False

6. 911 is available in all areas.
False

7. Not every jobsite needs first-aid supplies.
False

8. Employers must have employees on hand who are trained in basic first aid and CPR unless a hospital or clinic is in near proximity.
True

9. If 911 is not available in the jobsite area, what should be done before on-site work begins?
The telephone numbers of physicians, hospitals, or ambulances must be conspicuously posted.

Answers-Lifting safety

1. Back injuries account for one of every five workplace injuries or illnesses.
True

2. Most back injuries are the result of a single factor.
False

3. Back belts are considered personal protective equipment (PPE) by OR-OSHA.
False

4. Name three points of proper lifting technique.
Use your legs. Maintain your curves. Don't twist.

5. How many natural curves are in your back?
Three.

6. It is easier and safer to lift from an elevated surface.
True

7. Stretching should be done once at the end of the day.
False

Answers-Ladder safety

1. Can a step ladder be used to access the roof?
No.

2. How can you tell if the ladder is set up at the proper angle?
4-1 rule or stand straight and reach rule.

3. When using a ladder during construction work, under what conditions is it required to be secure against tipping?
All.

4. How many points of contact should you have when working from a ladder?
Three .

5. The body should be centered between the rails of a ladder while climbing or working from the ladder. *True*

6. Ladders are safe in windy conditions.
False

7. When should ladders be inspected?
Prior to use/after dropping...

8. You can safely carry objects while climbing a ladder.
False

9. An aluminum ladder should not be used when?
When any electrical lines or energized equipment are present.

Answers-Fall protection and jobsite trip hazards

1. Falls are the leading cause of work-related deaths among construction workers.
True

2. A fall hazard is anything in the workplace that could cause an unintended loss of balance or bodily support and result in a fall.
True

3. What is the purpose of identifying roof and fall safety hazards?
To determine how to eliminate or control them before they cause injuries.

4. What factors can increase the risk of falls?
e. is the correct answer

5. What is fall protection?
e. is the correct answer

6. What does a personal fall-arrest system do?
Arrests a fall.

7. What does a personal fall-restraint system do?
Prevents a fall.

8. What does "prompt rescue" mean?
Rescuing without delay.

9. What can happen to a worker suspended in a harness after a fall?
The worker can lose consciousness if the harness puts too much pressure on arteries. A worker suspended in a body harness must be rescued in time to prevent serious injury.

Answers-Solar plumbing safety

1. What plumbing activity is unique to solar contractors?
Working from rooftops and heat from solar collectors.

2. Solar collectors remain cool until fluid is added.
False

3. Covering a solar collector with opaque material prevents sunlight from heating the elements inside.
True

4. When choosing a fire extinguisher, a good option for most situations in solar plumbing is what type?
ABC

5. What are the most common plumbing hazards?
Burns and eye injuries.

6. The direct application of ice is not recommended for burns.
True

7. When soldering joints above eye level, what are three ways to reduce risk of injury?
Try to position yourself above the joint, use eye protection gear, wear long-sleeved shirts and gloves.

8. Solar collectors that are exposed to direct sunlight cool down quickly when they are covered.
False

Answers-Solar electrical safety

1. What are the three things to know the location of to be prepared for an emergency?
Electrical shut off location, First aid supplies, telephone.

2. Overhead power lines are dangerous and can kill.
True

3. Solar PV panels can product electric current with very little sunlight or other light source.
True

4. What is the minimum distance to stay away from overhead power lines?
10 ft.

5. AC current is more dangerous than DC.
False

6. DC current is more dangerous than AC.
False

7. GFCI is required for contractors unless you are using extension cords?
False

8. Working around electrical circuits when wet is more dangerous than when dry?
Not necessarily. If you rare sweating you are wet...

1 Exam Prep
Solar Water and Pool Heating
Questions and Answers

1. According to the *Solar Water and Pool Heating Manual*, a _________ collector captures the sun's electromagnetic energy and converts it to heat energy.

   A. Solar

   B. Focusing

   C. Flat-Plate

   D. Tracking

2. According to the *Solar Water and Pool Heating Manual*, the average value in Florida, at about sea level, we receive a maximum of __________ Btuh/ft2 hr at high noon on the day of the summer's equinox.

   A. 295

   B. 300

   C. 428

   D. 746

3. According to the Solar *Water and Pool Heating Manual*, in Orlando the seasonal variation is approximately __________ latitude.

   A. 18 degrees

   B. 28 degrees

   C. 38 degrees

   D. 48 degrees

4. According to the *Solar Water and Pool Heating Manual*, which of the following concerning heat loss in a pool is incorrect?

   A. Up to 70 percent of a swimming pools heat energy loss results from evaporation.

   B. Evaporation losses are directly proportional to wind velocities at the pool surface.

   C. Evaporative losses are higher from cool pools than from warmer pools.

   D. As much as 20 percent of a swimming pools thermal energy is caused by convection.

5. According to the *Solar Water and Pool Heating Manual*, the purpose of a system components check valve is ______ to prevent ?

A. Forward-flowing

B. Back-flowing

C. Being pumped

D. Thermo siphoning action

6. According to the *Solar Water and Pool Heating Manual*, the factor for standby heat loss from a hot water system storage tank when insulated in one inch of foam, (as in insulated tanks R-8-9. is ________ .

A. 1.00

B. 1.20

C. 1.18

D. 1.30

7. According to the Solar Water and Pool Heating Manual, a four-bedroom home with 5 people should have a water system, a water heater tank to accommodate the use of ______ gallons of hot water per day

A. 20

B. 40

C. 80

D. 85

8. When the collector sensor senses temperatures _____ degrees F hotter than the tank sensor the pump is turned on. Assume a differential controller was installed.

A. 3 degrees F.

B. 4 degrees F.

C. 5 to 20 degrees F.

D. 30 to 35 degrees F.

9. A solar collector oriented 30 degrees east or west of due south will require times the collector area of a system oriented due south.

A. 1.1

B. 1.3

C. 1.5

D. 1.7

10. The optimum collector tilt for year-round use for domestic solar water heating in Jacksonville, Florida would be __________ .

A. 25

B. 30

C. 38

D. 86

11. What is the angle of incidence when the sun is directly overhead?

A. 0 degrees

B. 90 degrees

C. 180 degrees

D. 270 degrees

12. How many heat traps should be installed on the storage tank piping?

A. 1

B. 2

C. 3

D. 4

13. Which collectors accept both direct and diffused radiation?

A. Focusing type

B. Storage tank

C. Evacuated tube

D. Flat plate

14. What is the maximum btu per square foot per hour of diffused and direct radiation that reaches the earth in Florida?

A. 295

B. 305

C. 350

D. 428

15. What percentage of solar energy is lost in the upper atmosphere?

A. 10%

B. 20%

C. 30%

D. 50%

16. On a daily basis, the "solar window" offers ___ hours of "usable" solar energy.

A. 3

B. 6

C. 9

D. 12

17. Corrosion caused by the contact between dissimilar metals is called_________ ?

A. Rust

B. Galvanic corrosion

C. Cathodic protection

D. Anodizing

18. A solar water heating system would have its air vent located _____________ ?

A. At the midpoint of the storage tank

B. Vertical, in the uppermost part

C. Immediately above the drain valve

D. Air vents are not part of the system

19. Where is the storage tank located on a thermo siphon system?

A. Above the collector

B. Below the collector

C. Beside the collector

D. Within the collector

20. Temperature differential is sometimes referred to as _____________ .

A. TD

B. Temp D

C. Delta T

D. DT

21. What is the most commonly used heat-transfer fluid for indirect solar water heating systems?

A. Water

B. Effluent

C. Silicone

D. Glycols

22. Ideally, a solar collector should face due south, but facing a collector 40 degrees either east or west of due south will reduce the performance by about _______ percent.

A. 13%

B. 25%

C. 40%

D. 50%

23. Most active direct solar water heating systems supplied by pressurized water will have valves on the roof to aid in venting and filling. Those air vents should be located _______

A. Below the inlet to the storage tank

B. Immediately above the drain valve

C. Between the temperature and pressure valves

D. Anywhere air could be trapped in pipes

24. What is the recommended depth of the pitch pan used where the collector leg attaches to a flat roof?

A. 4 inches

B. 3 inches

C. 2 inches

D. 1-1/2 inches

25. Component of the solar water heating system should be protected from freezing. How many methods of freeze protection are there?

A. 6

B. 5

C. 4

D. 2

1 Exam Prep

Solar Water and Pool Heating

Answers

1. A Section 2 Page 2-1
2. B Section 1 Page 1-3
3. B Section 1 Page 1-8
4. C Section 5 Page 5-1
5. D Section 2 Page 2-41
6. B Appendix 1 Page A-4
7. C Appendix 1 Page A-3
8. C Page 3-25
9. A Page 1-10, Figure 7, 30 degrees, move up to line, about 1.1
10. B Page 1-11, North Florida
11. A Page 1-5, Figure 3, 0 degrees
12. B Page 3-23, #4 (1-cold water inlet) (1-hot water supply)
13. D Page 1-4 and Section 2, System Components, Page 2-1
14. A Page 1-4 Figure 2
15. C Page 1-4 Figure 2
16. B Page 1-4
17. B System Components, Page 2-26
18. B System Components, Page 2-37, Figure 24
19. A System Types, Page 2-9
20. C Page 1-6
21. D System Components, Page 2-35
22. A Page 1-10, Figure 7, 40 degrees, move up to line, 1.13
23. D System Components, Page 2-37
24. D Page 3-11
25. B System Types, Page 2-12

Solar Water and Pool Heating Manual (UCF) Questions and Answers (Plumbing)

1. For year-round use, a collector tilt of __________ degrees work best for a project located in Tampa, Florida.

   A. 28
   B. 31
   C. 38
   D. 43

2. When the collector sensor senses temperatures __________°F hotter than the tank sensor, the pump is turned on. Assume a differential controller was installed.

   A. 3
   B. 4
   C. 5 to 20
   D. 30 to 35

3. A mounted collector, exposed to wind forces, and its mounting structure need to be able to withstand wind loads up to __________ mph.

   A. 120
   B. 130
   C. 140
   D. 146

4. When installing collector to storage piping, the minimum thickness of the rubber type insulation necessary on the piping is __________ inches.

   A. ½
   B. ¾
   C. 1
   D. 1 ½

5. A solar collector oriented 30 degrees east or west of due south will require __________ times the collector area of a system oriented due south.

   A. 1.1
   B. 1.3
   C. 1.5
   D. 1.7

6. A multiple collector system has 3 collectors piped in parallel. The collector to storage piping for the feed and return lines should be __________ inches or larger in diameter.

   A. ½
   B. ¼
   C. ¾
   D. 1

7. The optimum collector tilt for year-round use for domestic solar water heating in Jacksonville, Florida would be __________.

   A. 25
   B. 30
   C. 38
   D. 86

8. The angle of incidence when the sun is directly overhead is __________ degrees.

   A. 0
   B. 90
   C. 180
   D. 270

9. The solar return on a standard electric water heater should have a dip tube to return heated water approximately __________ inches below the upper element's thermostat.

   A. 2
   B. 3
   C. 4
   D. 6

10. The turnover time for a pool heating system using a gas or oil heater with 100 feet of 2-inch diameter pipe and a 1 hp pump is __________ hours.

    A. 9
    B. 8
    C. 7.2
    D. 8.6

11. __________ heat traps should be installed on the storage tank piping.

    A. 1
    B. 2
    C. 3
    D. 4

12. __________ collectors accept both direct and diffused radiation.

A. Focusing type
B. Storage tank
C. Evacuated tube
D. Flat plate

13. __________ is the maximum BTU per square foot per hour of diffused and direct radiation that reaches the earth in Florida.

A. 295
B. 305
C. 350
D. 428

14. __________ of solar energy is lost in the upper atmosphere.

A. 10%
B. 20%
C. 30%
D. 50%

15. On a daily basis, the "solar window" offers __________ hours of "usable" solar energy.

A. 3
B. 6
C. 9
D. 12

16. Corrosion caused by the contact between dissimilar metals is called __________.

A. Rust
B. Galvanic Corrosion
C. Cathodic Protection
D. Anodizing

17. A solar water heating system would have its air vent located __________.

A. At the midpoint of the storage tank
B. Vertical, in the uppermost part
C. Immediately above the drain valve
D. Air vents are not part of the system

18. The storage tank located __________ on a thermo siphon system.

A. Above the collector
B. Below the collector
C. Beside the collector
D. Within the collector

19. In an active direct solar water heating system, the pump must have a __________ housing and impeller to prevent corrosion from water chemistry.

   A. Bronze
   B. Aluminum
   C. Steel
   D. Cast-Iron

20. The most commonly used heat-transfer fluid for indirect solar water heating systems is __________.

   A. Water
   B. Effluent
   C. Silicone
   D. Glycols

21. The type of isolation valve that is used to manually isolate the various subsystems is the __________, which provides a complete flow barrier.

   A. Gall
   B. Globe
   C. Ball
   D. Drain

22. In order to prevent thermosiphoning action in a solar water heating system, many types of check valves are available. __________ is not a type of check valve.

   A. Vertical Check Valve
   B. Tempering Valve
   C. Horizontal Swing Check Valve
   D. Motorized Check Valve

23. The flow meter is located __________ in a solar water heating system.

   A. In the collector discharge piping
   B. In the collector feed line, below the pump
   C. In the collector feed line, above the pump
   D. At the highest point in the system

24. Ideally, a solar collector should face due south, but facing a collector 40 degrees either east or west of due south will reduce the performance by about __________.

   A. 13%
   B. 25%
   C. 40%
   D. 50%

25. In a gravity type system, it is recommended that piping slope at least __________ inch(es) per foot to allow for gravity draining.

A. 1/8
B. ¼
C. ½
D. 1

26. Most active direct solar water heating systems supplied by pressurized water will have valves on the roof to aid in venting and filling. Those air vents should be located __________.

A. Below the inlet to the storage tank
B. Immediately above the drain valve
C. Between the temperature and pressure valves
D. Anywhere air could be trapped in pipes

27. The temperature and pressure relief valve installed for a solar water heating system is __________.

A. At the highest point in the system
B. At the top of the solar storage tank
C. In the collector piping
D. On the collector loop

28. The recommended depth of the pitch pan used where the collector leg attaches to a flat roof is __________ inches.

A. 4
B. 3
C. 2
D. 1 ½

29. Component of the solar water heating system should be protected from freezing. There are __________ methods of freeze protection.

A. 6
B. 5
C. 4
D. 2

30. The friction loss or pressure drop experienced through a 1-inch, 90-degree long radius copper elbow is equivalent to that of __________ feet of straight 1-inch pipe.

A. 1
B. 1.7
C. 3
D. 2.3

31. Sand, gravel or anthracite filters are sometimes operated at a flow rate of 20 GPM per square foot. Some jurisdictions limit the flow rate through these filters to __________ gpm per square foot.

A. 8
B. 5
C. 3
D. 2

32. When sizing connecting pipes, excessive flow rates that cause erosion of the interior surfaces should be avoided. Some code jurisdictions limit the rate of water flow through copper pipes to __________ FPS.

A. 8
B. 5
C. 3
D. 2

33. A swimming pool circulation pump is to maintain a flow rate of 65 gpm against a total head of 60 feet. The pump's horsepower is __________ hp.

A. ¾
B. 1
C. 1 ½
D. 2

34. Estimate the volume of water in a pool which measures sixty feet in length, thirty-two feet in width and has an average depth of five feet. This pool would contain __________ gallons when filled flush to the top.

A. 9,600
B. 14,361
C. 71,808
D. 36,336

35. The friction loss experienced when water flows through a 2-inch diameter swing check valve is equal to that of __________ feet of 2-inch diameter pipe.

A. 1.15
B. 3.0
C. 11
D. 13

36. Temperature differential is sometimes referred to as __________.

A. TD
B. Temp D
C. Delta T
D. DT

37. Regarding climatic zones in Florida, Gainesville is located in the _________.

A. North Central Zone
B. Northern Zone
C. Central Zone
D. Mid-Central Zone

****Please see Answer Key on the following page*****

Solar Water and Pool Heating Manual (UCF)
Questions and Answers (Plumbing)
Answer Key

	Answer	Page#
1.	A	1-11, 25 degrees for S. Fl. and 30 degrees for N. Fl.
2.	C	3-25
3.	D	3-2
4.	A	3-21, #9
5.	A	1-10, Figure 7, 30 degrees, move up to line, about 1.1
6.	C	3-20
7.	B	1-11, North Florida
8.	A	1-5, Figure 3, 0 degrees
9.	D	3-23, #7
10.	C	5-21, Table 7.1, gas or oil, 100' - 2", 1 hp, 7.2
11.	B	3-23, #4 (1-cold water inlet) (1-hot water supply)
12.	D	1-4 and Section 2, System Components, Page 2-1
13.	A	1-4, Figure 2
14.	C	1-4, Figure 2
15.	B	1-4
16.	B	2-26
17.	B	2-37, Figure 24
18.	A	2-8
19.	A	2-25
20.	D	2-35
21.	C	2-40 and 2-41
22.	B	2-42 and 2-43
23.	C	2-46
24.	A	1-10, Figure 7, 40 degrees, move up to line, 1.13
25.	B	3-18, Figure 24
26.	D	2-37
27.	B	2-37, 2-38
28.	D	3-11

	Answer	Page#
29.	B	2-11
30.	B	5-22, 1", 90-degree elbow, copper, intersect lines
31.	C	5-14
32.	B	5-15
33.	C	5-15, Intersect 65 GPM with 60' head
34.	C	See example on Page: 5-18 Math – 60 ft x 32 ft x 5 ft = 9,600 ft^3 x 7.48 gallons per ft^3 = 71,808 gallons
35.	D	5-22, Table 7.2, Swing Check Valve, under 2 inches
36.	C	1-6
37.	A	5-6

State Solar
Practice Exam 1

1. When matching the inverter and the utility, ___________________________.

   A. Input voltage and frequency should be within prescribed limits of the corresponding utility values
   B. Output voltage and frequency should be within prescribed limits of the corresponding utility values
   C. Voltage and amps should be within prescribed limits of the corresponding utility values
   D. Wattage and voltage should be within prescribed limits of the corresponding utility values

2. A system with a measured amount of water and a measured amount of air in the system is a/an _____________system.

   A. Drainback
   B. Integral collector storage
   C. Gravity action
   D. Batch

3. The maximum water velocity in copper tubing shall not exceed _______ feet per second.

   A. 5
   B. 8
   C. 10
   D. 12

4. A solar energy technology that uses unique properties of semiconductors to directly convert solar radiation into electricity is a ____________________.

   A. Solar Array
   B. Photovoltaics
   C. Solar Cell
   D. Photodiodes

5. The instrument that measures light reflected or emitted from a surface, typically in units of footlamberts is a ________.

   A. Illuminance Meter
   B. Luminance Meter
   C. Luminaire
   D. Ballast

6. The preferred type of connection is _______________.

A. Crimped Terminals
B. Twist-on Wire Splices
C. Plug and Receptacle Type Connectors
D. Binding Post Terminals

7. When considering wind loading, the contractor should use _______________.

A. Good common sense
B. The manufacturer's recommendation
C. The Florida Building Code
D. The local code requirements

8. A device that converts AC power to DC power is a _________________.

A. Transformer
B. Converter
C. Maximum power point tracker
D. Rectifier

9. Copper tubing 2 inches in diameter shall be supported horizontally every _________feet.

A. 5
B. 10
C. 15
D. 20

10. The solar contractor decided a 6 foot by 8-foot collector would work the best with correct orientation. The owner wants the collector located 20 degrees west of due south to achieve the same energy output. The collector size the contractor should use is _________ sq. ft.

A. 50.88
B. 50
C. 40.88
D. 40

11. When collector temperature drops, the differential controller automatically _________________.

A. Maximizes pool heat
B. De-energizes the valve and flow bypasses the collector
C. Energizes the valve and flow bypasses the collector
D. Closes the collector loop

12. The use of a pool cover in Palm Beach for 14 hours a day should extend the use of the pool by ________ days per year.

A. 62
B. 75
C. 83
D. 96

13. A tilt angle of site latitude minus 15 degrees will optimize ________ performance.

A. Winter
B. Summer
C. Solstice
D. Energy array induction

14. When a system uses a freeze protection valve, the valve will be installed ________________.

A. At the top of the collector loop
B. On the collector return plumbing line beyond where the line penetrates the roof
C. On the collector plate at the middle or bottom of the collector near the collector inlet
D. Adjacent to the manual pump

15. Solar photovoltaic system dc circuits on or in one- and two-family dwellings shall be permitted to have a MAXIMUM voltage of _____ volts or less.

A. 125
B. 250
C. 300
D. 600

16. Sensors used with differential controllers are thermal resistors commonly called _____________.

A. Thermistors
B. Temperature resistors
C. Tristers
D. Consistors

17. Steel should be protected by any of the following except ___________.

A. Plating
B. Galvanizing
C. Cold spotting
D. Painting

18. The anode rod should be replaced _____________.

A. Yearly
B. Every 3 years
C. Periodically
D. As required

19. A 60 square foot solar panel should have a flow rate of less than gallons ________ per minute.

A. 0.6
B. 1.0
C. 1.5
D. 2.0

20. Passive systems use _______________.

A. Collector loops
B. Fluid loops
C. No pumps or controllers
D. Discharge tanks

21. ___________ is the reciprocal of resistance and is expressed in units of mhos, now called siemens.

A. Capacitance
B. Conductor
C. Conductance
D. Inductance

22. To get the most of a solar collector in central Florida, the fixed collector should be tilted up at an angle of about ___________.

A. 28 degrees to the vertical
B. 28 degrees to the horizontal
C. 50 degrees to the vertical
D. 50 degrees to the horizontal

23. The array tilt angle is the _____________.

A Vertical angle between the azimuth and the incidence
B The vertical angle between horizontal and the array surface
C The horizontal angle between vertical and the array surface
D The azimuth and the incidence angle

24. Energy is expressed in units of ____________.

A. Ohm
B. Coulomb
C. Joules
D. Hertz

25. Given 9,750 watt-hours, a module energy output of 180 watt-hours and a derating factor of 0.90 for non-critical application, the modules required are ______________.

A. 49
B. 61
C. 55
D. 58

26. _______________ valves must be used in all systems with freeze-protection valves.

A. Ball
B. Check
C. Gate
D. Meter

27. Photovoltaic cells primarily use ________________.

A. Invisible radiation
B. Light irradiation
C. Visible radiation
D. Negative irritation

28. When installing the collector loop, drain valves should be provided on ______________.

A. The high and low side
B. Back flush side
C. The left and upper side
D. Both sides

29. USE is normally used for a (an) ______________ PV application.

A. Array wiring
B. BOS interconnects
C. Interior exposed
D. Battery interconnects

30. To prevent collector water from backwashing through the filter and flushing trash into the pool from the strainer when the pump is shut down, the contractor should insure ___________.

A. All skimmers are operational
B. A spring-loaded check valve is installed upstream from the filter
C. The bypass valve is in the closed position
D. A spring-loaded check valve is installed downstream from the filter

31. For Jacksonville, Florida or north Florida, a year-round collector tile of __________ degrees works best.

A. 15
B. 25
C. 30
D. 40

32. Connecting photovoltaic devices in series involves connecting the _________________.

A. Positive terminal of one to the positive terminal of the other
B. Negative terminal to the positive terminal of the other
C. Negative terminal of one to the negative terminal of the other
D. Positive terminal of one to the negative terminal of the other

33. Fastener spacing for gasketed fasteners used to install roof mounted PV arrays on EPDM roof types is generally, between _______ and _______ inches.

A. 3; 6
B. 6; 12
C. 8; 24
D. 12; 16

34. All of the following hardware has proven itself for use in photovoltaic systems except_______.

A. Hot-dipped galvanized steel
B. Corrosion resistant aluminum
C. Cadmium
D. PVC wire ties

35. ____________ arrays use both diffuse and direct sunlight and can operate in either a fixed orientation or in a sun-tracking mode.

A. Fixed
B. Tracking
C. Flat-plate
D. Concentrator

36. Differential controlled systems use a circulating pump when sensors located at the top of the collector indicate a temperature difference of ________ to ________ degrees.

A. 0; 30
B. 10; 20
C. 5; 30
D. 5; 20

37. During the charging cycle, lead acid batteries emit _______________.

A. Hydrogen sulfide
B. Hydrogen gasses
C. Muriatic acid
D. Sulfuric acid

38. _______ is a wire-wound coil that induces a voltage as the rate of current changes through the coil.

A. Transformer
B. Inductor
C. Capacitor
D. Resistor

39. The pump draws water from the ______________ and main drain and forces it through the filter.

A. Well
B. Spa
C. Collector
D. Skimmer

40. There are _________ basic ways that photovoltaic generated power can be interconnected to the utility power in a residence.

A. One
B. Two
C. Four
D. Three

41. It is recommended all sensor circuits be wired for ________________ or less.

A. 24 VAC
B. 24 VDC
C. 110 VDC
D. 110 VAC

42. In series connections, the voltages ____________________.

A. Add and the current is limited to the total of the array
B. Diminish and the current is limited to the least of any device in the string
C. Increase and the current is limited to the least of any device in the string
D. Warble and the current is limited to the least of any device in the string

43. The use of ethylene glycol should be used only with a/an ______________.

A. Single wall heat exchanger
B. Double wall heat exchanger
C. ICS system
D. Single or double wall system

44. A meter used to measure the current flow or amperes through an electric circuit is a (an) __________.

A. Voltmeter
B. Ohmmeter
C. Ammeter
D. Watt-Hour

45. Air locks can prevent any flow if the pump does not have _______________.

A. The capacity to compress the air completely and force it through the system
B. A swing check valve at the top of the collector loop
C. A swing check valve at the bottom of the collector loop
D. A diverter capacity for air diversion

46. __________ loads are typically the highest of the load types.

A. Snow
B. Live
C. Wind
D. Dead

47. The battery system must include a disconnect when more than ________volts.

A. 6
B. 12
C. 24
D. 48

48. A faulty freeze sensor operation may result in ___________________.

A. Pump intermittent operation
B. Collector loop passage
C. Air vent malfunction
D. Burst collector tubes

49. Some special characteristics of drainback systems include all of the following except ____.

A. Collectors and pipe drains must be installed to allow proper and unimpeded drainage back to the drainback reservoir
B. Interlock blocking connectors
C. Pumps must be sized correctly to overcome gravity and friction losses
D. Expansion tanks, check valves or fill and drain valves are not required

50. As the liquid in the active system collector loop becomes cooler, the pump may ______.

A. Fail to start
B. Run continuously
C. Seize
D. Run intermittently

51. If batteries or cells are connected in series, the capacity of the string is limited to the ______.

A. Lower battery capacity
B. Higher battery capacity
C. Total voltage of the combined batteries
D. Total amps

52. The energy demand is 9,400 watt-hours, using a 24-volt battery bus voltage, the amp hours are ____.

A 3.92
B 39.2
C 392
D 3920

53. The utility service voltage is nominally sinusoidal at _____________ Hz.

A. 60
B. 80
C. 65
D. 70

54. A reservoir used to collect the heat-transfer fluid that drains from the collector loop each time the pump turns off is found in ______________systems.

A. Drain-back
B. Batch
C. Photovoltaic controlled
D. Timer controlled

55. If the PV system uses net metering, the utility electricity meter runs ________________ when power is exported from the PV system to the utility.

A. Forward
B. Backward
C. Forward and backward
D. At a constant speed

56. Heat exchanger materials must be compatible with the systems' fluid and piping and _____________ is by far the most common.

A. Copper
B. Aluminum
C. Steel
D. Bronze

57. The pool contains 23,075 gallons. The temperature of the pool water needs to be raised 3 degrees. The contractor has determined each 4 foot by 10-foot collector will deliver 850 Btu's per square foot. __________ collectors will be needed. BTU is the energy required to raise the temperature of 1 lb of water by 1 ºF.

A. 12
B. 17
C. 21
D. 30

58. Parallel reverse-return piping ensures a fairly uniform flow in each collector array with no more than _____collectors.

A. 2
B. 4
C. 6
D. 8

59. The overcurrent protection device has a rating of 60. The conductor size should be _____________.

A. 14
B. 12
C. 10
D. 8

60. In a differential controlled system, the circulating pump operates when sensors are located _________.

A. At the top of the collector
B. At the bottom of the collector
C. At the top of the collector and the bottom of the storage tank
D. At the bottom of the storage tank

61. The solar contractor should be able to inform the electrical contractor whether ___________.

A. 110 VAC is required
B. 220 VAC is required
C. 24 VAC, 110 VAC and/or 220 VAC is required
D. 110 VAC and/or 220 VAC is required

62. ____________ law states that for a steady-state current, the current in an electrical circuit is directly proportional to the voltage across the circuit and inversely proportional to the total resistance of the circuit.

A. Kirchhoff's
B. Ohm's
C. Faraday's
D. Ampere's

63. The total amp-hours are 4,200. The battery bus voltage is 24 volts. The kWh is____________.

A. 2,000
B. 100.8
C. 200.8
D. 1,000

64. Blue sky has a color temperature of between _________ and _________ degrees Kelvin (K).

A. 10,000; 30,000
B. 1,000; 3,000
C. 15,000; 20,000
D. 20,000; 30,000

65. The visible ________ consists of the colors of a rainbow, ranging from violet at one end to red at the other.

A. Efficacy
B. Color
C. Spectrum
D. Chromaticity

66. ____________ metering permits photovoltaic generated energy sent back to the utility to be valued differently than the energy supplied to the residence by the utility.

A Duel
B Simultaneous Buy/Sell
C. Dual
D. Single Net

67. A flat-plate solar collector installed in Miami, Florida, installed at latitude minus 15 degrees would have solar radiation in June of _________________.

A. 5.6
B. 5.5
C. 5.1
D. 4.5

68. The optimum tilt angle for Orlando, Florida is _____________ degrees.

A. 15
B. 28
C. 43
D. 52

69. To restore power, the contractor should push the __________ button.

A. Red
B. Blue
C. Yellow
D. Green

70. The amount of solar power striking the earth's surface at any given time is about ____________,

A. 2.1 X 1,017 watts
B. 1.2 X 1,017 watts
C. 1.2 X 1,017 volts
D. 2.1 X 1,017 volts

71. Single frequency harmonic components should be less than or equal to what percent for current distortion ______.

A. 1
B. 2
C. 3
D. 5

72. _______ is a term used to classify equipment, materials and hardware in a PV system, other than the PV array.

A. BOS
B. OBS
C. PVS
D. None of the above

73. The total amp-hours are 3,600. The battery bus voltage is 24 volts. The kWh is __________________.

A. 86.4
B. .15
C. 15
D. 8.64

74. A PV output circuit composed of four source circuits, each with a rated short-circuit current of 8 A, will have a maximum current of the output circuit of ____________________ .

A. 32 A
B. 40 A
C. 48 A
D. 64 A

75. The required working space for less than 150 V is at least ________ feet deep.

A. 1.5
B. 2
C. 3
D. 5

76. A good liquid film to use to retard evaporation is ______________.

A. Poly-glycol
B. Acetylsalicylic acid
C. Copolymers
D. Cetyl alcohol

77. The average yearly generator/battery charger on time is 3,200 hours. The average generator ac output power is 4,100 watts. The total kilowatt-hours are ___________.

A. 14,000
B. 12,120
C. 15,000
D. 13,120

78. Latitude _______________ mounting is best for summer energy collection.

A. plus 15°
B. minus 15°
C. plus 25°
D. minus 25°

79. The estimated friction loss for 4-inch PVC pipe delivering 280 gallons per minute is approximately _________ psi per 100 feet.

A. 2
B. 4
C. 6
D. 8

80. The ___________ is electrical information that is NOT required to appear on each module.

A. Open circuit voltage
B. Rated standby voltage
C. Operating voltage
D. Maximum power

81. To control temperature differential, a sensor should be tapped into the piping at a convenient place __________.

A. Ahead of the collector return line
B. Behind the collector discharge line
C. Either immediately after the collector return line or immediately before the collector loop
D. Before the collector bypass valve

82. A 10K thermistor at 77°F should have an ohm's resistance of ________________.

A. 3,000 or greater
B. 5,000 or greater
C. 7,500 or greater
D. 10,000

83. Indirect systems that use glycol as the heat transfer fluid use ______________ to remove any dissolved air left in the system after it has been pressurized or charged with heat-transfer fluid.

A. Check valve drains
B. Air vents
C. Purge controllers
D. Diluters

84. The common frequency for alternating current in the U.S. is _______________ hertz.

A. 50
B. 60
C. 70
D. 80

85. Support penetrations of an array module 18 inches wide on a metal roof, the vertical supports are flashed as small penetrations depending on configuration. The clearance recommended between the roof surface and the bottom of the array is ________ inches.

A. 14
B. 18
C. 24
D. 30

****Please See Answer Key on following page****

2/23/23

State Solar
Practice Exam 1

Answer		Reference	Section/Page#
1	B	Photovoltaic System Design (Course Manual)	11 - 10
2	A	Solar Water & Pool Heating Manual, 2006	2-9
3	B	Florida Building Code, Residential	R4501.6.3 and
		R4501.6.3, Figure AP103.3(2) Note, Figure AP103.3(3) Note, AP103.3(4) Note	
4	B	Photovoltaic Systems, 3rd Edition	4
5	B	Photovoltaic System Design (Course Manual)	10a-5
6	D	Photovoltaic System Design (Course Manual)	7-9
7	C	Solar Water & Pool Heating Manual, 2006	3-2
8	D	Photovoltaic Systems, 3rd Edition	224
9	B	Florida Building Code, Plumbing	Table 308.5
10	A	Solar Water & Pool Heating Manual, 2006	1-9
		6 x 8 x 1.06 = 50.88	
11	B	Solar Water & Pool Heating Manual, 2006	5-11
12	C	Solar Water & Pool Heating Manual, 2006	5-5 – Figure 4
13	B	Photovoltaic System Design (Course Manual)	8-5
14	B	Solar Water & Pool Heating Manual, 2006	2-16
15	D	NEC Handbook 2017	690.7
16	A	Solar Water & Pool Heating Manual, 2006	2-29
17	C	Solar Water & Pool Heating Manual, 2006	1-13
18	C	Solar Water & Pool Heating Manual, 2006	2-21
19	A	Solar Water & Pool Heating Manual, 2006	A-15
		60 sq ft of panel x 0.01 gallon per minute per square feet = 0.6 gallons per minute	
20	C	Solar Water & Pool Heating Manual, 2006	2-9
21	C	Photovoltaic System Design (Course Manual)	2a-1
22	D	Solar Water & Pool Heating Manual, 2006	1-8
23	B	Photovoltaic Systems, 3rd Edition	49
24	C	Photovoltaic System Design (Course Manual)	2a-2
25	B	Photovoltaic System Design (Course Manual)	6-10
		180 X .9 = 162	
		9,750 ÷ 162 = 60.18 = 61	

Answer		Reference	Section/Page#
26	B	Solar Water & Pool Heating Manual, 2006	2-17
27	C	Photovoltaic System Design (Course Manual)	2-8
28	D	Solar Water & Pool Heating Manual, 2006	3-21
29	A	Photovoltaic System Design (Course Manual)	7-6
30	D	Solar Water & Pool Heating Manual, 2006	5-9
31	C	Solar Water & Pool Heating Manual, 2006	1-11
32	D	Photovoltaic System Design (Course Manual)	4-1
33	C	NRCA Membrane Roof Systems, 2023 NRCA Membrane Roof Systems, 2019	309 292
34	D	Photovoltaic System Design (Course Manual)	8-3
35	C	Photovoltaic System Design (Course Manual)	2-10
36	D	Solar Water & Pool Heating Manual, 2006	2-3
37	B	Photovoltaic System Design (Course Manual)	9-1
38	B	Photovoltaic System Design (Course Manual)	2a-8
39	D	Solar Water & Pool Heating Manual, 2006	5-9
40	D	Photovoltaic System Design (Course Manual)	11-1
41	B	Solar Water & Pool Heating Manual, 2006	3-27
42	C	Photovoltaic System Design (Course Manual)	G-10
43	B	Solar Water & Pool Heating Manual, 2006	2-33
44	C	Photovoltaic System Design (Course Manual)	2a-11
45	A	Solar Water & Pool Heating Manual, 2006	4-6
46	C	Photovoltaic System Design (Course Manual)	8-1
47	D	Photovoltaic Systems, 3rd Edition	345
48	D	Solar Water & Pool Heating Manual, 2006	4-7
49	B	Solar Water & Pool Heating Manual, 2006	2-15
50	D	Solar Water & Pool Heating Manual, 2006	4-7
51	A	Photovoltaic System Design (Course Manual)	5-24
52	C	Photovoltaic System Design (Course Manual) 9,400 ÷ 2 = 391.6 = 392	6-5
53	A	Photovoltaic System Design (Course Manual)	11-10
54	A	Solar Water & Pool Heating Manual, 2006	2-15
55	B	Photovoltaic Systems, 3rd Edition	113
56	A	Solar Water & Pool Heating Manual, 2006	2-34

Answer		Reference	Section/Page#
57	B	Walker's Building Estimator's Reference	32nd Ed: 869 31st Ed: 1396
		BTU is the energy required to raise the temperature of 1 lb of water by 1 ^{o}F – Trade knowledge 23,075 gallons x 8.34 lb per gallon x 3 ^{o}F per lb per Btu = 577,336.5 Btu's 4 ft x 10 ft x 850 Btu's per sq ft = 34,000 Btu's 577,336.5 Btu's ÷ 34,000 Btu's = 16.9 = 17	
58	B	Solar Water & Pool Heating Manual, 2006	3-19
59	C	Photovoltaic Systems, 3rd Edition	341
60	C	Solar Water & Pool Heating Manual, 2006	2-3
61	D	Solar Water & Pool Heating Manual, 2006	3-22
62	B	Photovoltaic System Design (Course Manual)	2a-3
63	B	Photovoltaic System Design (Course Manual)	6-7
		24 X 4,200 ÷ 1,000 = 100.8	
64	A	Photovoltaic System Design (Course Manual)	10a-3
65	C	Photovoltaic System Design (Course Manual)	10a-3
66	C	Photovoltaic System Design (Course Manual)	11-4
67	B	Solar Water & Pool Heating Manual, 2006	1-11- Table 1
68	C	Solar Water & Pool Heating Manual, 2006	4-9
69	A	Solar Water & Pool Heating Manual, 2006	A-7
70	B	Photovoltaic System Design (Course Manual)	2-1
71	C	Photovoltaic System Design (Course Manual)	11-11
72	A	Photovoltaic System Design (Course Manual)	5-5
73	A	Photovoltaic System Design (Course Manual)	6-7
		3,600 X 24 + 1,000 = 86.4	
74	B	Photovoltaic Systems, 3rd Edition	312
		4 X 8 + 25 % is 40	
75	C	Photovoltaic Systems, 3rd Edition	388
76	D	Solar Water & Pool Heating Manual, 2006	5-6
77	D	Photovoltaic System Design (Course Manual)	6-21
		4,100 X 3,200 + 1,000 = 13,120	
78	B	Solar Water & Pool Heating Manual, 2006	1-10
79	A	Solar Water & Pool Heating Manual, 2006	5-16

Answer		Reference	Section/Page#
80	B	NEC Handbook 2017	690.51
81	A	Solar Water & Pool Heating Manual, 2006	5-11
82	D	Solar Water & Pool Heating Manual, 2006	2-29
83	B	Solar Water & Pool Heating Manual, 2006	2-37
84	B	Photovoltaic System Design (Course Manual)	2a-2
85	A	NRCA Metal Panel & SPF Roof Systems, 2020	152
		NRCA Metal Panel & SPF Roof Systems, 2016	141

State Solar
Practice Exam 2

1. Valves, gauges and meters used in solar systems serve to do all of the following except______.

   A. Prevent venting of air from the system
   B. Insolate parts of the system
   C. Prevent thermosiphon heat losses
   D. Provide freeze protection

2. The practical unit of electrical charge is the _____________.

   A. Current + D132
   B. Volt
   C. Power
   D. Coulomb

3. In stand-alone systems, the inverter is used to ________.

   A. Act as a grounding electrode
   B. Bypass the panel box
   C. Change direct current from a battery bank to nearly constant-output AC voltage
   D. Change alternating current from a battery bank to DC current

4. When measuring DC voltage with the VOM, the contractor should never measure circuits over ______volts.

   A. 500
   B. 700
   C. 850
   D. 1,000

5. To charge a nominal 12V battery, the array must be at least ____________.

   A. 12 V
   B. 14.5 V
   C. 18 V
   D. 24 V

6. A sensor that measures the total global solar irradiance in a hemispherical field of view is called a _______.

   A. Pyranometer
   B. Pyrheliometer
   C. Global meter
   D. Pyrometer

7. A 10-foot plastic collector may expand and contract as much as _______ inches in length.

A. 1
B. 2
C. 3
D. 4

8. The conducting medium allowing the transfer of ions between battery cell plates is called a (an) _________.

A. Electrolysis
B. Hydrochloric acid
C. Electrolyte
D. Array

9. Modules are typically connected together with _______________ .

A. Copper tightening bands
B. CPVC of PEX tubing
C. Internal enclosed connectors
D. External exposed connectors

10. Natural gas and propane system burners are located _______________.

A. At the mid-point of the system
B. At the bottom of the tank
C. At the top of the tank
D. Inside the tank

11. The term panel typically refers to _______________.

A. A group of judges usually consisting of at least one building official and one representative from the electric authority
B A larger group of modules in array usually three physically connected together as an installation unit
C An assembly of 2 or more modules mechanically and electrically integrated into a unit
D Usually three physically connected considered an installation unit

12. The type of system which prevents a fall from occurring is a____________.

A. safety system
B. personal fall-arrest system
C. personal fall-restraint system
D. positioning device

13. When full, a 4 foot by 5 foot by 7-foot collection tank will weigh ____________ pounds.

A. Less than 6,000
B. Between 6,000 and 7,000
C. Between 7,000 and 8,000
D. More than 8,000

14. To allow the owner to make seasonal adjustments, the contractor should ________________.

A. Check quarterly with the owner
B. Spend a little time on the automatic control
C. Leave the owner a complete checklist
D. Leave the owner a business card

15. Diatomaceous earth filters usually operate well at about ________________.

A. 2 gallons per minute per square foot
B. 2 gallons per minute per square yard
C. 4 gallons per minute per square foot
D. 2 gallons per minute per square yard

16. A second temperature differential sensor should be housed in a plastic block and placed near the________________.

A. Collector loop
B. 90 degrees to the collector outlet
C. Parallel to the collector outlet
D. In sequence with the collector inlet valve

17. The highest of the load types is typically?

A. Live load
B. Dead load
C. Wind load
D. Combined load

18. If the average solar irradiance is 800 W/m2 over 7 hours, what is the total solar irradiation over this period?

A. 8,700 Wh/m2 or 8.7 kWh/m2
B. 5,600 Wh/m2 or 5.6 kWh/m2 I
C. 4,800 Wh/m2 or 48.0 kWh/m2
D. 5,600 Wh/m2 or 56.0 kWh/m2

19. Which is not a requirement when installing connectors in a PV circuit?

A. Tool only opening when operating over 30 V dc or 15 V ac
B. Guarding and warning marking
C. Able to be opened under load when rated for interrupting current without hazard to the operator
D. Hand opening or disconnecting only permitted

20. The liquid in the active system collector loop in the evening will normally flow to the____________.

A. Low point in the loop
B. Storage tank
C. Pump housing
D. Thermosiphon

21. To be routed through an attic, PV conductors must be ________________ .

A. Grounded to the solar panel
B. Installed in a Schedule 80 conduit or greater
C. Metallic raceway following the point of first penetration of the building structure and the first disconnect
D. Contained in metal raceways between the point of first penetration of the building structure to the first readily accessible disconnecting means

22. The condition where essentially no electrical or chemical changes are occurring is known as __________.

A. Dead level state
B. Plus/minus voltage conditions
C. Roaming
D. Steady state

23. Installing expansion loops or offsets can accommodate piping ________________.

A. Temperature changes
B. Contractions
C. Air traps
D. Thermal expansion

24. Homeowners should be informed the water will be hottest ______________.

A. In the early morning
B. Late afternoon and early evening
C. Late evening
D. Right after sundown

25. Gas water heaters do not work well in single-tank solar systems because the ________________.

A. gas tank's burner heats the water entire tank of water from the top down
B. gas tank's burner heats the water entire tank of water from the bottom up
C. gas tank's burner heats the water entire tank of water any way
D. gas tank burner's heat ruptures the water entire tank eventually

26. Given a tank that is half full, 8 1/2 feet tall, 3 feet in diameter, the number of gallons is ___________.

A. Less than 475
B. Between 475 and 500
C. Between 500 and 550
D. More than 550

27. The ratio of light reflected from a surface to the incident light is ___________.

A. Transmittance
B. Absorptance
C. Luminance
D. Reflectance

28. The decomposition of water into hydrogen and oxygen gasses as the battery charges is known as ________.

A. Gassing
B. Phasing
C. Powering
D. Charging

29. The most popular storage tanks are made of _____________ with an inner glass, stone or epoxy lining.

A. Fiberglass
B. Steel
C. Stainless steel
D. Aluminum

30. ___________ valves must be used in all systems with freeze-protection valves.

A. Check
B. Gate
C. Bibb
D. Boiler

31. The incidence angle is the angle between the direction of ________________.

A. Radiation and a line exactly perpendicular to the azimuth surface
B. Radiation and a line exactly perpendicular to the array surface
C. Radiation and a line exactly vertical to the array surface I
D. Declination and the perpendicular tilt

32. The collectors in multiple-collector arrays should be plumbed ____________ unless the manufacturer specifies other.

A. In series
B. In parallel
C. According to contract specifications
D. According to Code

33. Given 3.25 therms, the number of Btu's is_____________.

A. 325,000
B. 250,000
C. 75,000
D. 125,000

34. The device used to admit atmospheric pressure into the system piping allowing the system to drain is the ___________.

A. Swing check valve
B. Gate valve
C. Vacuum breaker
D. Anti-suction device

35. A break in the associated wiring may be indicative of a/an ______________.

A. 120-volt circuit
B. 220 circuit
C. Zero reading
D. Infinite reading

36. The electronic controller requires ______________________.

A. 24-volt power and parallel connection
B. 120V minimum connection and parallel installation with the pool pump or timer
C. 220V minimum connection and parallel installation with the pool pump or timer
D. Swing check valve and collector loop vent protection

37. The light flux falling on a surface one square foot in area is___________.

A. Reflectance
B. Lumen
C. Refraction
D. Absorptance

38. Sizing PV systems for stand-alone operation involves ________ sets of calculations.

A. 2
B. 3
C. 4
D. 6

39. A/an _______________ is a carbon or wire-wound device that creates resistance to the flow of electrical current.

A. Capacitor
B Inductor
C. Transformer
D. Resistor

40. The two common types of isolation valves are ________ and ________ valves.

A. Ball; check
B. Gate; check
C. Ball; gate
D. Vacuum; gate

41. There are 4 fixtures using 40 watts each for 6 hours. The inverter efficiency is 0.85. The adjusted wattage is ___________.

A. 81.6-watt hours
B. 8.16 kvh
C. 11.29 kwh
D. 1,129 wh

42. The VOM measures a/an__________ circuit.

A. Closed
B. Open
C. Parallel
D. Series

43. Extension ladders have a movable____________.

A. Rope section
B. Fly section
C. Base section
D. Cap cover

44. A 5,420 W inverter outputting 220 V will have a listed continuous output rating of approximately _________amps.

A. 24
B. 25.53
C. 25
D. 24.63

45. The _________ is the basic building block of a photovoltaic module.

A. String
B. Series
C. Cell
D. Current

46. When installing water heaters, all except which of the following is important?

A. conveniently located on/off switch
B. R-value of the insulation blanket
C. Double pole 220 VAC switch
D. Informing the homeowner of the location of the water heater circuit breaker switch

47. Voltage unbalance should not be more than ________ percent.

A. 3
B. 2
C. 1
D. 10

48. When a collector is rack-mounted, the tilt angle should be verified so the collector will ___________.

A. Face due south
B. Drain by gravity
C. Face latitude plus 20 degrees
D. Wind forces will be controlled

49. A leaking check valve can cause the differential control to ___________.

A. Overheat the system
B. Increase scaling
C. Shut the collector loop down
D. Recycle the pump at night

50. Cetyl alcohol can reduce evaporation by as much as _______ percent.

A. 25
B. 40
C. 60
D. 80

51. The solar system must have insolation valves on ________________.

A. the converging side of the solar loop
B. the diverging side of the solar loop
C. one side of the solar loop
D. both sides of the solar loop

52. Differential controllers require ________________ sensor(s).

A. 1
B. 2
C. 3
D. 4

53. A condition occurring in a flooded battery when the concentration or specific gravity of the electrolyte increases from the bottom to the top of a cell is ____________.

A. Sulfation
B. Internal Resistance
C. Stratification
D. State of Charge

54. The vertical angle between the sun and the horizon is called the __________ angle.

A. Solar azimuth
B. Solar elevation
C. Solar zenith
D. Solar altitude

55. A 40 square foot solar collector should have a flow rate of _______ gallons in 20 minutes.

A. 4
B. 8
C. 20
D. 80

56. __________ laws are based on conservation of energy principles.

A. Faraday's
B. Newton's
C. Kirchhoff's
D. Ohm's

57. To keep water in the collector loop when the city water pressure is shut off the contractor should ___________________.

A. Close the collector loop
B. Open the collector loop
C. Purge all air from the collector loop
D. Open all vacuum breakers

58. ___________ cells are devices that convert light into electricity.

A. Energy
B. Photo
C. Power
D. Photovoltaic

59. ____________ control and condition the DC power from the array and either direct it to DC loads or convert it to AC power for use by AC loads.

A. Loads
B. Utilities
C. Arrays
D. Electrical components

60 Current in amperes is determined by __________________________.

A. Multiplying potential difference in volts by resistance in ohms
B. Dividing ohms by resistance
C. Subtracting potential difference in volts from ohms
D. Dividing potential difference in volts by the resistance in ohms

61. The most common type of pipe insulation used in solar systems is the ____________.

A. Closed cell flexible elastomeric foam
B. Open cell flexible elastomeric foam
C. Armatative flexible core device
D. Black tape compound system foam

62. If the average solar irradiance is 550 W/m2 over 6 hours, the total solar irradiation over this period in Wh/m2 and kWh/m2 is _____________.

A. 2,300 or 2.3
B. 2,000
C. 3,300 or 3.3 I
D. 3,000

63. Power is equal to ________.

A. El
B. PE
C. IR
D. ER

64. Which of the following is not a component of an active direct system?

A. Check valves to prevent thermosiphoning action
B. Isolation valves to isolate subsystem components for service
C. Air locks to prevent accidental discharge
D. Drain valves to drain the collector loop and tank

65. A pH level above 7.8 increases the ____________ .

A. Acidity
B. Alkalinity
C. Corrosivity
D. Chlorine level

66. In a (an)_____________________ system, the water storage tank is located above the collector.

A. Indirect pressurized
B. Drainback
C. Thermosiphon
D. Integral collector storage

67. Silicon PV modules operating at 20 to 24 degrees Celsius, use a correction factor of __________, when calculating voltage.

A. 1.02
B. 1.06
C. 1.18
D. 1.25

68. Which is a correct combination use of metals?

A. Aluminum and cast iron
B. Brass, copper and bronze
C. Brass, aluminum and copper
D. Magnesium and steel

69. PV modules in hot climates operate at temperatures of 60 degrees C to 80 degrees C, therefore conductors with insulation types rated at least _______ degrees C should be used.

A. 60
B. 75
C. 80
D. 90

70. Main drain systems and surface overflow systems which discharge to collector tanks shall be sized with a maximum flow velocity of _______________ ft. per second.

A. 2
B. 3
C. 4
D. 6

71. The resistance of conductors is generally expressed in ohms per __________ feet length.

A. 500
B. 1,000
C. 1,500
D. 2,000

72. All ungrounded conductors from the PV array should be protected by _____________.

A. THNN or better wire
B. Over-current devices
C. Grounding metal electrodes
D. Neutral ground

73. The insolation for Orlando, Florida during the month of August at a tilt of 20 degrees is _________.

A. 5.18
B. 4.24
C. 5.24
D. 4.07

74. The simplest way to find out if the system is working is by turning off or disconnecting the ___________.

A. Breaker
B. Electric back up element
C. Collector
D. Storage tank

75. The size of an interactive system is essentially limited by the _____________.

A. Azimuth
B. Tilt
C. Angle of incidence
D. Space

76. A common cause for an "open" condition may be any of the following except ______________.

A. broken connection between the wiring and the sensor
B. A piece of metal pinching the sensor wire
C. A disconnect at the water heater
D. A short

77. Connecting all of the positive terminals together and all of the negative terminals together placing the battery in ______________ condition.

A. Parallel
B. Series
C. Steady state
D. Charge

78. Unlisted grounding copper rods shall not be less than ____________ inch(es).

A. 1
B. 3/4
C. 5/8
D. 1/2

79. The typical correction factor for maximum power is ____________ for crystalline silicon cells.

A. -0.0041°C
B. 0.004/°C
C. -0.0031°C
D. 0.0031°C

80. When a system has two or more collectors, they should be plumbed in _____________.

A. Parallel
B. Series
C. Either parallel or series
D. Sequence

81. A timer controller requires the use of a special valve installed in the tank's common drain port to connect the ____________ line.

A. Feed
B. Return
C. Water intake
D. Feed and return

82. All air should be vented out of the collection loop except for ______________.

A. Drain-back systems
B. Batch collectors
C. Integral systems
D. ICS collectors

83. Photovoltaic cells primarily use _____________ radiation.

A. Visible
B. Ultraviolet
C. Infrared
D. Gamma

84. NRCA recommends that roof deck slopes intended for tile roofing systems be specified at ___________ or greater.

A. 2:12
B. 3:12
C. 4:12
D. 5:12

85. When the sensor's temperature increases, its resistance ___________.

A. Fluctuates
B. Goes down
C. Increases
D. Remains stable

*******Please see Answer Key on the following page*******

State Solar
Practice Exam 2

Answer		Reference	Section/Page#
1	A	Solar Water & Pool Heating Manual, 2006	2-36
2	D	Photovoltaic System Design (Course Manual) 2	a-1
3	C	NEC Handbook 2017	690.2
		See "Inverter" and "Stand-Alone System"	
4	D	Solar Water & Pool Heating Manual, 2006	A-9
5	B	Photovoltaic Systems, 3rd Edition	268
6	A	Photovoltaic Systems, 3rd Edition	40
7	A	Solar Water & Pool Heating Manual, 2006	5-24
8	C	Photovoltaic Systems, 3rd Edition	160
9	D	Photovoltaic Systems, 3rd Edition	144
10	B	Solar Water & Pool Heating Manual, 2006	2-21
11	C	Photovoltaic Systems, 3rd Edition	143
12	C	Solar Construction Safety 6	9
13	D	Walker's Building Estimator's Reference	32nd Ed: 869 31st Ed: 1396
		Volume = l x w x depth	
		4ft x 5ft x 7ft = 140 cubic feet x 7.48 gallons per cubic feet = 1047.2 gallons x 8.34 lbs per gallon = 8,734 lbs	
		OR	
		4ft x 5ft x 7ft = 140 cubic feet x 62.4 lbs per cubic feet =8736 lbs	
14	B	Solar Water & Pool Heating Manual, 2006	5-33
15	A	Solar Water & Pool Heating Manual, 2006	5-14
16	C	Solar Water & Pool Heating Manual, 2006	5-11
17	C	Photovoltaic System Design (Course Manual)	8-1
18	B	Photovoltaic Systems, 3rd Edition	32
		800 x 7 = 5,600	
		800 x 7 / 1,000 = 5.6	
19	D	NEC Handbook 2017	690.33(A-E)
20	B	Solar Water & Pool Heating Manual, 2006	4-7
21	D	NEC Handbook 2017	690.31(G)
22	D	Photovoltaic Systems, 3rd Edition	161
23	D	Solar Water & Pool Heating Manual, 2006	3-20
24	B	Solar Water & Pool Heating Manual, 2006	3-36

Answer		Reference	Section/Page#
25	B	Solar Water & Pool Heating Manual, 2006	3-22
26	A	Walker's Building Estimator's Reference	32nd Ed: 869 and 873 31st Ed: 1396 and 1401
		Volume of a cylinder = π x r^2 x h 1/2 full x 3.14 x 1.5 ft x 1.5 ft x 8.5 ft = 30.03 cubic feet x 7.48 gallons per cubic feet = 224.59 gal	
27	D	Photovoltaic System Design (Course Manual)	10a-2
28	A	Photovoltaic Systems, 3rd Edition	166
29	B	Solar Water & Pool Heating Manual, 2006	2-21
30	A	Solar Water & Pool Heating Manual, 2006	2-45
31	B	Photovoltaic Systems, 3rd Edition	50
32	B	Solar Water & Pool Heating Manual, 2006	3-19
33	A	Trade knowledge	
		3.25 x 100,000 = 325,000 BTU's	
34	C	Solar Water & Pool Heating Manual, 2006	2-40
35	C	Solar Water & Pool Heating Manual, 2006	A-10
36	B	Solar Water & Pool Heating Manual, 2006	5-30
37	B	Photovoltaic System Design (Course Manual)	10a-2
38	C	Photovoltaic Systems, 3rd Edition	250
39	D	Photovoltaic System Design (Course Manual)	2a-7
40	C	Solar Water & Pool Heating Manual, 2006	2-40
41	D	Photovoltaic System Design (Course Manual)	6-4
		4 x 40 x 6 / 0.85 = 1,129	
42	B	Solar Water & Pool Heating Manual, 2006	A-10
43	B	Solar Construction Safety	46
44	D	Photovoltaic Systems, 3rd Edition	479
		5,420 / 220 = 24.63	
45	C	Photovoltaic System Design (Course Manual)	4-4
46	B	Solar Water & Pool Heating Manual, 2006	3-22
47	C	Photovoltaic Systems, 3rd Edition	222
48	B	Solar Water & Pool Heating Manual, 2006	3-14
49	D	Solar Water & Pool Heating Manual, 2006	3-35
50	C	Solar Water & Pool Heating Manual, 2006	5-6
51	D	Solar Water & Pool Heating Manual, 2006	3-21
52	B	Solar Water & Pool Heating Manual, 2006	2-28

Answer		Reference	Section/Page#
53	C	Photovoltaic System Design (Course Manual)	5-12
54	D	Photovoltaic Systems, 3rd Edition	58
55	D	Solar Water & Pool Heating Manual, 2006	5-8
		40 sq ft x 1 gallon per minute per 10 sq ft x 20 minutes = 40 / 10 x 20 = 80 gallons	
56	C	Photovoltaic System Design (Course Manual)	2a-4
57	C	Solar Water & Pool Heating Manual, 2006	A-13
58	D	Photovoltaic System Design (Course Manual)	3-1
59	D	Photovoltaic Systems, 3rd Edition	4
60	D	Photovoltaic System Design (Course Manual)	2a-4
61	A	Solar Water & Pool Heating Manual, 2006	2-27
62	C	Photovoltaic Systems, 3rd Edition	32
		550 x 6 = 3,300 kWh/m2 = 3.3 kWh/m2	
63	A	Photovoltaic System Design (Course Manual)	2a-4
64	C	Solar Water & Pool Heating Manual, 2006	2-2
65	B	Solar Water & Pool Heating Manual, 2006	5-13
66	C	Solar Water & Pool Heating Manual, 2006	2-9
67	A	NEC Handbook 2017	690.7 Table
68	B	Solar Water & Pool Heating Manual, 2006	2-26
69	D	NEC Handbook 2017	Table 690.31(A)
70	B	Florida Building Code, Plumbing, 2017	454.1.6.5.8
71	B	Photovoltaic System Design (Course Manual)	7-7
72	B	Photovoltaic System Design (Course Manual)	7-8
73	A	Photovoltaic System Design (Course Manual)	6-37
74	B	Solar Water & Pool Heating Manual, 2006	4-8
75	D	Photovoltaic Systems, 3rd Edition	248
76	C	Solar Water & Pool Heating Manual, 2006	4-14
77	A	Photovoltaic Systems, 3rd Edition	177
78	C	NEC Handbook 2017	250.52(A)(5)(b)
79	B	Photovoltaic System Design (Course Manual)	3-6
80	A	Solar Water & Pool Heating Manual, 2006	3-19
81	D	Solar Water & Pool Heating Manual, 2006	2-30
82	A	Solar Water & Pool Heating Manual, 2006	3-29
83	A	Photovoltaic System Design (Course Manual)	2-8
84	C	NRCA Steep-slope Roof Systems, 2021	194
		NRCA Steep-slope Roof Systems, 2017	184
85	B	Solar Water & Pool Heating Manual, 2006	2-29

State Solar
Practice Exam 3

1 _____________is the capacity for doing work.

A. Power
B. Light
C. Energy
D. Irradiance

2. Snap-switches do not usually have a ____________.

A. Control box
B. Pass through control
C. Thermosiphon
D. Hot service connection

3. Feed and return lines to each collector should be ___________.

A. At least 8 feet
B. About the same length
C. Copper
D. PVC

4. _________ valves should be at all high points in the system where air is most likely to accumulate.

A. Swing check
B. Pressure relief
C. Elimination
D. Air-vent

5. Each piece of equipment in the PV system shall have _________________.

A. A copper grounding rod
B. A lead-acid battery backup
C. A high voltage relay switch
D. Readily accessible disconnect switches.

6. The tilt factor for an 8 in 12 roof pitch in Jacksonville, Florida is _______.

A. 1.09
B. 1.00
C. 1.01
D. 1.10

7. The ______________ requires utilities to interconnect any qualifying facility and pay for the cost of interconnection.

A. Public Regulatory Policy Act
B. Public Utilities Regulatory Policy Act
C. Department of Business and Professional Regulation
D. Department of Environmental Protection

8. Groups of cells connected in series are called ____________.

A. Series
B. Strings
C. Substring
D. Module

9. When using standoffs, the contractor should guarantee at least __________ clearance.

A. 1 inch
B. 1 foot
C. 2 inches
D. 3 inches

10. Orlando, Florida, has a latitude of approximately _________ degrees.

A. 6
B. 12
C. 28
D. 45

11. To determine the average condition of the fluid, take the sample from a point ______________________.

A. Above the bottom of the collector loop during a period when the system is at rest
B. Below the bottom of the collector loop during a period when the system is operating
C. Above the bottom of the collector loop during a period when the system is operating
D. Below the bottom of the collector loop during a period when the system is at rest

12. A 75 square foot solar panel should have a flow rate of less than _______ gallons per minute.

A. 0.75
B. 6.5
C. 7.5
D. 0.65

13. A/an ____________ is used to measure the current flow through an electrical circuit.

A. Voltmeter
B. Ammeter
C. Ohmmeter
D. Current shunt

14. The use of a photovoltaic controller offers ______________.

A. Decreased heat collection efficiency
B. Increased heat collection efficiency
C. Better battery range control
D. Freeze protection

15. The purpose of a battery is to ________________________.

A. Store energy for a later use
B. Convert DC current to AC current
C. Provide inexpensive voltage at the proper time
D. Convert electrical energy into chemical energy during the charging cycle

16. Thyristors have _______ leads.

A. 1
B. 2
C. 3
D. 4

17. For identical batteries connected in series, the total voltage is ____________________.

A. Determined by subtracting the plate voltage from the amperage
B. The sum of the combined battery voltages
C. Division of the combined battery voltages by the amps
D. The sum of the individual battery voltages and the total capacity is the same as for one battery

18. The minimum diameter in inches for an unlisted stainless steel grounding electrode is _______.

A. 1/2
B. 3/4
C. 5/8
D. 3/8

19. Which is not a common class of fire extinguisher?

A. A
B. B
C. C
D. D

20. Photovoltaic cells and batteries are _____________ current devices.

A. Alternating
B. Electrical
C. Wave
D. Direct

21. The proper way to remove outgassing deposits is to ____________________.

A. Clean with hydrochloric acid then wash with cool water
B. Use alcohol as much as possible
C. Bathe with hot soapy water for at least 1 hour
D. Scrape with a sharp blade at a 45-degree angle

22. A pH level below 7.1 is ___________.

A. Acidic
B. Alkaline
C. Drinkable
D. Balanced

23. The feed line should penetrate the roof ______________.

A. Parallel to the horizontal of the collector
B. Above the collector
C. Below the collector
D. 10 degrees below the mid-point of the collector

24. Electrolytes are a/an _____________.

A. Soft drink additive
B. Hydrochloric acid solution
C. Sulfuric acid solution
D. Amorphous solution

25. The booster pump should be placed in the ______________.

A. Main circulation line
B. Line feeding the collector loop
C. Line feeding the solar collectors
D. Bottom of the holding tank

26. ___________ not a basic method to prevent freeze damage.

A. Thermal mass
B. Draining
C. Water flow
D. Direct freeze fluids

27. A pool contains 47,124 gallons. The temperature of the pool water needs to be raised 2 degrees. The contractor has determined each 5 foot by 8-foot collector will deliver 1,000 Btu's per square foot. The number of collectors the contractor will need is ______. BTU is the energy required to raise the temperature of 1 lb of water by 1 ^{0}F.

A. 21
B. 19
C. 17
D. 20

28. In southern coastal climates corrosion rates may be as much as ________ times higher than in the arid desert areas.

A. 100
B. 200
C. 300
D. 400

29. Flat-plate connectors are designed to heat water to a medium temperature of ______ degrees.

A. 125
B. 140
C. 160
D. 212

30. A single 220 amp-hour, deep discharge, lead-acid battery should not be allowed to reach temperatures over ________ degrees Fahrenheit.

A. 90
B. 110
C. 120
D. 150

31. The angle at which electromagnetic energy falls on an object is known as _______________.

A. The angle of incidence
B. Declination
C. Azimuth
D. Tilt

32. Temperature rise even on a sunny day should be _____ to ______ degrees Fahrenheit.

A. 0; 5
B. 5; 10
C. 10; 15
D. 15; 20

33. The device that regulates the charging of a battery from the PV array by short-circuiting the array within the regulator is a/an ______________.

A. Shunt controller
B. Metering rod
C. Metal-oxide varistor (MOV)
D. Charge controller

34. All lines should be pitched at least ______ inch per foot.

A. 1/4
B. 1/2
C. 1/8
D. 3/4

35. To charge the batteries the array voltage must be ____________________.

A. At or equal to the battery-bank voltage
B. No more than 15 percent below the battery-bank voltage
C. No more than 15 percent above the battery-bank voltage
D. Higher than the battery-bank voltage

36. The angle between a ray striking a surface and a line perpendicular to that surface is known as __________.

A. Angle of incidence
B. Azimuth
C. Adjustable tilt control index
D. Path of declination

37. _______________ should be installed on the highest collector group.

A. A swing check valve
B. Ball valves and gate valves
C. A vacuum relief valve
D. A bypass switch

38. A 3,000-ohm thermistor with a resistance of 1,830 would have a temperature of __________ degrees.

A. 94
B. 96
C. 98
D. 100

39. The type of system that requires an interface with the utility grid to operate is _______________.

A. Stand-alone
B. Direct-coupled
C. Utility-interactive
D. Hybrid

40. In both new and retrofit applications with sloping roofs, _________ mounts work best.

A. Roof
B. Rack
C. Integral
D. Standoff

41. A bad sensor will be indicated by which of the following readings?

A. High
B. Zero
C. Infinite
D. 210 or more

42. A PV output circuit composed of four source circuits, each with a rated short-circuit current of 6 A will have a maximum current of the output circuit of _________.

A. 24
B. 25
C. 30
D. 26

43. A/An _____________ is a voltmeter that measures and displays a voltage signal with respect to time and is particularly useful for examining alternating current waveforms.

A. Watt-Hour meter
B. Oscilloscope
C. Ohmmeter
D. Current shunt

44. Copper tubing 2 inches in diameter shall be supported horizontally every __________feet.

A. 5
B. 10
C. 15
D. 20

45. The *National Electrical Code (NEC)* recommends ____________ diode(s) per 12-18 series cells.

A. Two
B. Four
C. One
D. Three

46. A building is 16 feet tall. To access the building, the minimum ladder length should be _____ feet.

A. 16
B. 17
C. 18
D. 19

47. A problem that should be considered when installing modules directly on the roof is ________.

A. Hurricane frequency
B. Angle and dangle
C. Array alignment
D. Heat transfer

48. Long-term high temperatures can also lead to premature degradation of ______________.

A. Photovoltaic cell alignment
B. Module encapsulation
C. Array distortion
D. Panel complacence

49. The solar contractor decided a 4 foot by 10-foot collector would work the best with correct orientation. The owner wants the collector located 20 degrees west of due south. Which selection compensates for the owner's request?

A. One 4 foot by 10-foot collector
B. One 4 foot by 10-foot collector and one 4 foot by 8-foot collector
C. One 4 foot by 6-foot collector and one 4 foot by 8-foot collector
D. Two 4 foot by 10-foot collectors

50. Single-conductor cable Type _____ shall be permitted in exposed outdoor locations in photovoltaic source circuits for photovoltaic module interconnections within the photovoltaic array.

A. UF
B. THHN
C. USE-2
D. THWN

51. For grounded systems the insulation on grounded conductors must be _____________.

A. Green
B. White or grey
C. Red
D. Black

52 The minimum rating for a DC receptacle used in PV systems shall be ________amps.

A. 5
B. 10
C. 15
D. 20

53. A 60 square foot solar collector should have a flow rate of _______ gallons in 30 minutes.

A. 380
B. 180
C. 480
D. 280

54. When the thermistor drifts, the contractor should ________________.

A. Correct by adding 10 percent
B. Recalibrate the thermistor
C. Replace the thermistor
D. Turn off the thermistor and turn it back on after a 10 second wait

55. The valve assuring accurate flow adjustments may be made is the _____________ valve.

A. Double check
B. Ball cock
C. Air release
D. Balancing

56. Why should the owner of the PV system be carefully instructed on the operation of the system?

A. So the homeowner can repair the system at will
B. To avoid "false alarm" callbacks
C. In order for the homeowner to properly diagnose the problems
D. To allow you time to install other units and make higher profits

57. ___________ insolation is determined by summing solar irradiance over time and it is usually expressed in units of kWh/m2 per day.

A. Solar
B. Irradiance
C. Direct
D. Diffuse

58. Given a tank that is half empty, 9 feet tall, 3 feet in diameter, the number of gallons is _______.

A. 327.8
B. 237.8
C. 337.5
D. 237.5

59. _____________ is a device consisting of two conductors separated by a dielectric material.

A. Capacitor
B. Inductor
C. Resistor
D. Transformer

60. A parallel connection without reverse return leads to _____________.

A. Uneven flow throughout the entire array
B. Water reaching less than the desired temperature
C. Bubbles in the discharge
D. Static regain

61. NRCA recommends that roof deck slopes intended for tile roofing systems be specified at ___________ or greater.

A. 2:12
B. 3:12
C. 4:12
D. 5:12

62. In 3 wire DC systems, the ___________ conductor supplying premises wiring shall be grounded.

A. Red
B. White
C. Black
D. Neutral conductor

63. A tank 6 feet in diameter and 3 feet high will hold ______ gallons of water.

A. 211.3848
B. 634.1544
C. 70.4616
D. 600.1544

64. The efficiency of a solar collector depends on all of the following except ______________.

A. Size
B. Tilt
C. Orientation
D. Wire diagramming

65. All PV systems regardless of voltage, shall have a/an __________ system for exposed noncurrent-carrying metal parts of PV module frames, electrical equipment, and conductor enclosures of PV systems.

A. Metal raceway
B. Conductor
C. Shut-off
D. Equipment-grounding

66. The P and T valve usually has a manufacturer seating of _______________.

A. 140 psi and 210°F
B. 100 psi and 212°F
C. 150 psf and 210°C
D. 150 psi and 210°F

67. Most of the daily solar radiation occurs between ________________.

A. Dawn and dusk
B. 10:30 am to 5 pm EST
C. 9:00 am and 3 pm
D. 8:30 am and 4:30 pm

68. Paralleling similar photovoltaic devices causes the individual currents to ___________.

A. Add
B. Subtract
C. Multiply
D. Divide

69. Flexible connectors have a tendency to ____________.

A. Last longer than normal connectors
B. Fail over time
C. Have fewer leaks
D. Kink

70. To properly size pumps the contractor must establish the ________________.

A. Time sequence of the pumping action
B. Flow rate in gpm
C. Pressure drops in the collector loop
D. System flow rate

71. An average value of __________ air masses has been chosen as a standard atmosphere.

A. 5.1
B. 1.4
C. 3.1
D. 1.5

72. The sun's total energy is composed of __________ % ultraviolet radiation, _______ % visible radiation and _________ % infrared radiation.

A. 46; 47; 7
B. 7; 74; 64
C. 5; 45; 44
D. 7; 47; 46

73. A meter used to measure the resistance in ohms between two points in an electrical circuit is a/an ______________.

A. Voltmeter
B. Shunt
C. Oscilloscope
D. Ohmmeter

74. The solar energy reaching the earth's surface is/are ___________.

A. Ultra-violet rays
B. Sunrays
C. Heat
D. Terrestrial solar radiation

75. Copper grounding rods shall not be less than _______ inches in diameter and _______feet long, unless listed.

A. 5/8; 8
B. 5/8; 6
C. 3/8; 6
D. 3/8; 8

76. An intermittent wind load up to 146 miles per hour is equivalent to ______ pounds per square foot.

A. 25
B. 50
C. 75
D. 100

77. The contractor is using undressed 2 X 9-inch planking. The load imposed will be 50 pounds per square foot.
The maximum span is _______ feet.

A. 6
B. 8
C. 10
D. 12

78. Gas back up systems may use ____________ for proper operation.

A. Check flow orifices
B. Thermosiphon solar preheating plumbed in series
C. Differential control units
D. Static relay devices

79. For solar plumbing the contractor should choose which of the following fire extinguishers?

A. ABC
B. CO2
C. BC
D. Halide

80. A semiconductor device that converts solar radiation into direct current electricity is a/an___________.

A. Inverter
B. Converter
C. Array
D. Photovoltaic cell

81. The valve allowing flow in only one direction is the _____________ valve.

A. Ball
B. Check
C. Float
D. Gate

82. A/an ___________ is used to measure the resistance in ohms between two points in an electrical circuit.

A. Ohmmeter
B. Ammeter
C. Voltmeter
D. Watt-Hour

83. A/an __________ is used to measure the potential difference between two points in an electrical.

A. Amp meter
B. Voltmeter
C. Circuit meter
D. Resistance meter

84. To reduce the flow in the collector of least resistance the contractor should use _______________.

A. Discharge valves
B. Flow-balancing valves
C. Swing check valves
D. Discharge retardation envelopment

85. _____________ arrays use optical lenses and mirrors to focus sunlight onto high-efficiency cells.

A. Fixed
B. Concentrator
C. Tracking
D. Flat-plate

Please See Answer Key on following page

ALH01/04/2021

State Solar
Practice Test 3

Answer		Reference	Section/Page#
1	C	Photovoltaic System Design (Course Manual)	2-1
2	A	Solar Water & Pool Heating Manual, 2006	4-11
3	B	Solar Water & Pool Heating Manual, 2006	5-27
4	D	Solar Water & Pool Heating Manual, 2006	3-17
5	D	NEC Handbook 2017	690.13
6	C	Solar Water & Pool Heating Manual, 2006	A-5
7	B	Photovoltaic System Design (Course Manual)	11-3
8	B	Photovoltaic System Design (Course Manual)	4-4
9	A	Solar Water & Pool Heating Manual, 2006	3-14
10	C	Solar Water & Pool Heating Manual, 2006	1-8
11	C	Solar Water & Pool Heating Manual, 2006	4-15
12	C	Solar Water & Pool Heating Manual, 2006	5-8
		75 sq ft x one gallon per minute per 10 sq ft of collector area = 75 / 10 = 7.5 gallons per minute	
13	B	Photovoltaic System Design (Course Manual)	2a-11
14	B	Solar Water & Pool Heating Manual, 2006	2-15
15	D	Photovoltaic Systems, 3rd Edition	99
16	C	Photovoltaic Systems, 3rd Edition	230
17	D	Photovoltaic System Design (Course Manual)	5-24
18	C	NEC Handbook 2017	250.52(5)(b)
19	D	Solar Construction Safety	87
20	D	Photovoltaic System Design (Course Manual)	2a-2
21	B	Solar Water & Pool Heating Manual, 2006	4-18
22	A	Solar Water & Pool Heating Manual, 2006	5-13
23	C	Solar Water & Pool Heating Manual, 2006	3-14
24	C	Photovoltaic System Design (Course Manual)	5-9
25	C	Solar Water & Pool Heating Manual, 2006	5-9
26	D	Solar Water & Pool Heating Manual, 2006	2-12

Answer		Reference	Section/Page#
27	D	Walker's Building Estimator's Reference	32nd Ed: 869
		`	31st Ed: 1396
		BTU is the energy required to raise the temperature of 1 lb of water by 1 ^{0}F – Trade Knowledge	
		47,124 gallons x 8.34 lb per gallon x 2 ^{0}F per lb per Btu = 785,085.84 Btu's	
		5 ft x 8 ft x 1,000 Btu's per sq ft = 40,000 Btu's	
		785,085.84 Btu's ÷ 40,000 Btu's = 19.627 = 20	
28	D	Photovoltaic Systems, 3rd Edition	288
29	B	Solar Water & Pool Heating Manual, 2006	2-1
30	B	NEC Handbook 2017	480.10(C) Information Note
31	A	Solar Water & Pool Heating Manual, 2006	1-4
32	B	Solar Water & Pool Heating Manual, 2006	5-32
33	A	Photovoltaic System Design (Course Manual)	5-39
34	A	Solar Water & Pool Heating Manual, 2006	3-14
35	D	Photovoltaic Systems, 3rd Edition	266
36	A	Photovoltaic System Design (Course Manual)	G-1
37	C	Solar Water & Pool Heating Manual, 2006	5-29
38	C	Solar Water & Pool Heating Manual, 2006	3-31
39	C	Photovoltaic System Design (Course Manual)	5-1
40	D	Photovoltaic System Design (Course Manual)	8-6
41	A	Solar Water & Pool Heating Manual, 2006	A-10
42	C	Photovoltaic Systems, 3rd Edition	312
		4 X 6 X 125% is 30	
43	B	Photovoltaic System Design (Course Manual)	2a-11
44	B	Florida Building Code, Plumbing, 2017	Table 308.5
45	C	Photovoltaic System Design (Course Manual)	7-18
46	D	OSHA 29 CFR	1926 .1053(b)(1)
47	D	Photovoltaic Systems, 3rd Edition	278
48	B	Photovoltaic Systems, 3rd Edition	139
49	C	Solar Water & Pool Heating Manual, 2006	1-9
		4 ft x 10 ft x 1.06 = 42.4 sq ft	
		(4 x 6) + (4 x 8) = 56 sq ft – choose the next larger square footage – can not be smaller	
50	C	NEC Handbook	690.31(C)(1)

Answer		Reference	Section/Page#
51	B	Photovoltaic System Design (Course Manual)	7-6
52	C	NEC Handbook 2017	406.3(B)
		There is no separate listing or required rating for DC PV systems.	
		The NEC requires a minimum rating of 15 Amps for ANY receptacle.	
53	B	Solar Water & Pool Heating Manual, 2006	5-8
		60 sq ft x 0.10 gallons per square per minute x 30 minutes = 180 gallons	
54	C	Solar Water & Pool Heating Manual, 2006	A-1 0
55	D	Solar Water & Pool Heating Manual, 2006	3-19
56	B	Solar Water & Pool Heating Manual, 2006	3-35
57	A	Photovoltaic System Design (Course Manual)	2-12
58	B	Walker's Building Estimator's Reference,	32nd Ed: 869 and 873 31st Ed: 1396 and 1401
		Volume of a cylinder = π x r^2 x h 1/2 full x 3.14 x 1.5 ft x 1.5 ft x 9 ft = 31.79 cubic feet x 7.48 gallons per cubic feet = 237.80 gal	
59	A	Photovoltaic System Design (Course Manual)	2a-8
60	A	Solar Water & Pool Heating Manual, 2006	3-19
61	C	NRCA Steep-slope Roof Systems, 2021 NRCA Steep-slope Roof Systems, 2017	194 184
62	D	NEC Handbook	250.162(B)
63	B	Walker's Building Estimator's Reference	32nd Ed: 869 and 873 31st Ed: 1396 and 1401
		Volume of a cylinder = π x r^2 x h 3.14 x 3 ft x 3 ft x 3 ft = 84.78 cubic feet x 7.48 gallons per cubic feet = 634.154 gal	
64	D	Solar Water & Pool Heating Manual, 2006	1-7
65	D	NEC Handbook 2017	690.43(A)
66	D	Solar Water & Pool Heating Manual, 2006	2-23
67	C	Photovoltaic Systems, 3rd Edition	76
68	A	Photovoltaic System Design (Course Manual)	4-2
69	B	Solar Water & Pool Heating Manual, 2006	3-19
70	B	Solar Water & Pool Heating Manual, 2006	5-15
71	D	Photovoltaic System Design (Course Manual)	2-9

Answer		Reference	Section/Page#
72	D	Photovoltaic System Design (Course Manual)	2-8
73	D	Photovoltaic System Design (Course Manual)	2a-11
74	D	Photovoltaic Systems, 3rd Edition	37
75	A	NEC Handbook 2017	250.52(5)(a)(b)
76	C	Solar Water & Pool Heating Manual, 2006	3-2
77	B	OSHA 29 CFR 1926	Subpart P App. A
78	B	Solar Water & Pool Heating Manual, 2006	2-22
79	A	Solar Construction Safety	87
80	D	Photovoltaic Systems, 3rd Edition	489
81	B	Solar Water & Pool Heating Manual, 2006	2-26
82	A	Photovoltaic System Design (Course Manual)	2a-11
83	B	Photovoltaic System Design (Course Manual)	2a-10
84	B	Solar Water & Pool Heating Manual, 2006	3-19
85	B	Photovoltaic System Design (Course Manual)	2-11

Made in United States
Orlando, FL
24 July 2025